GLOBALIZING JUSTICE

SUNY series in the Foundations of the Democratic State

William Crotty, editor

GLOBALIZING JUSTICE

*Critical Perspectives on Transnational Law
and the Cross-Border Migration
of Legal Norms*

Edited by

DONALD W. JACKSON
MICHAEL C. TOLLEY
MARY L. VOLCANSEK

STATE UNIVERSITY OF NEW YORK PRESS

Published by
STATE UNIVERSITY OF NEW YORK PRESS, ALBANY

© 2010 State University of New York

For information, contact
State University of New York Press, Albany, NY
www.sunypress.edu

Production, Laurie Searl
Marketing, Michael Campochiaro

Library of Congress Cataloging-in-Publication Data

Globalizing justice : critical perspectives on transnational law and the cross-border migration
    of legal norms / Edited by Donald W. Jackson, Michael C. Tolley and Mary L. Volcansek.
        p. cm.
    Includes bibliographical references and index.
    ISBN 978-1-4384-3069-0 (hardcover : alk. paper)
    1. International and municipal law. 2. Justice. 3. Globalization. 4. Conflict of laws.
I. Jackson, Donald W.   II. Tolley, Michael Carlton.   III. Volcansek, Mary L., 1948–

    K302.G56 2010
    341—dc22   2009023200

10 9 8 7 6 5 4 3 2 1

Contents

List of Tables

Preface and Acknowledgments

Globalization is a far-reaching, multifaceted phenomenon whose consequences on law are just beginning to be studied and understood more fully. The fourteen original studies collected here build on Mary Volcansek and John Stack's edited volume *Courts Crossing Borders: Blurring the Lines of Sovereignty* (2005), one of the first works by social scientists on the transnational influences on domestic law and courts in the United States and abroad. They are the result of works first presented by scholars at the 20th World Congress of the International Political Science Association (Fukuoka, Japan), the annual meetings of the Research Committee on Comparative Judicial Studies (Naples, Italy; Tempe, Arizona; and Melbourne, Australia), and the American Political Science Association (Philadelphia, Pennsylvania). Together these new works make an important contribution to the literature by assessing the scope and impact of the cross-border migration of legal ideas and norms on the United States, the United Kingdom, Australia, Argentina, and countries in Central America and Europe.

While not ignoring the legitimate concerns of those who fear some aspects of globalization, especially the blurring of the lines of state sovereignty, increasing criticism of global governance and the so-called democratic deficit, and the growing divide between rich and poor nations of the world, the works collected here demonstrate the powerful and often positive impact transnational forces can have on domestic law and the work of national courts. This edited volume documents how various aspects of legal globalization today, including the transnational spread of constitutional and human rights norms, the rise of universal criminal jurisdiction, and the role of both international nongovernmental organizations and domestic human rights commissions, have advanced freedom, rule of law, and democracy around the globe.

We would like to thank several individuals without whom this volume would not have come together. First, thanks to William Crotty, the Thomas P. O'Neill Chair in Public Life at Northeastern University and series editor, for his support of this project from the beginning. We would also like to acknowledge the contributions of Elisabetta de Franciscis of the University of Naples, Doris Marie Provine of Arizona State University, and Brian Galligan of the University of Melbourne, who graciously hosted the meetings of the Research Committee on Comparative Judicial Studies, where the

CONTENTS

issues of transnational law and the global spread of human rights norms were raised and debated. And special thanks to Sarah DeCapua, who edited all the manuscripts into their present form, and to Joan McEvoy, who carefully prepared the manuscript for publication. We are very grateful for their devoted assistance to this project.

Editors
Donald W. Jackson, Texas Christian University
Michael C. Tolley, Northeastern University
Mary L. Volcansek, Texas Christian University

Introduction

The studies collected in this volume examine the effects of various aspects of globalization today on law and legal systems around the world. The term *globalization* has many meanings, but for present purposes it is being used to refer to the process of increasing interconnectivity and interdependence among nation-states and the development of what Anne-Marie Slaughter calls a "global community of courts."[1] Arguably the forces of globalization have been at work for centuries, gradually shaping law and legal processes within sovereign nations. For example, the development of the *lex mercatoria*, or law merchant, is a story of how early norms and practices of the trading community became the law governing the resolution of commercial maritime disputes in courts both foreign and domestic. What is new today is the nature of the interconnections and extent of the interdependence among nation-states.

The nature and extent of legal globalization may be different today, but the central questions that this phenomenon raises remain the same: How are the forces of globalization today, including the global spread of international human rights norms, the rise of universal criminal jurisdiction, and the pressure for the establishment of rule of law and good governance in the developing world, affecting domestic law, courts, and processes? Are the effects the same in all places at all times? To what degree, if any, has the reception of international human rights norms and universal criminal jurisdiction undermined national authority and the concept of the nation-state?

This volume is divided into four parts: Transnational Influences on the U.S. Supreme Court; The Rise of Transnational Criminal Jurisdiction; Transnational Influences on Rights, Citizenship, and Democratization; and Transnational Law and the Boundaries of Sovereignty. The authors employ a variety of methodological approaches—historical, comparative, normative, and empirical—in an attempt to shed light on the three questions mentioned above.

In chapter 1, "The U.S. Supreme Court's Use of Comparative Law in the Construction of Constitutional Rights," David M. O'Brien assesses the influence of transnational human rights norms on the work of the U.S. Supreme Court. The U.S. Supreme Court, O'Brien argues, has come late to the new, global community of courts, and with considerable controversy both within the Court and in the American political system. Whereas O'Brien focuses on "the Rehnquist Court's use of comparative law in the construction of individual rights," Francine Banner, Ken Miller, and Doris Marie Provine take a wider view in chapter 2, "Foreign Law in American Jurisprudence: An Empirical Study," examining the transnational influences on rights and other areas of law. Based on their close analysis of the 2003–2004 Supreme Court term, Banner, Miller, and Provine show that "foreign law and foreign materials" have found their way into the briefs filed by litigants and amici and, as a result, have appeared with increasing frequency in the opinions of the Court. Christopher Whytock rounds out Part I with chapter 3, "Foreign Law in Domestic Courts: Different Uses, Different Implications." He develops a typology of the various uses of foreign and international law in U.S. law and examines "the empirical implications of different uses of foreign law that may be useful to a wide range of scholars."

Part II includes three chapters devoted to the rise of universal criminal jurisdiction and the global efforts to hold individuals responsible for war crimes, crimes against humanity, and genocide. This section commences with Donald Jackson's chapter 4, "Legitimacy and the Exercise of Universal Criminal Jurisdiction." In it he examines the "foundations for the legitimacy of criminal prosecutions brought in transnational tribunals exercising universal jurisdiction" and explores some of the "practical problems" encountered in key prosecutions before the ad hoc tribunals for Yugoslavia and Rwanda. In chapter 5, "International and Transnational Law, Sovereignty, and Hegemonic Power," Jackson addresses the problems in persuading the United States to accept fully the idea of universal criminal jurisdiction and ratify the treaty (the Rome Statute) establishing the International Criminal Court (ICC). The key problem, Jackson argues, is U.S. hegemonic power and unilateralism in a post-9/11 world. In chapter 6, "The Promotion of International Criminal Law: Evaluating the International Criminal Court and the Apprehension of Indictees," Lilian Barria and Steven Roper pick up where Jackson leaves off and closely examine the work of the ICC. Their aim is to gauge the effectiveness of the ICC by measuring its record in apprehending and prosecuting suspected war criminals.

Part III begins with an evaluation of the literature on this global phenomenon. Hans Peter Schmitz's chapter 7, "The Globalization of Human Rights Norms: Understanding the Opportunities and Limits of International Law and Transnational Activism," provides a critical, state-of-the-art review of "the contributions of political science scholarship to our understanding of the role of human rights ideas in global affairs," giving special emphasis to the key roles played by "transnational advocacy networks." The three chapters that follow show just how influential these networks can be. In chapter 8, "Rights and the Limits of Transnational Solidarity in Europe," Lisa Conant examines the evolution of social rights in Europe, defined as rights to the resources to promote social welfare, and shows how the European Court of Justice (ECJ) and the European Court of Human Rights (ECtHR) have forged what she calls a new "transnational social citizenship" that provides social benefits and protection to citizen and foreigner alike. In chapter 9, "International Imposition and Transmission of Democracy and Rule of Law: Lessons from Central America," Rachel Bowen details the effect of transnational advocacy networks on democratization processes in several countries in Central America; and in chapter 10, "The Role of International Actors in Promoting Rule of Law in Uganda," Joseph Isanga describes the same for Uganda.

Part IV includes four chapters that show how the cross-border migration of legal norms has altered the ideas of nation-state and sovereignty. In some areas of law, especially those related to human rights, global legal forces have eroded many of the barriers that separated national and international law. As a result, international and, in the case of Europe, supranational law are able to penetrate deeper into national law. In chapter 11, "Blurring Sovereignty: The Human Rights Act of 1998 and British Law," Mary Volcansek describes how the United Kingdom's membership in the Council of Europe and its obligations under the European Convention on Human Rights (ECHR) pressured it to adopt its first bill of rights, the Human Rights Act, in 1998. After closely examining the impact of this reform on the judicial protection of rights, she argues that the penetration of European human rights law and principles into British law has had the inevitable effect of "blurring" the concept of parliamentary sovereignty. In chapter 12, "Fundamental Rights, the European Court of Justice, and European Integration," Michael Tolley examines "the transnational flow of human rights norms among the European Court of Justice, the European Court of Human Rights, and the constitutional courts of member states of the EU." He argues that the ECJ's development of a rights jurisprudence helped to consolidate common principles of liberty, respect for human rights, and rule of law, and altered the way national constitutional courts give meaning to fundamental rights. The final two chapters of this volume describe how international human rights law was introduced and received in Australia and Argentina. In chapter 13, "Spreading the Word: Australia's National Human Rights and Equal Opportunity Commission as Transnational Legal Entrepreneur," Rhonda Evans Case examines the work of the NHREC and finds that it serves as an important conduit, or what the literature calls a "norm portal," through which international human rights principles flow. And in chapter 14, "Judicial Globalization: How the International Law of Human Rights Changed the Argentine Supreme Court," Walter Carnota shows how the court's "new norms and canons of constitutional interpretation" were the direct result of the court's willingness to give the prominent human rights treaties of the twentieth century constitutional status. With its new "internationalist" orientation, the Argentine Supreme Court, Carnota argues, joins the new global community of constitutional courts, increasingly engaged in transnational discourse on human rights.

In addition to enlightening readers to globalization's effects on law and courts both in the United States and abroad, our aim has been to encourage others to examine transnational legal influences and the cross-border migration of legal ideas in other contexts. The fourteen studies collected here are only the beginning.

Editors
Donald W. Jackson, Texas Christian University
Michael C. Tolley, Northeastern University
Mary L. Volcansek, Texas Christian University

NOTE

1. Anne-Marie Slaughter, "A Global Community of Courts," *Harvard International Law Journal* 44 (2003): 191–219.

PART I

Transnational Influences on the U.S. Supreme Court

The U.S. Supreme Court's Use of Comparative Law in the Construction of Constitutional Rights

DAVID M. O'BRIEN

In recent years, national high courts' use of comparative judicial opinions and law in the construction of individual rights has commanded greater attention. That is in no small part due to the increasing use of comparative legal analysis in rulings handed down by, for instance, the Supreme Court of Canada;[1] constitutional courts in western, central, and eastern Europe,[2] along with transnational courts like the ECtHR; as well as the Supreme Court of Israel;[3] and the Constitutional Court of the Republic of South Africa (which is required by its constitution to consider comparative and international law),[4] among other high courts. Court watchers and scholars have argued that a new paradigm for the construction of constitutional rights is emerging, based on and promoting the rise of "world constitutionalism."[5] Indeed, in the 1990s and 2000s, the number of citations to foreign legal sources increased in briefs filed and oral arguments before the Supreme Court of the United States.[6] At the same time, there are those who lament courts' increasing reliance on comparative constitutional law in constructing constitutional rights.[7]

The Supreme Court of the United States has been drawn into, rather than played a leading role in, the debate about the use of comparative law in the construction of constitutional rights. Foreign jurists have criticized the Court for its reluctance to engage in such an analysis.[8] Members of the Court are sharply divided on the matter, both in their off-the-bench comments and in their opinions. Justices Ruth Bader Ginsburg and Stephen Breyer have been the most outspoken in their embrace of comparative legal analysis when "interpreting constitutions and enforcing human rights."[9] By contrast, Justice Antonin Scalia has spoken out against the use of such sources. This is because he is a self-described "originalist"[10] with regard to constitutional interpretation and generally deems foreign materials irrelevant, because in his view such sources may encourage counter-majoritarian judicial decisions.

Members of the Rehnquist Court (1986-2005) have at times rather hotly contested the use of comparative judicial opinions and legal practices. The disagreement is evident in decisions ranging from the Court's role in policing the boundaries of federalism to the constitutionality of the death penalty and *Lawrence v. Texas*,[11] which struck down a state law criminalizing homosexual sodomy. In *Printz v. United States*,[12] for example, a bare majority invalidated a provision of the Brady Handgun Violence Prevention Act as an infringement on "states' rights," prompting dissenting Justice Breyer to question the majority's analysis and to highlight competing federal principles in Germany and the European Union. He noted that "their experience may . . . cast an empirical light on the consequences of different solutions to a common legal problem."[13] Yet, in delivering the opinion for the Court in *Printz*, Justice Scalia responded bluntly: "Comparative analysis is inappropriate to the task of interpreting a constitution."[14]

Justice Scalia's ire intensified in *Atkins v. Virginia*. There, writing for the Court, Justice John Paul Stevens cited the "world community" in support of what he claimed was an emerging "national consensus" against the execution of murderers who are mentally retarded. He also cited, along with states' execution practices, an amicus brief filed by the European Union. Dissenting Justice Scalia shot back, observing that "the Prize for the Court's Most Feeble Effort to fabricate 'national consensus' must go to its appeal . . . to the views of assorted professional and religious organizations, members of the so-called 'world community,' and respondents to opinion polls."[15]

No less opposed to the use of comparative legal materials, Justice Clarence Thomas, in a concurring opinion in the denial of certiorari in another death penalty case, *Knight v. Florida*,[16] criticized the petitioners for citing foreign sources in support of the claim that twenty years on death row amounts to cruel and unusual punishment under the Eighth Amendment. Likewise, in another concurring opinion on the denial of review, in *Foster v. Florida*,[17] Justice Thomas challenged Justice Breyer's citation of findings of European and Canadian courts, in a dissenting opinion from the denial of review, as irrelevant "foreign moods, fads, or fashions."

Still, perhaps, the most widely noted controversy related to the Rehnquist Court's drawing on comparative judicial decisions remains the majority's citing of a decision of the ECtHR in support of overruling a prior decision, *Bowers v. Hardwick*,[18] and in striking down Texas' law penalizing homosexual sodomy in *Lawrence v. Texas*. Writing for the Court, Justice Anthony Kennedy observed:

Almost five years before *Bowers* was decided the European Court of Human Rights considered a case with parallels to *Bowers* and to today's case ... [and] held that the laws proscribing the conduct were invalid under the European Convention on Human Rights, *Dudgeon v. United Kingdom*, 45 Eur. Ct. H.R. (1981) P52. Authoritative in all countries that are members of the Council of Europe (21 nations then, 45 nations now), the decision is at odds with the premise in *Bowers* that the claim put forward was insubstantial in our Western civilization.[19]

Justice Kennedy proceeded to emphasize that "other nations have taken action consistent with an affirmation of the protected right of homosexual adults to engage in intimate, consensual conduct."[20] Ironically, dissenting in *Lawrence v. Texas*, Justice Scalia cited a Canadian court decision[21] barring discrimination against homosexuals and warned of the judicial imposition of homosexual marriage.

Not surprisingly, Court watchers are no less divided about the incorporation of comparative legal analysis into the U.S. Supreme Court's opinions and constitutional law. Some supporters embrace the use of such foreign sources of law as pragmatic and functional in promoting the expansion of individual rights.[22] By contrast, others contend that comparative legal analysis has no place in constitutional interpretation.[23] They also argue that foreign law leads to antidemocratic and counter-majoritarian results.

Rather than engage in the normative debate about the propriety of the Court's reliance on comparative constitutionalism, the aim here is simply to examine and assess the Rehnquist Court's use of comparative law in the construction of individual rights, and specifically its reliance on foreign judicial opinions. Section One discusses briefly the Court's uses of comparative law. Section Two turns to an examination of competing uses of foreign judicial opinions. Section Three provides some concluding observations, but the basic conclusion may be stated at the outset. In spite of the controversy about the Court's reliance on foreign legal materials, the justices' uses of those materials remain very limited, certainly in comparison to other national high courts.

SOURCES AND USES OF COMPARATIVE AND INTERNATIONAL LAW

The Court has long drawn on sources of comparative law, ranging from observations on comparative legal practices, to works by foreign commentators,[24] to constitutional and statutory provisions, to international treaties and declarations,[25] to other high courts' judicial decisions. Chief Justice John Marshall, for example, writing in an admiralty case, *Thirty Hogsheads of Sugar v. Boyle*,[26] observed: "The decisions or the courts of every country, so far as they are founded upon a law common to every country, will be received, not as authority, but with respect."[27] Although he did not regard them as authority, Chief Justice Marshall nonetheless emphasized that "the rules established in British courts, and those established in the courts of other nations" constitute sources for judicial decision making and for developing workable rules of law. In addition, the supremacy clause in Article VI of the Constitution requires the courts to consider international treaties to which the United States is a party as binding and authoritative; however, that is a very different matter from citing foreign judicial decisions in the construction of constitutional rights, as in *Lawrence v. Texas*.

Admittedly, the Court's use of comparative law sources may prove misguided and in other ways problematic, but the same is true with regard to its reliance on history or social science data. As a result, scholars have analyzed the uses of comparative law sources and argued for the need for a more general theory of the use of comparative legal sources.[28]

The Court historically has employed comparative materials in four basic ways. First, the Court has referenced comparative legal materials in *dicta*, presenting a comparative context and legal contrasts that nevertheless appear not essential to resolving the issue presented. Second, the Court has taken "judicial notice" of the fact of differing foreign laws, legal systems, and decisions in its construction of constitutional rights. Third, the Court has cited foreign judicial decisions as precedents in its construction of individual rights and, alternatively, rejected or adopted them. Finally, on rare occasions, the Court has undertaken comparative constitutional analysis in order to provide a more persuasive rationale for its ruling.

Admittedly, these categories are not hard and fast. They are often matters of degree rather than differences in kind. Justice Harry A. Blackmun's citations to and discussion of Persian, Greek, Roman, and English laws in *Roe v. Wade*[29] in support of the proposition that abortion prior to quickening was not an indictable offense, for instance, might be considered taking "judicial notice" of comparative legal practices or dismissed as *dicta*. In any event, some examples of these different uses of foreign sources may prove useful in clarifying each category.

The Court has long included as *dicta* comparative references to the legal practices of the "English-speaking people."[30] It has done so often in order to highlight differences between the common law system versus the Continental inquisitorial system[31] or to emphasize democratic constitutional values in contrast with those of totalitarian regimes.[32] Besides drawing comparisons to emphasize the constitutional value and scope of individual rights, the Court has employed such materials in *dicta* when determining the constitutional boundaries of the national government's power and the scope of permissible governmental regulations.[33]

The citation in *dicta* or taking judicial notice of foreign legal sources and practices has, arguably, been invited by some of the Court's own standards for determining the scope of constitutional rights and powers. Foreign legal sources have been cited when applying, for example, the standard of "reasonableness"[34] and Justice Benjamin Cardozo's standard for selectively incorporating into the Fourteenth Amendment due process clause only those guarantees of the Bill of Rights "implicit in the concept of ordered liberty."[35]

Another source of continuing controversy is the "evolving standards of decency that mark the progress of [our] maturing society"[36] when determining the application of the Eighth Amendment's ban on "cruel and unusual punishment" to the imposition of capital punishment. Notably, Justice Arthur J. Goldberg, dissenting from the denial of certiorari in *Rudolph v. Alabama*,[37] invoked that standard and "standards of decency more or less universally accepted,"[38] citing United Nations (UN) surveys, reports, and foreign laws in support "of the trend ... throughout this world" against the imposition of the death penalty. On that basis, he specifically invited attorneys to challenge the constitutionality of imposing capital punishment for the crime of rape. It also seems fair to state that his opinion in *Rudolph v. Alabama* sparked a national debate about the death penalty, leading to a ten-year moratorium as well as encouraging comparative analysis in the Court's opinions on capital punishment.

Hence, writing for a plurality of the Court in *Coker v. Georgia*[39] in striking down the imposition of capital punishment for the crime of rape, Justice Byron White took notice of the fact that out of sixty major nations in the world surveyed in 1965, only three retained the death penalty for rape when death did not ensue.[40] Subsequently, writing for a bare majority of the Court in holding that the Eighth Amendment bars the imposition of capital punishment for those who abet, but do not commit, a felony murder, Justice White reaffirmed the relevance of foreign practices by adding that it was "worth noting that the doctrine of felony murder has been abolished in England and India, severely restricted in Canada and a number of other Commonwealth countries, and is unknown in continental Europe."[41] More recently, the Council of Europe filed "friend of the court" briefs urging the Court to take judicial notice of foreign laws barring the execution of the mentally retarded[42] and minors.[43]

The briefs filed before the Supreme Court by the European Union in opposition to the imposition of the death penalty not only build on Justice Goldberg's opinion in *Rudolph v. Alabama*. They are in the tradition of progressive attorney and later Supreme Court Justice Louis D. Brandeis, who urged the Court to take judicial notice of comparative laws and legal practices in *Muller v. Oregon*.[44] There, in the now-famous "Brandeis Brief," he cited not only social science data on the effect of long working hours on women's health, but also foreign laws and practices in Austria, France, Germany, Great

Britain, Holland, Italy, and Switzerland in support of Oregon's law limiting the hours women could work. He did so because at the time, a bare majority of the Court was striking down such progressive legislation for running afoul of the liberty of contract. His strategy was to show the reasonableness of the legislation and to persuade a majority of the Court not to second-guess the state legislature on the appropriateness of the law. Writing for the Court in *Muller*, Justice David Brewer took judicial "notice [of comparative] legislation as well as expression of opinion from sources other than judicial sources" in upholding the reasonableness of Oregon's law.

The Court also has cited foreign judicial opinions in adopting a rule of law—a rule of law, though, that also may ultimately reject the reasoning and holding of foreign courts. As earlier noted, the Court often has cited English precedents in its opinions. The nineteenth-century English standard for judging obscenity laid down in *Regina v. Hicklin*,[45] for instance, was adopted by many state and federal courts and used in the United States well into the twentieth century. In *Roth v. United States*,[46] Justice William J. Brennan Jr. cited and discussed that decision but ultimately held the "Hicklin Rule" to be inconsistent with the First Amendment's guarantee for free speech and press.

The Court nevertheless has rarely cited or analyzed foreign judicial opinions and comparative constitutional law in its construction of constitutional rights, at least in comparison with high courts in Canada,[47] South Africa,[48] and elsewhere. An exception is Chief Justice Earl Warren's opinion for the Court in *Miranda v. State of Arizona*,[49] in which Chief Justice Warren cited laws and judicial opinions handed down in England, Scotland, India, and Ceylon. That proved controversial. In a dissenting opinion, Justice John M. Harlan, for one, specifically objected to invoking foreign legal practices. Justice Harlan also took issue with Chief Justice Warren's summary of the rights of the accused accorded in other countries.

In sum, despite the controversy regarding the Court's incorporating legal sources in opinions, such usages are not unprecedented, even though they are infrequent and limited.

THE REHNQUIST COURT'S USE OF
FOREIGN JUDICIAL OPINIONS AND LEGAL SOURCES

Members of the Rehnquist Court were divided about the use of foreign legal sources. As already noted, Justice Thomas remains an outspoken opponent of the inclusion of such materials. Not surprisingly, he rarely cites such materials. Notably, though, in his concurring opinion on the denial of review in *Foster v. Florida*,[50] he cited Sir William Blackstone recommending "only a 48-hour delay between [a death] sentence and [the] execution" when criticizing Justice Breyer's dissenting opinion from the denial of review that cited a Supreme Court of Canada decision expressing concerns about lengthy delays in the administration of capital punishment. Apparently for Justice Thomas, as for Justice Scalia, Blackstone is in the same league as the founding fathers, even though he was a foreign commentator on foreign law. Nonetheless, Justice Thomas, concurring in *Holder v. Hall*,[51] cited in *dicta* secondary sources discussing ethnic representation in other countries when assessing minority–majority voting districts.

Ironically, Justice Ginsburg, who in off-the-bench remarks has embraced a comparative constitutional dialogue and lamented that the Supreme Court has referred to the UN's 1948 Universal Declaration of Human Rights only six times,[52] has made only one reference to comparative legal practices in her opinions, although she did cite foreign judicial decisions in an opinion for the Court in a case dealing with the interpretation of a treaty.[53] Concurring in the decision upholding the University of Michigan Law School's affirmative action policy in *Grutter v. Bollinger*,[54] Justice Ginsburg took judicial notice of UN conventions on racial and gender discrimination when emphasizing that the majority's ruling "accords with the international understanding of the office of affirmative action."

Likewise, in spite of some favorable off-the-bench comments about the value of looking to comparative constitutional practices, Justice Sandra Day O'Connor made only a passing reference to foreign legal sources in *dicta*—in *dicta* pertaining to the Nuremberg Tribunals as a precedent[55]—and to the elimination or restriction of felony murder in most commonwealth nations in support of the Court's ruling.[56]

Justice David H. Souter has said little about comparative constitutionalism. The sole exception is his taking note of the Dutch practice of permitting physician-assisted suicide in his concurring opinion in *Washington v. Glucksberg*,[57] in which he deferred to the ongoing political debate about the issue.

Although Justice Breyer has made clear his openness to considering comparative legal experiences, he has cited foreign sources and studies in only five opinions. Three of these are opinions dissenting from the denial of review of death penalty cases, in the tradition of Justice Goldberg (for whom he served as a law clerk) dissenting in *Rudolph v. Alabama*. All three involved claims that lengthy delays on death row amount to cruel and unusual punishment.[58] In *Elledge v. Florida*,[59] Justice Breyer cited English and other recent European court decisions holding lengthy delays in carrying out executions impermissible and refusing to extradite individuals to the United States on the ground that they might face undue delays in their executions. In that decision, he also emphasized that "British jurists have suggested that the Bill of Rights of 1689, a document relevant to the interpretation of our own Constitution, may forbid, as cruel and unusual, significantly less delays" than the twenty-three years spent on death row by the petitioner. The following year, in *Knight v. Florida*,[60] he pressed further in stressing that "A growing number of courts outside the United States—courts that accept or assume the lawfulness of the death penalty—have held that lengthy delay in administering a lawful death penalty renders ultimate execution inhuman, degrading, or unusually cruel." And he cited in support not only English court decisions but also those of the supreme courts of Canada, India, and Zimbabwe, as well as the European Court of Human Rights (ECtHR). Again dissenting from the Court's refusal to address the matter in *Foster v. Florida*,[61] Justice Breyer added to his citation of foreign judicial decisions quotations from *The Federalist* in support of taking judicial notice of those sources and in countering Justice Thomas's criticisms of the relevance of comparative legal materials. In Justice Breyer's view, "Just as 'attention to the judgment of other nations' can help Congress determine 'the justice and propriety of [America's] measures,' so it can help guide this Court when it decides whether a particular punishment violates the Eighth Amendment."[62] In short, in a pragmatic manner, Justice Breyer has taken judicial notice of comparative judicial rulings for broadening the scope of constitutional protection for individual rights. He has sought to defend reliance on such materials using an originalist argument to respond to Justice Thomas's criticisms of reliance on foreign legal sources.

In addition to taking judicial notice of foreign legal practices to call into question the Court's refusal to address the issue of lengthy delays in the implementation of death sentences, Justice Breyer also cited in dissent, in the tradition of Justice Brandeis, comparative legal experiences to debunk the reasoning and holding of a bare majority of the Court in *Printz v. United States*,[63] which struck down a provision of the Brady Act requiring state and local law enforcement officials to conduct background checks on handgun purchasers as an unfunded federal mandate. In his dissent, Justice Breyer cited several secondary studies of comparative federalism in support of his view of congressional power and federalism. He explained the use of those sources:

> Of course, we are interpreting our own Constitution, not those of other nations, and there may be relevant political and structural differences between their systems and our own. But their experience may nonetheless cast an empirical light on the consequences of different solutions to a common legal problem....[64]

Finally, in a concurring opinion in *Nixon v. Shrink Missouri Government PAC*,[64] upholding campaign contribution limits, Justice Breyer noted in *dicta* that the Court's First Amendment rulings on the matter were consistent with those of other constitutional courts, citing in support decisions of the Supreme Court of Canada and the ECtHR.

For his part, Chief Justice Rehnquist, on one hand, criticized his colleagues' reliance on foreign judicial decisions, and on the other, cited such sources in his own opinions—opinions both for the Court and those dissenting from the Court's decisions. Dissenting from the majority's holding and citing of foreign legal practices in support of declaring unconstitutional the execution of mentally retarded convicted murderers in *Atkins v. Virginia*,[65] Chief Justice Rehnquist observed, "I fail to see, however, how the views of other countries regarding the punishment of their citizens provide any support for the Court's ultimate determination."

Nonetheless, writing for the Court in denying congressional standing to challenge the constitutionality of legislation giving the president the power of the line-item veto in *Raines v. Byrd*,[66] Chief Justice Rehnquist referred to the procedures of "some European constitutional courts" in support of the view that a statute providing standing to sue might not be "irrational." Moreover, writing for the Court in its decision on the right to physician-assisted suicide in *Washington v. Glucksberg*,[67] the chief justice took judicial notice of foreign legal approaches to the matter, notably citing foreign judicial decisions that limited claims of individual rights—decisions of Canadian and Indian courts upholding the criminalization of assisted suicide.[68]

More curious is Chief Justice Rehnquist's dissent in *Planned Parenthood of Southeastern Pennsylvania v. Casey*[69] in criticizing the plurality for upholding the landmark ruling on a woman's right to have an abortion in *Roe v. Wade*,[70] from which he also had dissented. In a footnote, the chief justice cited in *dicta* a decision two years after *Roe* by the then–West German constitutional court striking down a law liberalizing access to abortion "on the grounds that life developing within the womb is constitutionally protected."[71] However, in the same footnote, he also cited a Canadian court decision "that followed reasoning similar to that of *Roe* in striking down a law that restricted abortion."[72] It is hard to make much of such references other than that the chief justice wanted to emphasize that comparative constitutional law points in conflicting directions, rather than necessarily establishes the "universalizability" of a rights claim.

As noted earlier, Justice Stevens created a controversy in *Atkins v. Virginia* when he took notice of the view of the "world community" in support of what he deemed an emerging "national consensus" in the United States, based on states' execution practices, against the execution of mentally retarded death row inmates. Yet he had previously done likewise in *Thompson v. Oklahoma*,[73] when also noting the practices of other countries, specifically "leading members of the Western European community," in support of the Court's holding that the Eighth Amendment bars the execution of minors fifteen years of age and younger. Justice Stevens also rather frequently has issued memoranda or dissenting opinions respecting the denial of review in death penalty cases involving delays in carrying out executions[74] and the execution of minors fifteen years of age and younger.[75]

Yet outside the area of death penalty appeals, and with the exception of *dicta* in another dissenting opinion referring to Fourth Amendment rules as "bulwarks against police practices that prevail in totalitarian regimes,"[76]

Justice Stevens cited foreign judicial decisions in only one other decision, the "enemy combatant" case, *Rasul v. Bush*.[77] Although deciding the case on federal statutory grounds in holding that alien "enemy combatants" held at the U.S. Naval Base in Guantánamo Bay, Cuba, are entitled to hearings on the basis for their detention, Justice Stevens's opinion for the Court discussed extensively English court rulings on the writ of habeas corpus. Moreover, he engaged dissenting Justice Scalia in a debate about the holdings and the scope of English court decisions on access to habeas corpus relief in places under national domination or territorial sovereignty. Notably, each justice charged the other with misreading and misrepresenting those precedents. Still, *Rasul v. Bush* remains Justice Stevens's only opinion to employ foreign judicial opinions as precedents in the construction of individuals' right of access to federal courts.

Justice Kennedy's opinion for the Court in *Lawrence v. Texas*, as noted, also stirred the controversy. Significantly, though, Justice Kennedy's reliance on a decision of the ECtHR, along with other foreign legal practices recognizing the rights of homosexuals, aimed to undermine the factual premises of Justice White's opinion for the Court, and Chief Justice Warren E. Burger's concurring opinion, in *Bowers v. Hardwick*. Contradicting their opinions in *Bowers*, Justice Kennedy emphasized that "other nations have taken action consistent with an affirmation of the protected right of homosexual adults to engage in intimate, consensual conduct." In other words, in the tradition of Justice Brandeis, Justice Kennedy drew on foreign judicial decisions in order to undermine the factual basis for and rationale of a majority of the Court in *Bowers*.

In only two other opinions for the Court, in *Loving v. United States*[78] and *Roper v. Simmons*,[79] did Justice Kennedy rely so extensively on foreign judicial opinions and legal practices. However, in two dissenting opinions,[80] he noted in *dicta* comparative legal practices. Also, in one other opinion for the Court, *Hiibel v. Sixth Judicial District Court of Nevada*,[81] he cited and discussed a U.S. precedent that quoted from an 1861 English court decision bearing on the Fifth Amendment's self-incrimination clause.

Writing for the Court in *Loving v. United States*, Justice Kennedy discussed foreign law—notably, English law at the time of the adoption of the U.S. Constitution—as relevant to deciding the constitutional boundaries between the powers of Congress and the president with respect to courts-martial and punishment under military law. As in *Lawrence v. Texas*, Justice Kennedy's reliance on foreign judicial decisions and legal practices provoked sharp criticism from Justice Scalia. Concurring in *Loving*, Justice Scalia agreed that English law at the time of the founding might be relevant to constitutional interpretation, but not in deciding the issue before the Court.[82]

Writing for a bare majority in *Roper v. Simmons*, Justice Kennedy cited several international treaties and foreign legal practices in overruling *Stanford v. Kentucky*,[83] which had upheld the execution of convicted murders who were older than fifteen but younger than eighteen at the time of their crimes. As in *Lawrence*, he marshaled such sources to undermine the Court's reasoning in *Stanford*. Although he emphasized that the Court, in determining evolving standards of decency, "has referred to the laws of other countries and to international authorities as instructive for its interpretation of the Eighth Amendment's prohibition," Justice Kennedy followed Justice Stevens's lead in *Atkins v. Virginia* in resting the primary basis for the ruling on state practices with respect to the execution of juveniles. In other words, Justice Kennedy simply took judicial notice of foreign legal practices to support the reasonableness of the majority's decision.

Justice Scalia repeatedly has chastised colleagues for relying on foreign judicial decisions and legal practices in their opinions. Dissenting from the Court's rulings in *Lawrence v. Texas* and *Roper v. Simmons*, he dismissed Justice Kennedy's discussion of foreign judicial opinions and laws as "dangerous *dicta*." Justice Scalia leveled his sharpest criticism, however, when colleagues cited foreign legal practices in support of the application of standards for applying the due process clause, like that of "implicit in the concept of ordered liberty" and that of "the evolving standards of decency" in determining the scope of the Eighth Amendment. Dissenting from the Court's holding the Eighth Amendment to bar the execution of individuals who were fifteen years old or younger at the time of their conviction for murder in *Thompson v. Oklahoma*, Justice Scalia argued that the citation of foreign legal practices in support of the ruling was "totally inappropriate as a means of establishing the fundamental beliefs of this Nation."[84] A year later, writing for the Court's majority in *Stanford v. Kentucky*,[85] holding the Eighth Amendment to permit the execution of convicted murderers who were at least sixteen years of age at the time of their crime, he elaborated, observing, "In determining what standards have 'evolved,' however, we have looked not to our own conceptions of decency, but to those of modern American society as a whole."[86] As discussed earlier, dissenting in *Atkins v. Virginia*, he maintained his opposition to the Court's reliance on foreign sources in holding that the Eighth Amendment bars the execution of mentally retarded individuals.

In spite of such occasionally rather caustic criticism of the Court's invoking foreign judicial decisions and legal practices, Justice Scalia has cited such sources in support of his own positions. He dissented from the Court's ruling that the First Amendment protects anonymous leafleting at election sites in *McIntyre v. Ohio Elections Commission*[87] and marshaled historical evidence in support of his view that at the time of the founding, the prohibition of anonymous speech was permissible. In opposing the majority's holding and, in particular, concurring with Justice Thomas's historical evidence supporting an originalist interpretation of the amendment's protection for such speech, Justice Scalia added to his list of evidence for his position citations to laws in Australia, Canada, and England that prohibit anonymous campaign speech.

Likewise, in opinions dissenting from the Court's rulings on the rights of enemy combatants, Justice Scalia discussed extensively English commentators and judicial decisions prior to and at the time of the adoption of the Constitution in support of his view of the "original understanding" of the writ of habeas corpus.[88] Finally, dissenting in *McCreary v. ACLU of Kentucky*,[89] he cited the French constitution, which proclaims France a "secular" state, in drawing a contrast with the U.S. Constitution and in criticizing Justice Souter's opinion for a bare majority holding that the posting of the Ten Commandments in courthouses runs afoul of the First Amendment's disestablishment clause. In short, although Justice Scalia argues against the Court's reliance on foreign judicial decisions and legal practices, he nonetheless has cited such foreign legal sources to support his positions and interpretation of the "original understanding" of the Constitution, though only in dissenting opinions. In short, what Justice Scalia opposes is reliance on contemporary comparative judicial decisions when construing constitutionally protected rights.

CONCLUSION

The controversy about the Rehnquist Court's incorporation of foreign legal practices in opinions appears on closer examination to be more smoke than fire. The Court's references to foreign legal sources are not historically unprecedented and remain infrequent and limited. Moreover, those references are most often in *dicta* or in opinions taking judicial notice of foreign legal practices (see Tables 1.1 and 1.2).

Furthermore, foreign judicial decisions and legal practices have appeared in only eight opinions for the Court. In spite of the controversy sparked by Justice Kennedy's citing such materials in *Lawrence v. Texas* and *Roper v. Simmons*, only Justice Stevens's opinion for the Court in *Rasul v. Bush* undertook

Table 1.1. Uses of Foreign Law, Practices, and Judicial Decisions in Opinions of the Rehnquist Court

	Dicta	*Judicial Notice*	*As Precedents*	*Total*
Rehnquist	2	2		4
Stevens	1	2	1	4
O'Connor	2			2
Scalia		2	2	4
Kennedy	2	3	1	6
Souter		1		1
Thomas	1	1		2
Ginsburg	1			1
Breyer	2		3	5
Totals:	11	11	7	29

Table 1.2. Number of Opinions Citing Foreign Legal Practices and Judicial Decisions

	Legal Practices	Judicial Decisions	Total
Rehnquist	2	2	4
Stevens	3	1	4
O'Connor	2		2
Scalia	2	2	4
Kennedy	3	3	6
Souter	1		1
Thomas	2		2
Ginsburg	1		1
Breyer	1	4	5
Totals:	17	12	29

a rather detailed comparative analysis of foreign precedents. And notably, Justice Stevens examined only old English common law decisions, not contemporary foreign practices and judicial decisions, to support his interpretation of the framers' understanding of the writ of habeas corpus and to rebut dissenting Justice Scalia's rival reading of those precedents and understanding of the writ at the time of the adoption of the Constitution.

In addition, the Court's reliance on foreign law, practices, and judicial decisions has been primarily in dissenting opinions—opinions filed most frequently by Justices Breyer and Scalia, followed by Justices O'Connor, Kennedy, and Thomas (see Table 1.3). In the tradition of Justice Brandeis, those

Table 1.3. Citations of Foreign Law, Practices, and Judicial Decisions in Opinions for the Court and in Concurring and Dissenting Opinions*

	Opinions for the Court	Concurring or Dissenting Opinions	Total
Rehnquist	2	2	4
Stevens	3	1	4
O'Connor		2	2
Scalia		4	4
Kennedy	4	2	6
Souter		1	1
Thomas		2	2
Ginsburg		1	1
Breyer		5	5
Totals:	9	20	29

*Excludes opinions criticizing the use of such materials.

citations generally aimed to call into question the reasoning of a ruling or the refusal to grant review of death penalty cases.

Finally, there are a number of ironies in the Rehnquist Court's citation of foreign legal practices and judicial decisions. First, those members of the Court (Chief Justice Rehnquist and Justices Stevens and Kennedy) who were the least outspoken about the usage and controversy about incorporating foreign legal sources in opinions construing the scope of individual rights most frequently cited those foreign legal materials. By contrast, Justice Ginsburg, who publicly endorsed comparative constitutional analysis, in only one opinion took notice of foreign legal practices in *dicta*. Likewise, Justice Breyer, who also in off-the-bench comments argued for the relevance of comparative constitutional practices, only cited in *dicta* or took judicial notice of foreign judicial decisions and legal practices, and notably only in dissenting opinions. Justice O'Connor only noted foreign legal practices in two opinions, and for his part, Justice Souter only once cited foreign legal practices in *dicta*. The two most outspoken critics of the use of foreign legal materials in the Court's opinions, Justices Scalia and Thomas, nonetheless took judicial notice of foreign legal practices and judicial precedents in support of their interpretation of the original understanding of constitutional guarantees. In sum, for better or worse, the Court has been reluctant to engage in the so-called global dialogue about the use of comparative constitutionalism in the construction of individual rights.

NOTES

1. See, e.g., Peter McCormick, "The Supreme Court of Canada and American Citations, 1945–1994: A Statistical Overview," *Supreme Court Law Review* 8 (1997): 527.

2. See, e.g., Stephen J. Breyer, "Changing Relationships among European Constitutional Courts," *Cardozo Law Review* 21 (2000): 1045.

3. See, e.g., *United Mizrachi Bank plc v. Migdal Cooperative Village*, 48 (iv) P.D. 221 (1995), printed in *Israel Law Review* 31 (1997): 754.

4. One notable decision, striking down capital punishment based on an exhaustive comparative law analysis, is *The State v. T. Makwanyane and M Mchnunu*, 1995 (3) SA 391 (Const. Ct.).

5. See Bruce Ackerman, "The Rise of World Constitutionalism," *Virginia Law Review* 83 (1997): 771; Anne-Marie Slaughter, "Judicial Globalization," *Virginia Journal of International Law* 40 (2000): 1103; Anne-Marie Slaughter, "A Global Community of Courts," *Harvard International Law Journal* 44 (2003): 191; and Ken I. Kersch, *Constructing Civil Liberties* (New York: Cambridge University Press, 2004), at 338–362.

6. See Jerry Goldman and Timothy Johnson, "Exploring the Use of Foreign Law and Foreign Sources in the U.S. Supreme Court's Decision Making Process," paper presented at the American Political Science Association national convention (Sept. 1–4, 2005).

7. See Robert H. Bork, *Coercing Virtue: The Worldwide Rule of Judges* (Washington, D.C.: American Enterprise Institute, 2003).

8. See, e.g., Claire L'Heureux-Dube, "The Importance of Dialogue: Globalization and the International Impact of the Rehnquist Court," *Tulsa Law Journal* 34 (1998): 15. (Justice L'Heureux-Dube retired from the Supreme Court of Canada in 2002.)

9. Ruth Bader Ginsburg and Deborah Hones Merritt, "Affirmative Action: An International Human Rights Dialogue," *Cardozo Law Review* 21 (1999): 253, at 282; and Ruth Bader Ginsburg, "A Decent Respect to the Opinions of [Human]kind: The Value of a Comparative Perspective in Constitutional Adjudication," Address before the Constitutional Court of South Africa (Feb. 7, 2006), online at http://www.supremecourtus.gov/publicinfo (visited Apr 26, 2006).

10. See, e.g., Antonin Scalia, "Originalism: The Lesser Evil," *University of Cincinnati Law Review* 57 (1989): 849.

11. *Lawrence v. Texas*, 539 U.S. 558 (2003).

12. *Printz v. United States*, 521 U.S. 898 (1997).

13. *Printz v. United States*, 521 U.S. 898, at 997 (Breyer, J., dis. op.).

14. *Printz v. United States*, 521 U.S. 898, at 921 n. 11.

15. *Atkins v. Virginia*, 536 U.S. 304 (Scalia, J., dis. op.).

16. *Knight v. Florida*, 528 U.S. 990 (1999), at 990.

17. *Foster v. Florida*, 537 U.S. 990, 990 (2002) (Thomas, J., con. in denial of cert.).

18. *Bowers v. Hardwick*, 478 U.S. 186 (1986).

19. *Lawrence v. Texas*, 539 U.S. 558, at 576–578.

20. Ibid., at 573.

21. *Halpern v. Toronto*, 2003 WL 34950 (Ont Ct. App., June 10, 2003).

22. See, e.g., Mark Tushnet, "Transnational/Domestic Constitutional Law," *Loyola of Los Angeles Law Review* 37 (2003): 239; Mark Tushnet, "Returning With Interest: Observations on Some Putative Benefits of Studying Comparative Constitutional Law," *University of Pennsylvania Journal of Constitutional Law* 1 (1998): 325; Mark Tushnet, "The Possibilities of Comparative Constitutional Law," *Yale Law Journal* 108 (1999): 1225; and Harold Honju Koh, "The United States Constitution and International Law," *American Journal of International Law* 98 (2004): 43.

23. See Bork, *Coercing Virtue*, see note 7; Christopher McCrudden, "A Common Law of Human Rights? Transnational Conversations on Constitutional Rights," *Oxford Journal of Legal Studies* 20 (2000): 499; Roger P. Alford, "Misusing International Sources to Interpret the Constitution," *American Journal of International Law* 98 (2004): 57.

24. Sir William Blackstone's *Commentaries on the English Common Law*, for example, is frequently cited by the Supreme Court. One study found that between 1900 and 2003, the Court cited Blackstone 309 times. See Donald Childress, "Using Comparative Constitutional Law to Resolve Domestic Federal Questions," *Duke Law Journal* 53 (2003): 193, at 201 n. 50.

25. The Court thus noted in an international law case, *The Paquete Habana*, 175 U.S. 677, 708 (1900), that "[i]nternational law is part of our law, and must be ascertained and administered by the courts of justice...." Also as noted earlier, the supremacy clause of Article VI of the Constitution requires the Court to follow international treaties to which the United States is a party.

26. *Thirty Hogsheads of Sugar v. Boyle*, 13 U.S. (9 Cranch) 191 (1815). Elsewhere, Chief Justice Marshall observed that "the Court is bound by the law of nations which is a part of the law of the land." *The Nereide*, 13 U.S. (9 Cranch) 388, 423 (1815). See also *Murray v. The Schooner Charming Betsy*, 6 U.S. 64, 118 (1804) (observing that "an act of Congress ought never to be construed to violate the law of nations if any other possible construction remains").

27. Ibid. at 198.

28. For a thoughtful analysis, see Sujit Choudhry, "Globalization in Search of Justification: Towards a Theory of Comparative Constitutional Interpretation," *Indiana Law Review* 74 (1999): 819. See also William Twining, *Globalization and Legal Theory* (Evanston: Northwestern University Press, 2001); and David Fontana, "Refined Comparativism in Constitutional Law," *UCLA Law Review* 49 (2001): 539.

29. *Roe v. Wade*, 410 U.S. 113, 129–133 (1973).

30. See, e.g., *Rast v. Van Deman & Lewis Co.*, 240 U.S. 342, 366 (1916) (observing that the Constitution embraces "relatively fundamental rules of right, as generally understood by all English-speaking communities"); *Malinski v. New York*, 324 U.S. 401, 413–414 (1945) (Frankfurter, J., con. op.) (observing "The safeguards of 'due process of law' and 'the equal protection of the laws' summarize the history of freedom of English-speaking peoples running back to Magna Carta and reflected in the constitutional development of our people"); *Rochin v. California*, 342 U.S. 165, 169 (1952) (whether a police practice runs afoul of "canons of decency and fairness which express the notions of justice of English-speaking peoples"); *Quinn v. United States*, 349 U.S. 155, 167 (1955) (holding a practice "supported by long-standing tradition here and in other English-speaking nations"); *Poe v. Ullman*, 367 U.S. 497, 548 (1961) (Harlan, J., dis. op.) (supporting the idea of privacy in terms of the "common understanding throughout the English-speaking world"); *Roe v. Locke*, 423 U.S. 48, 50 (1975) ("crimes against nature" is not ambiguous among "English speaking people"); and *Ingraham v. Wright*, 430 U.S. 651, 673 n. 42 (1977) (quoting *Wolf v. Colorado*, 338 U.S. 25, 27–28 (1949). More recently, the Court has not taken such a limited view and cited "civilized societies"; see, e.g., *Ford v. Wainwright*, 477 U.S. 399, 409 (1986), and the discussion in the text and cited in notes 57 and 89.

31. See, e.g., *Betts v. Brady*, 316 U.S. 455, 465–472 (1942); and *Stein v. New York*, 346 U. 156, 199 (1953) (Frankfurter, J., dis. op.).

32. See, e.g., *Terminiello v. Chicago*, 337 U.S. 1, 4 (1949) ("The right to speak freely and to promote diversity of ideas and programs is therefore one of the chief distinctions that sets us apart from totalitarian regimes."); *Tenney v. Brandhove*, 341 U.S. 367, 381 (1951) (Black, J., con. op.) (noting the use of congressional committees in Argentina to suppress dissidents); *Dennis v. United States*, 341 U.S. 494, 584 (1951) (Douglas, J., dis. op.) (pointing up the association between free speech and democracies); *Joint Anti-Facist Refugee Committee v. McGrath*, 341 U.S. 123, 189 (1951) (Reed, J., dis. op.) (citing other democracies and their efforts to control governmental disloyalty); *Brown v. Allen*, 344 U.S. 443, 512 (1953) (noting that the writ of habeas corpus is "one of the decisively differentiating factors between our democracy and totalitarian governments"); *Shaughnessy v. United States ex rel. Mezei*, 345 U.S. 206, 226 (1953) (Jackson, J., dis. op.) (observing that the detention of aliens without a hearing has "overtones of the 'protective custody' of Nazis"); *Sweez v. New Hampshire*, 354 U.S. 234, 262 (1957) (Frankfurter, J., con. op.) (noting an argument for academic freedom

in South Africa); *Ker v. California*, 374 U.S. 23, 62 (1963) (Brennan, J., dis. op.) (observing that a police practice at issue was "usually associated with totalitarian police"); *United States v. White*, 401 U.S. 745, 764–765 (1971) (Douglas, J., dis. op.) (criticizing the majority for permitting the kind of police surveillance associated with "totalitarian countries"); *Karlan v. City of Cincinnati*, 416 U.S. 924, 926–927 (1974) (Douglas, J., dis. op.) (freedom of speech in the United States contrasts with totalitarian countries); *Elrod v. Burns*, 427 U.S. 347, 353 (1976) (noting that political patronage was associated with the Nazi rise to power in Germany); *Ward v. Rock Against Racism*, 491 U.S. 781, 790 (1989) ("The totalitarian states in our own times . . . have censored musical compositions to serve the needs of the state."); and *Holland v. Illinois*, 493 U.S. 474, 507–508 n. 6 (1990) (Marshall, J., dis. op.) (drawing analogies between South Africa and Nazi Germany to U.S. practices in the racial composition of juries).

    33. See, e.g., *New York v. United States*, 326 U.S. 572, 580, and 583 (1946) (citing laws in Argentina, Canada, and Australia in upholding congressional taxing power over state objections). See also *CBS v. Democractic National Committee*, 412 U.S. 94, 158 n. 9 (1973) (Douglas, J., con. op.).

    34. See, e.g., *Adkins v. Children's Hospital*, 261 U.S. 525, 570–571 (1923) (Holmes, J., dis. op.) (pointing out that the practice of other nations, including Great Britain and Australia, indicated the reasonableness of minimum wage laws for women that the majority struck down as unconstitutional).

    35. *Palko v. Connecticut*, 302 U.S. 319, 325 (1937). The Court also noted comparative constitutional law when it confronted the incorporation question in *Hurtado v. California*, 110 U.S. 516, 522–532 (1884).

    36. *Trop v. Dulles*, 356 U.S. 86, 101 (1958).

    37. *Rudolph v. Alabama*, 375 U.S. 889 (1963) (Goldberg, J., dis. op. from denial of cert.).

    38. Ibid., quoting *Francis v. Resweber*, 329 U.S. 495, 469 (1947) (Frankfurter, J., con. op.).

    39. *Coker v. Georgia*, 433 U.S. 584 (1977).

    40. Ibid., at 596 n. 10.

    41. *Enmund v. Florida*, 458 U.S. 782, 797 n. 22 (1982).

    42. Brief of the European Union, amicus curiae, *McCarver v. North Carolina*, 533 U.S. 975 (2001) (No. 00-8727), available in 2001 WL 648609, resubmitted in *Atkins v. Virginia*, 536 U.S. 304 (2002).

    43. Brief of the Council of Europe in *Roper v. Simmons* (No. 03-633).

    44. *Muller v. Oregon*, 208 U.S. 412 (1908).

    45. *Regina v. Hicklin*, [1868] L.R. 3 Q.B. 360.

    46. *Roth v. United States*, 354 U.S. 476 (1957), at 489.

    47. See, e.g., *Regina v. Keegstra*, 2 SCR 697 (1990) (analyzing and rejecting U.S. Supreme Court holdings on obscenity); and *Regina v. Butler*, 1 SCR 452 (1992) (ruling on the permissibility of punishing "hate speech").

    48. See, e.g., *The State v. T. Makwanyane and M. Mchnunu*, 1995 (3) SA 391 (Const. Ct.).

    49. *Miranda v. State of Arizona*, 384 U.S. 436 (1966).

    50. *Foster v. Florida*, 537 U.S. 999 (2000) (Thomas, J., con. op. on denial of cert.).

    51. *Holder v. Hall*, 512 U.S. 874, 907 n. 14 (1994) (Thomas, J., con. op.).

52. See Justice Ruth Bader Ginsburg, "Looking Beyond Our Borders: The Value of a Comparative Perspective in Constitutional Adjudication," *Idaho Law Review* 40 (2003): 1. Justice Ginsburg also emphasizes that a majority of the Court has cited the U.N. Declaration of Human Rights only twice in majority opinions: *Zemel v. Rusk*, 381 U.S. 1, 4, 15 n. 13 (1965); and *Kennedy v. Mendoza-Martinez*, 372 U.S. 144, 161 n. 16 (1963). The other citations are in *American Federation of Labor v. American Sash & Door Co.*, 335 U.S. 538, 550 n. 5 (1949) (Frankfurter, J., con. op.); *International Association of Machinists v. Street*, 367 U.S. 740, 776 (1961) (Douglas, J., con. op.); *Dandridge v. Williams*, 397 U.S. 471, 521 n. 14 (1970) (Marshall, J., dis. op.); and *Knight v. Florida*, 528 U.S. 990, 996 (1999) (Breyer, J., dis. op. from the denial of review). Subsequently, Justice Souter cited and discussed the Universal Declaration on Human Rights in his opinion for the Court in *Sosa v. Alvarez-Machain*, 542 U.S. 692 (2004), rejecting a claim to sue for damages under the laws of nations and the Alien Tort Statute.

53. See *El Al Israel Airlines, Inc. v. Tsui Yuan Tseng*, 525 U.S. 155, 176 (1999). See also *Barclays Bank v. Franchise Tax Board*, 512 U.S. 298, 324 n. 22 (1994) (citing government briefs opposing California's tax scheme).

54. *Grutter v. Bollinger*, 539 U.S. 306, 344 (2003) (Ginsburg, J., con. op.).

55. *United States v. Stanley*, 483 U.S. 669, 710 (O'Connor, J., con. and dis. op.).

56. *Enmund v. Florida*, 458 U.S. 782, 796–797 n. 22 (1982).

57. *Washington v. Glucksberg*, 521 U.S. 702, 785–787 (1997) (Souter, J., con. op.).

58. Justice Breyer also noted his agreement with Justice Stevens's memorandum respecting the denial of certiorari *Lackey v. Texas*, 514 U.S. 1045 (1995) (Stevens, J., dis. op.), which indicated "the issue is an important undecided one."

59. *Elledge v. Florida*, 525 U.S. 944 (1998) (Breyer, J., dis. op.).

60. *Knight v. Florida*, 528 U.S. 990, 997 (Breyer, J., dis. op.).

61. *Foster v. Florida*, 537 U.S. 990 (2002) (Breyer, J., dis. op.).

62. Alexander Hamilton, James Madison, and John Jay, *The Federalist Papers*, ed. Isaac Kramnick (New York: Penguin Classics, 1987) (first published in 1788), no. 63, 369.

63. *Printz v. United States*, 521 U.S. 898 (1997).

64. *Nixon v. Shrink Missouri Government PAC*, 528 U.S. 377, 403 (2000) (Breyer, J., con. op.).

65. *Atkins v. Virginia*, 536 U.S. 304, at 337 (Rehnquist, C.J., dis. op.).

66. *Raines v. Byrd*, 521 U.S. 811, 821 (1997).

67. *Washington v. Glucksberg*, 521 U.S. 702, 710 no. 8, and 718 no. 16.

68. Ibid., citing *Rodriguez v. British Columbia* [1993] D.L.R. 342 (Can.); and *Gian Haur (Smt) v. State of Punjab* [1996] 2 L.R.C. 264 (India).

69. *Planned Parenthood of Southeastern Pennsylvania v. Casey*, 505 U.S. 833 (1992).

70. *Roe v. Wade*, 410 U.S. 113 (1973).

71. Ibid., at 945 n. 1 (Rehnquist, C. J., dis. op.), citing Judgment of February 25, 1975, 39 BVerfGE 1.

72. Ibid., citing *Morgentaler v. Queen*, 1 S.C.R. 30, 44 D.L.R. 4th 385 (1988).

73. *Thompson v. Oklahoma*, 487 U.S. 815, 830–833 (1988).

74. See, e.g., *Lackey v. Texas*, 514 U.S. 1045, 1045 (1995) (Stevens, J., memorandum respecting the denial of cert.).

75. See, e.g., *Patterson v. Texas*, 536 U.S. 984, 984 (2002) (Stevens, J., dis. op. respecting the denial of cert.).

76. *California v. Acevedo*, 500 U.S. 565, 586 (1991) (Stevens, J., dis. op.).

77. *Rasul v. Bush*, 542 U.S. 466 (2004).

78. *Loving v. United States*, 517 U.S. 748 (1996).

79. *Roper v. Simmons*, 543 U.S. 551 (2005).

80. See *Metro Broadcasting, Inc. v. FCC*, 497 U.S. 547, 633 no. 1 (1990) (Kennedy, J., dis. op.) (noting race-conscious definitions in Nazi Germany and the former South Africa); and *American Dredging Co. v. Miller*, 510 U.S. 443, 466 (1994) (Kennedy, J., dis. op.) (citing foreign decisions on admiralty law as relevant to federal court jurisdiction).

81. *Hiibel v. Sixth Judicial District Court of Nevada*, 542 U.S. 177 (2004).

82. *Loving v. United States*, 517 U.S. 748, at 775–776 (Scalia, J., con. op.).

83. *Roper v. Simmons*, 543 U.S. 551, at 574–575.

84. *Thompson v. Oklahoma*, 487 U.S. 815, at 868 no. 4 (Scalia, J., dis. op.).

85. *Stanford v. Kentucky*, 492 U.S. 361 (1989).

86. Ibid., at 369.

87. *McIntyre v. Ohio Elections Commission*, 514 U.S. 334 (1995).

88. See *Hamdi v. Rumsfeld*, 542 U.S. 507, 554–560 (2004) (Scalia, J., dis. op.); and *Rasul v. Bush*, 542 U.S. 466, 503–506 (2004) (Scalia, J., dis. op.).

89. *McCreary v. ACLU of Kentucky*, 125 S.Ct. 2722, 2748 (2005) (Scalia, J., dis. op.).

CHAPTER TWO

Foreign Law in American Jurisprudence

An Empirical Study

FRANCINE BANNER, KEN MILLER, AND DORIS MARIE PROVINE

INTRODUCTION

The use of legal references from outside the United States in judicial opinions interpreting the U.S. Constitution has become a controversial political issue and, remarkably, even a litmus test of suitability for membership on the Supreme Court in the estimation of some members of the U.S. Senate. The most recent nominees, John Roberts, Samuel Alito, and Sonia Sotomayor, each were questioned about their views on this topic in their confirmation hearings. The House of Representatives expressed its position in a March 2004 resolution complaining that "inappropriate judicial reliance on foreign judgments, laws, or pronouncements threatens the sovereignty of the United States, the separation of powers and the President's and Senate's treaty-making authority."[1] This resolution attracted dozens of cosponsors and a warning from its sponsor, Florida Republican Tom Feeney, that judges who base decisions on foreign precedents risk the "ultimate remedy" of impeachment.[2] Foreign law is clearly a lightning rod for congressional anxieties about judicial policy making and the growing importance of international law in world affairs.

Although this debate is illuminating regarding contemporary Court-congressional relations, it is extraordinarily misleading as an indication of the actual role of foreign legal citations in Supreme Court decision making. In the spotlight are judicial remarks in a few cases, as explained in chapter 1, that support controversial interpretations of broad clauses of the Constitution like "cruel and unusual punishment." What remains obscure is the role that foreign law plays in the overall pattern of decision making on the Supreme Court. How often do the justices consider arguments based on the law of other nations when it is not essential to resolve the case? Are advocates, through their briefs, frequently pressing arguments based on foreign legal authority on the justices to supplement positions based on domestic law? What kinds of legal problems evoke references to foreign law? Are the justices following the lead of advocates in this area or developing their own standards for these references?

A number of legal scholars have argued the pros and cons of foreign law citations in constitutional decision making. Our goal is somewhat different. We seek to better understand the empirical reality of foreign law penetration into Supreme Court decision making. To accomplish this goal, we must look at the docket as a whole. We begin by noting that the Court historically has been open to reviewing many kinds of information in considering constitutional issues, including not just social science research and scientific data but also all variety of creative works when they shed light on an issue. It has been liberal in permitting briefs from groups and individuals with no direct interest in a case. Its rules for accepting cases to review on the merits are also liberal, suggesting openness to new issues, including perhaps arguments based on the law of other nations. There is, in short, a fundamentally inductive quality in the Court's approach to information, as befits constitutional adjudication in a common-law system.[3]

The Court receives an enormous amount of information from litigants and amici. Detailed briefs are present in almost every case that the Court accepts for review.[4] The Court's openness to information helps it stay abreast of relevant legal, social scientific, and political information not easily found elsewhere while giving the justices an indication of the level of public interest in a case.[5]

Our research strategy was to study briefs filed in the 2003-2004 Supreme Court term for evidence of foreign law arguments. We chose to examine a full term, rather than selected cases, because it allowed us to get a slice-of-life view of the Court. Those who have focused on individual cases generally have chosen the most controversial ones the Court has decided in recent terms; for example, the juvenile death penalty or rights to homosexual sex. That approach helps to show why citations to foreign law have drawn critical attention from Congress, but it cannot provide a sense of emergent themes in litigation or the frequency with which the Court engages with foreign law in its day-to-day work. Nor does it give a sense of the foreign law arguments arising from the briefs the Court receives. We do not suggest that the period we studied was either typical or atypical because we have not done the longitudinal research that would be necessary to make such a claim. But we do assert that 2003 has emerged as a relatively normal term, albeit with more foreign law activity than some others because of several cases arising from the Guantánamo detentions.

Our definition of foreign law is intentionally broad. It includes citations to non-U.S. legal decisions and to non-U.S. statutes, including decisions and legislation from individual nations and regional and supranational bodies like the European Court of Human Rights, the European Parliament, and European Community institutions. We also include international human rights accords and declarations in this category, as well as citations to nonlegal authorities, including books and even newspaper articles from the foreign press. Our interest is in the nonessential citation of foreign authority, so we do not count citations to international treaties that are essential to the resolution of a controversy. In short, we looked for evidence in the briefs of what observers have found controversial in the Court's opinions: citation to foreign authority to bolster an argument that could be grounded in domestic law.

THE CONTROVERSY ABOUT FOREIGN LAW:
A BRIEF DESCRIPTION

The genesis of the political controversy about the Supreme Court's use of foreign law is generally understood to lie in *Lawrence v. Texas*,[6] a 2003 decision in which the Court cited European precedents and British statutory law in ruling that Texas's antisodomy law was unconstitutional. In dissent, Justices Scalia and Thomas and Chief Justice Rehnquist drew attention to the majority's invocation of foreign law, complaining that the discussion of foreign views was not only "meaningless *dicta*" but also "dangerous *dicta*," because "this Court should not impose foreign moods, fads, or fashions on Americans."[7] The objection was not to foreign law per se, but to its inclusion in a decision elucidating the meaning of the Fourteenth Amendment of the United States Constitution.

By all accounts, the justices appear to be enjoying the controversy they have generated. Justice Scalia and Justice Stephen Breyer, for example, gamely debated the issue before a live television audience at American University's Washington College of Law in January 2005, and more recently, Justice Scalia traded views on foreign law in front of a television audience with American Civil Liberties Union (ACLU) president Nadine Strossen. Justice Ruth Bader Ginsburg occasionally has weighed in to favor references to foreign case law in speeches before legal audiences and in her writing, and while she was on the Court, Justice Sandra Day O'Connor referred in positive terms to citations to foreign law. Even Justice Scalia, the Court's most outspoken opponent of foreign law references, has outlined the circumstances under which he would rely on foreign law. Citation of foreign legal authority is appropriate, he has argued, though perhaps not strictly necessary, in interpreting treaty obligations. He argued for respect for "our sister signatories" in *Olympic Airways v. Husain*,[8] playfully chiding the majority for its "new abstemiousness with regard to foreign fare."

On the recently reformulated Court, Justice Anthony M. Kennedy is likely to play a key role with regard to foreign law. He has already established himself as the swing voter who most often tips the scales in the close cases that divide liberal and conservative members of the Court. Even before Justices Alito and Roberts joined the Court, however, Kennedy had been singled out by some members of Congress as leading the United States toward an undesirable "internationalization" of its judicial system, and he was excoriated by former House Majority Leader Tom DeLay for his "incredibly outrageous" and "activist" opinions that arise from his "do[ing] his own research on the Internet!"[9] It was Kennedy who authored the majority opinion in *Lawrence v. Texas*. He also wrote in *Roper v. Simmons*[10] that the "world community's" prohibition of the juvenile death penalty provided "respected and significant confirmation" for the Court's own conclusion that the juvenile death penalty is unconstitutional. At least one legal commentator sees him as sending "a powerful new message about weight to be given international law" by U.S. courts.[11]

Although the members of the Court appear quite relaxed about the foreign law controversy, debate among legal scholars has been heated, which is a bit surprising because *Lawrence*, as many observers have pointed out, was not the first time members of the Supreme Court used foreign law to bolster their opinions.[12] As Kersch observes, the *Lawrence* decision made apparent a "trend of going global" that was anything but new,[13] whereas Cleveland describes such citations as "the culmination of a battle raging" since the 1980s.[14] Morag-Levine reaches back even further in her analysis of today's controversy, observing that the recent vehement disagreement about the legitimacy of citation to non-U.S. sources resembles nineteenth-century disputes among the justices in *Printz v. United States*.[15] Calabresi and Zimdahl also see long-term continuity, noting that "references to foreign sources of law . . . have been somewhat commonplace" during the past two hundred years:

> [T]he Lawrence and Roper Court's reference to foreign sources of law reflects an old tradition of such references which can be found in many nineteenth century Supreme Court opinions, including opinions written by such historical titans as Chief Justice Marshall and Justice Story.[16]

There is long-standing practice of using these citations to support highly controversial opinions. Foreign law was referenced, for example, in both concurring and dissenting opinions in *Dred Scott v. Sandford*, upholding slavery, and deployed in *Reynolds v. United States*, a case addressing polygamy.[17] International rules regarding territorial jurisdiction helped the Court determine the reach of state personal jurisdiction in the classic civil procedure case *Pennoyer v. Neff*.[18]

Despite this venerable history of foreign law citations, the matter remains controversial in legal, as well as political, circles. Many commentators have been dubious of, or even hostile to, the idea of foreign citations. Alford, for instance, notes that where domestic consensus on issues like the death penalty may be lacking, foreign law may embolden the Court to render a decision that has little public or legal support: "One might say that the Court recognizes that exotic suspenders take on increasing importance when one's trusty belt is threadbare."[19] Glendon complains that foreign material has been used inappropriately by the Court to "buttress the court's own decision to override legislation."[20] In a similar vein, Robert Bork worries that there has been a qualitative change in the type of cases citing non-U.S. authority, noting a "recent tendency" of courts to "cite the decisions of foreign courts in applying their own constitutions," a trend he considers to be antidemocratic.[21] Calabresi and Zimdahl echo Bork, noting that "in controversial social issue cases, like *Lawrence* . . . the Court should not impose secular European values on the American citizenry in the guise of constitutional interpretation."[22] Kersch, too, argues that the Court's recent "transnational turn" is distinct from earlier citation to foreign authority because it is tied to reformist political goals.[23] Cleveland, on the other hand, calls such criticism "ahistorical and misguided" in failing to acknowledge a "rich historical relationship between the Constitution and international law."[24]

There does appear to be a common sentiment among both proponents and critics that the Court lacks a systematic approach to foreign law citation. Justice Breyer acknowledged this in suggesting that the Court's current practice of citation to non-U.S. authority is analogous to the way judges treat legislative history: "It's like looking at a cocktail party, you look over the cocktail party to identify your friends."[25] Young recommends that a system similar to the preemption doctrine governing state and federal law be devised to determine when non-U.S. law should be applied.[26] Waldron suggests that citation to foreign law can stem from the "law of nations."[27]

There have been some attempts to determine how frequently foreign law citations occur in the Supreme Court's opinions. Calabresi and Zimdahl reviewed decisions by the Court from 1789 to 2005, demonstrating that, although the Court's recent citation to foreign law is not "unprecedented," there does appear to have been a "steady escalation" in recent years, particularly in criminal and in controversial cases.[28] Anderson argues that, even though a "handful" of cases contained citation to non-U.S. law prior to the *Roper v. Simmons* decision, the post-Roper era has ushered in a "new era of constitutional comparativism."[29]

Although these scholars give us a much-needed historical perspective on whether and how the Court's citation to foreign law qualitatively and quantitatively may have changed during the past two hundred years, nowhere have we found a systematic, empirical study of the role that non-U.S. law currently plays in the day-to-day operation of the Supreme Court. One might surmise from the discussion among the justices and from the many contacts they have with foreign judges and lawyers—and from comments regarding "escalation" of reliance on non-U.S. authority—that citations to foreign law have become a relatively frequent phenomenon in Supreme Court opinions. This is not the case. Even the most ardent defenders of foreign law do not invoke it very often. Professional norms not fully elucidated in the debate about foreign law appear to discourage these references, even as dicta. We take up this issue in the next section, which examines the 2003 docket in detail.

OUR STUDY

We began by examining the Table of Authorities in each of the briefs that litigants and amici filed in the cases that the Court decided in 2003. We looked for any reference to foreign law or foreign materials, including foreign technical material and newspaper articles in the foreign press. This process involved reviewing 722 briefs, a laborious exercise but one we thought necessary in order not to prejudge a case as either "foreign" or "domestic" on the basis of the Court's eventual resolution of the conflict. This initial review eliminated sixty-seven of the eighty cases the Court decided that term.

Eleven of the thirteen cases that remained involved issues that might engage the justices in consideration of foreign law. An example is *Sosa v. Alvarez-Machain*,[30] in which Drug Enforcement and Administration (DEA)-hired agents abducted a Mexican national in Mexico and delivered him to authorities in the United States.[31] The two remaining cases did not appear to have international implications but nevertheless contained at least one citation to foreign materials in one of the briefs filed in each case.[32]

We then took a closer look at all of the briefs in our thirteen-case sample. We analyzed the arguments in each of these documents, noting whether they rested on domestic or international authority and whether they were strictly legal arguments or broader and more policy oriented. We noted the individuals and organizations filing amicus briefs to see whether they were domestic or foreign. We tabulated the proportion of U.S. to non-U.S. cases cited in each brief as well the proportion of other than U.S. legal authority.

After a thorough review of the briefs, we turned to the on-the-merits decisions in these cases, looking for references to foreign law in any of the opinions. Our procedure of working "forward" from filings to opinions, rather than "backward" from opinions to submitted materials, helped to ensure that we did not miss any relevant material in the somewhat tedious process of sifting through the numerous amicus and litigant briefs.

FINDINGS

The thirteen cases in which foreign law made an appearance, either in the briefs or opinions or both, included three cases regarding some aspect of the detention of enemy combatants:

- *Hamdi v. Rumsfeld*, 124 S.Ct. 2633,
- *Rasul v. Bush*, 124 S.Ct. 2686,
- *Rumsfeld v. Padilla*, 124 S.Ct. 2711.

The other ten cases raised a variety of issues:

- The environmental impact of additional trucks being allowed into the United States pursuant to the North American Free Trade Agreement (NAFTA) (*DOT v. Public Citizen*, 124 S.Ct. 2204)
- International price fixing of vitamin sales (*F. Hoffman-La Roche Ltd. et al. v. Empagran SA, et al.*, 124 S.Ct. 2359)
- Reparations for art stolen by the Nazis during World War II (*Republic of Austria v. Altman*, 124 S.Ct. 2240)
- Applicability of the Warsaw Convention to a passenger's accidental death on an airline (*Olympic Airways v. Husain*, 124 . S.Ct. 1221)
- Whether a Mexican national abducted by the DEA in Mexico has a cause of action against the DEA under the Alien Tort Claims Act (*Sosa v. Alvarez-Machain*, 124 S.Ct. 2739)
- Drug searches of gas tanks at the Mexican border (*U.S. v. Flores-Montano*, 124 S.Ct. 1582)
- Discovery issues in a European competition claim against a U.S. corporation (*Intel v. Advanced Micro Devices*, 124 S.Ct. 2466)
- Municipal provision of telecommunications services (*Nixon v. Missouri Municipal League*, 124 S.Ct. 1555)
- Whether failure to give a suspect a Miranda warning requires suppression of the physical fruits of a suspect's unwarned but voluntary statements (*U.S. v. Patane,* 124 S.Ct. 2620)

- Whether diversity jurisdiction exists in a breach of contract action brought by two Mexican partners against a Mexican corporation in U.S. district court (*Grupo Dataflux v. Atlas Global Group, LP*, 124 S.Ct. 1920).

The brief writers in these cases were diverse. In *Rasul v. Bush,* which involved the rights of prisoners held at Guantánamo Bay, the amici included U.S. ambassadors to various nations, the Slavic and European Centres for Law and Justice, former American prisoners of war, international law experts, the international bar association, a coalition of international nongovernmental organizations (NGOs), members of the Houses of Parliament in the United Kingdom and Northern Ireland, the International Commission of Jurists, the family members of various detainees, and the plaintiffs in a Nazi "stolen art" case. In *F. Hoffman-La Roche*, the vitamin price-fixing case, amicus briefs were filed by the governments of Germany, the Netherlands, Northern Ireland, the United Kingdom, Japan, Canada, and Belgium. In *Republic of Austria v. Altman*, the case involving art allegedly stolen by the Nazis, an international group of artists filed a brief. Fred Korematsu, who was detained in a U.S. internment camp during World War II, filed amicus briefs in all three cases dealing with detention—*Rasul v. Bush, Hamdi v Rumsfeld,* and *Rumsfeld v. Padilla*. In each case, he noted that the United States should not use a time of war as an excuse to restrict civil liberties.

There was a wide range of sources in the briefs studied. Cases involving foreign detainees often cited the Geneva Convention, the International Convention for Civil and Political Rights, the European Convention for the Protection of Human Rights, and various other UN resolutions. The case involving the international vitamin cartel, *F. Hoffman-La Roche*, cited numerous treaties among foreign governments and the United States, as well as various non-U.S. statutes in support of free trade and protecting non-U.S. consumers. Interestingly, some litigants and amici cited newspapers, including sources from as far away as Africa, Saudi Arabia, and Korea. In *Rasul v. Bush*, for example, a few parties cited news articles describing the unfair detention or poor conditions at Guantánamo Bay: "Briton Claims Racial Abuse"[33] and "Legal Limbo of Guantánamo's Prisoners."[34] Others cited articles describing the fine time and great meals prisoners were having in custody: "I Had a Good Time at Guantánamo, Says Inmate."[35]

We found an assortment of foreign legal materials on both sides of disputed issues in some cases. In the *Hamdi* case, Robert Bork, no fan of the International Criminal Court, cited that court's founding principles in support of his argument for maintaining custody of the Guantánamo detainees. Opposing sides cited the Geneva Convention as support in *Rasul v. Bush*. Former legal advisors to the U.S. State Department, the European Centre for Law and Justice, and the Slavic Centre for Law and Justice argued that the convention showed that detention in times of war without access to a tribunal was consistent with the rule of law and law of armed conflict, whereas the opposing side relied on the convention to show that detaining individuals was "anathema" to the rule of law.

Table 2.1 (next page) summarizes some of these findings. Note the degree to which references to U.S. law predominated in the briefs, both in case citations and in citations to secondary forms of authority, such as treaties, constitutions, statutes, law review articles, addresses before the UN, and newspapers. Although U.S. materials were preponderant in the briefs, there were sufficient foreign materials in almost all of these cases to permit the Supreme Court to cite foreign law in its opinions. A significant number of briefs had extensive citations to foreign authority, including cases, statutes, treaties, and other secondary legal materials.

The overall picture, however, was one of analysis based on U.S. domestic law. Far more than 90 percent of cases cited and at least 70 percent of secondary material cited were from the United States (see Table 2.1). Some of the U.S. citations contained references to foreign law within them. Thus in *Olympic Airways*, we found briefs that cited both U.S. and foreign cases that previously had interpreted the Warsaw Convention. In an interesting variation on this theme, two briefs in *Rasul v. Bush* cited two American cases that have become famous for their reference to foreign law: *Atkins v. Virginia* and *Lawrence v. Texas*. The argument in these briefs was that these cases were right in using world standards in constitutional interpretation.[36]

Litigants and their allies are clearly incorporating foreign law as they see fit—there is no developed jurisprudence in this area, nor much self-discipline in citation or argument based on foreign law. The brief writers tend to be policy oriented and not particularly careful about citing material directly relevant to the case. In *Rasul v. Bush*, for example, the governors' brief argued that the "war on terror" made it more difficult for governors to respond to emergencies. Former American POWs argued that a decision against access to habeas corpus might endanger U.S. POWs currently held around the world. Relatives of detainees argued that they were being held in violation of Islamic law. NGOs argued that a decision against detainees could undermine their activities. Potential claimants under the Alien Tort Claims Act argued that "alien friends" should be entitled to assert claims in U.S. courts. Cases in other areas were similar. For example, in *Altman v. Austria*, a case requesting compensation for Jewish-owned art stolen by Nazi sympathizers in Austria, some amici focused on the evil the Nazis had produced. Litigants and the amici left the Court to make its own assessment of the relevance of such material.

No brief writer addressed the question of when foreign law should be incorporated into a Supreme Court decision. This question—a preoccupation among legal scholars and some members of the Court—could have

Table 2.1. Citations to Foreign Law in Amicus and Party Briefs

Case	Number of Amici	Citations to Foreign Case Law as a percentage of all legal citations	Citations to Foreign Secondary Authority as a percentage of all nonlegal citations
DOT v. Public Citizen, 124 S. Ct. 2204	5	0%	0%
Hamdi v. Rumsfeld, 124 S. Ct. 2633	17	5%	13%
Olympic Airways v. Husain, 124 S. Ct. 1221	2	9%	0%
Republic of Austria v. Altman, 124 S. Ct. 2240	7	3%	6%
Rasul v. Bush, 124 S. Ct. 2686	37	15%	35%
F. Hoffman-La Roche Ltd. v. Empagran S.A., et al., 124 S. Ct. 2359	23	6%	29%
U.S. v. Flores-Montano, 124 S. Ct. 1582	2	0%	0%
Sosa v. Alvarez-Machain, 124 S. Ct. 2739	24	11%	14%
Intel v. Advanced Micro Devices, 124 S. Ct. 2466	7	18%	19%
Rumsfeld v. Padilla, 124 S. Ct. 2711	31	7%	6%
Nixon v. Missouri Municipal League, 124 S. Ct. 1555	12	0%	2%
U.S. v. Patane, 124 S. Ct. 2620	4	1%	0%
Grupo Dataflux v. Atlas Global Group, L.P., 124 S. Ct. 1920	0	0%	0%

been usefully discussed in introducing foreign material. The brief writers could have at least explained the criteria they used in their own selection of materials. The explanation for this omission may lie in the ignorance of some of the brief writers of the debate about foreign law or possibly in the narrow conception of argument that pervades these briefs. The tone of these documents, we found, was uniformly practical and adversarial, not broadly conceptual and abstract. The evident goal, not surprisingly, was to persuade by whatever means possible.

Perhaps our most significant finding is that the brief writers generally failed to persuade the justices on the grounds of foreign law–based arguments. If the opinions of the justices are a reasonably reliable barometer of their reasoning process, foreign law materials had little impact on the decisions reached in the 2003 term. Even in the three cases involving detainees whom the government deemed enemy combatants, in which many amici and some litigants focused significantly on foreign law, most of the justices restricted themselves to solely domestic sources. Only in *Hamdi v. Rumsfield* did a four-justice plurality rely on law–of–war principles found in international law, including the Third Geneva Convention Related to the Treatment and Punishment of Prisoners during War.[37] *Hamdi*, like *Padilla* and *Rasul*, was ultimately decided exclusively on U.S. legal grounds. The many transnational concerns expressed in the briefs in these cases were completely ignored by most of the justices.

The only case that did include an extensive discussion of issues raised by foreign law was *F. Hoffman-La Roche*, the vitamin case. The case addressed whether the Court could apply the Sherman Anti-Trust Act to redress foreign injury that occurred as a result of international price-fixing. The Court examined two primary questions: (1) Did the Foreign Trade Antitrust Improvements Act of 1982 (FTAIA) apply to claims of foreign plaintiffs whose injuries did not arise from the effects of antitrust violations on United States commerce? and (2) Did these foreign plaintiffs have standing to sue under the Clayton Act, 15 U.S.C. § 15(a)? Although the case ultimately was decided on the basis of U.S. law as arising under the FTAIA, Justice Breyer devoted a significant portion of the majority opinion to a discussion of sovereignty issues raised in foreign briefs.[38] He discussed arguments made by the Respondents, as well as those from amicus briefs filed by the governments of Germany, Canada, and Japan, that application of the U.S. antitrust statute in this instance would interfere with states' ability to regulate their own commercial affairs. He contrasted these arguments with those made by the Petitioners that injured plaintiffs should be permitted to benefit from the treble damages provision included in the U.S. statute.[39] Ultimately, the Court resisted what it called "legal imperialism" and declined to impose U.S. antitrust laws on the international market.[40]

Looking at the briefs in each case and comparing them with the Court's opinions suggests that the Court is almost never *obliged* to use foreign law in reaching a decision. Even treaties, such as the Warsaw Convention, can be interpreted solely in terms of references to U.S. case law and norms. When the Court elects to refer to foreign law, as Justice Breyer did in *F. Hoffman-La Roche*, or, more strikingly, as Justice Kennedy did in *Lawrence* and *Roper* in prior terms, it does so quite tentatively. Generally, the justices use international law not as a basis for their decisions but as an ancillary proposition confirming established U.S. norms, as Justice O'Connor has suggested they should.

Our study thus suggests that claims of a foreign law invasion are seriously misleading. In fact, the foreign law penetration into American jurisprudence is slight, occasional, and more often than not grounded in nonconstitutional concerns. No one on the Court appears to be using foreign law as the primary basis for interpreting any U.S. statutes or our Constitution or even treaties and international conventions. Rather the picture that emerges is more conversational, with the justices drawing parallels to situations in other nations to bolster points already established with American sources, and not doing even this very often.

This movement is, above all, a tentative exploration of options, not a movement away from traditional decisional norms. As a practical matter, the justices have much more foreign law available to them than they actually use, indicating sensitivity to the limited role foreign sources typically play in deciding cases. Even the foreigners who file briefs attempting to convince the Court of their position typically rely most heavily on American law to make their arguments.

CONCLUDING OBSERVATIONS

No one should be surprised that foreign law sometimes makes its way into American judicial opinions. The United States was founded with international norms in mind. The Constitution contains a number of clauses designed to appeal to foreign investors and reassure our overseas creditors. Judges have been obliged to study foreign law in interpreting treaty obligations and international understandings since our earliest days. These are respected precedents. Some of these early decisions appeared in the briefs and opinions in the 2003 term.

Individual rights also have been debated in global terms and not only recently. A famous example is the Truman administration's request that the Court outlaw racial segregation in the 1940s and 1950s on the grounds that it offended world opinion and weakened our effort to rid the world of communism. As Dudziak reports: "[T]hrough a series of *amicus* briefs detailing the effect of racial segregation on U.S. foreign policy interests, the Administration impressed upon the Supreme Court the necessity for world peace and national security of upholding black civil rights at home."[41] The Court did not mention these concerns in its desegregation opinions, but it must have been aware of them.

Explicit references to foreign law in deciding a matter of individual rights, however, are something new, representing an increasingly open acknowledgment among members of the Supreme Court that many democratic nations in the industrialized world are struggling with the same problems. Such citations also implicitly acknowledge that courts around the world have been referencing, and sometimes relying upon, Supreme Court jurisprudence for some time. The right to silence in criminal proceedings announced in *Miranda v. Arizona*, for example, has been imitated by nations such as China. Brazil, India, and Russia that have also looked to U.S. decisions for guidance in affirmative action and desegregation cases.[42]

It is evident from our research that the justices are quite selective in the actual deployment of foreign law in their opinions. Even when the Court has an obvious opportunity to use foreign law, and is encouraged to do so by amici, it will probably demur, instead focusing its analysis inward toward federal legislation or executive action. The justices appear to be more inclined to talk with foreign judges about common legal concerns than to reference those concerns in their own opinions. They have done nothing to discourage foreign law arguments from litigants or amici, but they are obviously reluctant to use these materials in their opinions.

It seems unlikely that the Court will soon develop a jurisprudence to indicate when foreign law sources might be relevant, either in constitutional interpretation or in applying treaty law. The fault line between those who favor a more originalist or textual approach to the Constitution and those who take a more functional, contemporizing view of their role is unlikely to go away. As Justice Breyer noted in his televised discussion with Justice Scalia, differences over textualism reflect differences in the weighing of evils to be avoided in constitutional interpretation, a matter on which reasonable minds can, and do, differ.

It would be more accurate to characterize what is happening as a conversation. The question that has drawn most public attention is where foreign law fits in the consideration of individual-rights questions that admit of no easy answers. But this is not the only area where judicial views differ. The 2003 term data reveal that there is also disagreement among the justices on whether and how to assimilate foreign judicial decisions in interpreting treaty obligations. As the *Olympic Airways* litigation demonstrates, the split on the Court on treaty issues is different from the division of opinion in individual rights cases. Treaty cases allow a justice claiming an originalist approach to adjudication to demonstrate a cosmopolitanism that would be inapposite in individual rights cases.

In this conversation about the value of foreign law in American jurisprudence, one thing that all the participants would probably agree upon is that references to foreign law are not a "remarkable" departure from established judicial patterns of thought. Participants might also agree that there is increasing pressure to include references to foreign law. The amount of relevant and available foreign materials is growing dramatically with the rise of active constitutional courts at the national level and of meta-national courts at the regional and international level. Human rights discourse is an expanding global phenomenon with important implications for legal systems. Judges are in more contact with each other than in earlier times, and legal materials from all over the world are much easier to access than ever before. A multitude of voices invoking a wealth of international and supranational law, in short, are vying for the Court's attention. And a growing number of controversies that arguably implicate international law are making their way before the Court. The justices are quite appropriately thoughtful in considering whether and how to engage with this material.

NOTES

1. H.R. 568.
2. Linda Greenhouse, "Rehnquist Resumes His Call for Judicial Independence," *New York Times* (January 1, 2005), A10. Senator Tom Coburn made a similar threat at the Roberts confirmation hearings. Mary Ann Glendon, "Judicial Tourism: What's Wrong with the U.S. Supreme Court Citing Foreign Law," *Wall Street Journal* (WSJ. com), online at http://www.opinionjournal.com/forms/printThishtm1?id=110007265 (September 17, 2005).
3. See, for example, Melissa A. Waters, "Meditating Norms and Identity: The Role of Transnational Judicial Dialogue in Creating and Enforcing International Law," *Georgetown Law Journal* 93 (2005): 487–574; Janet Koven Levit, "The Supreme Court, Constitutional Courts and the Role of International Law in Constitutional Jurisprudence: A Tale of International Law in the Heartland: Torres and the Role of State Courts in Transnational Legal Conversation," *Tulsa Journal of Comparative and International Law* 11 (2005): 163–187; Gerald Neuman, "The Uses of International Law in Constitutional Interpretation," *American Journal of International Law* 98 (2004): 82–90; and Lori Fisler Damrosch and Bernard H. Oxman, "Agora: The United States Constitution and International Law," *American Journal of International Law* 98 (2004): 42.
4. Lee Epstein and Jack Knight, *Choices Justices Make* (Washington, D.C.: Congressional Quarterly Press, 1998); Joseph D. Kearney and Tomas W. Merrill, "The Influence of *Amicus Curiae* Briefs on the Supreme Court," *University of Pennsylvania Law Review* 148 (2000): 743–855; and Forrest Maltzman, James F. Spriggs, and Paul J. Wahlbeck, *Crafting Law on the Supreme Court* (Cambridge: Cambridge University Press, 2000).
5. Paul M. Collins Jr., "Friends of the Court: Examining the Influence of Amicus Curiae Participation in U.S. Supreme Court Litigation," *Law and Society Review* 38 (2004): 807–32 and see Epstein and Knight; Marie Hojnacki, " 'Interest Groups' Decisions to Join Alliances or Work Alone," *American Journal of Political Science* 41 (1997): 67–87; Stephen L. Wasby, *Race Relations Litigation in an Age of Complexity*

(Charlottesville: University Press of Virginia, 1995); and Bruce L. Ennis, "Effective Amicus Briefs," *Catholic University Law Review* 33 (1984): 603–609.

6. 539 U.S. 558 (2003).

7. *Lawrence v. Texas,* 539 U.S. 558 (2003), citing *Foster v. Florida,* 537 U.S. 990 (2002).

8. 124 S. Ct. 1221 (2003).

9. Associated Press, "DeLay Slams Supreme Court Justice Kennedy," MSNBC. com (April 20, 2005), online at http://www.msnbc.msn.com/id/7550959/.

10. 125 S. Ct. 1183 (2005).

11. Richard Dieter, "International Influence on the Death Penalty in the U.S.," *Foreign Service Journal* (October 2003).

12. Conservative as well as liberal justices have used foreign law to support their arguments in a variety of decisions. See Chief Justice Rehnquist's use of foreign law in *Washington v. Glucksberg,* 521 U.S. 702 (1997) and *Vacco v. Quill,* 521 U.S. 793 (1997). Justices Ginsburg and Breyer cited international law in their concurrence in *Grutter v. Bollinger* at 123 S. Ct. 2325 (2003), and see *Coker v. Georgia,* 433 U.S. 584, 596 n. 10 (1977); *Thompson v. Oklahoma,* 487 U.S. 815, 830 (1988). Justice Breyer also cited foreign law in a dissent from the denial of certiorari in a death penalty appeal in *Knight v. Florida,* 528 U.S. 990 (1999). And see *Atkins v. Virginia* and *Roper v. Simmons.*

13. Ken Kersch, "Essay: The New Legal Transnationalism, the Globalized Judiciary, and the Rule of Law," *Washington University Global Studies Law Review* 4 (2004): 345–387.

14. Sarah H. Cleveland, "Our International Constitution," *Yale Journal of International Law* 31 (2006): 1–125.

15. Noga Morag-Levine, "Judges, Legislators, and Europe's Law: Common Law Constitutionalism and Foreign Precedents," *Maryland Law Review* 65 (2006): 34–48.

16. Steven G. Calabresi and Stephanie Dotson Zimdahl, "The Supreme Court and Foreign Sources of Law: Two Hundred Years of Practice and the Juvenile Death Penalty Decision," *William and Mary Law Review* 47 (2005): 743–909, at 907.

17. Ibid., 753–754.

18. Cleveland, 50.

19. Roger P. Alford, "Agora: The United States Constitution and International Law: Misusing International Sources to Interpret the Constitution," *American Journal of International Law* 98 (2005): 57–68.

20. See Glendon, note 2.

21. Robert H. Bork, *Coercing Virtue: The Worldwide Rule of Judges* (Washington, D.C.: American Enterprise Institute, 2003), 17.

22. Calabresi and Zimdahl, 754.

23. Kersch, 346.

24. Cleveland, 124.

25. Stephen Breyer, "Keynote Address" 97 ASIL Proceedings (Discussion) (2003).

26. Ernest A. Young, "Institutional Settlement in a Globalizing Judicial System," *Duke Law Journal* 54 (2005): 1177–1178.

27. Jeremy Waldron, "The Supreme Court, 2004 Term: Foreign Law and the Modern *Ius Gentium*," *Harvard Law Review* 119 (2005): 129–147. For a comprehensive discussion of the views of opponents and proponents of constitutional comparativism, see Alford (2006, 558–659).

28. Calabresi and Zimdahl, 848–849, 903.

29. Kenneth Anderson, "Foreign Law and the U.S. Constitution," *Policy Review* (2005): 146–147. More generally, see Louis J. Blum, "Mixed Signals: The Limited Role of Comparative Analysis in Constitutional Adjudication," *San Diego Law Review* 39 (2003): 157–200; Harold Koh, "Agora: The United States Constitution and International Law: International Law as Part of Our Law," *American Journal of International Law* 98 (2004): 43–57; Joan Larsen, "Importing Constitutional Norms from a 'Wider Civilization': *Lawrence* and the Rehnquist Court's Use of Foreign and International Law in Domestic Constitutional Interpretation," *Ohio State Law Journal* 65 (2004): 1283–1327; Donald E. Childress, "Using Comparative Constitutional Law to Resolve Domestic Federal Questions," *Duke Law Journal* 53 (2003): 193–221; and Alford.

30. 124 S. Ct. 2739 (2004).

31. We initially identified one case involving the constitutionality of the Child Online Protection Act that we thought might have attracted foreign amici; however, we eliminated that case from our sample because the opinions and briefs focused entirely on domestic-law issues, and the case attracted no foreign amici.

32. One case was *Nixon v. Missouri Municipal League*, 541 U.S. 125 (2003), Brief of the High Tech Broadband Coalition and the Fiber-To-The-Home Council as Amici Curiae in Support of Respondents, 2003 WL 22466045. The coalition cited UN statistics on broadband penetration to suggest the preemptive effect of the Telecommunications Act. These statistics were not ultimately referenced by the Court in the published decision. The other case, *U.S. v. Patane*, 542 U.S. 630 (2003), concerned the limits of the *Miranda* decision. The brief of the Brennan Center for Justice, 2003 WL 22197346, referenced a British decision and an Israeli decision for the proposition that inhuman or degrading treatment should be prohibited, regardless of the use to be made of the information sought. The Court did not reference either of these decisions in its opinion.

33. Tania Branigan, "Camp Delta Briton Claims Racial Abuse," *The Guardian* (January 12, 2004), online at http://www.guardian.co.uk/guantanamo/story/0,13743,1121046,00.html.

34. Monica Whitlock, "Legal Limbo of Guantanamo's Prisoners," BBC News (May 16, 2003), online at http://news.bbc.co.uk/2/hi/americas/3034697.stm.

35. Rajeev Syal, "I Had A Good Time at Guantánamo, Says Inmate," *London Telegraph* (January 9, 2004), online at http://www.telegraph.co.uk/news/main.jhtml?xml=/news/2004/02/08/wguan08.xml&sSheet=/portal/2004/02/08/ixportal.html.

36. *Rasul v. Bush*, 124 S.Ct. 2686, *Petitioners' Brief on the Merits*, 2004 WL 162758 at 29 and *Brief of Amicus Curiae in Support of Respondents of Citizens for the Common Defense*, 2004 WL 442301 at 26.

37. See Rebecca Lefler, "Note: A Comparison of Comparison: Use of Foreign Case Law as Persuasive Authority by the United States Supreme Court, the Supreme Court of Canada and the High Court of Australia," *Southern California Interdisciplinary Law Journal* 11 (2001): 592–594.

38. Justice Breyer, it should be noted, also discussed foreign law in a case that was not part of our sample because it did not get the four votes necessary for review under the Court's certiorari rules. Breyer framed his dissent from this decision with reference to foreign law in *Torres v. Mullin*, 540 U.S. 1035, *cert. denied* (2003), which concerned the right of arrested foreign nationals to have their consulates informed of their arrests.

39. *F. Hoffman-La Roche Ltd. v. Empagran SA, et al.*, 124 S. Ct. at 2373.

40. Ibid., 2373.

41. Mary L. Dudziak, "Desegregation as a Cold War Imperative," *Stanford Law Review* 41 (1988): 61–120.

42. Ricardo Henriques, "Race, Inequality and Education: Challenges for Affirmative Action in Brazil and the United States," presented at the Woodrow Wilson International Center for Scholars (April 11, 2005); and Thomas Sowell, "International Affirmative Action," online at http://www.townhall.com (visited June 3, 2003).

CHAPTER THREE

Foreign Law
in Domestic Courts

Different Uses, Different Implications

CHRISTOPHER A. WHYTOCK

One can be forgiven for wondering if the debate about references to foreign law in U.S. court opinions is much ado about nothing.[1] In none of the cases that sparked the debate—*Atkins v. Virginia*,[2] *Lawrence v. Texas*,[3] and *Roper v. Simmons*[4]—did the U.S. Supreme Court treat foreign law as binding law that could override U.S. law. Nor, as two recent articles empirically demonstrate, is the use of foreign law by U.S. courts anything new.[5] For courts in other countries, the use of foreign law is "decidedly commonplace."[6] Yet "[t]here is little evidence to suggest parallel mobilization in opposition to foreign citations by courts abroad"[7]—which suggests that the controversy in the United States indeed might be disproportionate to the problems posed by comparativism in judicial decision making. As Noga Morag-Levine states, "Supreme Court opinions are replete with references to extra-legal sources such as philosophical treatises and social science research. Why single out foreign case law as deserving of special condemnation?"[8] After a careful analysis of the debate, Mark Tushnet concludes that what really is motivating critics of foreign law in U.S. courts is concern about the appropriate scope of judicial power, not foreign law per se.[9]

Nevertheless, the question of foreign law in domestic courts is an important one. Skeptics correctly warn that the use of foreign law—at least in the context of constitutional interpretation—raises serious issues of constitutional theory[10] and comparative methodology.[11] Those more sympathetic to the use of foreign law not only disagree with skeptics' arguments that there is no "constitutional license" to use foreign law,[12] but also claim that a greater willingness of domestic courts to use foreign law can improve the quality of constitutional decision making. The focus of existing research and commentary on both sides of this debate is on the constitutional issues associated with references to foreign law in U.S. court opinions and, more generally, on the important normative concerns about whether and how domestic courts should use foreign law.

This work, however, focuses little attention on the actual consequences of domestic court references to foreign law and therefore eventually relies on untested empirical assumptions about what those consequences might be.[13] Nonconsequentialist reasons to favor or disfavor foreign law in domestic courts exist, of course. Yet a well-informed, normative dialogue must be attentive to consequences, at least if it is to extend beyond the narrow confines of more formal variants of constitutional theory. The use of foreign law in domestic courts also raises interesting questions of positive theory—particularly about the relationship between different uses of foreign law and the cross-border migration of legal norms that so far are unexplored. For these reasons, this chapter proposes a social science approach that focuses on the empirical implications of foreign law in domestic courts.

Unfortunately, the existing literature does not provide the conceptual foundations for exploring these implications. Scholars generally appreciate that domestic courts can use foreign law in different ways and that these differences are analytically significant, but the result has been an overabundance of typologies of different uses and a lack of conceptual clarity. Therefore, in the main part of this chapter, I will attempt to take a small conceptual step forward by consolidating into a single, manageable typology the many different uses of foreign law in domestic courts that already have been identified by scholars. No single typology can be useful for all purposes, and ultimately an empirical project motivated by a particular theory calls for concepts that are motivated by the same theory. Thus the goal is modest: to provide a language for a preliminary exploration of the empirical implications of different uses of foreign law that may be useful to a wide range of scholars. Next, I will build on the typology by considering the consequences of different uses of foreign law in domestic courts and the role of domestic courts as agents in processes of norm internalization and transnational policy diffusion. In particular, I will use the typology to examine the claim made by some critics that foreign law references in U.S. court opinions lead to the internalization of non-U.S. norms into U.S. society by changing domestic law or policy. Finally, I will suggest several avenues for future research on foreign law in domestic courts and domestic courts as institutional pathways for norm internalization. The central message is simple: Different uses of foreign law have different implications for the cross-border migration of legal norms, and both normative theory and positive theory should take these differences into account.[14]

DIFFERENT USES OF FOREIGN LAW IN DOMESTIC COURTS

"Stable concepts and a shared understanding of categories are routinely viewed as a foundation of any research community."[15] If this view is correct, then the emerging community of scholars studying foreign law references in U.S. court opinions is being built on somewhat shaky foundations; the scholarly conversation about how domestic courts use foreign law suffers from a cacophony of categories. Richard Posner distinguishes informational and precedential citations to foreign law.[16] Anne-Marie Slaughter distinguishes between using foreign law as coercive authority and using it as persuasive authority.[17] Vicki Jackson takes Slaughter's category of persuasive authority and breaks it into more than a dozen specific ways that domestic courts have used foreign law.[18] Kenneth Anderson distinguishes the use of foreign law to help interpret the U.S. Constitution from other uses of foreign law.[19] Still others—including David Fontana and Kim Scheppele—distinguish between using foreign law in a positive way, as an example of what a domestic court should do, and in a negative way, as an example of what a domestic court should not do.[20] Fontana also distinguishes "genealogical comparativism" from "ahistorical comparativism," as well as three other ways domestic courts may use foreign law: in *dicta*, to create a principle of law, and to prove a constitutional fact.[21]

For Sujit Choudhry, foreign law can be used in one of three modes—universalist, genealogical, and dialogical[22]—whereas Mark Tushnet identifies functionalism, expressivism, and bricolage as three ways of using foreign law in constitutional interpretation.[23] Harold Koh refers to three situations in which the U.S. Supreme Court has referred to foreign law: when a U.S. law parallels the law of another country; to learn about the possible consequences of a particular solution to a common legal problem; and when a U.S. constitutional concept refers to a community standard such as "cruel and unusual," "due process," or "unreasonable."[24] Kai Schadbach, using a more traditional comparative law perspective, emphasizes the use of foreign law for enhancing knowledge and understanding and as a source of ideas and solutions.[25] More empirically oriented scholars have categorized uses of foreign law more exhaustively. David Zaring identifies five uses: to interpret domestic law, interpret foreign law, interpret treaties, interpret customary international law, and help coordinate litigation.[26] Steven Calabresi and Stephanie Zimdahl discern five "thematic categories" of foreign law use: use in "reasonableness" determinations; interpretation of ambiguous phrases; evidence in criminal law cases; logical reinforcement for judicial opinions; and illustrations of possible consequences of a legal decision.[27]

Social science methodologist John Gerring emphasizes that "[c]oncept formation concerns the most basic question of research: What are we talking about?"[28] Legal scholars generally have a shared understanding of what is meant by "foreign law."[29] They appreciate that domestic courts can use foreign law in different ways, thus avoiding the pitfall of lumping together all uses of foreign law.[30] However, as demonstrated by the foregoing tour of typologies, scholars are classifying these different uses very differently, resulting in a proliferation of categories that blurs the fundamental "what are we talking about" question. The lack of agreement about how to categorize the different ways that domestic courts use foreign law risks hindering productive scholarly dialogue and retarding theoretical progress.

With these concerns in mind, I propose a five-part conceptual typology of the different ways that domestic courts can use foreign law: as (1) binding law, (2) a nonbinding norm, (3) an interpretive aid, (4) a basis for functional comparison, and (5) factual information.[31] The immediate consequence inevitably is to add to the already long list of typologies. However, the typology proposed here seeks to consolidate existing categories, and to the extent it succeeds in doing so, the result is integration rather than further proliferation. More fundamentally, the typology attempts to strike an appropriate balance between capturing analytically relevant differences, on one hand, and avoiding digression into an unmanageable and conceptually useless list on the other.

First, courts can use foreign law as binding law to help answer the question, "What must we decide?" This use occurs when a domestic court makes a legal decision by applying foreign law to a given set of facts based on an implicit or explicit claim that the foreign law is a binding legal rule in the domestic forum. Such a claim in turn depends on the application of a "rule of recognition," to use H. L. A. Hart's terminology, that specifies "some feature or features possession of which by a suggested rule is taken as a conclusive affirmative indication that it is a [legal] rule."[32] The underlying logic can be called a "logic of necessity:" the court uses a particular legal rule because the rule of recognition demands it.[33]

Most legal scholars understand that in none of the cases that have led to the current controversy has a court used foreign law as binding law. However, this type of use is more than a theoretical possibility. In many cases, U.S. state and federal courts dealing with transnational litigation apply foreign law as the binding law in the case after engaging in choice-of-law analysis.[34] Similarly, U.S. courts frequently recognize and enforce the judgments of foreign courts.[35] An example is *Silverman v. Rosewood Hotels & Resorts*, in which the plaintiff filed a suit in a U.S. district court against the company that managed a Mexican hotel, claiming that she was injured while staying there.[36] The plaintiff argued that New York law should apply to the case, and the defendant argued that Mexican law should apply. In its choice-of-law analysis, the court considered a number of factors, including the general principle that the law of the place of the injury should govern. It then concluded that Mexican law applied and used that law to determine the amount of damages owed to the plaintiff.

Second, judges can use foreign law as a nonbinding norm—as a source of answers to the question, "What should we decide?" This use occurs when a domestic court refers to foreign law to make or support a normative argument but does not treat it as binding law. Whereas the use of foreign law as binding law relies on the claim that the foreign law is, according to the rule of recognition, binding law in the domestic forum, the use of foreign law as a nonbinding norm relies on an argument—again, either implicit or explicit—that the foreign law has some normative force. Such a claim may, for example, be rooted in the intrinsic normative value of the foreign law's content, such as its rationality or resonance within a particular set of moral values or on the law's provenance.[37] The underlying logic is a logic of appropriateness:[38] foreign law is used as a norm to suggest which decision is appropriate, not which one is legally necessary.[39]

Use of foreign law as a nonbinding norm includes a number of uses described by other scholars, all of which involve references to foreign law to make or reinforce a normative argument: use as evidence of reasonableness,[40] community standards,[41] or natural[42] or universal law;[43] use of foreign law in an expressive,[44] aversive, aspirational,[45] or genealogical mode;[46] and more generally, use as what Calabresi and Zimdahl call "logical reinforcement."[47] However, use as a nonbinding norm is not intended to include all uses of foreign law that are covered by Slaughter's concept of "persuasive authority."[48] Foreign law may be persuasive because of its normative force, in which case it is used as a nonbinding norm; because it is deemed relevant to the interpretation of a legal text, in which case it is used as an interpretive aid; or because it provides information about the consequences of a particular legal decision, in which case the foreign law is being used for functional comparison.[49]

An example of foreign law being used as a nonbinding norm is the U.S. Supreme Court's 2005 decision in *Roper v. Simmons*. In that case, the Court referred to foreign law to provide normative support for the legal analysis of the Eighth Amendment that led it to conclude that the death penalty is cruel and unusual punishment when applied to minors: "Our determination that the death penalty is disproportionate punishment for offenders under 18 finds confirmation in the stark reality that the United States is the only country in the world that continues to give official sanction to the juvenile death penalty." The Court continued: "[O]nly seven countries other than the United States have executed juvenile offenders since 1990: Iran, Pakistan, Saudi Arabia, Yemen, Nigeria, the Democratic Republic of Congo, and China. . . . The opinion of the world community, while not controlling our outcome, does provide respected and significant confirmation for our own conclusions."[50]

Third, judges can use foreign law as an interpretive aid—as a tool for answering the question, "What does it mean?" This use occurs when a domestic court refers to foreign law to make or support an argument about the meaning of a legal text. There is a reliance on the claim that there is some relationship—whether textual, procedural, or historical—between the text being interpreted and the foreign law that makes the foreign law appropriate as an interpretive aid. For some purposes, it may prove analytically helpful to divide this use into three subcategories: use of foreign law to interpret (1) domestic law, (2) foreign law, or (3) international law.[51]

An example of foreign law being used as an aid in interpreting domestic law is *Crawford v. Washington*, which the Supreme Court decided in 2004. The Court extensively discussed English common law to establish the historical context in which the Sixth Amendment was adopted in order to establish the meaning of the confrontation clause originally intended by the drafters of the U.S. Bill of Rights.[52] An example of the use of foreign law as an aid in interpreting foreign law is *Torah Soft v. Drosnin*, in which a U.S. district court, after applying choice-of-law analysis, used the Israeli Commercial Torts Law as binding law in the case and then consulted Israeli case law to help interpret it.[53] Finally, an example of using foreign law as an aid in interpreting international law is *Air France v. Saks*, in which the U.S. Supreme Court faced the task of interpreting the word "accident" in the Warsaw Convention.[54] As an interpretive aid, the Court examined a decision of a French court that had interpreted the same provision of the Warsaw Convention. The U.S. Supreme Court noted that, "[i]n determining precisely what causes can be considered accidents, we 'find the opinions of our sister signatories to be entitled to considerable weight.' "[55]

Fourth, foreign law can be used as a basis for functional comparison—as evidence to help answer the question, "What are the likely consequences of our decision?"[56] This use occurs when a domestic court refers to foreign law and the apparent consequences of that law to make inferences about the consequences of a possible decision.[57] This usage relies on the implicit assumption or explicit claim that the foreign experience is sufficiently comparable to the domestic experience to make the domestic court's analysis of likely consequences more accurate or reliable than it would be without considering foreign legal experience.[58] Unlike the use of foreign law as a nonbinding norm, which follows a logic of appropriateness, the use of foreign law for functional comparison follows a logic of consequences.[59] The focus is not on the foreign law's intrinsic normative value, but rather on its effects and what can be inferred from them about the likely effects of the domestic court's decision.

An example of the use of foreign law as a basis for functional comparison is the U.S. Supreme Court's landmark decision in *Miranda v. State of Arizona*.[60] The Court looked to the experience of other countries to bolster its claim that to require what have come to be known as Miranda warnings would not have a substantial detrimental effect on law enforcement. The Court first noted that the law of England, Scotland, and India requires equally or more comprehensive warnings to be given to an accused. It then explained: "There appears to have been no marked detrimental effect on criminal law enforcement in these jurisdictions as a result of these rules. Conditions of law enforcement in our country are sufficiently similar to permit reference to this experience as assurance that lawlessness will not result from warning an individual of his rights or allowing him to exercise them."[61]

Finally, domestic courts can use foreign law as factual information to answer factual questions. Not at issue is the foreign law's domestic legal or normative force, its bearing on the interpretation of a legal text, or its consequences. Rather, foreign law is used as a fact necessary for the application of a domestic legal principle[62] or for a domestic court to understand foreign legal proceedings according to what might be called a "logic of information." For example, a defendant's prior conviction in a foreign country may be a relevant fact in determining whether criminal prosecution in the United States is barred by the constitutional prohibition of double jeopardy;[63] in choice-of-law analysis, foreign law may be relevant in determining the extent of a foreign government's interest in having its law apply to transnational litigation filed in a domestic court. The adequacy of a foreign court as an alternative to the domestic court is a standard element of *forum non conveniens* analysis, and facts about the status of foreign legal proceedings are essential for judicial efforts to coordinate transnational litigation.

These five categories—use as binding law, as a nonbinding norm, as an interpretive aid, for functional comparison, and as factual information—inevitably occupy a somewhat uncomfortable middle ground between the inductivism and proliferation of categories beyond which this chapter attempts to move and the precisely tailored and theoretically motivated approach to concept formation and typologies that ultimately will be necessary for the most rigorous analytical work.[64] It is clear that no typology can work for all purposes. Nevertheless, this typology encompasses most of the uses of foreign law that other scholars have deemed important, organizes them analytically, and does so in a manageable way, using only a small number of categories. It is offered as a common language for scholars interested in exploring the implications of foreign law in domestic courts and as a starting point for further conceptual refinement.[65]

DIFFERENT USES, DIFFERENT IMPLICATIONS: DOMESTIC COURTS AS AGENTS OF NORM INTERNALIZATION

Do references to foreign law in domestic court opinions cause changes in domestic law or policy? This is one of the great concerns of critics of foreign law citations.[66] For example, Justice Scalia, citing Justice Thomas, argued in his dissent in *Lawrence* that the Court's references to foreign law in that case were "dangerous" because "this Court ... should not impose foreign moods, fads, or fashions on Americans."[67] Yet there is no simple answer to this question,

Table 3.1. Different Uses of Foreign Law by Domestic Courts

Type of Use	Associated Question	Associated Logic	Underlying Claim
Binding Law	What must we decide?	Logic of Necessity	The foreign law is applicable binding law in the case.
Nonbinding Norm	What should we decide?	Logic of Appropriateness	The foreign law has normative force.
Interpretive Aid	What does it mean?	Logic of Interpretation	There is a textual or historical relationship between the foreign law and the text being interpreted.
Functional Comparison	What are the consequences?	Logic of Consequences	The foreign legal experience is comparable to domestic experience.
Factual Information	What are the relevant facts?	Logic of Information	The foreign law is a fact that is relevant to the legal analysis.

because different uses of foreign law imply different degrees and different kinds of cross-border norm migration.

It is worth emphasizing what is at stake here. The criticism rests on an empirical assumption, namely that the use of foreign law in domestic courts results in norm internalization. Whether this assumption is sound raises a formidable counterfactual question: But for the use of foreign law, how would the Court's decision, or the consequences of the Court's decision, be different, if at all? Little progress can be made toward answering this question here. My goal is more modest: to explore the intuition that emerges from the categorization of different uses of foreign law and how these differences have implications for norm internalization.

The use of foreign law as binding law involves direct but usually very limited degrees of norm internalization. It is direct because it involves the application of foreign law as the basis for an authoritative decision by a domestic court. However, it generally indicates a very limited degree of internalization. When a domestic court enforces a foreign judgment, it typically binds only the parties to the litigation giving rise to that judgment. Likewise, when choice-of-law analysis leads a domestic court to apply foreign law as binding law, it ordinarily applies only to the specific parties and facts of the case. In neither case is foreign law incorporated into generally applicable domestic law or used to change domestic policy.[68] Rather, internalization is limited to the specific case at hand.

Somewhat counterintuitively, then, the use of foreign law as a nonbinding norm or for functional comparison may in practice result in a higher degree of internalization than its use as binding law. In contrast to one-shot applications of foreign law to specific litigants, use as a nonbinding norm or for functional comparison may be associated with significant changes in domestic policy, even if it is not the primary basis for the Court's decision. In *Roper*, for example, the U.S. Supreme Court did not base its decision primarily on its use of foreign law as a nonbinding norm, but the decision changed U.S. policy regarding the punishment of criminal offenders. In *Miranda*, the Court did not base its decision primarily on its use of foreign law for functional comparison, but that decision resulted in important changes in criminal procedure. As already noted, to estimate how much different uses of foreign law affect judicial decision making would involve very difficult counterfactual reasoning. However, the foregoing analysis suggests that the distinction between the use of foreign law as binding law, on one hand, and as a nonbinding norm or for functional comparison, on the other, is a distinction with a theoretical and practical difference.

Moreover, internalization is likely to be qualitatively different depending on whether foreign law is used as a nonbinding norm or for functional comparison. In the first instance, to the extent that a norm is internalized, it is because of its normative salience according to a logic of appropriateness—

normative values associated with societal ends are being introduced domestically. In the case of functional comparison, internalization occurs instead because of a norm's functionality—because it is an effective means to a given end—according to a logic of expected consequences. In that case, solutions are being introduced domestically. In the *Roper* case, foreign law was used as a nonbinding norm to support the Court's conclusion that applying the death penalty to minors was unconstitutional. To the extent that there was internalization, it was internalization of a norm about appropriate forms of punishment. In *Miranda*, on the other hand, foreign law was used for functional comparison. Although the Court's decision obviously had normative content, to the extent that this particular functional use of foreign law resulted in internalization, it was internalization of a method for pursuing a societal goal—in this case, a solution to the problem of protecting suspects' constitutional privilege against self-incrimination without impeding law enforcement. Of course, different normative values may have different consequences, and different solutions are likely to have different normative implications—the line between ends and means rarely is obvious. Nevertheless, these different uses of foreign law imply different modes of internalization with qualitatively different impacts on domestic law and policy.

The use of foreign law as factual information generally should not lead directly to norm internalization, although it may do so indirectly; for example, as part of a choice-of-law analysis. The use of foreign law as an interpretive aid, however, may lead to incidental norm internalization. Take, for example, a domestic court that is applying a provision of its own country's constitution, using it as the binding law in the case, and assume that there is a range of interpretations considered *ex ante* by the sitting judge to be reasonable. If the use of foreign law as an interpretive aid moves the judge in favor of a particular interpretation or even merely narrows the scope of interpretations under consideration, then there has been internalization at the margins, with the possible result—again, difficult to estimate because of the challenges of counterfactual reasoning and causal inference—that the domestic court's decision is closer to that of another country than it would have been without the interpretive use of foreign law.

Given the plausibility of these relationships, international relations and comparative politics scholars should pay close attention to the role of domestic courts in transnational processes of norm internalization and policy diffusion. Leading approaches to norm internalization and policy diffusion focus on interactions between unitary states, treating them either as rational actors who incorporate norms in response to altered payoffs or new information[69] or as agents who internalize norms through processes of socialization.[70] For example, in the work of Beth Simmons and Zachary Elkins on the diffusion of liberal economic policies, the unit of analysis is the state, and the key explanatory variables generally relate to the choices of other states and various qualities associated with those other states. Promising as these approaches may be, they tend to neglect domestic political variables that may determine the conditions under which norms or policies are likely to spread from one country to another. For this reason, state-centric versions of diffusion and norm internalization theory have been criticized for failing to explain the actual causal links between external rules and domestic policy choices[71] and for being vague: "[F]ew [studies] focus on the diffusion mechanism, or how it might vary cross-nationally. Large-N studies of global norm diffusion offer little additional insight, as they are quantitative and correlational in design. Missing is the detailed process tracing and case research needed to explore actual diffusion mechanisms."[72] Systematic study of the role of domestic courts as institutional pathways for the cross-border migration of norms would be one way to respond constructively to these criticisms.

Other approaches drop the unitary state actor assumption and look at how domestic actors and political structures provide pathways whereby external norms can be internalized—yet the role of domestic courts remains neglected. Andrew Cortell and James Davis emphasize two characteristics of domestic political structure that can increase the likelihood of norm internalization: decentralized decision-making authority based on separation of powers, with the reasoning that separation of powers provides more independent institutional pathways for norm internalization, and incorporation of international norms into domestic law.[73] The authors do not explore the role of domestic courts in their theory, but it would seem that domestic courts could play a central role in Cortell and Davis's causal story. To the extent that courts enjoy judicial independence, they offer a distinct institutional pathway for introducing external norms into domestic society and incorporating them into domestic law.[74] Thus international relations and comparative politics scholars could improve their understanding of cross-border norm migration by exploring the role of domestic courts in transnational processes of norm internalization and policy diffusion.

For their part, scholars specifically interested in the consequences of foreign law in domestic courts could benefit from exploring political science theories of diffusion and norm internalization.[75] For example, Cortell and Davis emphasize the domestic salience or legitimacy of a norm: In general, the greater a norm's domestic salience, the greater its impact is likely to be on domestic policy.[76] They suggest that an international norm is likely to have more domestic salience when there is a "cultural match"—that is, when it resonates "with domestic norms, widely held domestic understandings, beliefs, and obligations."[77] This reasoning would seem equally plausible when applied to foreign law and has several interesting implications. The higher the domestic salience of a foreign law, the greater its domestic impact is likely to be if used by a domestic court. References to foreign law that do not enjoy domestic salience are less likely to have significant domestic normative consequences. In this way, even if a domestic court uses foreign law with the intention of changing domestic norms, the normative fabric of domestic society places a check on the court's ability to do so: If the norms it attempts to import by using foreign law do not resonate domestically, they are less likely to have domestic impact than if they do resonate with existing domestic norms.[78] As suggested by a long tradition of comparative law scholarship, it is far from obvious that formal introduction of external norms necessarily results in domestic normative change.[79]

Because different uses of foreign law in domestic courts are associated with different degrees and qualities of norm internalization and because norm internalization depends on domestic salience, across-the-board critiques of foreign law references based on concerns about judicial imposition of "foreign fads and fashions" miss the mark. The foregoing analysis suggests that if these concerns are valid, they probably are most justified in certain cases in which courts use foreign law as a nonbinding norm and less so under other circumstances. The analysis also suggests that even when domestic courts use foreign law with the goal of internalizing a foreign norm, such efforts are likely to have limited domestic consequences unless the foreign law has sufficient legitimacy under existing domestic norms. Ultimately, assessing the consequences of foreign law in domestic courts depends on addressing the formidable challenges of causal inference posed by the following counterfactual question: But for a court's use of foreign law, how would its decision, or the consequences of its decision, be different, if at all? Notwithstanding these challenges, the validity of untested assumptions about the consequences of foreign law references in domestic court opinions should not be taken for granted. Instead, they should be subjected to careful scrutiny.

CONCLUSION

The foregoing discussion of the different consequences of different uses of foreign law is not intended to be more than exploratory. Although motivated by empirical concerns, the analysis has been primarily conceptual. This is a necessary first step, given the absence of conceptual foundations in the existing literature, but the results are at best suggestive. An important line of further research is to more exhaustively examine the implications of different uses of foreign law and move beyond conceptual work to theory building and hypothesis testing.

In addition, this chapter surely raises more questions than it answers about the role of domestic courts as agents in processes of norm internalization and policy diffusion. For example, what determines whether and how domestic courts use foreign law? This implies a second avenue of further research: Under what conditions are domestic courts likely to use foreign law in different ways?[80] Several hypotheses from the work of Beth Simmons and Zachary Elkins on diffusion might be adapted to address this question. For example, a domestic court may be more likely to use (1) foreign law that has been widely used by other states; (2) the foreign law of states that are economic competitors; or (3) that have the best economic performance. A domestic court also may be more likely to use foreign law of states from which the domestic court has the most extensive opportunities to obtain information about the consequences of the foreign law or that have a cultural affinity with the domestic court's state.[81] Recent work by Lee Epstein and Jack Knight illustrates another way of answering this question that pays closer attention to the judicial micro-foundations of diffusion. According to them, whether or not actors involved in the design of constitutions use foreign constitutional models depends on their strategic choices, which in turn reflect their "relative influence, preferences, and beliefs."[82] Although their empirical analysis does not extend to judicial decision making, they argue that their theory does—when courts decide whether or not to use foreign law, they are making decisions about the "design [of] institutions to govern their societies," and these decisions are a product of judges' strategic considerations given their preferences and the preferences of other political actors.[83] Epstein and Knight's approach, perhaps combined with a typology of different uses of foreign law, such as the one proposed in this chapter, might help lead scholars toward a theory of cross-border norm migration that provides a rigorous account of the judicial pathway that is missing from state-centric theories of diffusion and even theories of norm internalization that emphasize domestic political structures.

Moreover, although the debate about foreign law in domestic courts prompted this chapter, limiting the analysis to foreign law is—at least from the perspective of positive theory—somewhat arbitrary. My typology of different uses of foreign law may also be analytically helpful for understanding the role of international law in domestic courts, and to the extent it is, it may for some purposes be more productive to use a single concept of nondomestic, external, or "outside" law rather than separate concepts of foreign law and international law. Thus, although the foreign law/international law distinction clearly has important implications for legal theory, the distinction may be less important for, and perhaps even an impediment to, positive theories of norm internalization. Different ways of using "outside" law may do a better job of explaining different empirical consequences than whether that law is foreign or international. This reasoning suggests a broader research agenda that would bring legal scholars and political scientists interested in comparative legal analysis together with those interested in international legal analysis in domestic courts.[84] The central premise, however, would remain the same: Different uses of "outside" law have different implications for processes of cross-border norm migration and for our understanding of the role of domestic courts in these processes.

NOTES

1. For concise overviews of the debate—in which recent references to foreign law in prominent U.S. Supreme Court decisions have been strongly criticized by some judges, legal scholars, and politicians, and defended by others—see Sujit Choudhry, "Migration as a New Metaphor in Comparative Constitutional Law," in *The Migration of Constitutional Ideas*, ed. Sujit Choudhry (Cambridge: Cambridge University Press, 2006), 1–13, and David S. Law, "Generic Constitutional Law," *Minnesota Law Review* 89 (2005): 653–657.

2. 536 U.S. 304 (2002) (holding that the death penalty applied to the mentally retarded is unconstitutional).

3. 539 U.S. 558 (2003) (holding that a Texas statute criminalizing same-sex sodomy is unconstitutional).

4. 543 U.S. 551 (2005) (holding that the death penalty applied to juvenile offenders is unconstitutional).

5. Steven G. Calabresi and Stephanie Dotson Zimdahl, "The Supreme Court and Foreign Sources of Law: Two Hundred Years of Practice and the Juvenile Death Penalty Decision," *William and Mary Law Review* 47 (2005): 743–910, and David Zaring, "The Use of Foreign Decisions by Federal Courts: An Empirical Analysis," *Journal of Empirical Legal Studies* 3 (2006): 297–331. But see Ken I. Kersch, "The New Legal Transnationalism, the Globalized Judiciary, and the Rule of Law," *Washington University Global Studies Law Review* 4 (2005): 346 (arguing that "the current transnational trend amongst judges and scholars is not . . . business as usual in the American courts").

6. Melissa A. Waters, "Mediating Norms and Identity: The Role of Transnational Judicial Dialogue in Creating and Enforcing International Law," *Georgetown Law Journal* 93 (2005): 491.

7. Noga Morag-Levine, "Judges, Legislators, and Europe's Law: Common-Law Constitutionalism and Foreign Precedents," *Maryland Law Review* 65 (2006): 102.

8. Ibid. Similarly, Vicki Jackson notes that the nonbinding use of foreign law "shares characteristics of other forms of persuasive authority used in Supreme Court decisions" such as state and lower court opinions, law review articles, and literature. Vicki Jackson, "Yes Please, I'd Love to Talk with You," *Legal Affairs* (July/August 2004), online at http://www.legalaffairs.org/issues/July-August-2004/feature_jackson_julaug04. msp. In his empirical study, Zaring found thirty-three federal court citations to Bruce Springsteen, twenty-seven to Bob Dylan, and ten to John Updike. Zaring, 327.

9. Mark Tushnet, "Transnational/Domestic Constitutional Law," *Loyola of Los Angeles Law Review* 37 (2003): 248. See also Choudhry, 6.

10. Roger P. Alford, "In Search of a Theory for Constitutional Comparativism," *UCLA Law Review* 52 (2005): 639–714.

11. Michael D. Ramsey, "International Materials and Domestic Rights: Reflections on Atkins and Lawrence," *American Journal of International Law* 98 (2004): 69–82.

12. Mark Tushnet, "The Possibilities of Comparative Constitutional Law," *Yale Law Journal* 108 (1999): 1225–1308.

13. For a recent collection of essays that begins to explore the implications of judicial comparativism for the migration of constitutional ideas, see Sujit Choudhry, ed., *The Migration of Constitutional Ideas* (Cambridge: Cambridge University Press, 2007).

14. To be clear, I do not in any way intend to minimize the importance of the normative concerns raised by foreign law in domestic courts. Rather, I wish to highlight the need to assess the empirical assumptions on which these concerns rest.

15. David Collier and James E. Mahon Jr., "Conceptual 'Stretching' Revisited: Adapting Categories in Comparative Analysis," *American Political Science Review* 87 (1993): 845.

16. Richard Posner, "No Thanks, We Already Have Our Own Laws," *Legal Affairs* (online at July/August 2004), http://www.legalaffairs.org/issues/July-August-2004/feature_posner_julaug04.msp.

17. Anne-Marie Slaughter, *A New World Order* (Princeton: Princeton University Press, 2004), 69. See also Laurence R. Helfer and Anne-Marie Slaughter, "Toward a Theory of Effective Supranational Adjudication," *Yale Law Journal* 107 (1997): 320–321.

18. Vicki Jackson, "Transnational Discourse, Relational Authority, and the U.S. Court: Gender Equality," *Loyola of Los Angeles Law Review* 37 (2003): 282–287.

19. Kenneth Anderson, "Foreign Law and the U.S. Constitution: The Supreme Court's Global Aspirations," *Policy Review*, no. 131 (June–July 2005), online at http://www.hoover.org/publications/policyreview/2932196.html.

20. See David Fontana, "Refined Comparativism in Constitutional Law," *UCLA Law Review* 49 (1999): 551 (distinguishing "positive" and "negative comparativism") and Kim Lane Scheppele, "Aspirational and Aversive Constitutionalism: The Case for Studying Cross-Constitutional Influence through Negative Models," *International Journal of Constitutional Law* 1 (2003): 299–301 (distinguishing "aspirational" and "aversive constitutionalism").

21. Fontana, 550–551.

22. Sujit Choudhry, "Globalization in Search of Justification: Toward a Theory of Comparative Constitutional Interpretation," *Indiana Law Journal* 74 (1999): 825.

23. Tushnet, "Possibilities," 1228.

24. Harold Hongju Koh, "International Law as Part of Our Law," *American Journal of International Law* 98 (2004): 45–46.

25. Kai Schadbach, "The Benefits of Comparative Law: A Continental European View," *Boston University International Law Journal* 16 (1998): 331–422.

26. Zaring, 306–307. He adds a sixth category to capture "passing references" to foreign law.

27. Calabresi and Zimdahl, 884.

28. John Gerring, *Social Science Methodology: A Criterial Framework* (Cambridge: Cambridge University Press, 2001), 35.

29. Nevertheless, Frederic Kirgis, an honorary editor of the *American Journal of International Law*, noted that some commentators were confusing foreign law with international law and thus deemed it appropriate to publish a brief explanation. Frederic L. Kirgis, "Is Foreign Law International Law?" *ASIL Insights* (October 31, 2005), online at http://www.asil.org/insights/2005/10/insights051031.html. For the purposes of this chapter, foreign law means the law of a country other than the country of the court using it, including constitutions, legislation, regulations, case law, judgments, and proceedings.

30. This is a pitfall because domestic courts use foreign law in different ways, and as this chapter seeks to demonstrate, these differences are important in both theory and practice.

31. This typology represents only one dimension along which uses of foreign law may vary. In addition, there may be interesting variations in which courts use foreign law, which foreign law is used, and whether foreign law is being used to support or oppose the domestic status quo. I thank Mark Axelrod for pointing out these possibilities.

32. H. L. A. Hart, *The Concept of Law*, 2d ed. (Oxford: Oxford University Press, 1994), 94–95. A rule of recognition is what Hart calls a "secondary" rule—a "rule about rules"—that identifies valid "primary" legal rules by reference to specific texts or by their characteristics, such as "the fact of their having been enacted by a specific body, or their long customary practice, or their relation to judicial decisions." Ibid.

33. This definition is similar to Helfer and Slaughter's term "coercive authority," which is associated with "an argument of authority." Helfer and Slaughter, 320–321. Using this chapter's definition of binding law, the relevant "argument of authority" would be that the rule of recognition requires (or bars) application of a particular legal rule.

34. See George A. Bermann, *Transnational Litigation* (St. Paul: West, 2003), chap. 7, and Gary B. Born and Peter B. Rutledge, *International Civil Litigation in United States Courts*, 4th ed. (New York: Aspen Publishers, 2007), chap. 8.

35. See Bermann, chap. 10, and Born and Rutledge, chap. 12.

36. 2004 U.S. Dist. LEXIS 16110 (2004).

37. See Anne-Marie Slaughter, "A Typology of Transjudicial Communication," *University of Richmond Law Review* 29 (1994): 124 (domestic courts are unlikely to use foreign law as persuasive authority unless "they are persuaded or if they conclude that either the content of the idea and/or its source will enable them better to persuade their own audience").

38. March and Olsen explain the logic of appropriateness as follows: "actions are seen as rule-based. . . . Action involves evoking an identity or role and matching the obligations of that identity or role to a specific situation. The pursuit of purpose is associated with identities more than with interests, and with the selection of rules more than with individual rational expectations." James G. March and Johan P. Olsen, "The Institutional Dynamics of International Political Orders," *International Organization* 52 (1998): 951. Use as binding law according to what I have called a logic of necessity can be understood as a special case of the logic of appropriateness, one based on the rule of recognition.

39. By way of example, a court might use foreign law in this manner in order to choose among multiple legally permissible decisions or, in the words of Sujit Choudhry, to help "decid[e] hard cases where the positive legal materials run out." Choudhry, 4.

40. Calabresi and Zimdahl, 884.

41. Koh, 45–46.

42. Alford, 659–673.

43. Choudhry, 825.

44. Tushnet, 1228.

45. Fontana, 551; Scheppele, 299–301.

46. Choudhry, 825; Fontana, 550.

47. Calabresi and Zimdahl, 884.

48. Slaughter, *New World Order*, 75–78.

49. These last two uses are described below.

50. 543 U.S. 551, at 575–578. It is interesting to note that a genealogical claim underlies one element of the court's use of foreign law as a nonbinding norm: "[T]he United Kingdom abolished the juvenile death penalty. . . . The United Kingdom's experience bears particular relevance here in light of the historic ties between our countries and in light of the Eighth Amendment's own origins. . . ." 543 U.S. 551, at 577.

51. See Zaring, 306.

52. 541 U.S. 36 (2004).

53. 224 F. Supp. 2d 704 (2002).

54. 470 U.S. 392 (1985).

55. Ibid., at 403–404.

56. Functionalism is a venerable methodology in comparative legal studies. For a classic statement of functionalism, see Konrad Zweigert and Hein Kötz, *Introduction to Comparative Law*, 3d ed. (Oxford: Oxford University Press, 1998), and for recent overviews of functionalism, see Michele Graziadei, "The Functionalist Heritage," in *Comparative Legal Studies: Traditions and Transitions*, ed. Pierre Legrand and Roderick Munday (Cambridge: Cambridge University Press, 2003), 100–130, and Ralf Michaels, "The Functional Method of Comparative Law," in *Oxford Handbook of Comparative Law*, ed. Mathias Reimann and Reinhard Zimmermann (Oxford: Oxford University Press, 2006): 339–382.

57. This use is what Tushnet calls "functionalism"; what Koh, drawing on Justice Breyer's work, calls "empirical light"; and what Calabresi and Zimdahl call "empirical consequences." Tushnet, *Possibilities*, 1238–1269; Koh, *International Law*, 45–46; Calabresi and Zimdahl, 884. As with the use of foreign law as a nonbinding norm, foreign law can be used either aspirationally or aversively in the functional mode.

58. This is an exercise in causal inference; and causal inference requires data. When attempting to infer the likely consequences of a particular legal decision, the relevant data would include other instances in which similar legal decisions were made, in other places or in other times. If there is no similar earlier decision that has been made domestically, it may be necessary to look to foreign legal experience for relevant data. Even if there have been similar domestic decisions, it may be useful to look to foreign legal experience as well, because increasing the number of cases in one's analysis can increase the confidence one can reasonably have in the resulting causal inference. The challenges of making sound causal inferences—especially using cross-national data—are, of course, formidable. Yet there is an enormous literature in both comparative politics and comparative law (literatures that so far have evolved separately) aimed at addressing these challenges. See Ran Hirschl, "The Question of Case Selection in Comparative Constitutional Law," *American Journal of Comparative Law* 53 (2005) and Christopher A. Whytock, "Taking Causality Seriously in Comparative Constitutional Law: Insights from Comparative Politics and Comparative Political Economy," *Loyola of Los Angeles Law Review* 41 (2008): 629 (reviewing these literatures with an emphasis on qualitative and quantitative approaches, respectively). An important issue, and one I hope to pursue in future work, is the extent to which judges, either directly or through expert social science testimony, are equipped to make these types

of causal inferences. My intuition is that causal inferences are unavoidable in judicial decision making and that more attention should be devoted to figuring out how to make these inferences as sound as possible given the limitations of judicial capacity.

59. According to March and Olsen, "Those who see actions as driven by expectations of consequences imagine that human actors choose among alternatives by evaluating their likely consequences for personal or collective objectives." March and Olsen, 949. The logic of appropriateness and the logic of consequences approximately correspond to the two elements of ends–means analysis in constitutional interpretation: The ends are determined by the former logic, and the means by the latter.

60. 384 U.S. 436 (1966).

61. 384 U.S. 436, at 487–490 [footnotes omitted].

62. This includes using foreign law as "datum" and the preliminary and incidental application of foreign law in resolving questions of private international law, including choice-of-law rules. Hans W. Baade, "The Operation of Foreign Public Law," *Texas International Law Journal* 30 (1995): 448 and 458.

63. Ibid., 450.

64. See Gerring, chap. 3, and Colin Elman, "Explanatory Typologies in Qualitative Studies of International Politics," *International Organization* 59 (2005): 293–326.

65. This typology might also be useful as a categorical variable—either one to be explained or one that might help to explain varying consequences of using foreign law in domestic courts. It also may be useful for refining normative and legal theories of comparativism, because different uses of foreign law have different normative and legal implications.

66. And, with respect to international norms, it is one of the great hopes of some international legal scholars. See, for example, Koh, "Transnational Legal Process," *Nebraska Law Review* 75 (1996): 181.

67. 539 U.S. 558, 598 (Scalia, joined by Rehnquist and Thomas, dissenting) (quoting from Justice Thomas's concurring opinion in *Foster v. Florida*, 537 U.S. 990 (2002) (Thomas, J., concurring in denial of certiorari).

68. However, in deciding such cases, domestic courts send signals to transnational actors about how they might decide similar foreign judgment and choice-of-law issues under similar circumstances in the future. Christopher A. Whytock, "Transnational Law, Domestic Courts, and Global Governance" (March 15, 2007), online at http://ssrn. com/abstract=976274. Moreover, such decisions may contribute to the shaping of domestic common law principles relating to the recognition and enforcement of foreign judgments or to choice of law.

69. See, for example, Beth A. Simmons and Zachary Elkins, "The Globalization of Liberalization: Policy Diffusion in the International Political Economy," *American Political Science Review* 98 (2004): 171–189.

70. See, for example, Alexander Wendt, *Social Theory of International Politics* (Cambridge: Cambridge University Press, 1999).

71. Andrew P. Cortell and James W. Davis Jr., "How Do International Institutions Matter? The Domestic Impact of International Rules and Norms," *International Studies Quarterly* 40 (1996): 451.

72. Jeffrey T. Checkel, "International Norms and Domestic Politics: Bridging the Rationalist-Contructivist Divide," *European Journal of International Relations* 3 (1997): 476.

73. Cortell and Davis, 471.

74. A focus on courts as important domestic structures in Cortell and Davis's account would be consistent with Harold Koh's transnational legal process theory, which argues that courts play an important role in the process of incorporating international law into domestic law. Koh, *Transnational Legal Process*, 204.

75. Similarly, William Twining argues that diffusion theory might provide important insights for comparative legal scholars interested in the transnational spread of laws and legal institutions. William Twining, "Diffusion of Law: A Global Perspective," *Journal of Legal Pluralism* 49 (2004): 1–45, and William Twining, "Social Science and Diffusion of Law," *Journal of Law and Society* 32 (2005): 203–240.

76. Cortell and Davis, 456–457; Andrew P. Cortell and James W. Davis Jr., "Understanding the Domestic Impact of International Norms: A Research Agenda," *International Studies Review* 2 (2000): 65–90.

77. Cortell and Davis, "Domestic Impact," 73.

78. In fact, this would further imply that domestic courts, concerned about maintaining their legitimacy, would be disinclined to use foreign law in the first place if they did not expect it to have domestic resonance. On the other hand, it is likely that the legal imprimatur of a domestic court on a foreign legal principle could itself increase its domestic salience, at least in rule-of-law societies.

79. Mark Tushnet refers to this as the "organicist" critique of legal transplants and attributes it to Montesquieu and Hegel. Mark Tushnet, "Returning with Interest: Observations on Some Putative Benefits of Studying Comparative Constitutional Law," *University of Pennsylvania Journal of Constitutional Law* 1 (1998): 333. The basic logic is that only legal institutions that emerge organically within a society will be accepted by that society.

80. Although this chapter focuses on U.S. courts, this research question implies eventual comparative study: The factors that influence judicial decision making may vary cross-nationally.

81. Simmons and Elkins, 172–176. These are the hypotheses applied by Simmons and Elkins to the diffusion of liberal economic policies based on the logics of altered payoffs and new information. Their empirical findings support the hypotheses about economic competitors and cultural peers (for which common religion is used as a proxy).

82. Lee Epstein and Jack Knight, "Constitutional Borrowing and Nonborrowing," *International Journal of Constitutional Law* 1 (2003): 209–210.

83. Ibid., 197.

84. According to this perspective, domestic courts play a role not only in norm internalization, as discussed in this chapter, but also in the interpretation and shaping of international law—thus domestic courts play a role in both "second image reversed" (Peter Gourevitch's term) accounts of world politics that I have emphasized here and "second image" (Kenneth Waltz's term) accounts, which I have discussed elsewhere. See Christopher A. Whytock, "Foreign Law, Domestic Courts, and World Politics" (paper presented at the annual conference of the International Studies Association, San Diego, Calif., March 22–25, 2006).

PART II

The Rise of Transnational Criminal Jurisdiction

CHAPTER FOUR

Legitimacy and the Exercise of Universal Criminal Jurisdiction

DONALD W. JACKSON

In the era of globalization, mostly characterized by the fact that time and space are collapsed through instant communications, by rapid transportation, and the massive and relatively free flow of people, goods, and money across state boundaries, the concept of absolute sovereignty no longer exists.

Jackson Nayamuya Maogoto[1]

This chapter focuses on issues concerning the legitimacy of criminal prosecutions under international law (war crimes, crimes against humanity, genocide, and other offenses) and on the practical problems that so far have been encountered, especially in key prosecutions before the ad hoc tribunals for Yugoslavia and Rwanda.

CONCEPTUALIZING LEGITIMACY

David Beetham's reformulation of the traditional approach to studying legitimacy argues that instead of simply assessing public opinion regarding the legitimacy of authority, we should ask whether that authority conforms to the values and standards of a society—whether it satisfies "the normative expectations they have of it." Thus, he says, "We are making an assessment of the degree of congruence, or lack of it, between a given system of power and the beliefs, values and expectations that provide its justification."[2] In other words, we can study the beliefs and values that people have and from those we can assess their congruence with a system, rather than assessing individuals' diffuse system support directly as an indication of legitimacy.

In Beetham's formulation, power is legitimate when:

1. It conforms to established rules.

2. The rules can be justified by reference to beliefs shared by both dominant and subordinate interests.

3. There is evidence of consent by the subordinate to the particular power relation.

Evaluation of these three criteria can be made, in his view, by examining evidence in the public domain, though not solely (and perhaps not primarily) by public opinion (the proper evidence is "not in the private recesses of people's minds").[3] Indeed, this approach offers an alternative methodology for answering questions about legitimacy. The first question—whether the use of power conforms to established rules—may be one chiefly for lawyers and judges, but certainly social scientists have a contribution to make as well. The second question—the congruity between rules and beliefs shared by both dominant and subordinate interests—can be answered both by philosophers and social scientists and by survey research, but Beetham suggests that the question of legitimacy ought not be answered by mass public opinion alone. The third question—that of expressed consent—is more complicated. Clearly some sort of democratic or democratic/representative accountability is suggested, but the form is indeterminate. Beetham does argue that today it must be mass consent, given that popular consent is a contemporary democratic standard, perhaps only sometimes achieved, but aspired to by most people.[4]

Beetham concludes, "The legitimacy or rightfulness of power, then, provides an explanation for obedience through the obligation it imposes on people to obey, and through the *grounds* or *reasons* it gives for their obedience."[5]

The key difficulty with the legitimacy of prosecutions under universal criminal jurisdiction is that the traditional units of analysis in international law have been sovereign states. In international law, a sovereign state is a unit or collectivity that claims the exclusive right to the legitimate use of physical force within a society,[6] and international law ordinarily recognizes the exclusive territorial rights and political independence of those units. Yet prosecutions under universal criminal jurisdiction represent a form of humanitarian intervention that is held to be justifiable when a sovereign state fails to fulfill the duty owed by a state to its citizens or subjects. This perspective on duty is becoming commonplace in international circles[7]—governments today are viewed as having a duty to protect their citizens against serious abuses of their rights. These duties may be those contained within international covenants or they may be transmitted within the provisions of customary international law that have developed incrementally, chiefly during the past two centuries. These include war crimes, crimes against humanity, and genocide and are part of the peremptory norms of international law (*jus cogens*).[8] The key issue with the legitimacy of such prosecutions is that they run counter to the claims of those who continue to assert the prerogatives of unrestricted sovereignty.

Max Weber's formulation of legitimacy provides an essential background for Beetham's reformulation. Whereas Beetham's categories include recognition and adherence to rules, resting, ultimately, on the consent of disputants, Weber's formulation is broader. Thus a government's policy is effective either because the government has sufficient coercive power to make it so or because a sufficient number of people regard the policy as legitimate and willingly, or even reluctantly, obey. If for no other reasons than economy and the avoidance of conflict, effectiveness through legitimacy is usually preferable to coercion or the frequent use of threats of coercion.

The legitimacy of a governmental policy (order) may be upheld for a variety of reasons, including personal loyalty, support for the values represented by the action, faith-based imperatives, or indeed through perceived self-interest.

Weber classifies these foundations for legitimacy to include:

1. Tradition: "a belief in the legitimacy of what has always existed."

2. Affectual attitudes: "especially emotional, legitimizing the validity of what is newly revealed or a model to imitate."

3. Rational belief in an absolute value: such as belief in "natural law."

4. Legality: "the readiness to conform with rules which are formally correct and have been imposed by accepted procedure."

He then argues that, in modern times, the most common basis for legitimacy lies in legality. A belief in legality provides a strong foundation for the legitimate authority of the source imposing an order. For the purposes of this paper, legality as a foundation of legitimacy is clearly the most important element.[9] Institutions and processes governed by law are supposed to operate in a fair and impartial manner, independent of coercion or pressure from powerful individuals or interests. Indeed, judicial independence is a hallmark of legality, however difficult it may be to achieve in practice,[10] and it is a key ingredient of the rule of law.

As the vastness of the literature on the topic attests, the concept of "the rule of law" raises more questions that it answers. Still, it can be said that where the concept prevails, governance operates, for the most part, on the basis of openly articulated commands and standards that are implemented in a predictable manner and maintained as authoritative, even vis-à-vis the executive power (notwithstanding leeway for some range of discretion), by the countervailing power of independent courts.[11]

APPLYING THE ELEMENTS OF LEGITIMACY

Perhaps I am going too far to explain the obvious. Legality—the rule of law—would represent the foundation for the legitimacy of criminal prosecutions brought in transnational tribunals exercising universal jurisdiction, but to be seen as legitimate, such prosecutions must be widely accepted as being congruent with widely shared beliefs and values, and broad consent to the exercise of such jurisdiction is seen as necessary.

Such prosecutions might *not* be legitimate if:

1. The substantive rules applied are seen to represent the values of a dominant culture, but not that of a "subordinate" culture that is engaged in a conflict with a dominant culture. (This is especially problematic if the rules applied are mostly those of a hegemonic power.)

2. The procedures followed are perceived to be biased rather than fair and impartial.

3. The judges are perceived to be biased rather than fair and impartial.

4. The prosecutions chiefly represent a form of "victor's justice."

5. The purposes of such prosecutions are seen as having no purpose other than that of affirming the preferences of a dominant culture.

6. The purposes of such prosecutions are seen as having no purpose other than vengeance, but this raises a question: Is there a useful distinction between vengeance and retribution? Retribution is often a purpose of punishment.

7. There are no appropriate measures or procedures in place to ensure that none of the six preceding problems exists in fact.

In the broadest sense, the legitimacy of transnational prosecutions thus may depend on the quality of a tribunal's engagement with the nation-states and people who will be most affected by its decisions.[12]

THE VALUES OF DOMINANT CULTURES OR COUNTRIES

One of the most compelling arguments questioning the legitimacy of trans-national prosecutions under universal jurisdiction is contained in Anthony Anghie's recent book *Imperialism, Sovereignty and the Making of International Law*.[13] Anghie writes chiefly from a third-world perspective, arguing that the traditional legal justifications of sovereignty, as well as those underlying the contemporary transnational intrusions on sovereignty, are mostly founded on the interests of Western societies. Although I think his argument is overdrawn, it nonetheless is worthy both of due consideration and of an honest effort to provide a sufficient answer.

Anghie reviews five historic "episodes," beginning with what he calls the "colonial origins of international law" and concluding with the contemporary "episodes" of globalization and the war on terrorism. He suggests that sovereignty was defined, especially in the period of Spanish colonization, to justify sovereignty for Spanish civilization but to withhold sovereignty from the native people of the New World because they were pagans. Anghie argues that the work of sixteenth century jurist Francisco de Vitoria[14] accounts for the differences between the two societies as justification for the waging of war against the nonsovereign Indians by the Spaniards whenever Indians resisted Spanish intrusions on their lands and cultures. This view, Anghie argues, extends through the nineteenth century because colonies were forced "to comply with authoritative European standards in order to win recognition and assert themselves."[15] This can be seen as well in the post–World War I system of mandates through the League of Nations, under which the development of mandated territories was monitored for the "well-being and development" of their people.[16] For the new states that eventually gained their independence, "sovereignty [wa]s the hard won prize for their long struggle for emancipation. It is the legal epitome of the fact that they are masters in their own house."[17] Anghie's interpretation is that globalization links good governance with international human rights law.[18] Good governance, in turn, is founded on liberal democracy, which was established as the universal model to be emulated after the Cold War ended. The next step was that liberal democracy was linked to the rule of law and to the development of free market capitalist economies. The International Monetary Fund, the World Bank, and the World Trade Organization (WTO) are key institutions that seek to advance these linkages. Societies that do not rely on liberal democracy and free market capitalism and that do not respect the rule of law must be disciplined and/or reformed—so runs the argument.

Anghie sees the potential for the war on terrorism to continue this development process through the identification of "rogue states"—the worst ones constituting an "Axis of Evil"—that are to be transformed by the active promotion of liberal democracy.[19] The end is that preemptive self-defense (PESD) measures are seen as entirely legal and that overseeing the transformation of rogue states in liberal democracies is the best way to remove their threat: "War waged in the PESD mode may now become the vehicle for a new form of imperialism, defensive imperialism."[20]

It certainly is easy to apprehend the thread of Anghie's argument in the development of U.S. strategic security policies since 9/11, and he is not alone in making such inferences about the imperialistic strain in the promotion of liberal democracy by the United States.

David Chandler, writing from his perspective as a British academic, is even more critical than Anghie. Chandler sees the decline in the weight accorded state sovereignty as an opportunity most likely to be seized by Western-led interventions:

> The growing acceptance of a moral right of some states to unilaterally or collectively exercise military power to uphold "international justice" and human rights indicates that sovereignty, or the exercise of state power, is being transformed. While, for some states, sovereignty is being limited, for others, it is increasingly free from traditional international constraints. This could be clearly seen in the Western response to the New York and Washington attacks in September 2001, where it was assumed that the US and Britain had the right to remove the Taliban from power in Afghanistan. . . .[21]

According to this argument, the duty to intervene usually is invoked only by powerful states or by coalitions of states that together are led by the powerful. Although President George W. Bush referred to his coalition for invading Iraq as a "coalition of the willing," Chandler contends that the coalition requires a mighty senior member and that such coalitions usually are far less inclusive than those that might be formed under United Nations (UN) auspices. Still, such coalitions often claim to act on behalf of an international human rights community. Chandler argues that no such community exists except in the imagination of certain human rights activists. Such an extension of "international justice" represents, in his view, the "abolition of international law" because "there can be no international law without equal sovereignty, no system of rights without equality between rights bearing subjects."[22] He believes that the assumption underlying most international interventions is that the people and governments concerned were not capable of acting without international supervision. Thus, in his view, interventions deny the opportunity for the people concerned to seek the solutions to their own problems and shortcomings through political processes. Chandler cites Geoffrey Robertson, a leading human rights advocate, who believes that even the International Criminal Court (ICC) "will be little more than the backdrop for show trials against countries like Rwanda and the former Yugoslavia where none of the combatants have superpower support."[23]

However critical or pessimistic David Chandler and his cohorts may be, they recognize that true universality might offer the answers to such objections. It is important also to recognize that Anthony Anghie believes that the best challenge to these trends in which powerful countries often dominate interventions is to develop a system of human rights that serves to protect human dignity and social justice, especially in states that encourage or tolerate grossly inequitable economic systems.[24] There are other paths for the development of human rights that may transcend dominance by powerful nations that insist on sovereignty only for themselves. We will now analyze what qualities are essential for legitimate prosecutions for war crimes and crimes against humanity.

UNIVERSALITY

Prosecutions for war crimes and crimes against humanity that transcend not only traditional national boundaries, but that can be brought successfully against both powerful and weak interests or nations, offer the best answer to critics such as Anghie and Chandler. This prospect is represented by what John Hagen and Gary Bass call "liberal legalism."[25] Hagen views liberal legalism as progressing from the Nuremberg precedent up to the creation of the permanent ICC. Although the United States at present continues to work against this progression, most of our European allies, Canada, and New Zealand are among the countries that endorse it. During the negotiations at the Rome Conference in the summer of 1998, the proponents of the ICC were referred to as the "like-minded nations," while the United States was the principal obstacle to their purposes. Hagen describes John Bolton, then-undersecretary of state for arms control and international security, and, subsequently, President George W. Bush's UN ambassador, as the "point person" for the U.S. advocacy for "legal exceptionalism," so that the agents of the United States would be immune from prosecution before the ICC.[26] Liberal legalism, however, stands for the universal rule of law, multilaterism, and a permanent and freestanding ICC.[27] Bass sees a continuing struggle between the principles of liberal legalism and the self-serving pursuit of interests, even among the advocates for an ICC. He sees the creation of the ad hoc tribunals for the former Yugoslavia and Rwanda as the expression of legal liberalism but recognizes that if a permanent ICC is to be taken seriously, the advocates of legal liberalism "will have to make a far stronger commitment to international justice" than they did in the 1990s.[28] In the end, it remains highly questionable whether such commitments can prevail against the continued opposition of the United States. Surely success is much likelier in the long term than it seems at present.

IMPARTIALITY

It is also unlikely that victor's justice will contribute to the eventual success of legal liberalism. Thus the prosecution of Saddam Hussein before an Iraqi court instituted and sustained by the United States is not a great step forward. Likewise, one of the problems with the long-standing position of U.S. governments that all prosecutions before the ICC ought be brought by resolutions of the UN Security Council is that the United States and other permanent members of the security council would be able to veto any prosecutions seen as threatening or counter to their interests. Although that may be seen as a virtue, particularly by the administration of George W. Bush, it means that the ICC is vulnerable to objections such as those raised by Anghie and Chandler. There can be no real impartiality when powerful countries can determine by themselves when, where, and how such prosecutions shall take place while insisting on their own exemptions.

THE PURPOSES OF PUNISHMENT

Why should we seek criminal punishment for the perpetrators of serious breaches of human rights and humanitarian law? The traditionally cited purposes of punishment are either utilitarian or retributive. Utilitarian punishment includes rehabilitation, although usually that is not pertinent to the prosecution of those who commit serious war crimes or crimes against humanity. Utilitarian punishment of such individuals usually is based on deterrence. On the other hand, retribution (accountability might suffice as a more positive term) holds that those who commit intentional crimes deserve to be punished. This position assumes both that individuals have free will and that they are morally responsible for their actions.

Deterrence usually is divided into its general and specific forms. Of these, specific deterrence (keeping particular individuals from repeating the same crimes) seems less pertinent than general deterrence (deterring others from committing similar crimes) with respect to war crimes or crimes against humanity.[29] When considering general deterrence for "ordinary" crimes, most theorists argue that swift and certain arrests, prosecutions, and punishment are the most likely to deter.[30] Usually these are more important than the severity of punishment, although the punishment must be proportionate in severity to the offense if it is to be taken seriously. Proportionality of punishment is imponderable when the most serious war crimes, crimes against humanity, or genocide are concerned, because no punishment will be seen as sufficient for such crimes that impact hundreds or thousands. Even so, if we take these ideas about deterrence into account, how likely is it that the successful prosecution of those who commit war crimes and crimes against humanity will deter others from committing comparable crimes? Based on human experience with such prosecutions to the present, effective deterrence seems improbable because impunity has been far likelier than sure and certain punishment. There is no solid, empiric evidence for effective deterrence.[31] Although the efficacy of deterrence has always been difficult to assess, it is fair to say that punishment for war crimes, crimes against humanity, and genocide would have to be swift and more certain than has been the case to the present—for example, in the prosecutions of perpetrators from the former Yugoslavia or Rwanda.[32] If effective deterrence is unlikely, it is probably better to consider the retributive purposes of such prosecutions. The notion that the criminals should get their "just desserts" has an ancient lineage, but vengeance and retribution have something in common. Yet Justice Robert Jackson's opening statement at Nuremberg suggested that justice and vengeance are contradictory.[33] However, there is another option in current thinking about punishment.

Within the past few years, restorative justice has been a popular topic among criminal justice professionals. This contemporary understanding of restorative justice emphasizes the prospect of emotional restoration to the victims of crime, or to their survivors,[34] and this is likely to be viewed more positively than retribution as a reason for punishment. Restorative justice has been sought in alternative venues as well, probably the best-known venue being the Truth and Reconciliation Commission of South Africa, whose report was published in 1998.[35] However, reconciliation also has its limits,[36] and most international lawyers seem to agree that in cases involving the most serious crimes—genocide, for example—"lasting peace and justice require some form of criminal accountability."[37]

RESOURCES: TIME, MONEY, AND PERSONNEL

The issues reviewed thus far in this chapter are theoretical, but there also are important practical issues with regard to the efficacy of transnational prosecutions. The UN Security Council referred issues involving Darfur (Sudan) to the ICC in 2005, but because there have been no completed prosecutions in the ICC, the only substantial evidence about actual practice comes from the ad hoc tribunals for the former Yugoslavia and Rwanda.

TIMELY JUSTICE

The trial of Slobodan Milosević, who was taken into custody in 2001, took place before the International Criminal Tribunal for the Former Yugoslavia (ICTY) and was nearing the end of its third year when Milosević died. It presented some vexing issues regarding timely justice. The complete online listing of those accused before the ICTY included eighty-one names as of late January 2006.[38] Two high-level individuals indicted for major violations, Radovan Karadžić, former president of the Bosnian Serbian Republic, and Ratko Mladić, leader of the Army of the Republika Srpska, remained at large.

By September 1, 1996, approximately ninety thousand people were imprisoned in Rwanda for trial at Arusha, Tanzania.[39] The first trial began in January 1997, and by November 2005, the International Criminal Tribunal for Rwanda (ICTR) had handed down twenty judgments involving twenty-six accused people. The judgments included one prime minister, four ministers of state, and others who held leadership positions during the genocide of 1994. The completion strategy filed by the ICTR with the UN reported that as of November 2005, there were twenty-six people standing accused in ten separate trials. The estimate concluded that the tribunal would have completed trials of sixty-five to seventy people through 2008[40] so the great preponderance of trials will have been in Rwandan domestic courts rather than in the ICTR.

Two problems clearly emerge for the outcomes reported in the previous two paragraphs. The first is that when grave violations of international law involve thousands of perpetrators, as was the case especially in Rwanda, an international criminal tribunal, ad hoc or permanent, may be incapable of coping with the caseload without the introduction of huge resources, including a quite large commitment of personnel. The second problem is the inverse: If international prosecutions chiefly focus on the high officials responsible for grave violations of international law, rather than trying the many lower-level perpetrators, the trials of high-level officials are likely to be politically charged, complex, and long. The outcomes with the ICTY may seem more encouraging than those with the ICTR, probably because of their higher visibility, but the Milosević trial is not likely to represent a precedent that others will choose to follow, the trial of Saddam Hussein being the most obvious example. Timely justice will most likely continue to be a serious problem.

MONEY: HOW MUCH?—AND ITS SOURCES

The projected budget for the ICTY for 2006 to 2007 was more than $267 million, while the total expenditures from the first budget year from 1993 through the latest projections for 2006 to 2007 will total more than $1 billion. The budget for the ICTY is set by the Fifth Committee of the UN General Assembly and is paid for by assessments to UN members. However, NATO and several Muslim countries also make voluntary contributions. As of December 21, 2005, the ICTY employed 1,146 staff members from 79 countries. In addition to the costs directly associated with the court, the budget includes its detention unit, the provision of legal aid, the witness protection and assistance program, translation and interpretation, travel expenses, and the costs of securing evidence.[41] Although that is a great deal of money, to put it in perspective, it is less than the approximate cost of four U.S. B-1 bombers.[42]

The UN appropriation for fiscal year 2004-2005 was approximately $250 million. It is also funded by assessments of UN member states and by voluntary contributions.

In absolute terms, the resources required for an effective ICC, although substantial, are manageable, except in the prosecutions of mass offenders, but only if the political will exists to make the necessary payments.

PERSONNEL

The ICTY consists of three trial chambers with nine judges and one appellate chamber with seven judges. In addition, nine *ad litem* judges have been assigned to trial chambers. The ICTR consists of nine judges in its trial chamber and an additional nine *ad litem* judges assigned to trial chambers, with a total of eighteen. The seven judges assigned to the appellate chamber also sit as the appellate chamber for the ICTY. The judges of the ICTY and ICTR do indeed represent much of the world,[43] although of the judges of the ICTY, only one comes from eastern Europe, none comes from orthodox-predominant countries in the Balkans, and the only large Muslim-dominant country represented is Egypt. There is a community of lawyers and associated professionals trained in public international law, especially international human rights and humanitarian law, who can be recruited for positions in institutions like the ICTY and ICTR. Many of them have had experience with international nongovernmental organizations (NGOs) or with various agencies of the UN. The developments in transnational justice described in this essay are familiar and integral to the professional lives of such lawyers. There is clearly a congruence between their values and the values represented in transnational prosecutions that provides a background of legitimacy for ad hoc or permanent transnational or international courts. However, it seems unlikely that any of the developments just reviewed has much visibility beyond the community of lawyers and associated professionals just described. Visibility is especially problematic in the United States.

OTHER CRITIQUES

When genocide, war crimes, or crimes against humanity are alleged, the ICC at The Hague may exercise supranational authority and jurisdiction. Among the most cogent arguments concerning the legitimacy of such jurisdiction is that of Madeline Morris.[44] If a crime covered by the Rome Statute for the

ICC occurs within a state that is a party to the statute or within a state that consents ad hoc to the jurisdiction of the ICC, the ICC will have authority to adjudicate, even if one of the defendants is a national of a nonmember or nonconsenting state, such as the United States. Morris argues that although there has been much discussion of the "democratic deficit" in the WTO, there has been almost no discussion of the democratic legitimacy of the ICC. States that are parties to the ICC treaty will have the right to partici-pate in the Assembly of States Parties created by the Rome Statute,[45] but for nonparty states, such as the United States, there will be no state consent to the jurisdiction of the court and no democratic linkage to the ICC. Thus, as in Beetham's formulation above, there will have been no consent, so no legitimacy can be inferred.[46] The thread of the argument is quite logical.

As to lessons learned from the experience of the ICTR, Jose Alvarez[47] concludes his long review with the following:

> Effective international criminal law enforcement requires international efforts directed at prosecuting crimes such as genocide by the most effective means any of us are likely to see in our lifetimes—by local police, local prosecutors and local courts. While international tribunals need to be kept as an option of last resort, good faith domestic pros-ecutions that encourage civil dissensus may better preserve collective memory and promote the mollification of victims, the accountability of perpetrators, the national (and even the international) rule of law and national reconciliation.[48]

With regard to the Milosević trial, its length threatened to make the trial a theater of the absurd, and the reputation of the tribunal may have been helped by his demise. The trials of the major Nazi leaders at Nuremberg were based on documentary history, which the Nazis had been careful to archive. No such documentary record exists for the crimes for which Milosević stood accused. His guilt had to be built on a testimonial record that was long and complex and from many eyewitnesses. Milosević was able to drag out his defense and intimidate witnesses in cross-examinations while the prosecution tried to link his conduct through several levels of subordinates. If such trials drag on for years, can they possibly be seen as relevant or legitimate?[49]

The forum for the trial of Saddam Hussein surely did not satisfy the conditions for a multilateral transnational tribunal. Although it was nominally in an Iraqi court, it depended almost entirely on American planning, resources, and security. The enduring divisions among Sunni, Shia, and Kurdish segments of the Iraqi people and the outlawing of the Baathists made impartiality elu-sive, if not impossible. Most problematic was that Saddam could emulate the Milosević strategy of delay and harassment, while the Iraqi court could not entirely constrain his defense in the interest of securing a manageably shorter trial. In the end, it is difficult to imagine how Saddam's prosecution before a crudely improvised Iraqi court could meet the conditions for legitimacy proposed in Beetham's formulation.[50]

CONCLUSION

It is somewhat heartening that in March 2005, the UN Security Council referred the situation in Darfur, Sudan, to the prosecutor of the ICC. This was accomplished with eleven votes in favor and with the abstentions of Algeria, Brazil, China, and the United States.[51] This suggests, at least, that the United States is willing to tolerate the ICC when it poses no danger to U.S. interests. While these developments indicate that the ICC will not exist only on paper, whether it will be able to exercise its jurisdiction over more powerful nations or interests remains to be seen.

It is easy to understand why the idealistic proponents of transnational justice dream of an effective and legitimate ICC. They share an ethos that no person exercising political authority—and no nation—should be above the law. Their worldview also is consistent with the trends toward globalization that have occurred during the past two decades—in the sense that human rights are understood to be universal. However, issues about the legitimacy of an International Criminal Court may involve a serious disconnect between ordinary citizens, especially in the United States—whose view of justice usually is rooted exclusively in local courts—and transnational institutions. How serious is this disconnect in the United States and elsewhere? We do not have sufficient data to answer such questions, so much research is yet to be done. These questions transcend social science: they have serious political implications.

NOTES

1. From *State Sovereignty and International Criminal Law: Versailles to Rome.* Ardsley (New York: Transnational Publishers, 2003), ix. My essay on the relative decline of Westphalian sovereignty, "Sovereignty, Transnational Constraints and Universal Criminal Jurisdiction," was included in Mary L. Volcansek and John F. Stack Jr., eds., *Courts Crossing Borders: Blurring the Lines of Sovereignty* (Durham, NC: Carolina Academic Press, 2005), chap. 9.

2. David Beetham, *The Legitimation of Power* (Atlantic Highlands, N.J.: Humanities Press International, 1991), 11.

3. Ibid. at 13.

4. Ibid. at 94.

5. Ibid. at 26 (Emphasis in original).

6. See Max Weber, "Politics as a Vocation," in Max Weber, *Essays in Sociology* (Boston: Routledge & Kegan Paul, 1958), 77. For more extensive discussion, see Brad R. Roth, *Governmental Illegitimacy in International Law* (Oxford: Oxford University Press, 2000), 8–15.

7. See, for example, Amitai Etzioni, "From Right to Responsibility, the Definition of Sovereignty is Changing," in *The Interdependent,* vol. 3, no. 4 (2005–2006), 35.

8. "[T]here are some atrocities, such as genocide and slavery, that go to the core of shared humanitarian values, and are recognized as violating peremptory norms of international law (*jus cogens*). It is on these grounds that the advocates of humanitarian intervention must make their case, as they do in criticizing the failure of the international community to act against the mass killings of Tutsis by the Hutu rulers of Rwanda in 1994." Roth, see note 6 at 32.

9. Max Weber, *The Theory of Social and Economic Organization* (New York: The Free Press, 1947), 126–132.

10. See especially Peter Russell and David O'Brien, eds., *Judicial Independence in the Age of Democracy: Critical Perspectives from Around the World* (Charlottesville: University Press of Virginia, 2001).

11. Roth, see note 6 at 50.

12. See the discussion in Section II of Janet Iontcheva Turner, "Nationalizing International Criminal Law." *Stanford International Law Journal* 41 (2005): 1.

13. Cambridge: Cambridge University Press, 2005. His overall argument is "that the non-European world is different, that the governance of these societies has been intimately shaped, since the very beginning of the colonial encounter, by international actors, imperial European states, whose actions have been sanctioned and enabled by international law" (p. 253).

14. Vitoria's two lectures, "On the Indians Lately Discovered," and "On the Law of War Made by the Spaniards on the Barbarians," can be found in Ernest Nys, ed., *Indis et de Ivre Belli Reflectiones* (Washington, D.C.: Carnegie Institution of Washington, 1917). In Anghie's discussion, see chap. 1.

15. See note 13 at 107.

16. Ibid. at 149.

17. Ibid. at 196, citing R. P. Anand, "Role of the 'New' Asian-African Countries in the Present International Legal Order." *American Journal of International Law* 56 (1962) 383 at 390.

18. Anghie, see note 13, chap. 5.

19. Anghie cites George W. Bush's "Axis of Evil" speech on page 277. "States like these, and their terrorist allies, constitute an 'Axis of Evil,' arming to threaten the peace of the world. By seeking weapons of mass destruction, these regimes pose a grave and growing danger. They could provide these arms to terrorists, giving them the means to match their hatred. They could attack our allies or attempt to blackmail the United States. In any of these cases, the price of indifference would be catastrophic."

20. Ibid. at 294. Also see the conclusion at page 309: "My broad argument is that the [war against terrorism] represents a set of policies and principles that reproduces the structure of the civilizing mission. Further, it is precisely by invoking the primordial, imperial structures latent within international law that this supposedly new initiative seeks to disrupt and transform existing international law. It is a novel initiative that relies for its power on a very ancient set of ideas—regarding self-defence, humanitarian intervention, and conquest."

21. David Chandler, *From Kosovo to Kabul: Human Rights and International Intervention* (London: Pluto Press, 2002), 122.

22. Ibid. at 135–137.

23. Ibid. at 147–148.

24. Anghie, see note 13 at 271.

25. John Hagen, *Justice in the Balkans: Prosecuting War Crimes in the Hague Tribunal* (Chicago: University of Chicago Press, 2003), chap. 7; Gary Jonathan Bass, *Stay the Hand of Vengeance: The Politics of War Crimes Tribunals* (Princeton: Princeton University Press, 2000), 278–283.

26. Ibid. at 206.

27. Ibid. at 207.

28. Bass, see note 25 at 282.

29. Most war crimes and crimes against humanity are contextual, which is to say that they are contingent on particular sequences of events, rather than representing purposive career criminality.

30. Franklin E. Zimring and Gordon J. Hawkins, *Deterrence: The Legal Threat in Crime Control* (Chicago: University of Chicago Press, 1973), 246 et seq.

31. See Theodor Meron, "From Nuremberg to the Hague," *Military Law Review* 149 (1995): 107 at 110.

32. David Wippman, "Atrocities, Deterrence and the Limits of International Justice," *Fordham Law Journal* 23 (1999): 473.

33. "That four great nations, flushed with victory and stung with injury, stay the hand of vengeance and voluntarily submit their captive enemies to the judgment of the law is one of the significant tributes that Power has ever paid to Reason." This was quoted on the frontispiece, and provided the title for Gary Bass's book, *Stay the Hand of Vengeance*, see note 25.

34. See, for example, Heather Strang, *Repair of Revenge: Victims and Restorative Justice* (Oxford: Clarendon Press, 2002).

35. An important assessment of truth and reconciliation commissions is that by Priscilla B. Hayner, *Unspeakable Truths: Confronting State Terror and Atrocity* (New York and London: Routledge, 2001).

36. Roy L. Brooks, ed., *When Sorry Isn't Enough: The Controversy over Apologies and Reparations for Human Injustice* (New York: New York University Press, 1999).

37. Jose E. Alvarez, "Crimes of States/Crimes of Hate: Lessons from Rwanda," *Yale Journal of International Law* 24 (1999): 365 at 482.

38. Online at http://www.un.org/icty (visited June 4, 2007).

39. Alvarez, see note 37 at 393.

40. The completion report and much additional information are online at www.ictr.org (visited June 4, 2007).

41. See the background information online at http://www.un.org/icty/cases-e/index-e.htm (visited June 4, 2007).

42. The unit cost for a B-1 bomber was $283.1 million, based on fiscal 1998 constant dollars. Seventy-two of these bombers were deployed. Online at http://www.darkgovernment.com/b1.html (visited June 4, 2007).

43. The appellate chamber (for both the ICTY and the ICTR): United States, Italy, Senegal, Turkey, Germany, Guyana, and Zambia. The ICTY trial chambers: Jamaica, Malta, China, Egypt, the Netherlands, South Korea, France, and Australia. The ICTY ad hoc judges, as of this writing, are from: Spain, Madagascar, the Netherlands, Sweden, Belgium, Denmark, Germany, France, and Hungary. The ICTR trial judges: Norway, Fiji, Russia, Tanzania, Madagascar, Sri Lanka, Uganda, Kenya, Ghana, Jordan,

South Korea, Argentina, Pakistan, St. Kitts and Nevis, Italy, Cameroon, Sweden, and Burkina Faso.

44. Professor of Law, Duke University.

45. Article 112 of the Rome Statute. See the Web site of the ICC, including the Rome Statute, online at www.un.org/icc.

46. Beetham, see note 1.

47. Professor of law, University of Michigan Law School.

48. Alvarez, see note 37 at 483.

49. *The Times of London*: Peter Quayle, "How long should it take to try a man for genocide?" June 21, 2005.

50. See page 68.

51. Resolution 1593 (2005), Press Release SC/8351, online at www.un.org/News/Press/docs/2005/sc8351.doc.htm (visited June 4, 2007).

CHAPTER FIVE

International and Transnational Law, Sovereignty, and Hegemonic Power

DONALD W. JACKSON

Law above the level of the nation-state is on the rise, though sometimes constrained by the political, economic, and military power of certain nations. Indeed, universal criminal jurisdiction may even be invoked by courts of nation-states—or by emergent international tribunals with criminal jurisdiction—to prosecute crimes committed in other nations that are recognized under international law.[1] Most crimes so recognized flow from the key precedents of prosecutions in Germany and Japan following World War II, but some crimes, including piracy on the high seas, which is classified as a crime against humanity, and the international slave trade are older than World War II.[2] In chapter 4, after reviewing contemporary events concerning the evolution and growth of universal criminal jurisdiction,[3] I suggested that most American scholars who study justice systems have not paid sufficient attention to the transformations that universal jurisdiction (which is one aspect of globalization) is bringing to the manner through which justice is sought or determined. Moreover, I noted that issues involving the perceived legitimacy of criminal prosecutions under universal jurisdiction mostly remain unexplored. Those suggestions were written in 2002, after the terrorist attacks of 9/11 and about a year before the beginning of the U.S. intervention in Iraq and also before the May 1, 2003, proclamation by President George W. Bush that "[m]ajor combat operations in Iraq have ended." The central point of this chapter is that events since the terrorist attacks of September 11, 2001, have seriously threatened the prospects for universal criminal jurisdiction and for the growth of the more effective global rule of law. That threat chiefly comes from the power and policies of the United States.

This chapter will examine the serious difficulties that U.S. hegemonic[4] power and its related strategic security policies have raised against the prospects for any foreseeable achievement of a reasonably objective[5] global rule of law. I certainly do not mean to suggest that such difficulties represent a Manichean global conflict between good and evil, although some neoconservative analysts do see conflicts between the United States and its enemies in such terms.[6] Instead, I propose to study what is a grave conflict between, on one hand, current U.S. power and policy and, on the other hand, the evolution of universal standards of justice that otherwise have developed from transformative events of the past sixty years, some of which were intentional, but many which were driven by material and technological development.

GLOBALIZATION AND UNIVERSAL JUSTICE STANDARDS: THEORETICAL PERSPECTIVES

Martin Shapiro has described a "prototype of courts," which represents an ideal process for conflict resolution. The essential ideal is based on a "triad" in which two people, who encounter a conflict they cannot resolve, resort to a third person for help. Shapiro argues:

> So universal across time and space is this simple social invention of triads that we can discover almost no society that fails to employ it. And from its overwhelming appeal to common sense stems the basic legitimacy of courts everywhere. In short, the triad for purposes of conflict resolution is the basic social logic of courts, a logic so compelling that courts have become a universal political phenomenon.[7]

It is important to stress that the social logic of conflict resolution by a third party rests on the fairness of the third party to both sides of the unresolved conflict. One way of putting this is that the role of the third party—the essential role of a judge[8]—requires that the agent for conflict resolution be as fair, impartial, and objective as is humanly possible. Of course, that is the second-best solution. Each party to the conflict would really prefer for the third party to be biased in his or her favor, but the conflicting preferences of the two parties lead naturally to the second-best solution for both of them, which is fairness and impartiality toward both sides. Obviously, in criminal cases, the defendant usually does not elect to submit to the jurisdiction of the judge, and the power of state police to arrest and hold defendants for trial is essential; nonetheless, both the prosecution and the defendant have the same second-best preference for a fair and impartial hearing.

In a recent essay by Kenneth Abbott and others, the triad is combined with two other principles to describe the "Concept of Legalization" in world politics: "obligation" represents the agreements by nation-states or other international actors to be bound by a rule or a set of rules; "precision" means that as much ambiguity as possible has been resolved to create precise, elaborated rules; and "delegation" means that actors have granted authority to a third party (the triad again) to apply the rules and resolve disputes.[9] For the purpose of this essay, only the ideals of obligation and delegation will be considered. Although there are important issues of precision, such as the definition of torture or aggression under international law, those will be the subject of another book.

Those who seek to create institutions through which universal standards of justice may be applied are trying to extend the ideal of triadic conflict resolution—or the three elements of legalization—beyond the level of the nation-state. Peter Singer, in his book on the ethics of globalization, wrote, "Support for an effective universal prohibition on genocide and crimes against humanity shows more clearly than any other issue how our conception of the sovereign rights of states has changed over the past fifty years."[10] The International Criminal Tribunal for the Former Yugoslavia (ICTY), the International Criminal Tribunal for Rwanda (ICTR) (both created by United Nations [UN] Security Council resolutions), and the International Criminal Court (ICC) (created by the Rome Statute of 1998 but extant by state ratifications only since July 1, 2002) are three examples of legalization, the first two being geographically and time bound, whereas the third is—in principle if not yet in reality—global and forward looking, with no foreseen expiration. The impulse for these institutions was that grave injustices (so grave that they represented crimes like those prosecuted against the leaders of German National Socialism in Nuremberg in 1945 and after) were being committed by persons who exercised state power against their perceived or real enemies. The problem always has been that those exercising state power usually have had impunity for the crimes they commit. Usually, only warfare voided such impunity—and then the victors imposed justice on their defeated enemies—certainly not the ideal forum for fair and impartial justice, even though sometimes it is unavoidable. Nonetheless, the aftermath of World War II involved an effort to transcend victors' justice by creating universal institutions, such as the various organizations that would be associated with the UN, and universal standards of justice represented in various international covenants and treaties, and, more recently, by the Rome Statute of the ICC. Just as warfare has sometimes produced victors' justice, the legitimacy of international tribunals is contingent on their recognition by nation-states as fair and impartial tribunals and eventually on their effective power to order the arrest of and hold for trial those accused of crimes.

Although there are many examples of the shortcomings of efforts to establish effective transnational justice—the failure to prosecute genocide effectively and in a timely fashion is the most serious example—one recent illustration of absence of objectivity and fairness in criminal prosecutions can be found in President George W. Bush's executive order of November 2001 that established military commissions for the prosecution of alleged international terrorists. In his initial public proposal, executive authority was responsible both for the prosecution and judging by such commissions. Moreover, President Bush claimed authority to order indefinite detention of prisoners, lowered the standards for the admission of evidence, provided for hearings in camera, and withdrew the presumption of innocence. Only public objections from the legal community and others led to the initial revision of the president's order.[11]

Just as globalization—at its best—would mean policies and institutions that would support fairness in world trade, world banking, and world finance, since World War II there has been an impulse as well for fairly administered world justice. However, none of these global outcomes will suffice if, in the long run, they are dominated by the interests of a single nation or by a singular source of economic or military power. Domination would mean that lesser participants cannot rely on the fairness or impartiality of such institutions. Instead, the domination of global institutions by a single source of power might represent a contemporary version of imperialism, although that concept is no longer entirely appropriate.[12] Indeed, we need a new concept to fit the occasion.[13] Ideally, global standards of justice administered through transnational institutions would involve triadic justice meted out by fair and impartial third parties (tribunals), and everyone and every nation would recognize and be subject to the jurisdiction of these institutions. Thus the principles of obligation and delegation as integral aspects of legalization, proposed by Abbott et al.,[14] would be met. Those are deceptively simple ideals; achieving them in practice is quite another matter.

The United States, for one, resists most efforts to subject its representatives or military personnel to obligatory international jurisdiction. Although President Bill Clinton signed the Rome Statute of the ICC on December 31, 2000 (the last day it was open for signature), President George W. Bush withdrew the signature in May 2002, and since then the Bush administration has continued to oppose the ICC and has worked through various means to secure immunity from its jurisdiction for U.S. personnel.

THE FIRST KEY PROBLEM: U.S. HEGEMONIC POWER AND UNILATERALISM

This problem represents the current unwillingness of the United States to delegate authority over its conduct to transnational institutions.

In September 2002, the administration of George W. Bush published its *National Security Strategy*. Its perspective—flowing in large part from the terrorist attacks of September 11, 2001—is that the United States has many dangerous enemies, so "[d]efending our Nation against its enemies is the first and fundamental commitment of the Federal Government." The strategy argues that our enemies are "shadowy networks" of terrorists, so "to defeat this threat we must make use of every tool in our arsenal—military power, homeland defenses, law enforcement, intelligence, and vigorous efforts to cut off terrorist financing."[15] The Bush administration's idea of preemptive action is set forth in the following paragraph:

> The United States has long maintained the option of preemptive actions to counter a sufficient threat to our national security. The greater the threat, the greater is the risk of inaction—and the more compelling the case for taking anticipatory action to defend ourselves, even if uncertainty remains as to the time and place of the enemy's attack. To forestall or prevent such hostile acts by our adversaries, the United States will, if necessary, act preemptively.[16]

We should note that even some of the strongest advocates of Bush's 2002 policy statement acknowledge that preemption as embraced in the statement violates the provisions of the UN Charter. For example, writing in the *Los Angeles Times*, David Frum and Richard Perle recognized that Article 51 of the charter acknowledges a right of self-defense only against an actual attack. It duly notes, "In all other cases where a nation feels threatened, it is supposed to go to the UN Security Council to seek authorization before it takes military action—even action that might forestall an attack."[17]

But that recognition is not meant as a concession to the UN Charter as imposing de facto limits on U.S. power. In an essay in *Foreign Affairs* in 1996, Robert Kagan and William Kristol argued that the United States needed to take advantage of the "unipolar moment" following the demise of the Soviet Union to develop a new strategic policy. The United States should increase its defense budget and should use its power unabashedly to pursue a foreign policy that pressures dictators and authoritarian regimes.[18] Views such as those urged by Kagan and Kristol have been described as a "neocon" worldview, but they were the inheritors of a view from the other end of the American political spectrum. A recent book by George Packer has put it well:

> The idea was that governments should not be allowed to abuse their own citizens on a massive scale; that sovereignty did not excuse rape, torture, murder, and genocide; that it was the world's interest and obligations to end these crimes. This new kind of war became known as humanitarian intervention, and in this country its advocates

acquired the name *liberal interventionists*, or, in shorthand, *liberal hawks* [emphasis added].[19]

Packer duly notes that liberal interventionists were multilateralists who preferred to intervene through the UN, but that the failure of the UN to act decisively, especially in Bosnia and Rwanda in 1994, enabled and strengthened the unilateralist preferences of the neocons, such as Kagan and Kristol, who, according to Packer, responded to the following questions:

> What should the United States do about threats that the world insists on ignoring? Is it necessary for war to have the sanction of an international body? What are the limits of sovereignty? Can democracy be brought by force?: Whose responsibility does a defeated country become after a war? Most of all: What role should America's power play in shaping the answers?[20]

Kagan and Kristol called their response—their form of intervention—"benevolent hegemony:"

> Having defeated the "evil empire," the United States enjoys strategic and ideological predominance. The first objective of U.S. foreign policy should be to preserve and enhance that predominance by strengthening America's security, supporting its friends, advancing its interests, and standing up for its principles around the world.[21]

It was unilateralist, if need be (but a "coalition of the willing" was most welcome), and its occasion was Iraq.

One of the most comprehensive statements of the neocon position is contained in David Frum's and Richard Perle's *An End to Evil: How to Win the War on Terror* (2003).[22] There are several prominent themes in the book; one of them is the broad rejection of constraints due to multilateralism and the disdain for UN interventions. The authors argue that the UN Charter is entirely inadequate to deal with stateless terrorism. Of course, this disregards the fact that the Security Council may nonetheless authorize an appropriate response to terrorism, as it did in the instance of Afghanistan. That members of the Security Council sometimes may have ideas that diverge from the official position of the United States and that we may not always get our way is, of course, entirely consistent with the design of the UN Charter, even if its U.S. sponsors in 1945 did not expect such outcomes. Frum and Perle see the United States as being single-handedly responsible for preserving world peace and justice, as revealed in the concluding paragraph of their book:

> ...A world at peace; a world governed by law; a world in which all peoples are free to find their own destinies: That dream has not

yet come true, it will not come true soon, but if it ever does come true, it will be brought into being by American armed might and defended by American might too. America's vocation is not an imperial vocation. Our vocation is to support justice with power. It is a vocation that has earned us terrible enemies. It is a vocation that has made us, at our best moments, the hope of the world.[23]

It is doubtful that most people in other countries are reassured by the expression of such "noble" sentiments. Responding appropriately to the call of Frum and Perle for a "Pax Americana" requires that the contradictions within their position—as least with previous policies of the United States—be examined. Although it may be true that at its best moments, the United States has embodied high hopes for much of the world (as it did after December 7, 1941), achieving its aspirations for the world through unchecked and unrestrained unilateral American military power in the twenty-first century is quite problematic. To be sure, the political climate of the United States when the UN Charter was conceived following World War II—when the only other significant military power in the world was the Soviet Union—was a very different one.

From the beginning of U.S. participation in World War II, President Franklin Roosevelt did view the United States as one of the "four policemen" that would collaboratively maintain peace and security in the world. Although the United States clearly was to be in a prominent leadership role, there was no intention evidenced for the unilateral exercise of police power by the United States except, perhaps, when acting under the Monroe Doctrine within the confines of the Western Hemisphere.[24]

The Atlantic Charter of August 14, 1941, marked the movement of the United States from a position of neutrality and relative isolation from Europe toward eventual alliance with the United Kingdom and other Western allies.[25] The closing paragraph of the charter, agreed to by President Roosevelt and Prime Minister Winston Churchill, expressed the aspiration for the nations of the world that all might abandon the use of force, calling for the establishment of a "wider and permanent system of security."[26]

The key conference on the creation of a postwar international security agency was held at Dumbarton Oaks in Washington, D.C., and led to the proposal of October 1944. The document proposed as the principal organs of the international agency a general assembly, a security council, and a secretariat headed by the secretary general and an international court of justice. The Security Council of eleven members was to include as permanent members the United States, the United Kingdom, the Soviet Union, the Republic of China, and—eventually—France. The six nonpermanent members were to be elected by the general assembly. Substantive decisions of the Security Council were to require at least seven votes, including the votes of the five permanent members. The Security Council was empowered to act when there was a determined threat to peace or an act of aggression. These features were essentially approved at the Yalta Conference in February 1945, and Roosevelt, Churchill, and Stalin called a UN conference to be held in San Francisco in September 1945.

When U.S. Secretary of State Edward Stettinius addressed the opening of the San Francisco Conference, President Roosevelt recently had died; Stettinius quoted from Roosevelt's words at the Yalta Conference:

> The structure of world peace cannot be the work of one man, or one party or one nation. It cannot be an American peace, or a British, a Russian, a French or a Chinese peace. There cannot be the peace of large nations—or of small nations. It must be the peace which rests on the cooperative efforts of the whole world. . . . There can be no middleground here. We have to take responsibility for world collaboration, or we shall have to bear the responsibility for another world conflict.[27]

The difference between Roosevelt's words and those of Frum and Perle, who argue that peace and justice will be realized only as a consequence of American armed might and the will to use it, is profound and troubling, but the difficulty that unilateralism creates for transnational justice is even more problematic.

The Bush administration sought Bilateral Immunity Agreements (BIAs) through which nation-states guarantee not to render U.S. personnel to the jurisdiction of the ICC. It also has suspended military assistance to nation-states that do not enter into such agreements. The American Service Members' Protection Act (2002), which was first strongly supported by then-chair of the Senate Foreign Relations Committee, Jesse Helms, authorizes the president of the United States to use any means necessary to free U.S. citizens from custody in The Hague, and the Nethercutt Amendment of December 2004, allows the cutting off of aid to countries that have not signed BIAs. The United States has also successfully sought immunity for U.S. participants in UN peacekeeping missions through Security Council Resolution 1422, first enacted in July 2002 and extended through July 2004 but withdrawn from further extension when the United States saw that it was not likely to be renewed.[28] It is evident that current U.S. policy does not envision for itself, or its representatives, the prospect of criminal prosecution through transnational courts.

We should note that India, both Koreas, the Russian Federation, and the People's Republic of China have not ratified the Rome Statute for the ICC. In the Middle East, only Jordan and Yemen have ratified. Obviously, it is a matter of grave concern should several of the most powerful and populous countries of the world, or countries in high-conflict regions, fail to accede to the jurisdiction of the ICC. In the instances of Russia and China, however, there is no clear evidence that they are intractable opponents of the ICC. By the middle of 2007, 105 countries had ratified the Rome Statute.

CONTEMPORARY CRITIQUES OF HEGEMONY AND UNILATERALISM

Most of the United States' European allies, even the United Kingdom, are much stronger supporters of international law and institutions than is the United States. The members of the European Union have created strong transnational institutions in the economic sphere, and the members of the Council of Europe have accepted constraints on their sovereignty through their adherence to the European Convention on Human Rights, which allows their nationals to complain about violations of the convention directly to the European Court of Human Rights in Strasbourg. One consequence is that the United States is sometimes viewed as a country that views international law and institutions as good for others, but not for itself.[29]

George Soros brings an interesting critical perspective to neoconservative views on the role of the United States in world politics. As a disciple of Karl Popper, Soros is suspicious of claims of ultimate truth. Instead, he is committed to what he calls the principle of "radical fallibility," which is premised on Popper's philosophy of science. All scientific knowledge is eternally tentative and open to the disconfirmation by the presentation of contrary evidence, and an open society makes possible the pursuit and presentation of contrary evidence. The twentieth century too often demonstrated the consequences of ideologues who, encountering the inconsistencies between their ideologies and reality, attempted to remake the world to conform to their ideology. Millions of humans who got in their way were ruthlessly eliminated by Hitler, Lenin, Stalin, Mao, and others. Soros views the neoconservative ideology as simply holding that because we are stronger than others, we must know better and we must have right on our side. He quoted the national security strategy of George W. Bush:

> The greatest struggles of the twentieth century between liberty and totalitarians ended with a decisive victory for the forces of freedom—and a single sustainable model for national success: freedom, democracy and free enterprise.[30]

Although Soros is no apologist for the United Nations, he notes, "the advocates of American supremacy have developed an ideological aversion to the UN Security Council because it gives other permanent members equal rights."[31]

One of the most cogent reviews of the strategic policy of the administration of George W. Bush is that by Ivo Daalder and James Lindsay in

America Unbound: the Bush Revolution in Foreign Policy.[32] Perhaps their most salient comment is:

> Bush's way was not America's only choice. In fact, Washington had chosen differently before. When America emerged from World War II as the predominant power in the world, it could have imposed an imperium commensurate with its power. But Franklin Roosevelt and Harry Truman chose not to. They recognized that American power would be more acceptable and more effective and lasting if it were folded into alliances and multilateral institutions that served the best interests of many countries. So they created the United Nations to help ensure international peace and security, set up the Breton Woods system to help stabilize international economic interactions and spent vast sums of money to help rebuild countries (including the vanquished foes) that had been devastated by the war. It was not just America's victory in war, but also its magnanimity in peace, that made the twentieth century the American century.

The national security policy of the second Bush administration clearly diverged from that tradition.

THE SECOND PROBLEM: THE AMERICAN PRESIDENCY AND THE EXERCISE OF UNCONSTRAINED INHERENT POWER

This problem represented the unwillingness of the administration of George W. Bush to recognize that it—or more precisely the president of the United States—is always legally bound by the rules of international law, even including rules the United States has agreed to by the ratification of conventions or treaties. At the same time, the Bush administration asserted that a proper interpretation of the president's power under Article II of the U.S. Constitution supports the conclusion that Congress has no power to limit or define the president's war-making powers.

John Yoo's recent book provides insight to the constitutional powers perspective of George W. Bush's administration.[33] Yoo argues that a "flexible, dynamic approach is required to interpreting the constitutional provisions regarding presidential and congressional powers over questions of war and peace," leading to the interpretation that "the Constitution allows the political branches to shape a variety of processes for deciding on matters ranging from war and peace to international cooperation."[34] The crux of his argument for inherent presidential power, adapted to the necessities of the occasion, rest on his view that Article II vests the greatest powers over foreign affairs to the executive; that is, to the president. Although that is not a surprising or unusual argument, his next step is the assertion that we need to understand executive authority as it was understood at the writing of the Constitution. According to Yoo, English constitutional understanding at the time of the writing of the U.S. Constitution was that foreign affairs was the province of the Crown, to the virtual exclusion of Parliament, which had only the power of the purse held by the House of Commons. Thus Yoo's argument runs that the framers intended to follow the English allocation of powers—the foreign affairs power of King George III presumably passed to the president of the United States, subject only to the express provisions of the U.S. Constitution. In support of this position, Yoo cites Alexander Hamilton and Chief Justice John Marshall, both of them strong Federalists.

Of course, the express constitutional provisions conceived by the framers of our Constitution are important: providing for congressional declaration of war, for congressional power over foreign commerce, and for the ratification of treaties by an extraordinary majority of the Senate. Moreover, the Congress was given the power of the purse that had been held also by the House of Commons relative to the British Crown, but Yoo does not see these as serious limitations on inherent executive power. It should be noted that Louis Fisher, one of the leading scholars on the constitutional powers of the president, has concluded that Yoo's argument "contradicts not only statements made at the Philadelphia convention and at the contemporary state ratification debates but also the text of the Constitution.[35]

To be sure, Yoo is not alone in making such an argument for presidential powers; it is the context of his position—having formerly participated in advising President Bush on post-9/11 decisions—that makes his book interesting. Several of his memorandums, sometimes cowritten with others, are in the public domain. His memo of September 25, 2001, immediately following 9/11, focused on the president's constitutional authority to conduct military operations against terrorists and nations supporting them and is his first relevant to this analysis:

> [W]e think it beyond question that the President has the plenary constitutional powers to take such military actions as he deems necessary and appropriate to respond to the terrorist attacks upon the United States of September 11, 2001.... In both the War Powers Resolution and the Joint Resolution [following 9/11], the Congress has recognized the President's authority to use force in circumstances such as those created by the September 11 incidents. *Neither statute, however, can place any limits on the President's determinations as to any terrorist threat, the amount of military force to be used in response, or the method, timing, and nature of the response. These decisions under our Constitution are for the President alone to make* [emphasis added].[36]

Does it follow then, that if the Congress cannot place any limits on the president's powers as commander in chief, provisions of international law also do not apply? While not making quite that point, in a memo of January 9, 2002, concerning the application of treaties and laws to al Qaeda and Taliban detainees, Yoo and Robert Delahunty, another Justice Department attorney, argued that al Qaeda "would not be included in non-international forms of armed conflict to which some provisions of the Geneva Convention might apply." Neither were members of the Taliban militia protected: "First, the Taliban was not a government and Afghanistan was not—even prior to the beginning of the present conflict—a functioning State during the period in which they engaged in hostilities against the United States and its allies." Second, Yoo and Delahunty conclude that "customary international law, whatever its source and content does not bind the President, or restrict the actions of the United States military, because it does not constitute federal law recognized under the Supremacy Clause of the Constitution.[37] This was followed on January 25, 2002, by a memo for the president from Alberto Gonzalez, then-counsel to the president, largely confirming the position taken in the Yoo-Delahunty memorandum.

One more memo should be sufficient to illustrate the breadth and preemptive quality of the president's powers as seen by John Yoo (and others within the administration of George W. Bush): Yoo's memo of August 1, 2002, on the standards to be followed in interrogations conducted outside the United States. The particular concern of the memo was the application of Title 18, sections 2340[38] through 2340a[39] of the U.S. Code, the provisions that implemented the Convention Against Torture and Other Cruel, Inhuman and Degrading Treatment into federal law.[40]

Yoo's memo took a narrow view of torture as defined by section 2340a, concluding that to constitute torture the conduct:

> "must inflict pain that is difficult to endure. Physical pain amounting to torture must be equivalent in intensity to the pain accompanying serious physical injury, such as organ failure, impairment of bodily function or even death." For purely mental pain or suffering to amount to torture under Section 2340, it must result in significant psychological harm of sufficient duration, e.g., lasting for months or even years. . . . We conclude that the statute, taken as a whole, makes plain that it prohibits only extreme acts.[41]

But that restrictive definition of torture is not the most important aspect of Yoo's memo for the purposes of this paper. Part V of his memo concludes that, given the circumstances of the war against terrorism, prosecution under Section 2340a may be barred because enforcement of the statute would "represent an unconstitutional infringement of the president's authority to conduct war." Furthermore, according to Yoo, the decisions of the U.S. Supreme Court have recognized that the "President enjoys complete discretion in the exercise of his Commander in Chief authority and in conducting operations against hostile forces."[42] Finally, "[a]ny effort by Congress to regulate the interrogation of battlefield combatants would violate the Constitution's sole vesting of the Commander-in-Chief authority in the President."[43] In Part VI of the memo, Yoo also concludes that under the circumstances of the war against terrorism, the defenses of necessity and self-defense would both justify interrogations that might otherwise be illegal under Section 2340a.[44]

As noted in the May 2005 report by Amnesty International, the U.S. Second Periodic Report to the Committee Against Torture (required by the UN Convention Against Torture) noted that concerns generated by the August 1, 2002, memo (the John Yoo memo reviewed above) caused it to be withdrawn on June 22, 2004, two months after the photographs from Abu Ghraib become public.[45] These quotes from advocates for the Bush administration are recited here to demonstrate that there have been strong and consistently expressed statements by high officials of the administration of George W. Bush in support of the view that neither international nor American constitutional law ought to impose any enforceable constraints on presidential war-making power.

Yet that has not been the end of the matter. Another occasion for the assertion of executive authority has been the claim of inherent authority to eavesdrop on persons within the United States, without any prior authorization by warrant. The usual practice has been to secure a warrant from a special (secret) federal court that operates under the authority of the Foreign Intelligence Surveillance Act, a process that was created in response to the excesses of the Nixon administration that was required should one party to an electronic exchange (these days including e-mail) be within the United States. The administration of George W. Bush continued to assert the president's prerogative to eavesdrop without warrant. Vice President Cheney, often the point person called on to defend controversial practices of the administration, was quoted in the *New York Times*, after having expressed his respect for Congress:

> But I do believe that especially in the day and age we live in, the nature of the threats we face, the president of the United States needs to have his constitutional powers unimpaired, if you will, in terms of the conduct of national security policy.[46]

Cheney concluded that the War Powers Resolution (1973) also was "an infringement on the authority of the presidency" and said that it could be unconstitutional.[47] John Yoo also argued in favor of such warrantless eavesdropping in a memo of September 21, 2001.[48] That these views represented the consistent position of the administration of George W. Bush is also reflected in an essay that most likely was written with White House approval for an op-ed in the *New York Times*. David Rivkin and Lee A. Casey, both former Justice Department attorneys for both the Reagan and George H. W. Bush administrations, affirmed their support for warrantless searches of conversations including at least one person within the Untied States to acquire foreign intelligence information.[49] It seems clear that it is not just the constraints of international law that the George W. Bush administration opposed; any legal constraints on executive power were rejected, even in the face of strong opposition, including some opposition within the Republican Party itself.

CONCLUSION

This chapter has not been meant as a diatribe against the administration of George W. Bush. It is intended only as a description of important obstacles—those that are the consequence of current U.S. policies—against the exercise of universal criminal jurisdiction and the more effective achievement of the global rule of law. Nonetheless, there are some important contradictions in the U.S. position that should be noted.

In supporting the prosecution of the surviving leaders of National Socialist Germany, the United States asserted that there were certain universal principles of justice that could be applied to them, even if the conduct of German leaders was made legal, under German law, during the Nazi regime. These universal standards included war crimes, crimes against humanity, and the newly named crime of genocide. For officials of the administration of George W. Bush to suggest that there are no universal provisions of customary international law that ought to be applied to the United States directly contradicts the position the United States took at the end of World War II toward Hitler and his minions.

Another contradiction can be found in the fact that the United States continues to support the prosecution of serious violations of international law for other countries. This is represented by UN Security Council Resolution 1593, which, with the assent of the United States, referred the situation in Darfur, Sudan, to the ICC.[50]

The argument that the president of the United States ought to have essentially the same power over foreign and military policy that the British Crown (King George III) had at the time of the writing of the U.S. Constitution ignores the fact that popular democracy was not achieved in the United Kingdom until the passage of several electoral reform bills (the first important one in 1837). With the rise of the House of Commons following the eventual achievement of the franchise for all adult subjects of the United Kingdom, the power of the Crown was rendered entirely symbolic, and the political constraints on the governments of the day by a majority of Parliament became real. It would indeed be an ironic outcome if the president of the United States should achieve virtually unchecked power over foreign and military affairs, while the power of the British monarch, against which we, in large measure, rebelled, should become symbolic, rather than real.

The lesson we learned long ago, chiefly from James Madison, the chief architect of our Constitution, was that no political power ought to be entirely unchecked. However, the lesson to be learned from this chapter is that triadic dispute resolution is an unlikely solution when one of the parties to a dispute or conflict is so powerful that it can insist on having its own way, regardless of the intrinsic merits of the dispute. The United States most likely is not unique in this respect; rather it is only the current and most highly visible hegemon. This point is well made in the recent book by Gerry Simpson, *Great Powers and Outlaw States*, in which he notes that great powers have often claimed "the right to intervene in the affairs of other states in order to produce some proclaimed community goal."[51] In the U.S. constitutional context, Schwarz and Huq, in their book, *Unchecked and Unbalanced: Presidential Power in a Time of Terror*,[52] refute the George W. Bush administration's view that national security concerns make the "Constitution's structure of separated branches sharing powers inadequate," so that "we must place unfettered, absolute trust in the executive branch." Presumably this would be an executive branch that would rarely, if ever, be constrained by international law. The Bush administration often was unwilling to recognize its obligations under international law or to delegate to an impartial third party the right to make binding decisions that may affect the United States.

NOTES

1. Such as war crimes, crimes against humanity, and genocide.

2. Piracy by state authorization (privateers) against state enemies was abolished under international law by the Declaration of Paris in 1856; the first comprehensive, international treaty on the slave trade was agreed to in 1890.

3. "Sovereignty, Transnational Constraints and Universal Criminal Jurisdiction," in Mary L. Volcansek and John F. Stack Jr., eds., *Courts Crossing Borders: Blurring the Lines of Sovereignty* (Durham: Carolina Academic Press, 2005), chap. 9.

4. Here, hegemonic power is intended chiefly to refer to the power of the United States to insist that it be exempted from the rules of international law that apply to other nations.

5. Here I use the word *objective* only in the sense of what may be humanly possible, rather than in an absolute or ontological sense. However, I do argue that objectivity, in the sense intended here, is not likely to be founded on the pursuit of a single nation's interests, however noble its claimed objectives might be.

6. See, for example, Samuel P. Huntington, *The Clash of Civilizations and the Remaking of World Order* (New York: Touchstone Books, 1997).

7. Martin Shapiro, *Courts: A Comparative and Political Analysis* (Chicago: University of Chicago Press, 1980), 1.

8. Donald W. Jackson, "Salient Interactions: The State Trial Judge and the Legal Profession." *The Justice System Journal* 1, no. 2 (1975): 24.

9. Kenneth W. Abbott, Robert O. Keohane, Andrew Moravcsik, Anne-Marie Slaughter, and Duncan Snidal, "The Concept of Legalization," in Judith L. Goldstein, Miles Kahler, Robert O. Keohane, and Anne-Marie Slaughter, *Legalization and World Politics* (Cambridge: MIT Press, 2001), 17–20.

10. *One World: The Ethics of Globalization* (New Haven: Yale University Press), 106.

11. Richard J. Goldstone, "International Law and Justice and America's War on Terrorism," in *Social Research* 69, no. 4 (2002): 1051.

12. See the recent book by Michael Mandelbaum, *The Case for Goliath: How America Acts as the World's Government in the 21st Century* (New York: Public Affairs Books), 2005.

13. Imperialism does not fit the occasion because the nature of productive capacity and the distribution of raw materials and final products are quite unlike those of the nineteenth century. European powers exercised imperial power to control both raw materials and the productive capacities of those who lived under their rule. Except perhaps for oil, that is no longer the case. Hegemony, rather than imperialism, is a better concept.

14. See Kenneth Abbott, et al., "The Concept of Legalization," in Judith L. Goldstein, et al., *Legalization and World Politics* (Cambridge: MIT Press, 2001).

15. These quotes are from President Bush's preamble to the policy statement, September 17, 2002: *The National Security Policy of the United States of America*, 1, online at www.whitehouse.gov/nsc/nss.html (visited May 31, 2007).

16. Ibid. at 15.

17. *Los Angeles Times*, "The UN Must Change or the U.S. Must Quit," January 26, 2004, online at http://www.frontpagemag.com/Articles/Printable.asp?ID=11910 (visited May 31, 2007).

18. William Kristol and Robert Kagan, "Toward a Neo-Reaganite Foreign Policy," *Foreign Affairs* 75, no. 11 (1996), online at http://www.carnegieendowment.org/publications/index.cfm?fa=view&id=276 (visited May 31, 2007).

19. George Packer, *The Assassins' Gate: America in Iraq* (New York: Farrar, Straus and Giroux, 2005), 33.

20. Ibid. at 35.

21. Kristol and Kagan, see note 18.

22. New York: Random House, 2003.

23. Ibid. at 279.

24. The Act of Chapultepec (March 6, 1945) declared that in the event of an act of aggression against the sovereignty or political independence of any American state, the other American signatories would consult and determine the measures that might be taken. Under the UN Charter, such regional arrangements apply only to measures of self-defense, and only in the failure of the Security Council to act. Of course, these are pious aspirations, not often matched by actual practice, but so are the aspirations of Frum and Perle.

25. The Neutrality Act of 1935 was designed to keep the United States out of a European war. The exchanges between the United Kingdom and the United States of destroyers (to the United Kingdom) for bases (for the United States) occurred in

September 1940. The Lend-Lease Act of 1941 was enacted on March 11, almost nine months before the attack on Pearl Harbor.

26. Online at http://www.internet-esq.com/ussaugusta/atlantic1.htm (visited May 31, 2007).

27. Online at http://www.trumanlibrary.org/whistlestop/study_collections/un/large (click on Address of Secretary of State Stettinius of April 25, 1945) (visited May 31, 2007).

28. Additional information regarding these developments regarding the International Criminal Court online at http://iccnow.org/ (visited May 31, 2007).

29. For an assessment that the United States deserves more credit, see John F. Murphy, *The United States and the Rule of Law in International Affairs* (Cambridge: Cambridge University Press, 2004), 355.

30. George Soros, *The Bubble of American Democracy: Correcting the Misuse of American Powers* (New York: Public Affairs Books), 10.

31. Ibid. at 116.

32. Washington, D.C.: Brookings Institution Press, 2003.

33. Formerly (2001–2003) the deputy assistant attorney general in the Office of Legal Counsel of the Department of Justice.

34. *The Powers of War and Peace: The Constitution and Foreign Affairs After 9/11* (Chicago: University of Chicago Press, 2005), 293.

35. Louis Fisher, *Presidential War Powers*, rev. ed. (Lawrence: University Press of Kansas, 2004), 15. See also Louis Fisher, "Unchecked Presidential Wars." *University of Pennsylvania Law Review* 14 (2000): 1658.

36. "Memorandum Opinion for the Deputy Counsel to the President," September 25, 2001, online at http://www.usdoj.gov/olc/warpowers925.htm, 16 (visited May 31, 2007).

37. "Application of Treaties and Laws to al Qaeda and Taliban Detainees" (January 9, 2002, John Yoo and Robert J. Delahunty to William J. Haynes II, general counsel, Department of Defense), online at http://fl1.findlaw.com/news.findlaw.com/hdocs/docs/doj/bybee12202mem.pdf (visited May 31, 2007).

38. Section 2340 defines the act of torture as an "act committed by a person acting under the color of law specifically intended to inflict severe pain or mental pain or suffering (other than pain or suffering incidental to lawful sanctions) of another person within his custody or physical control."

39. Section 2340a provides that "to convict a defendant of torture, the prosecution must establish that: (1) the torture occurred within the United States; (2) the defendant acted under color of law; (3) the victim was within the defendant's custody or physical control; (4) the defendant specifically intended to cause severe physical or mental pain or suffering; and (5) the act inflicted severe physical or mental pain or suffering."

40. The United States Senate ratified the Convention Against Torture on October 21, 1994.

41. "Memorandum for Alberto Gonzalez, Counsel to the President," August 1, 2002, page 1, online at http://washingtonpost.com/wp-srv/politics/documents/cheney/torture_memo_aug2002.pdf (visited July 27, 2009).

42. Ibid. at 31, 33.

43. Ibid. at 39.

44. Ibid.

45. Amnesty International, "United States of America: Guantánamo and Beyond: The Continuing Pursuit of Unchecked Power." May 13, 2005 (AI Index: AMR 51-063/2005). Consideration of issues involving Guantánamo can be found online at http: www.amnestyusa.org (click on issues).

46. *New York Times,* "Cheney Defends Eavesdropping without Warrants," page A22, December 21, 2005.

47. Ibid., column 1.

48. Ibid., column 2.

49. *New York Times,* "Unwarranted Complaints," December 27, 2005, A23.

50. *Insight on the International Criminal Court,* "ICC Prosecutor Appeals to UN Security Council for International Cooperation on Darfur." Issue 5, July 2005, 1.

51. Gerry Simpson, *Great Powers and Outlaw States: Unequal Sovereigns in the International Legal Order* (Cambridge: Cambridge University Press, 2004), 3.

52. A. O. Schwarz Jr. and Aziz Z. Huq (New York: The New Press, 2007), 200.

CHAPTER SIX

The Promotion of
International Criminal Law

*Evaluating the International Criminal Court
and the Apprehension of Indictees*

LILIAN A. BARRIA AND STEVEN D. ROPER

Although much has been written about the formation of the International Criminal Court (ICC),[1] the court's relationship with the United States,[2] and the Rome Statute,[3] less attention has been focused on issues of state cooperation and the apprehension of indictees. In order to understand the legal basis and the actual power of the ICC to secure the arrest of indictees, this chapter considers some of the legal and the political issues associated with apprehension in international criminal cases. We examine some of the issues related to the arrest of indictees in the ad hoc tribunals to draw general lessons regarding when international criminal tribunals are more effective in arresting suspects. In addition, we examine the Rome Statute and the ICC's Rules of Procedure and Evidence to identify the different types of referrals, the role and the powers of the Office of the Prosecutor (OTP), and the different categories of crime. From these, we develop a classification of the issues with the greatest influence on the ability of the ICC to arrest indictees, and we apply this inventory to a study of the four ongoing African cases at the ICC exploring the political environment in which these legal principles operate. We conclude by comparing the four cases to determine patterns of state cooperation and ICC behavior.

DRAWING LESSONS FROM THE AD HOC TRIBUNALS

The history and the development of the ICC and the ad hoc tribunals are intertwined. Between 1994 and 1998, the historical lessons and practical issues associated with the International Criminal Tribunal for the Former Yugoslavia (ICTY) and the International Criminal Tribunal for Rwanda (ICTR) provided a backdrop for the various discussions about the creation of the ICC. During the diplomatic conference in Rome in 1998, one of the key concerns was the relationship of the ICC to states and the obligations that states would have to the court vis-à-vis their own citizens and citizens of other states.[4] For many, one of the lessons learned from the experiences of the ICTY and the ICTR was that the noncompliance of states, particularly in the failure to surrender indictees, greatly undermines the effectiveness of tribunals. Indeed, there were two distinct periods involving the ability of the ad hoc tribunals to apprehend suspects.[5] During the first period, from the mid- to late 1990s, both tribunals, especially the ICTY, were ineffective in apprehending suspects.[6] Most of those who were tried at the ICTY prior to 2000 were lower-rank indictees who were politically easier for states to surrender. In the second period, since the early 2000s, the tribunals have been much more successful in apprehending suspects. There are two reasons for this change. First, the use of military assets gave the tribunal coercive power to detain suspects. In Bosnia and Herzegovina (BiH), those who did not voluntarily surrender were subject to capture by the North Atlantic Treaty Organization-led Stabilization Force (SFOR). One of the lessons for the ICC from these early years of the ICTY is that the assistance from a military force with quasi-police power can greatly assist in the apprehension of suspects.

The success in arresting suspects in BiH compares favorably against the experience in apprehending suspects in Croatia and Serbia. In the case of these countries, state cooperation was more fundamental because of a lack of a military presence. For years, the ICTY was hampered in its efforts to obtain suspects from these two states. During the last few years, both states, however, have cooperated much more with the ICTY, leading to the important arrest of former Croatian general Ante Gotovina in December 2005. The reason for this change has been attributed to the insistence of European Union (EU) officials that accession talks with both states would move forward only after fugitives like Ratko Mladić and Radovan Karadžić were arrested. By July 2006, Serbian officials announced an "action plan" designed to actively assist in the arrest of Mladić. During the last two years, EU pressure and the promise of eventual membership have been instrumental in assisting the ICTY in the arrest and the surrender of high-ranking indictees.[7] However, Gallarotti and Preis note that arresting so-called "big fish" in the mid- to late 1990s would have undermined the peace process in the former Yugoslavia, as well as intensified hostility among the warring factions. They argue that "[i]ndicting but not arresting Karadžić promoted the peace accord and served to diffuse a potential powder keg in the region. . . . [A]rrests of indicted criminals in general have become more numerous as the peace further consolidated."[8] Their observation highlights the need to consider the status of the indictee, as well as the status of the conflict in any international criminal prosecution.

In the case of Rwanda, the initial effectiveness of the tribunal was also greatly undermined by the lack of cooperation from other states. Part of the reluctance to transfer suspects was due to the balance of power struggle that has engulfed central Africa since the mid-1990s.[9] The location of suspects in diverse states hindered the process of surrender, because arresting suspects in third-party states required coordinated cooperation from multiple states that had very different agendas and even hostility toward each other. The blurring of internal (civil) and interstate conflict made arrest and prosecution much more problematic.[10] However, as was the case with the ICTY, the early 2000s marked a new phase of state cooperation with the ICTR. By 2006, twenty-one countries had transferred indictees to the tribunal. Significantly, in 2002, the Democratic Republic of the Congo (DRC), a haven for Hutu refugees, surrendered its first two suspects. Approximately 89 percent of those indicted by the tribunal have been arrested. One of the lessons from the experience of the ICTY and the ICTR is that arresting indictees can be a lengthy, time-consuming process even with the obligation of state cooperation. As Goldstone and Bass argue, "[s]uch heel-dragging and outright obstruction [as in the case of the ad hoc tribunals] must not be allowed to become a feature of the ICC's proceedings. . . . One should not assume that an ICC will have it any easier."[11] Although certain elements of the Rome Statute were designed to ameliorate these types of problems, others create significant loopholes that ultimately impact the surrender of indictees.[12]

THE INFLUENCE OF THE ROME STATUTE ON STATE COOPERATION AND THE ARRESTING OF SUSPECTS

The Obligation of Non-Party and State Party Actors

During the early negotiations of the Rome Statute, representatives rejected the concept of ICC universal jurisdiction in which nonparty states had an absolute obligation to cooperate.[13] Therefore, the Rome Statute creates a treaty-based regime binding only on those states that formally join the ICC.[14] The court has jurisdiction only over crimes committed on the territory of a state party, or if the accused is a national of a state party (otherwise, the state must consent to the ICC's jurisdiction). The lone exception is when a case is referred to the ICC by the UN Security Council, which will be discussed in the next section. We make this point regarding jurisdiction to emphasize that nationals of an ICC state party, under most circumstances, have an incentive to flee to nonparty states. Because many states have a criminal code or even a constitutional prohibition against extradition, arresting nationals could prove extremely difficult.[15] Even in the case of a state party, there is a disagreement about the absolute requirement to arrest and to surrender a suspect. Oosterveld, Perry, and McManus argue that the statute is clear with regard to the obligation of state parties to arrest indictees.[16] However, Sarooshi[17] notes that the request for arrest and transfer is secondary to the legal procedures of the state.[18] Article 89 states that parties shall cooperate in the arrest and surrender of individuals "under their national law."

Therefore, for state parties, the ability to arrest and transfer suspects to the ICC requires either the creation of a separate legal procedure or the amendment of existing extradition laws. The situation becomes even more complex in situations of competing requests for the surrender of a suspect (Article 90) and provisional arrest (Article 92), which comprise Part 9 of the statute. As Sadat and Carden argue, "Part 9 is the least 'supranational' section of the Treaty. . . . [T]he articles that follow are so riddled with exceptions and qualifications that it is difficult to think of this as anything but an exhortation."[19] Assuming that a state party does not surrender a suspect and is found to be in noncompliance with its obligations under Article 89, there are no specific penalties attached to this behavior. Under Article 87, the ICC may refer the failure to comply with the Assembly of States Parties.[20] However, the Rules of Procedure of the Assembly does not prescribe any penalty for noncompliance (Rule 82). Gallarotti and Preis conclude that the "penalties for noncompliance are vague and unthreatening. . . . [The statute] lacks the level of specificity necessary to insure compliance with the spirit of the ICC's mandates."[21]

The Nature of the Referral and the Role of the Prosecutor

There are three procedures by which a case can be referred to the ICC. First, a case can be initiated by a request of a state party to the OTP. Second, a UN Security Council resolution under Chapter VII authority can refer a case to the OTP. Third, the chief prosecutor may initiate investigations *proprio motu* (of his own accord) and submit a request to authorize an investigation to the ICC Pre-Trial Chamber, which approves the request. In the first case, all state parties have a right to refer a situation to the OTP. The OTP then has the responsibility to investigate to determine if individuals should be charged with the crimes in which the ICC has jurisdiction. However, the statute is silent regarding whether a state party may request the return of a case it had earlier referred.[22]

Although the use of a UN Security Council resolution as a basis of referral was included early in the statute draft, the fact that three of the permanent members of the Security Council have not become parties to the ICC led to the belief that a Security Council referral would be difficult to accomplish.[23] However, if the Security Council did make a referral, it is unclear how UN Chapter VII authority would interface with the specific sections of the statute pertaining to state cooperation. Even more complex would be a situation in which the council referral was of a nonparty state, in which case only Chapter VII provisions regarding state cooperation would apply, as there would be no corresponding statute language dealing with the nonparty state.

Most of the discussion in Rome concerning the power of referral dealt with the ability of the prosecutor to initiate an investigation. Some states, such as the United States, regarded an independent prosecutor with *proprio motu* powers as creating a "global prosecutor" with no accountability and highly susceptible to political influence.[24] However, this concern fails to consider that the *proprio motu* powers fall under the judicial control of the Pre-Trial Chamber, which is responsible for authorizing a full investigation. Chief prosecutor Luis Moreno Ocampo has indicated that his preference is to defer to state judiciaries whenever possible.[25] The ICC prosecutor is dependent on state cooperation for investigations and the gathering of evidence, and there are numerous loopholes that allow the state to assert a right not to cooperate. For example, Article 93(4) provides the state an absolute right to refuse assistance to the OTP in cases of national security. For this reason, Danner argues that principled decision making is paramount, as is "impartiality [which] is critical in the context of the ICC because its absence constitutes the basis for the charge most frequently leveled at the Court: that it will become a source of 'politicized' prosecutions."[26]

One of the issues of discretion that confronts the prosecutor concerns the timing of an investigation and the issuing of arrest warrants. Should a prosecutor investigate a case and indict suspects during or after a conflict? From one perspective, indictments can serve notice to warring factions that the international community is engaged and can become part of the process of conflict resolution. On the other hand, "[o]ngoing disputes render investigation and enforcement difficult, and they make the calculation of the 'interests of justice' very difficult to assess. . . . Intervening in an ongoing conflict makes the political ramifications of any investigation more acute."[27]

The Definition of Crimes

A final issue that may influence the ability of the ICC to arrest suspects and garner state support concerns the nature of the charges against indictees. The ICC has jurisdiction over four broad categories of crime: genocide, crimes against humanity, war crimes, and the crime of aggression.[28] The crime of genocide was the least problematic at the Rome conference because it has been authoritatively defined in the Genocide Convention of 1948. In terms of war crimes, numerous instruments have elaborated the offenses in this category, but the Rome Statute is much more detailed in terms of the types of crimes, as well as the international and the internal character of the crimes. Ultimately, crimes against humanity proved to be one of the most difficult categories because of the problem of "distinguishing the crime from war crimes and from crimes under domestic law . . . [and] determining which acts are punishable under international law as a matter of individual criminal responsibility, as opposed to State responsibility."[29]

The three categories of crimes defined cover crimes that are inhumane and are violations of fundamental human rights; however, state parties may opt out of the jurisdiction of the ICC concerning war crimes. Article 124 allows a state up to seven years after it has become a party to the ICC not to accept the court's jurisdiction. In addition, the Rome Statute allows for the defense of superior orders and the defense of property only in cases concerning war crimes. For these reasons, Schabas concludes that, "[i]t might be argued that war crimes are less important than both genocide and crimes against humanity."[30] Whether this legal hierarchy is recognized by suspects is an open question; however, especially in regard to the charge of genocide, suspects and states might be much less willing to cooperate because of the gravity of the offense and the accompanying penalty.

ASSESSING THE EFFECTIVENESS OF THE ICC TO ARREST

Based on the lessons of the ad hoc tribunals and the institutional features and the jurisdiction of the ICC, we have developed a classification of the issues that we consider to have the greatest influence on the ability of the ICC to apprehend indictees. We examine the specific characteristics of the issue and assess whether it "enhances," "limits," or constitutes a "formal" form of influence by which the ICC can seek the apprehension of suspects. By formal influence, we mean that the characteristic denotes a formal authority (for example, Security Council Chapter VII power) that provides the ICC with legal power, but also indicates a reluctance of the state to cooperate (either because of a denial of the situation or a lack of resources). In this case, the ICC's formal authority is undermined by the lack of state cooperation. This classification scheme is not exhaustive, but it provides a set of the most important issues that influence ICC apprehension effectiveness. As a legal institution without the coercive powers of the state or certain intergovernmental organizations, the ICC is vulnerable to cooperation and coordination problems at the state and the international level.

The State as an Actor

Many of the issues that we consider important to examine in order to understand the effectiveness of the ICC involve the state because in almost all cases, it will be the state that will have to arrest and surrender suspects to the ICC. One of the first issues that we considered in explaining the effectiveness of the ICC concerns the nature of the conflict. Whether a conflict is internal or interstate influences a large number of issues, including the effectiveness of international institutions. Although the Rome Statute covers both forms of conflict, we believe that international conflict renders the successful apprehension of suspects more problematic. As we have seen in the wars in the former Yugoslavia, the ability to flee to another state in which extradition might not be possible makes apprehension more difficult.

As Gallarotti and Preis note, apprehending suspects during an ongoing conflict can exacerbate the conflict and render state cooperation all but impossible.[30] Therefore, we believe that the ICC will be more successful in gaining the surrender of suspects after hostilities have ended. The only exception would be cases in which the end of the conflict entailed the use of an amnesty. While the Rome Statute is silent on the use of amnesties, Article 27 eliminates the immunity *ratione personae*[31] and *ratione materiae*[32] of public officials, and the ICC would certainly not consider an amnesty law an impediment to prosecution. However, the use of amnesties is a continuous issue, which many state actors regard as a necessary evil.

The ICC will be most effective in securing the apprehension of suspects in cases involving state parties. Indeed, there are only two situations in which nonparty states cooperate with the ICC (on a voluntary basis and because of a Security Council resolution). Therefore, we anticipate that the ICC's success will be much more limited in situations involving nonparty states. In addition, we believe that the type of suspect has an impact on the apprehension ability of the ICC. While Rome Statute Article 27 waives national law immunities of state officials, Akande argues, "[b]ecause the Court does not have the independent powers of arrest and must rely on states to arrest and surrender wanted persons, the immunities of state officials in national jurisdictions become important."[33] Finally, domestic support for the ICC, from the government as well as civil society, clearly enhances the influence of the court to apprehend suspects. However, governments and civil society are not monolithic entities, but are composed of various individuals and institutions with their own interests. In many situations, we anticipate that *parts* of the government and certain *segments* of civil society will support the ICC while others may not. Thus, evaluating government and civil society support for the ICC requires sensitivity to competing claims and agendas.

The ICC as an Actor

In terms of the ICC, we regard two issues as central to the effectiveness of the court in obtaining the apprehension of suspects. First, we believe that the type of referral is an important *ex ante* characteristic that provides some basis for anticipating the future behavior of the state. In cases in which the state has referred the situation to the court, we expect greater state cooperation on a number of issues, including the surrender of suspects. While a referral by a UN Security Council resolution with Chapter VII authority reflecting a consensus of the permanent members of the Security Council would appear to provide more leverage to the ICC, the history of the ICTY and the ICTR demonstrates that this formal power still requires the genuine cooperation of the state. Finally, we consider a referral based on the prosecutor's *propio motu* power as providing the most limited amount of influence in obtaining suspects. If the national judiciary of the state is unwilling or unable to prosecute the situation, then it is doubtful that the ICC can rely on state resources for the arrest and the surrender of suspects.

As previously indicated, the creation of an opt-out clause for war crimes, as well as the use of court-sanctioned defenses, makes this category of crimes seemingly less significant compared to genocide and crimes against humanity. This being the case, we believe that suspects charged with war crimes will either be easier to arrest or more prone to voluntarily surrender because of the perception that these are lesser charges. In particular, charges based on genocide are viewed as more serious with a concomitant need for greater punishment. As Prunier discusses in relationship to Darfur, "whether the 'big-G word' [genocide] is used or not appears to make a considerable difference in terms of international reaction. . . . [W]e seem to think that the killing of 250,000 people in a genocide is more serious, a greater tragedy, and more deserving of our attention than the killing of 250,000 people in nongenocidal massacres."[34]

Third Parties as Actors

No discussion of the effectiveness of apprehending suspects would be complete without considering the role of third parties. As previously discussed in the case of the ICTY, third-party intervention and pressure has been fundamental to the success of the tribunal in obtaining the arrest and the surrender of indictees. However, the forms that this pressure takes have a differential impact. Condemnations by the international community, discussions at the Security Council, and diplomatic efforts have had a limited influence on the behavior of states to secure the surrender of suspects. Instead, we believe that military/peacekeeping pressure and especially economic pressure are the most successful tools available to third parties to encourage state cooperation.

For domestic judiciaries, the capture of suspects is the role of law enforcement agencies. Therefore, one might suppose that military/peacekeeping pressure would be the most effective tool for the surrender of suspects. However, we regard this form of pressure as having a formal influence because in most cases, sovereign states are extremely reluctant to allow foreign forces on their soil, and if they allow these forces, the formal mandate is often very restrictive. In the case of SFOR in Bosnia, the mandate was interpreted in a broad fashion to allow for the assistance with the capture of suspects. In Sudan, the African Union observer mission (AMIS) began with a very limited mandate that has been expanded, but has never included provisions that interfere with the primacy of the state.

Economic sanctions have long been used to promote state cooperation in regard to human rights while many find that the allocation of foreign assistance has also been used to influence human rights policy.[35] We believe that significant economic pressure may be one of the most effective tools available to third parties in order to support the activity of the ICC. In the case of the ICTY, the EU was very successful in assisting the tribunal because of the perceived economic benefits that states, such as Croatia, would gain with membership. In order to assess our classification scheme, we briefly examine the four situations currently at the ICC to determine those issues and characteristics that have been most likely to influence the effectiveness of the ICC in the apprehension of suspects.

THE CREATION OF INTERNATIONAL JUSTICE— THE CASES CURRENTLY BEFORE THE ICC

Central African Republic (CAR)

The conflict that engulfed the CAR in 2002 and which is the main focus of investigation of the ICC involved current President François Bozizé and former President Ange-Félix Patassé. Patassé became President of the CAR in 1993 in the first democratic election since independence in 1960. Most of his supporters lived in the northwestern savanna, whereas all previous presidents were either from the forest or Ubangi river regions in the south. Patassé began to replace southern government and military officials with northerners, which antagonized the Yakoma ethnic group (a southern ethnic majority) who had benefited from the patronage of former President André Kolingba. Soldiers who had been loyal to Kolingba were ferociously opposed to their loss of privilege, and the tense relations between the armed forces and the government were exacerbated by the irregular payment of salaries, which culminated in a series of coup attempts in the mid 1990s as parts of the armed forces sought to overthrow the government. Most of the military under army chief of staff François Bozizé supported Patassé and assisted him in suppressing these coup attempts; however, tensions between northerners and southerners greatly increased, polarizing society to a greater extent than before.

In May 2001, soldiers led by Kolingba attempted to overthrow Patassé. The government sought military assistance from the Congolese Liberation Movement (MLC), which had begun a rebellion in the DRC in late 1998 and controlled territory adjacent to the CAR. After this coup attempt failed, Patassé questioned Bozizé's loyalty and in October 2001, Bozizé was dismissed from his military position. By 2002, Bozizé led a coup attempt with the assistance of troops from Chad to overthrow the government. To fight Bozizé, Patassé again requested the assistance of the MLC to defeat the rebels.

Hundreds of MLC soldiers looted parts of the capital, Bangui, and as MLC and CAR government forces pursued Bozizé's forces, Amnesty International claims that war crimes and crimes against humanity, including crimes of sexual violence, were committed during the conflict. Human rights activists claim that about four hundred people were victims of atrocities.[36] The use of rape was partly intended to punish women for alleged assistance to the Bozizé-led combatants. Survivors and witnesses said they recognized members of the MLC by the fact that they did not speak Sango (a national language spoken by virtually all Central Africans), but instead spoke Lingala, which is the mostly widely spoken language in the DRC. Combatants loyal to General Bozizé, including their allies from Chad, are reported to have carried out rapes in the areas they occupied. In March 2003, President Patassé left the country for an international meeting, and Bozizé was able to enter Bangui and take control of the military and the government.

In July 2003, prosecutor Moreno Ocampo announced that he had already received 499 communications from various sources alleging human rights violations in the CAR related to the conflict. In January 2005, he revealed that the CAR government had referred the situation to the ICC (the referral was received in December 2004). While there have not been any indictments issued by the ICC, the CAR Supreme Court in February 2006 referred former President Patassé, as well as former MLC leader Bemba, to the ICC on charges of rape and murder. Also included in the referral are a French policeman and two aides of Patassé. Despite an Interpol red notice, none of the five has been arrested (for example, Patassé currently resides in Togo). The CAR Ministry of Justice stated that the "only way to prevent total impunity is to call for international help. The International Criminal Court should be the best route to follow."[37]

Democratic Republic of Congo

War raged in the DRC between 1998 and 2002 with over fifty thousand troops from seven different African states fighting along with the DRC army and numerous rebel factions and tribal militias. Angola, Zimbabwe, Namibia, and Chad supported the government of President Laurent Kabila. Uganda backed the Congolese Liberation Movement (MLC) rebel group, while Rwanda supported the Rally for Democracy-Goma (RCD-Goma) and the Union of Congolese Patriots (UPC) rebel groups. Burundi had deployed troops to the DRC to fight Hutu rebels.[38] During the conflict, clashes in the northeastern Ituri region between the minority Hema and the majority Lendu tribal militias killed more than fifty thousand people and displaced five hundred thousand. All the groups fighting in the Ituri region are accused of recruiting child soldiers to form the bulk of their troops. More than half the estimated fifteen thousand Hema fighters were younger than eighteen. Thomas Lubanga, the leader of the UPC (a Hema rebel group), emerged as one of the most notorious commanders in the war. Soldiers under his command are accused of murder, torture, rape, and the mutilation of their victims. Since the end of the war, some ten thousand people have been displaced by the continuous fighting, many fleeing to neighboring Uganda.

After the war ended in 2002, a transitional government was put in place that included President Joseph Kabila and four vice presidents, two of whom came from the ranks of the former rebels (Jean-Pierre Bemba, head of the MLC, and Azarias Ruberwa, leader of RCD-Goma). In September 2003, the UN officially took over peacekeeping operations in the province of Ituri from a French-led force that had been stationed there since June 2003. The UN Observer Mission for Congo (MONUC) was authorized under Chapter VII authority to locate, disarm, and repatriate thousands of Rwandan Hutus who fled to the DRC after the 1994 genocide in Rwanda.[39] Although there were efforts to disarm the DRC militias, many from the UPC retained their weapons and continued to fight. A UN investigation of the role of the foreign forces also revealed the systematic plunder by all parties of Congolese natural resources, particularly diamonds. Uganda allegedly was training local militias in order to maintain control of Ituri's resources and Rwanda was placing proxies in key positions (such as quasi-governmental firms with bosses from Kigali replacing Congolese).[40]

The OTP initially investigated the situation in the DRC, focusing on crimes committed in the Ituri region. In September 2003, the prosecutor informed the Assembly of States Parties that he was ready to request authorization from the Pre-Trial Chamber to use his own *proprio motu* powers to start an investigation, but that a referral and active support from the DRC would assist his work. In a letter in November 2003, the DRC government welcomed the involvement of the ICC, and by March 2004, the DRC referred the situation to the court (preempting an official *proprio motu* referral). In June 2004, the prosecutor announced the commencement of an investigation following a preliminary examination of the crimes committed in the country since July 2002.

In February 2005, nine Bangladeshi UN peacekeepers were killed, which increased the efforts of the DRC government to arrest militia leaders. In March 2005, Floribert Ndjabu of the Lendu Nationalist and Integrationist Front was arrested, as was Lubanga of the UPC. In February 2006, a sealed arrest warrant for Lubanga was issued at the ICC, which became public in March (the same day that Lubanga was handed over to the ICC by the DRC government). He was charged with three counts of war crimes, including the enlistment and conscription of children under the age of fifteen who participated actively in hostilities. To date, he is the only suspect at the ICC. The challenge for the DRC and the ICC is to arrest the other militia and rebel group leaders who committed crimes during the conflict. The UN has indicated that there were nine parties to the war who used child soldiers or committed war crimes against children.

Sudan

In Darfur (the western region of Sudan), an estimated two hundred thousand individuals have been killed, with millions displaced and approximately two hundred thousand refugees settled along Chad's border with Sudan, since 2003. The violence in Darfur erupted at a time in which the long-enduring conflict between the northern government in Khartoum and the rebel movements in the south headed by the Sudan People's Liberation Movement were finally being resolved. Prunier explains that the Darfuri rebels resented the peace deal between the north and the south because the tribes in Darfur "would most likely be completely excluded from the new power- and wealth-sharing arrangements. After years of marginalization, resentment, frustration, and increasing social troubles, the Darfuri revolted in their turn."[41]

Abdelmoula argues that the ruling National Islamic Front "equates Islam with Arabism. Among the practical implications of this attitude is that groups of non-Arab descent are treated as an inferior category of persons."[42] The insurgents in Darfur are black Muslims, whereas the ruling elite in Khartoum are Arab Muslims, and when the Darfuri insurgency began, the government was unable to send in the military to quell the uprising because many in the armed forces were from Darfur. Therefore, the government relied upon Darfuri Arab militia (known as the *janjaweed*) to carry out military operations on behalf of the government.[43] Udombana argues that the *janjaweed* have been incorporated into the Sudanese military structure.[44] While the Sudanese government has denounced the militia in Darfur, nongovernmental organizations have documented many instances in which the *janjaweed* acted with the assistance and supervision of the Sudanese military.[45]

The UN Commission of Inquiry, established in 2004 to investigate alleged human rights violations in Darfur, issued a report in January 2005 which found that government forces had been involved in various atrocities that it labeled crimes against humanity and war crimes, but not genocide.[46] The report also contained a sealed file of fifty-one individuals it recommended for prosecution. The speculation is that this list includes important policy makers in the government, military, intelligence services, and Parliament. Considering that the "Sudanese government is extremely hierarchical in many respects, and functions through a tight network of ruling insiders," it is difficult to imagine that events in Darfur are not being directed by officials in Khartoum.[47] While the ICC OTP was able to see the commission's file, prosecutor Moreno Ocampo has stated that he "does not consider this list of names to be binding; rather they represent the conclusions of the Commissions."[48]

In March 2005, UN Security Council Resolution 1593 referred the situation to the ICC. However, because this referral was made through a Security Council resolution rather than a self-referral of a state party, Sudan, which is not a state party to the ICC, has resisted repeated calls to cooperate with the court.[49] The ICC had a preliminary meeting with officials in Sudan in February 2006, but has not been able to conduct investigations in the capital or the Darfuri region.[50] Chief prosecutor Moreno Ocampo, in a report to the Security Council, indicated that "[g]iven the scale of the alleged crimes in Darfur, and the complexities associated with the identification of those bearing greatest responsibility for the crimes, my Office currently anticipates the investigation and prosecution of a sequence of cases, rather than a single case."[51]

Rather than cooperate with the court, the Sudanese government has repeatedly stymied efforts at ending impunity for officials. For example, the government announced the day after the ICC opened investigations in 2005 that it established a Special National Criminal Court for Darfur, which began hearing cases immediately. However, none of the indictees is a high-ranking official, nor has any been indicted or charged with war crimes or crimes against humanity.[20] Indeed, in August 2005, President Omar al-Bashir signed a law that provided a general immunity to any member of the armed forces for crimes committed. Even economic sanctions imposed as part of UN Security Council Resolution 1591 in March 2005 have not created conditions for more cooperation. Indeed, following the ICC's warrants of arrest issued in April 2007 for Ali Muhammad Ali Abd-Al-Rahman (a principal leader of the *janjaweed* militia) and Ahmad Muhammad Harun (Sudan's secretary of state for humanitarian affairs and a former minister in charge of Darfur), the government in Khartoum was quick to denounce the indictments, and many in the human rights community have expressed their frustration over the perceived inactivity of the ICC. However, because this referral was made by the UN Security Council, rather than a state party self-referral, the Darfur case was going to be more difficult than other cases before the ICC.

Uganda

The ongoing conflict in Uganda involves the government of President Yoweri Museveni and the Ugandan armed forces (known as the Uganda People's Defense Force or UPDF) pitted against the Lord's Resistance Army (LRA). The conflict has been raging for twenty years, and one of the reasons it has been difficult for the government to negotiate with the LRA is because the insurgents do not have a clear political, economic, or territorial agenda. The conflict has centered in the northern area of Acholiland (the Acholi are the dominant tribal group in the region). However, it has spilled into southern Sudan and the Sudanese government has been accused of supporting the LRA.

Doom and Vlassenroot argue that two historical trends assist in understanding the conflict in northern Uganda: first has been the widening economic and political gap between the north and the south, and second, the militarization of politics.[52] As part of its colonial policy, Britain introduced industry and cash crop production in the south, while the north became the source of cheap labor for southern industry. While people from the south held civil service positions, Acholi from the north were recruited into the armed forces. Museveni's rise to power in 1986 led to a change in the composition of the armed forces from being dominated by the Acholi to being primarily staffed and controlled by southerners. Many Acholi feared that the UPDF would take revenge for the acts committed by the Acholi-dominated army under the previous government of Milton Obote. Indeed, the UPDF engaged in a policy of violent reprisals including executions, torture, rape, and looting.

When Joseph Kony, the leader of the LRA, began his fight in 1986, he espoused the idea that only so-called "purified" Acholi like himself would be able to defeat the Museveni forces. Thus, the LRA targeted both the UPDF as well as Acholi civilians in order to eliminate those loyal to the government and create a new Acholi community based on Kony's vision. Generally, LRA operations were not very successful, and while they were almost defeated, the government inexplicably changed strategies and decided to engage in peace negotiations by 1994. However, the talks soon collapsed as Kony accused of disloyalty any Acholi who supported negotiations with the government. These events led Kony to increase his attacks on the Acholi, who became the victims of a number of LRA massacres starting in 1995.

In many cases, the victims were hacked or clubbed to death. The LRA also cut ears and lips to warn others of the consequences of being suspected as a government informant. Rape became commonplace, and the LRA increasingly engaged in the abduction of Acholi children who were seen as the basis for purifying Acholi society through Kony's indoctrination.[53] Humanitarian organizations estimate that more than twenty thousand children have been abducted by the LRA since 1986. The Acholi have been forced to leave their homes and move into protected villages, which are often located next to military bases. Approximately fifty thousand are internally displaced, while some fifteen thousand have fled the area, resulting in economic collapse.

In December 2003, President Museveni decided to refer the situation to the ICC and allow an investigation in northern Uganda. By October 2005, prosecutor Moreno Ocampo announced the unsealing of arrest warrants for five LRA members. Kony was charged with thirty-three counts, including twelve counts of crimes against humanity and twenty-one counts of war crimes. The other four indictees were charged with various counts for crimes against humanity and war crimes. Moreno Ocampo stated, "[t]he next step is arrest. . . . Reports indicate that the fugitives are moving between [sic] three countries: Uganda, DRC and the Sudan. These countries must work together, with the support of the international community, to carry out the arrests."[54]

The effort by the ICC to hold the LRA accountable has been hampered recently by the government, which has entered into peace negotiations with the LRA. President Museveni has offered the rebels a full and guaranteed amnesty as long as they renounce violence. The talks are being brokered by the government of southern Sudan. Acholi community leaders have supported the negotiations in order to end the violence and bring stability to the region. They have questioned the efforts of the ICC to provide justice, preferring local solutions to the conflict. However, their past attempts to broker talks have been unsuccessful due to the distrust between the Acholi elders, the LRA, and the government. Moreover, there is a widespread perception that elements in the government have blocked any effort toward a successful peace agreement in the pursuit of profiteering.

CONCLUSION: COMPARING THE EFFECTIVENESS OF THE ICC

As the ICC continues to issue indictments and seek the arrest of individuals suspected of human rights violations, it will encounter the constraints imposed by the need for state cooperation and international community support. What we have seen in the four cases so far is that the ICC faces a number of challenges. In the case of the CAR, there appears to be strong domestic support within the government and the population to cooperate with the ICC once indictments are issued. However, at this time, the location of the possible indictees is the greatest impediment to arrest. The individuals most likely to be indicted by the court are not in the CAR, and therefore third-party state cooperation will be necessary. As previously indicated, potential suspects have an incentive to flee to ICC nonparty states to avoid surrender.

The court has had some success in the DRC due to the cooperation of the government, as well as external pressure in the form of UN peacekeeping operations. However, as further indictments are possibly issued, it remains to be seen whether the DRC will continue to cooperate. In Uganda, the government is currently seeking to negotiate a peace agreement with the LRA. As Kaul states, if the Ugandan government were not able to surrender these indictees, then the "credibility of the Court would suffer if an arrest warrant issued by the judges of the Pre-Trial Chamber at the request of the prosecutor . . . remained ineffective over a long period because the states parties were slow, or failed, to execute it."[55] Although the government has not requested that the ICC indictments be withdrawn, the chances for apprehension have decreased with the offer of an amnesty to the LRA.

The issues that we have identified based on the experience of the ad hoc tribunals, as well as the ICC's institutional design, points to Sudan as the most challenging case for the ICC. At the state level, the characteristics of the conflict, as well as the types of suspects that could be indicted, have led to continual resistance by Khartoum. It is true that the international community has been much more vocal in its condemnation of the human rights abuses in Darfur, but more pressure will have to be exerted on the government of Sudan to end the violence and to secure the arrest of those who are indicted. As Danner argues, "pressure exerted by outside entities will be critical to the success of the ICC."[56]

NOTES

1. Hans-Peter Kaul, "Construction Site for More Justice: The International Criminal Court after Two Years," *American Journal of International Law* 99 (2005): 370; Eric Leonard, *The Onset of Global Governance: International Relations Theory and the International Criminal Court* (Adlershot, England: Ashgate Publishing, 2005).

2. Sarah B. Sewall and Carl Kaysen, eds., *The United States and the International Criminal Court* (Lanham, MD: Rowman & Littlefield Publishers, 2000).

3. Melissa K. Marler, "The International Criminal Court: Assessing the Juris-dictional Loopholes in the Rome Statute," *Duke Law Journal* 49 (1999): 825; Danesh Sarooshi, "The Statute of the International Criminal Court," *The International and Comparative Law Quarterly* 48 (1999): 387.

4. David J. Scheffer, "The U.S. Perspective on the ICC," in Sewall and Kaysen, eds., *The United States and the International Criminal Court* (Lanham, MD: Rowman & Littlefield Publishers, 2000).

5. Steven D. Roper and Lilian A Barria, *Designing Criminal Tribunals: Sovereignty and International Concerns in the Protection of Human Rights* (Aldershot, England: Ashgate Publishing, 2006).

6. Theodor Meron, "Answering for War Crimes: Lessons from the Balkans," *Foreign Affairs* 72 (1997): 2.

7. Interview with Carla Del Ponte, chief prosecutor, and David Tolbert, deputy prosecutor, ICTY (The Hague, July 12, 2006).

8. Giulio M. Gallarotti and Arik Y. Preis, "Politics, International Justice and the United States: Toward a Permanent International Criminal Court," *UCLA Journal of International Law and Foreign Affairs* 4 (1999): 1.

9. The refusal to transfer suspects is not specific to African countries. France and the United States have refused to surrender individuals to the ICTR. Moreover, there has been at least one case in which a country surrendered a suspect to a Rwandan national court rather than to the ICTR.

10. Both forms of conflict have been incorporated into the statute's definition of war crimes.

11. Richard J. Goldstone and Gary Jonathan Bass, "Lessons from the International Criminal Tribunals," in Sewall and Kayens, see note 2 at 57.

12. Technically, states do not "extradite" suspects to the ICC but rather surrender them to the Court. This language which is found in Article 91 of the Rome Statute was specifically included because extradition refers to a state-to-state process (see Valerie Oosterveld, Mike Perry and John McManus, "How the World Will Relate to the Court: The Cooperation of States with the International Criminal Court," *Fordham International Law Journal* 25 (2002): 767).

13. Marler, see note 3. Although the ICC does not have universal jurisdiction, certain categories of crimes in the Rome Statute have universal jurisdiction under international customary law; e.g., genocide and crimes against humanity.

14. As of this writing, the ICC includes 105 member-states.

15. This is one of the major problems confronting the prosecution of war crimes cases in the former Yugoslavia. For example, the Serbian criminal code forbids the extradition of nationals (interview with Del Ponte and Tolbert), see note 7.

16. See note 12.

17. See note 3.

18. Articles 89, 90, and 91 provide a clear procedure for the arrest and surrender of suspects. We are not arguing that the process is unclear, but rather that the process must ultimately conform to the laws of the state.

19. Leila Nadya Sadat and S. Richard Carden, "The New International Criminal Court: An Uneasy Revolution," *Georgetown Law Journal* 88 (2000): 444.

20. The Assembly of States Parties is an administrative and legislative organ of the ICC.

21. See note 8 at 29–30.

22. However, the statute does allow the state party to challenge a decision of the prosecutor not to prosecute a referred case.

23. Marler, see note 3.

24. Lawrence Weschler, "Exceptional Cases in Rome: The United States and the Struggle for an ICC," in Sewell and Kaysen, see note 2.

25. Interview with Rod Rostan, legal officer, Office of the Prosecutor, ICC (The Hague, July 11, 2006).

26. Allison Marston Danner, "Enhancing the Legitimacy and Accountability of Prosecutorial Discretion at the International Criminal Court," *American Journal of International Law* 97 (2003): 537.

27. Ibid., at 545.

28. The crime of aggression cannot be amended to include the necessary definition and condition for prosecution until the July 2009 review conference of the Rome Statute.

29. Sadat and Carden, see note 19 at 428.

30. William A. Schabas, *An Introduction to the International Criminal Court*, 2nd ed. (Cambridge: Cambridge University Press, 2004) at 30.

30. See note 8.

31. Determining the parties who will be covered.

32. Determining the subject matter that will be covered.

33. Dapo Akande, "International Law Immunities and the International Criminal Court," *American Journal of International Law* 98 (2004): 420.

34. Gérard Prunier, "The Politics of Death in Darfur." *Current History* 105 (2006): 201.

35. The effectiveness of sanctions, as well as the importance of human rights policy, on the allocation of foreign assistance are highly contested issues within the literature. A review of this literature is beyond the scope of this chapter.

36. Amnesty International 2004. "Central African Republic: Five Months of War against Women," online at web.amnesty.org/library/Index/ENGAFR190012004).

37. BBC 2006, "Hague Referral for African Pair," online at http://news.bbc. co.uk/1/Africa/4908938.stm (visited June 26, 2007).

38. Aid agencies have estimated that the war killed approximately three million people, with most of them succumbing to disease and famine.

39. By 2006, the DRC had 17,000 UN peacekeepers, which was the UN's largest peacekeeping operation.

40. UN Security Council, "Report From the Panel of Experts in the Illegal Exploitation of Natural Resources and Other Forms of Wealth of the Democratic Republic of Congo." (Document 2/2003/1027).

41. Gérard Prunier, "The Politics of Death in Darfur," *Current History* 105 (2006): 195.

42. Adam M. Abdelmoula, "The 'Fundamentalist' Agenda for Human Rights: The Sudan and Algeria," *Arab Studies Quarterly* 18 (1996): 18.

43. Ibid. He reports that the government has been supporting Arab Darfuri against non-Arab tribes in the region for many years.

44. Nsongurua J. Udombana, "When Neutrality is a Sin: The Darfur Crisis and the Crisis of Humanitarian Intervention in Sudan," *Human Rights Quarterly* 27 (2005): 1149.

45. Human Rights Watch 2005, "Entrenching Impunity: Government Responsibility for International Crimes in Darfur," 17 (2005): 1.

46. International Commission of Inquiry on Darfur, "Report of the International Commission of Inquiry on Darfur to the United Nations Secretary General" (2005).

47. Human Rights Watch 2005, see note 44 at 58.

48. Luis Moreno Ocampo, "Report of the Prosecutor of the International Criminal Court, Mr. Luis Moreno Ocampo to the Security Council Pursuant to UNSCR 1593," June 29, 2005 at 2.

49. Sudan has signed but not ratified the Rome Statute.

50. Interview with Rod Rostan, legal officer, Office of the Prosecutor, ICC (The Hague, July 11, 2006).

51. "Statement of the Prosecutor of the International Criminal Court, Mr. Luis Moreno Ocampo to the UN Security Council Pursuant to UNSCR 1593" (June 14, 2006).

52. Ruddy Doom and Koen Vlassenroot, "Kony's Message: A New *Koine?* The Lord's Resistance Army in Northern Uganda," *African Affairs* 98 (1999): 5.

53. Mohamed M. El Zeidy, "The Ugandan Government Triggers the First Test of the Complementarity Principle: An Assessment of the First State's Party Referral to the ICC." *International Criminal Law Review* 5 (2005): 83–199.

54. Luis Moreno Ocampo, "The Investigation in Northern Uganda," online at http://www.icc-cpi.int/NR/rdonlyres/2919856F-03E0-403F-A1A8-D61D4F350A20/277306/Uganda_PPpresentation7.pdf (visited August 7, 2009).

55. Kaul, see note 1 at 383.

56. Danner, see note 26 at 535.

PART III

Transnational Influences on Rights, Citizenship, and Democratization

CHAPTER SEVEN

The Globalization of Human Rights Norms

*Understanding the Opportunities and Limits of
International Law and Transnational Activism*

HANS PETER SCHMITZ

INTRODUCTION

By any measure, human rights have increased in importance in the last three decades to occupy a prominent place in global affairs.[1] As a result, analyzing the effects of international human rights treaties and concomitant transnational efforts to diffuse these norms has become an accepted and desirable research topic in political science[2] and neighboring disciplines. This development marks a significant change from a few decades ago, when mainstream political science largely ignored international law and nongovernmental activism. It also reflects a weakening of subdisciplinary boundaries within political science, in particular those between the study of international relations and comparative politics.[3] This chapter will also show how human rights research has recently become one of the most productive forums for scholars to bring diverse qualitative and quantitative skills to bear on key questions of domestic and global governance. Finally, the growing interest in human rights issues, and international law more broadly, draws a growing number of political scientists toward interdisciplinary research programs such as comparative judicial studies. In short, human rights claims are pervasive in past and current social and political struggles, and scholars are paying increasing attention to the effects of framing the development of societies in a language of rights.

This introduction to the subsection on "Transnational Influences on Rights, Citizenship, and Democratization" provides a brief summary of the current research on transnational human rights diffusion and introduces the following chapters by Lisa Conant (Chapter 8), Rachel Bowen (Chapter 9), and Joseph Isanga (Chapter 10). Conant's chapter shows how European courts recently have expanded social entitlements beyond national citizens and created a basic outline of transnational social citizenship. However, welfare reforms across European nations simultaneously have made the enjoyment of such entitlements contingent on economic activity. Although the courts have been successful in erasing the distinction between nationals and foreigners, domestic reforms establish new inequalities between those who participate in the workforce and those who do not. Conant persuasively argues that Europe moved closer to the United States model of separating citizenship from social rights but is unlikely to make the enjoyment of social rights entirely contingent on economic activity. The chapter shows in compelling ways how courts play a powerful role in the emergence of a transnational citizenship but are unable or unwilling to address new forms of inequality arising from the increasingly unequal distribution of wealth among the world's citizens. If rights can be fully enjoyed only by the economically secure, then the claim to their universality loses even more credibility.

Bowen effectively uses earlier research on the judicialization of politics and the role of transnational human rights activists to explain variation in the adoption of principles related to the rule of law in Guatemala and Nicaragua. Her research confirms the basic validity of Margaret Keck's and Kathryn Sikkink's "boomerang pattern"[4] as well as the "spiral model" developed by Thomas Risse and Sikkink based on cross-regional and comparative case studies of human rights change.[5] Yet Bowen's research goes much further and explains one of the crucial puzzles of the current human rights research within political science: What accounts for the persistent gap between a growing human rights *rhetoric* and the lack of progress in translating those norms into better human rights *practice*?[6] The chapter details how a weaker civil society and less developed ties to international supporters account for differences between Guatemala and Nicaragua, as well as for persistent human rights challenges in both nations.

Isanga's case study of Uganda also focuses on how domestic actors react to the external promotion of human rights ideas. He shows that Uganda's record of upholding the rule of law remains flawed largely as a result of a lack of consistency on the part of the international community. Because Uganda's president, Yoweri Museveni, has created conditions of lasting domestic stability (except in the northern and western border regions) and economic growth since 1986, donor governments have come to accept his "benevolent dictatorship" and refrained for a long time from applying consistent pressure to improve the rule of law, secure judicial independence, and transition toward a multiparty electoral system. In Uganda's case, the persistent gap between human rights rhetoric and practice reflects a lack of international attention, competing national security interests of Western donors (e.g., the war on terrorism), and the charismatic leadership of Museveni himself. Significant advances in fighting HIV/AIDS, as well as promotion of the social and economic welfare of Ugandan citizens after twenty years of civil war, also have helped Museveni to legitimize his open repression of domestic political dissent and his defiance of norms of democratic governance.

These three chapters fit well within the current state of political science research on the role of international law and transnational activism in promoting norms such as human rights and democratic governance. An initial wave of research published in the mid-1990s presented evidence for the independent power of human rights norms, courts, and transnational advocacy networks, but more recent studies have challenged this optimism and focused on the persistent gap between the growing rhetorical adoption of human rights norms by states and an apparent lack of actual human rights improvement on the ground. With few exceptions, qualitative case studies tend to confirm a more optimistic view of human rights progress, whereas quantitative methods have (more recently) been used to identify the persistence of human rights violations across countries despite increasing rhetorical commitments to human rights. Bowen and Isanga effectively use case studies to elaborate some of the factors that undermine human rights progress and the effectiveness of external promotional efforts. More subtly, Conant shows how European courts play a very active role in expanding the enjoyment of certain rights beyond national citizenship, but they do so within a larger context of increasing inequalities based on economic status. This threatens the universality of human rights and makes their enjoyment increasingly contingent on certain contractual obligations.

One of the major challenges for political scientists working in this area is to explain why this gap exists and decide if the institutionalization of human rights norms through international treaties actually represents a viable strategy for advancing those principles. The second research problem focuses on the role of nongovernmental actors and transnational relations in transmitting those norms from the global to the local level. Challenges to universalist claims and a real or perceived narrowing of the human rights discourse to "Western values" can undermine the legitimacy of activists who advance these norms primarily in non-Western societies. This chapter will provide a brief review of the existing literature on the external promotion of human rights. It will begin with a focus on the literature assessing the role of international law and human rights treaties as the structural framework of rights promotion and then move to a discussion of the burgeoning literature on the effectiveness and consequences of the key agents, transnational networks, and their principle-based mobilization.

NORMATIVE AND DOMESTIC BIASES: STATE-CENTRISM
AND MATERIAL INTERESTS

Before presenting current research on the role of human rights norms and transnational principled mobilization in global affairs, this introduction will briefly review the disciplinary and normative challenges this agenda presents to traditional political science. These challenges include persistent disciplinary boundaries between international relations and comparative politics, a pervasive state-centrism and normative bias in favor of sovereign domestic rule, and a primary focus on material forces in constructing interest-based explanations for human behavior. In the field of international relations (IR), the recent rise of the constructivist research agenda has drawn much (although certainly not all) of its strength from bringing transnationalism "back in"[7] and using human rights as a major empirical area of investigation. Those transnational and norms-driven analyses of the mid-1990s stood in stark contrast to the dominant rationalist approaches, which focus either on military competition (neorealism) or economic cooperation (liberal institutionalism).[8] During the next decade, constructivist methods and transnational perspectives have not only become part of the mainstream of IR theory, but rationalist scholars have also joined in and effectively challenged some of the earlier assumptions on the principled motives and roles of transnational activism in diffusing norms of democratic governance and human rights. This marks a significant shift from a time when human rights were either viewed as epiphenomenal (to economic development) by comparativists or openly rejected on various normative or utilitarian grounds by IR scholars.[9] Today, by contrast, explaining principled advocacy efforts and the effects of moral persuasion are accepted topics of research.[10]

The neorealist tradition in the field of IR takes an amoral and utilitarian view of the world and insists that concerns for human rights in other nations are likely to increase the potential for violent conflict among states. Neorealists insist that a respect for the sovereignty of other nations contributes to peace in an anarchic world because state leaders focus on their own security rather than on the domestic conditions of their neighbors. For neorealists, sovereignty and nonintervention are not principles competing with the idea of universal human rights, but a prudent guidance in an effort to tame a war-prone international system.

Institutionalist theories emerged during the 1970s and 1980s as the main challenge to neorealism. Institutionalists are more optimistic about the ability of states to overcome anarchy and establish international "cooperation under anarchy,"[11] but they share with neorealists the key ideas of state-centrism and sovereignty, as well as the rational pursuit of material interests. Institutionalists do not reject international human rights agreements as a threat to peace, but they have difficulties accounting for their emergence because the issue area of human rights, unlike trade, does not facilitate interstate cooperation through interdependence and reciprocity. With the exception of large-scale atrocities, human rights conditions in one nation do not necessarily affect the welfare of another nation. As a result, institutionalists have trouble identifying a set of rational preferences and interests that would sustain interstate cooperation in the issue area of human rights. The end of the Cold War and the failure of mainstream theories to predict and explain such a momentous event in global affairs provided the necessary window of opportunity to challenge the dominance of state-centrism and rational-materialist accounts dominant in the analysis of world politics.[12]

In comparative politics, the core limitations to taking human rights seriously are twofold. First, the disciplinary boundaries discourage a systematic inclusion of external influences such as transnational activists or promotional efforts by United Nations (UN) human rights institutions. Second, the mainstream in the field also prefers material and interest-driven explanations similar to neorealist and neoliberal institutionalist accounts in IR. In the key comparativist area of explaining regime types in general and democratization in particular, a long-dominant modernization perspective insisted that political change is largely driven by economic development. After decades of research, current scholarship continues to view domestic wealth as a powerful predictor for the survival of democracy[13] or even upholds the more expansive claim that economic growth always precedes sustainable democratic change.[14] More agency-driven perspectives on democratization emerging during the 1980s[15] discount underlying structural conditions in favor of bargains and pacts among elites; however, the literature on democratization remained largely focused on identifying the rational interest calculations of the domestic leadership.[16]

The domestic bias in analyzing human rights advances and democratic change is a natural result of real world political developments. Although the external promotion of human rights and democracy is a common practice of many liberal democracies and transnational nonstate actors today, such efforts were much less prominent in the past. Human rights promotion became a task for the newly created UN in 1945, but norms of state sovereignty and the Cold War effectively limited those efforts to standard-setting[17] until help arrived from increasingly prominent nongovernmental organizations (NGOs) such as Amnesty International (founded in 1961) and Human Rights Watch (founded in 1978). Today intergovernmental organizations and NGOs form a "*symbiotic* relationship of mutual growth and interdependence,"[18] and researchers can draw on decades of human rights reports and data to systematically explore the successes and failures of promotional efforts on behalf of selected rights.[19] But do international treaties have any positive effects on domestic human rights conditions, or are they empty promises shielding human rights violators from scrutiny? The subsequent section will focus on this question before moving on to evaluate the specific role of transnational advocacy networks and NGOs as key agents in the diffusion of norms such as human rights and democratic governance.

INTERGOVERNMENTAL ORGANIZATIONS AND HUMAN RIGHTS: EMPTY PROMISES OR LONG-TERM SOCIALIZATION?

International human rights treaties have proliferated since the adoption of the Universal Declaration of Human Rights by UN members on December 10, 1948. The Office of the UN High Commissioner for Human Rights identifies nine core human rights agreements with monitoring bodies and a total of approximately two dozen international human rights treaties open for states' signature and ratification.[20] Regional human rights treaties exist in Europe, the Americas, and Africa but still are absent in Asia and the Middle East. Traditional IR theories find the emergence and expansion of this global system of human rights agreements puzzling because they violate the basic norm of sovereignty by providing a rationale for external actors to intervene in the domestic affairs of a state. Additionally, neorealists view human rights treaties as a potential threat to international peace and national security, and neoliberal institutionalists doubt that human rights can provide a central force in creating material interdependence and incentives for rational cooperation among states.

Understanding the expansion of the global human rights regime requires looking beyond states and their material interests and accepting a more autonomous role for international institutions and transnational nonstate actors. International institutions and NGOs are frequently intimately linked in their goals and even organizational forms (e.g., in Keck and Sikkink's "transnational advocacy networks"), but more recent debates in political science have analytically separated the effects of state participation in international institutions from the effects of transnational mobilization by nonstate actors. The former research agenda, discussed here first, is driven by two key questions: (1) What are the origins of regional and global human rights institutions? and (2) Does state participation in those regional and global institutions improve human rights conditions?

What Accounts for the Emergence and Evolution of Global and Regional Human Rights Institutions?

Despite a general skepticism toward human rights treaties, IR theories emphasizing security (neorealism) or material well-being (neoliberal institutionalism) as key motives for state behavior can serve as a first cut for explaining the emergence and evolution of international institutions. Neorealists would emphasize the role and interests of powerful states and can easily explain why the United States government happily used human rights rhetoric against its ideological rivals while ignoring the same abuses committed by its allies.[21] Mark Mazower uses this logic to explain the creation of the UN human rights system as the lowest common denominator among major global powers with dismal domestic human rights records.[22]

Institutionalists focus less on the abuse of human rights rhetoric by the powerful but view it primarily as a signaling device in reciprocal and mutual beneficial relations with other nations. Andrew Moravcsik concludes, with regard to the European human rights regime, that new democracies were more proactive in pushing for strong supranational institutions because their leaderships had a strong incentive to bind their hands domestically and gain credibility internationally.[23] The key insight shared by rationalist IR theories is that human rights are a means serving more fundamental (national) interests, such as security or economic well-being.

The constructivist response to skeptical analyses of global and regional human rights regimes focuses on the role of individual and collective norm entrepreneurs[24] and takes a more long-term view of the evolution of those human rights ideas and agreements. Whereas rationalists tend to view international institutions primarily as an end result of state interests and actions, constructivists see them as a transitional stage marking an initial victory of norm leaders, which, in turn, provides a new and strengthened platform for transnational mobilization. Constructivists insist that human rights change "comes about because many individuals had similar experiences, not because they all inhabited the same social context but because through their interactions with each other and with their reading and viewing, they actually created a new social context."[25]

Neorealists and neoliberal institutionalists focus on states' continued exclusive control of the process of negotiating and adopting intergovernmental agreements and remain skeptical about the possibility of transforming the core interests of states in global affairs. Constructivists answer this skepticism by pointing to the principled and nongovernmental sources of the norms underlying state negotiations and by insisting that international institutions develop autonomy from their creators and substitute state interests as key motives with their mandate, internal bureaucratic culture,[26] or an external universal model of the "world polity."[27]

Both sides will usually find evidence for their respective optimism and pessimism analyzing the same international institutions and events. Take the example of the now-replaced United Nations Commission on Human Rights (UNCHR): Whereas realists will emphasize the hypocrisy of consistently ignoring certain human rights offenders (e.g., China or Saudi Arabia), constructivists see a long-term process of growing consistency and "forcing an increasing number of repressive regimes to defend their records in private and in public."[28]

What are the Effects of Global Human Rights Institutions?

The emergence of human rights institutions presents a new and vibrant interdisciplinary research area; however, political scientists are likely to focus with even more keen interest on the actual effects of such agreements. A 2007 special issue of the *Journal of Peace Research* summarizes nicely the current debate in this area, which has generated two contrasting views. As more political scientists have applied quantitative methods to the study of human rights and particularly the level of state compliance with international human rights obligations, the emerging consensus paints a pessimistic picture of increasing global human rights "talk" that is not necessarily followed by improvements in human rights conditions (even decades after joining a human rights treaty).[29]

These studies conclude that the weak enforcement mechanisms of international human rights treaties, combined with a lack of democratic governance and civil society, are likely to produce perverse results such as that a "nominal gesture of treaty ratification . . . can even lead to worse human rights records."[30] Although the presence of democratic governance and a strong civil society increase the likelihood of long-term domestic compliance with treaty obligations,[31] quantitative scholarship maintains that repressive governments no longer fear legal commitments to international human rights treaties and have learned how to avoid implementing those norms.

In contrast with the results from quantitative research, the qualitative literature, such as Rachel Bowen's comparison of Guatemala and Nicaragua, is more optimistic about the transformative effects of participating in global human rights regimes.[32] Qualitative scholarship typically focuses on the interactions between transnational networks and their domestic counterparts in pressuring and socializing repressive regimes into compliance with international norms (see "Nongovernmental Activism and Transnational Networks: From Establishing Their Significance to Understanding Their Limits"). What explains this significant gap between the qualitative and the quantitative literature?

To some degree, the qualitative literature has focused more attention on cases of successful human rights change, most prominently in Eastern Europe[33] and Latin America.[34] By contrast, qualitative studies can provide a more global and cross-regional perspective. However, even within the qualitative literature, scholars have made conscious efforts to go beyond cases confirming their optimism and explain the failures of the global human rights regime.[35] Hafner-Burton and Ron also suggest that qualitative scholars are more likely to pick up on the *process* and small movements toward positive human rights, whereas quantitative scholars will focus on comparable *outcomes* and ignore those changes in individual countries as "minor deviations."[36]

The gap between optimists and pessimists on the issue of global human rights institutions is not necessarily an artifact of the different qualitative and quantitative methods used. Scholars using qualitative methods have for some time explored the limits of international human rights institutions and produced the core critiques of the idea of human rights itself,[37] while the quantitative literature delivers a complex and mixed picture of successes and failures. Regional case selection and methods do matter, but in many cases scholars can easily come to opposite conclusions even when looking at the same institutions and historical processes.[38] The case of the death penalty and the role of the European Union as a key actor in promoting the global abolition of the practice provides another example of finding evidence for both optimism and pessimism with regard to the effectiveness of global human rights institutions.

In the case of the death penalty, human rights organizations played the central role in creating an unprecedented "norms cascade"[39] beginning in the mid-1970s. Following intense internal debates and dissent on the issue of expanding its mandate, Amnesty International decided in 1976 to promote the abolition of the death penalty as one of its core goals. By 1989, the UN General Assembly adopted the Second Optional Protocol to the International Covenant on Civil and Political Rights (ICCPR) calling on all member states to abolish the death penalty. In 1990, the Organization of American States (OAS) adopted a similar protocol to its human rights convention. In May 2002, the Council of Europe adopted Protocol 13 to the European Convention on Human Rights, which represents the first international treaty abolishing the death penalty with no exceptions. Today, the European Union is the key regional intergovernmental organization spreading the abolitionist movement beyond its borders to new and aspiring member states (including, most recently, Turkey and Ukraine).

According to Amnesty International,[40] three nations each year have abolished the death penalty in the past decade. In 1948, eight nations had abolished the death penalty for all crimes. This number increased to seventeen by 1977. Yet as Amnesty International began to mobilize on the issue during the late 1970s, the number of abolitionist nations increased more rapidly to sixty-three (1998), seventy-six (2002), and eighty-nine (2006). The total number of abolitionist nations in law or practice stands at 129 today, whereas 68 nations are qualified by Amnesty International as retentionist. In major retentionist nations such as the United States, the mobilization also has had a major impact, including the January 2003 decision of former Illinois governor George Ryan to commute all death sentences in his state; the March 2005 Supreme Court decision abolishing juvenile executions; and the continued legal challenges to the practice on the federal and state levels.

The case of the death penalty is a compelling example of transnational activism and the role of global and regional institutions. It is a "hard" case for transnational activists and scholars, because a majority of the public in most nations supports the death penalty by a wide majority.[41] The case also defies the simple dichotomy between democracies and authoritarian regimes[42] and provides an easy measurement of the dependent variable of human rights change. Skeptics will rightly point to the slow pace of the abolitionist movement and argue that any gains are easily reversible.

It is worthwhile to recount issues on which most scholars engaged in this debate can agree. First, democracy and a strong civil society are positively correlated with improved human rights conditions at home. Both quantitative and qualitative scholarship has found that domestic political space for human rights activism is a positive condition for further improvements. Within specific autocratic regimes, positive human rights change is also possible and can affect various areas of social, economic, political, and civil rights (short of full democratization).

Second, scholars agree that transnational networks of activists play a crucial role in the diffusion of global human rights standards. Those transnational activists are the key agents in transmitting still weakly enforced human rights agreements into a given domestic context. The effects of this transnational mobilization are not always positive or in line with the intent of the external norm promoters. The qualitative literature on transnational human rights activism has shown how frustration with the incapacitated UN human rights system motivated a new generation of norm entrepreneurs into founding organizations such as Amnesty International and Human Rights Watch. Those NGOs initially focused on shining a light on state failures to live up to their human rights rhetoric but since then have become the subject of scholarly and public scrutiny themselves. The following section will present a brief overview of the literature on the emergence and efficacy of transnational human rights activism.

NONGOVERNMENTAL ACTIVISM AND TRANSNATIONAL NETWORKS: FROM ESTABLISHING THEIR SIGNIFICANCE TO UNDERSTANDING THEIR LIMITS

The key agents for the global promotion of human rights are NGOs and their transnational networks. This section will focus on those nonstate actors with a primary purpose of advancing human rights, although many other nongovernmental activities by NGOs, multinational corporations (MNCs), rebel groups, or terrorist networks obviously also have significant ramifications for human rights conditions. In the past, Amnesty International, Human Rights Watch, and other advocacy groups have almost exclusively focused on the responsibility of states for the human rights conditions in their territory. More recently, the same organizations have expanded their targets to include other nonstate actors, signaling a pragmatic response to the inability of many governments (e.g., in failed states) to effectively shape human rights conditions within their territories. Human rights groups also for some time have targeted multinational corporations for their roles in supporting repressive governments or creating unacceptable working conditions in factories abroad.[43] While recognizing the increasing prominence of other nonstate actors in shaping human rights conditions, this section will primarily focus on the power and limits of transnational advocacy dedicated primarily to the promotion of human rights.

Almost ten years after its publication, Keck and Sikkink's *Activists Beyond Borders* remains the definitive statement on the role of human rights (and other) activists in global affairs. The relevance of the book is reconfirmed by current publications, which continue to build on or challenge key insights of the book, including the "boomerang model,"[44] the theory of issue emergence,[45] the respective strength of external and domestic mobilization,[46] or the assumption of unity and principled motives driving those advocacy networks.[47] The more recent literature building on *Activists Beyond Borders* is decidedly more skeptical about the motives and effects of transnational activism. Keck and Sikkink established a new research field, which is now populated by studies seeking to identify the sources of transnational activism as well as the conditions under which it yields specific results. I divide these efforts into two major but interrelated categories focusing, first, on how scholars have explored the role of the external environment of transnational activism and, second, on forms of internal contestation and conflict within transnational networks and NGOs.

Why Do Some Issues Get Adopted, While Others Do Not?

One key area of recent transnational research focuses on the question of how transnational actors select issues and decide to commit resources to specific causes. Keck and Sikkink viewed those networks primarily driven by principles and emphasized their focus on areas of greatest need (bodily harm and opportunities), a clear causal chain linking violations to a responsible agent, the availability of precedent in the form of a preexisting norm (resonance), and the presence of norm entrepreneurs.[48] By contrast, more recent scholarship has either questioned the principled character of NGO activism[49] or explored why some undoubtedly deserving causes fail to even get recognized by activist networks.[50]

Ron, Ramos, and Rodgers (2005, at 576) challenge the focus on principles in the earlier scholarship by comparing the human rights reporting practice of Amnesty International (from 1986 to 2000) with the actual severity of human rights conditions in countries.[51] The study confirms a strong correlation between Amnesty's target selection and state power, media exposure, and foreign aid levels. For example, the authors contrast a list of top-ten targets (based on Amnesty International background reports) with a ranking of countries with the greatest violations of personal integrity rights. The top four nations targeted by Amnesty International are Turkey, the U.S.S.R./Russia,

China, and the United States; however, those four countries do not appear in the top-twenty list of human rights–violating states. This leads the authors to conclude that human rights NGOs target states for reasons other than their human rights records, including the likelihood of gaining media attention and the relative power of the targeted state. The authors conclude that their research challenges NGOs to "ensure that strategic considerations do not play too large of a role" because this may "contribute to the marginalization of abuses in smaller, poorer or weaker countries." Clifford Bob's qualitative work confirms and complements this result with a "bottom-up" perspective by showing that not the most deserving human rights causes receive global attention, but instead those where local activists present their causes in ways compatible with the interests and needs of potential external audiences.[52]

Although this type of research corrects an overly principled view of transnational activism, it does not invalidate previous assumptions about the moral sources of human rights mobilization. A careful reanalysis of the data compiled by James Ron and his collaborators reveals at least two results challenging a purely strategic view of human rights groups. First, some countries end up high on the agenda of Amnesty International because the prevalent violations are of particular concern for the organization. China and the United States may be of greater media importance, but they are also prime targets for Amnesty International because they are global leaders in use of the death penalty. Second, many developed nations have become targets of reporting not only because of human rights conditions at home, but because of their involvement as weapons suppliers in armed conflicts elsewhere. Turkey, China, and Russia are regularly targets of Amnesty International because of their direct involvement in violent conflicts causing some of the worst human rights violations elsewhere (e.g., Democratic Republic of the Congo [DRC], Sudan, or Colombia). Finally, the dichotomy between principled and strategic motives is largely an academic exercise with limited relevance for practitioners. The environment of NGOs is of major importance in understanding their strategic choices, but any externally generated incentives are ultimately filtered in internal debates and contestation. As Stephen Hopgood's book on Amnesty International elaborates, transnational activists constantly face trade-offs and choices about the use of their limited resources. This kind of consequentialism does not necessarily compromise a commitment to underlying human rights norms, but it certainly requires researchers to better understand how social problems become campaign issues and what role the "domestic politics" of transnational activism plays.

Unpacking Transnational Activism: Contestation within NGOs and Across Networks

In addition to informing the debate on the external influences shaping transnational activism, Keck and Sikkink's original work also has motivated scholars to open the "black box" of principled activism and transnational advocacy networks. This is a key goal of Hopgood's recent ethnography of Amnesty

International, where he states that "we know next to nothing about what Amnesty is like on the inside."[53] Hopgood argues that Amnesty International is neither a typical NGO nor really a human rights organization, but is a secular religion primarily designed to provide a spiritual home to its membership. This insight has significant consequences for our understanding of transnational activism and the deeper causes of organizational and strategic change within individual organizations. This type of scholarship reduces transnational activism neither to principles nor to strategic interest, but understands NGOs as significant sites of (semi-)public discourse and political contestation.

The "domestic" is also at the center of recent studies investigating the effects (and unintended consequences) of transnational activism beyond individual organizations and their internal debates. In contrast to earlier, optimistic views of an emerging "global civil society" and a withering of the state, more recent research emphasizes the inherent fragility of transnational coalitions and the crucial role of domestic support as a key ingredient of successful transnational campaigns.[54] Others emphasize the relative autonomy of domestic activists and their ability to manipulate external campaigns to better suit their domestic needs.[55] Finally, researchers also have argued that transnational mobilization for human rights is most productive in challenging autocratic regimes but plays a much less significant role in latter stages of political regime change. Unintended consequences of such external interventions include distracting domestic allies from building effective coalitions at home and providing mobilizing opportunities to repressive elites and politically savvy autocratic leaders.[56]

Sometimes the limits of transnational activism have little to do with internal wranglings, strategic calculations, or countermobilization when a campaign is already under way. In some cases, transnational campaigns fail to emerge around an issue previously identified in the literature as particularly conducive to mobilization and network formation. Explaining cases of "non-emergence" requires exploring the role of norm entrepreneurs in defining an issue and the role of "domestic politics" within networks in adopting an issue for a campaign.[57]

The literature on transnational advocacy networks and principled human rights activism has begun to explore why campaigns succeed or fail, why some issues never turn into a campaign, and why some problems never become recognized as issues. Future research on transnational advocacy networks can gain much from the social-movement, agenda-setting, and gate-keeping literature, which have long explored why and how people come to realize that "a given state of affairs is neither natural nor accidental."[58]

CONCLUSIONS

The expansion of human rights "talk" in world politics has been followed during the past decade by a growth of human rights–related research within political science. More reliable and comprehensive data on human rights conditions in nations around the world have enabled a diversification of research methods in the field and generated exciting new research agendas and puzzles. The early literature primarily focused on challenging mainstream state-centric accounts by showing the independent influence of norms and nonstate actors in world affairs. As the research agenda gradually matured and became more accepted, a more diverse group of scholars began to take on questions about the relevance of global human rights institutions and transnational activism. Lisa Conant, Rachel Bowen, and John Isanga make significant contributions as part of this ongoing investigation into the transnational diffusion of global norms prescribing respect for human rights and democratic governance. Their studies elaborate on the problems encountered by transnational activists and international institutions in enforcing specific rights and the rule of law in a given domestic context. Chapters 8 through 10 address the two core questions emerging within the wider interdisciplinary debate in this area: First, do international human rights institutions have a measurable positive effect on domestic conditions? Second, what is the role of transnational nongovernmental activism in transmitting those norms?

A survey of the literature emerging with regard to the first question leads to two main conclusions. First, there is more agreement among scholars than some of the published rhetoric suggests. Most would agree that international human rights agreements (with the exception of the European system) are weak in terms of their enforcement mechanisms and have to rely for their effectiveness on the presence of transnational and, preferably, domestic nongovernmental mobilization and a relative openness of the political system. Conant's chapter adds to this general insight that even the well-established European human rights system is largely unable to prevent recent efforts to exclude citizens from certain social rights based on economic status. Although some may celebrate the courts' efforts to expand the rights enjoyed by noncitizens in Europe, parallel reforms of the welfare state introduce new discriminatory practices at the national level. The efforts of international institutions defending human rights have real consequences but do not obliterate the significance of domestic processes expanding or contracting the enjoyment of rights across different economic and social groups.

Second, disagreements about the role of international institutions do not necessarily follow methodological divides between quantitative and qualitative scholarship. Some of the more recent quantitative work shows a significant gap between rhetoric and compliance, but qualitative scholars have for some time taken this result for granted and begun to actually explain why such a gap may persist and how activists' choices and strategies in spreading human rights norms may affect those outcomes. Qualitative scholarship also is dominant in pushing beyond questions of effectiveness to explore the legitimacy of the current human rights discourse. Understanding the measurable effects of those institutions requires looking at their origins and their evolution within a system driven by a plethora of unequal participants in a global public discourse. This leads to the second question and the central role of transnational advocacy networks.

Human rights norms are diffused by specific actions of mostly nongovernmental advocates. Whereas the first generation of research assumed a close and unproblematic identity between norms and their promoters as well as between transnational activists and their domestic counterparts, more recent scholarship is unpacking those actors and exploring their organizations and networks as sites of intense political contestation and issue definition. The results of this research emphasize the role of norm entrepreneurs in the process of issue creation, focus on intra-organizational and -network conflicts in shaping issue adoption and strategic choices, emphasize the role of domestic support and autonomy in transnational activism, and recount how transnational mobilization can have unintended consequences undermining the original goals. In better specifying the conditions of transnational issue emergence, as well as campaign creation and success, this literature plays a crucial part in our understanding of global and domestic political and social change. The following two chapters make a strong case for the growing significance and vibrancy of this research agenda by elaborating the power and limits of global human rights norms and transnational activism.

NOTES

1. Howard Ramos, James Ron, and Oskar N. T. Thoms report that the median use of "human rights" in major global media outlets almost doubled between 1986 and 2000; Howard Ramos, James Ron, and Oskar N. T. Thoms, "Shaping the Northern Media's Human Rights Coverage, 1986-2000," *Journal of Peace Research* 44, no. 3 (2007): 385–406.

2. The American Political Science Association (APSA) added a human rights section in November 2001, whereas a similar section emerged within the International Studies Association (ISA) only in March 2006. Within the International Political Science Association (IPSA), a research committee on human rights was formed in 1987.

3. Mitchell A. Orenstein and Hans Peter Schmitz, "The New Transnationalism and Comparative Politics," *Comparative Politics* 38, no. 4 (2006): 479–500, and Bruce M. Russett, "Reintegrating the Subdisciplines of International and Comparative Politics," *International Studies Review* 5, no. 4 (2003): 9–12.

4. Margaret Keck and Kathryn Sikkink, *Activists Beyond Borders. Advocacy Networks in International Politics* (Ithaca: Cornell University Press, 1997), 13.

5. Thomas Risse and Kathryn Sikkink, "The socialization of human rights norms," in *The Power of Human Rights. International Norms and Domestic Change*, edited by Thomas Risse, Stephen Ropp, and Kathryn Sikkink (Cambridge: Cambridge University Press, 1999), 20; for a critique of the "spiral model" (and review of the field), see Todd Landman, "The Political Science of Human Rights," *British Journal of Political Science* 35, no. 3 (2005): 549–572.

6. *Journal of Peace Research* 44, no. 4 (2007): 379–384, special issue on "Protecting Human Rights," guest editors Emilie Hafner-Burton and James Ron.

7. Thomas Risse-Kappen, ed., *Bringing Transnational Relations Back In: Non-State Actors, Domestic Structures, and International Institutions* (Cambridge: Cambridge University Press, 1995).

8. Andreas Hasenclever, Peter Mayer, and Volker Rittberger, *Theories of International Regimes* (Cambridge: Cambridge University Press, 1997).

9. R. J. Vincent, *Human Rights and International Relations* (Cambridge: Cambridge University Press, 1986).

10. Joshua W. Busby, "Bono Made Jesse Helms Cry: Jubilee 2000, Debt Relief, and Moral Action in International Politics," *International Studies Quarterly* 51, no. 2 (2007): 247–275.

11. Kenneth A. Oye, *Cooperation Under Anarchy* (Princeton: Princeton University Press, 1986).

12. Jeffrey T. Checkel, "The Constructivist Turn in International Relations Theory: A Review Essay," *World Politics* 50, no. 2 (1998): 324–348.

13. Adam Przeworski and Fernando Limongi, "Modernization: Theories and Facts," *World Politics* 49, no. 2 (1997): 155–183.

14. Carles Boix and Susan C. Stokes, "Endogenous Democratization" *World Politics* 55, no. 4 (2003): 517–549.

15. Guillermo O'Donnell and Philippe C. Schmitter, *Transitions from Authoritarian Rule: Tentative Conclusions about Uncertain Democracies* (Baltimore: Johns Hopkins University Press, 1986).

16. Karen L. Remmer, "New Theoretical Perspectives on Democratization," *Comparative Politics* 28, no. 1 (1995): 103–122; Hans Peter Schmitz, "Domestic and Transnational Perspectives on Democratization," *International Studies Review* 6, no. 3 (2005): 403–426.

17. Jack Donnelly, "International Human Rights: A Regime Analysis," *International Organization* 40, no. 3 (1986): 599–642.

18. Kim Reimann, "A View from the Top: International Politics, Norms and the Worldwide Growth of NGOs," *International Studies Quarterly* 51, no. 4 (2006), 67.

19. This essay focuses primarily on external efforts to improve human rights conditions by intergovernmental and nongovernmental actors intervening in a relatively stable domestic setting. The discussion excludes cases of mass atrocities (e.g., genocide) and the extensive literature on humanitarian interventions and "democracy by force." The discussion also excludes literature focusing on the domestic effects of purely structural changes in the international system. A prominent example here is how the Cold War shaped the United States federal government's support for the civil rights movement at home; see Thomas Borstelmann, *The Cold War and the Color Line: American Race Relations in the Global Arena* (Cambridge: Harvard University Press, 2001); Mary L. Dudziak, *Cold War Civil Rights. Race and the Image of American Democracy* (Princeton: Princeton University Press, 2000).

20. International law section at the Office of the United Nations High Commissioner for Human Rights, online at http://www.ohchr.org/english/law/ (visited July 11, 2007).

21. James H. Lebovic and Erik Voeten, "The Politics of Shame. The Condemnation of Country Human Rights Practices in the UNCHR," *International Studies Quarterly* 50, no. 4 (2006): 861–888.

22. Mark Mazower, "The Strange Triumph of Human Rights, 1933–1950," *The Historical Journal* 47, no. 2 (2004): 379–398.

23. Andrew Moravcsik, "The Origins of Human Rights Regimes: Democratic Delegation in Postwar Europe," *International Organization* 54, no. 2 (2000): 217–252.

24. Examples of such norm entrepreneurship are prevalent throughout the history of human rights activism and include Henri Dunant/the International Committee of the Red Cross (rules of war, 1864); Eleanor Roosevelt (Universal Declaration of Human Rights, 1948); Raphael Lemkin (Genocide Convention, 1948); Amnesty International (UN Convention against Torture, 1984/87); Jody Williams (landmines, 1997); and Bono (debt relief, 2000s).

25. Lynn Hunt, *Inventing Human Rights. A History* (New York: W.W. Norton, 2007), 34. Elizabeth Borgwardt makes a similar claim about the role of collective "transformative experiences" in tracing how U.S. policy makers after 1945 projected the human rights ideas driving the New Deal onto the international arena; see Elizabeth Borgwardt, *A New Deal for the World: America's Vision for Human Rights* (Cambridge, Mass: Belknap Press, 2005), 86.

26. Michael Barnett and Martha Finnemore, *Rules for the World: International Organizations in Global Politics* (Ithaca: Cornell University Press, 2004).

27. John Boli and George M. Thomas, "World Culture in the World Polity," *American Sociological Review* 62, no. 2 (1997): 171–190.

28. James H. Lebovic and Erik Voeten, "The Politics of Shame," 884.

29. Oona Hathaway, "Do Human Rights Treaties make a Difference?" *The Yale Law Journal* 111, no. 8 (2002): 1935-2042; for a more optimistic view, see Todd Landman, *Protecting Human Rights. A Comparative Study* (Washington, D.C.: Georgetown University Press, 2005). A summary of this debate is provided by Emilie M. Hafner-Burton and Kiyoteru Tsutsui, "Justice Lost! The Failure of International Human Rights Law to Matter Where Needed Most," *Journal of Peace Research* 44, no. 3 (2007): 407–425.

30. Eric Neumayer, "Do International Human Rights Treaties Improve Respect for Human Rights?" *Journal of Conflict Resolution* 49, no. 6 (2005): 925–953.

31. Emilie Hafner-Burton and Kiyoteru Tsutsui, "Human Rights in a Globalizing World. The Paradox of Empty Promises," *American Sociological Review* 110, no. 5 (2005): 1373–1411; Steven C. Poe and C. Neal Tate, "Repression of Human Rights to Personal Integrity in the 1980s: A Global Analysis," *The American Political Science Review* 88, no. 4. (1994): 853–872.

32. Martha Finnemore and Kathryn Sikkink, "International Norm Dynamics and Political Change," *International Organization* 52, no. 4 (1998): 887–917 and Thomas Risse, Stephen Ropp, and Kathryn Sikkink, eds., *The Power of Human Rights*.

33. Daniel C. Thomas, *The Helsinki Effect: International Norms, Human Rights, and the Demise of Communism* (Princeton: Princeton University Press, 2001).

34. Kathryn Sikkink, "Human Rights, Principled Issue Networks, and Sovereignty in Latin America," *International Organization* 47, no. 3 (1993): 411–441.

35. For example, see the paired comparisons in Thomas Risse, Stephen Ropp, and Kathryn Sikkink, eds., *The Power of Human Rights*; for other qualitative works with a more pessimistic view of transnational activism, see Clifford Bob, *The Marketing of Rebellion: Insurgents, Media, and International Activism* (Cambridge: Cambridge University Press, 2005) and Sarah E. Mendelson and John K. Glenn, eds., *The Power and Limits of NGOs* (New York: Columbia University Press, 2002).

36. Emilie Hafner-Burton and James Ron, "Preventing Human Rights Abuse," *Journal of Peace Research* 44 (2007): 379–383, at 381.

37. Michael Ignatieff, *Human Rights as Politics of Idolatry*, edited by Amy Gutmann (Princeton: Princeton University Press, 2001); Stanley Cohen, *States of Denial: Knowing about Atrocities and Suffering* (Cambridge, UK: Polity Press, 2001); Pheng Cheah, *Inhuman Conditions: On Cosmopolitanism and Human Rights* (Cambridge: Harvard University Press, 2006).

38. Lebovic and Voeten provide such conflicting interpretations using the example of the United Nations Commission on Human Rights (UNCHR); James H. Lebovic and Erik Voeten, "The Politics of Shame."

39. Martha Finnemore and Kathryn Sikkink, "International Norm Dynamics and Political Change."

40. For current information on abolitionist and retentionist countries, see Amnesty International's Web site, "The Death Penalty," online at http://web.amnesty.org/pages/deathpenalty-countries-eng.

41. Sangmin Bae, *When the State No Longer Kills: International Human Rights Norms and Abolition of Capital Punishment* (Albany: State University of New York Press, 2007).

42. For a similar effort in disaggregating autocratic regimes with regard to their human rights records, see Christian Davenport, "State Repression and the Tyrannical Peace," *Journal of Peace Research* 44, no. 4 (2007): 485–504.

43. George Andreopoulos, Zahra F. Kabasakal Arat, and Peter Juviler, eds., *Non-State Actors in the Human Rights Universe* (Bloomfield, Conn.: Kumarian Press, 2006).

44. Naomi Roht-Arriaza, *The Pinochet Effect: Transnational Justice in the Age of Human Rights* (Philadelphia: University of Pennsylvania Press, 2005), chap. 8; Sidney Tarrow, *The New Transnational Activism* (Cambridge: Cambridge University Press, 2005), 143–160.

45. R. Charli Carpenter, "Setting the Advocacy Agenda: Theorizing Issue Emergence and Nonemergence in Transnational Advocacy Networks," *International Studies Quarterly* 51, no. 1 (2007): 99–120.

46. Shareen Hertel, *Unexpected Power. Conflict and Change among Transnational Activists* (Ithaca: Cornell University Press, 2006); Robert M. Press, *Peaceful Resistance: Advancing Human Rights and Democratic Freedoms* (Aldershot, UK: Ashgate, 2006).

47. Alexander Cooley and James Ron, "The NGO Scramble: Organizational Insecurity and the Political Economy of Transnational Action," *International Security* 27, no. 1 (2002): 5–39; Clifford Bob, *The Marketing of Rebellion*; Lisa Jordan and Peter Van Tuijl, "Political Responsibility in Transnational NGO Advocacy," *World Development* 28, no. 12 (2000): 2051–2065.

48. Richard Price, "Reversing the Gun Sights: Transnational Civil Society Targets Land Mines," *International Organization* 52, no. 3 (1998): 613–644.

49. James Ron, Howard Ramos, and Kathleen Rodgers, "Transnational Information Politics. NGO Human Rights Reporting, 1986–2000," *International Studies Quarterly* 49, no. 3 (2005): 557–587.

50. R. Charli Carpenter, "Setting the Advocacy Agenda."

51. Ron, Ramos, and Rogers, "Transnational Information Politics," at 576.

52. Clifford Bob, *The Marketing of Rebellion*.

53. Stephen Hopgood, *Keepers of the Flame: Understanding Amnesty International* (Ithaca: Cornell University Press, 2006), 3. Similarly, Michael Barnett and Martha

Finnemore argue with regard to intergovernmental organizations (IOs) that "we can better understand what IOs *do* if we better understand what IOs *are,*" Michael Barnett and Martha Finnemore, *Rules for the World*, 9.

54. Sidney Tarrow, *The New Transnational Activism*.

55. Shareen Hertel, *Unexpected Power*.

56. Hans Peter Schmitz, *Transnational Mobilization and Domestic Regime Change. Africa and Comparative Perspective* (Houndmills, UK: Palgrave Macmillan, 2006).

57. R. Charli Carpenter, "*Setting the Advocacy Agenda.*"

58. Margaret Keck and Kathryn Sikkink, *Activists Beyond Borders*, 19.

CHAPTER EIGHT

Rights and the Limits of Transnational Solidarity in Europe

LISA CONANT

EUROPEAN COURTS AND SOCIAL RIGHTS: A CASE OF U.S. JUDICIAL ACTIVISM OR SOCIAL DUMPING?

Courts contribute to the construction of citizenship by determining who enjoys rights to participate in a community. Carlos Ball credits the European Court of Justice (ECJ) with the creation of a transnational capitalist society in which rights to participate in the European Union's regional market generated broader rights to equal treatment, including access to domestic social benefits that foreign host states intended to reserve for their own nationals.[1] In this chapter, I explore how the evolution of social rights in two European legal venues is transforming the nature of solidarity and citizenship in Europe. I first argue that member states of the European Union (EU) and Council of Europe adopted legal texts that develop a *transnational civil citizenship* based on economic and civil rights. Second, I suggest that the ECJ and European Court of Human Rights (ECtHR) creatively interpreted EU law and the Convention for the Protection of Human Rights and Fundamental Freedoms (hereafter the convention) to expand entitlements to social rights, helping to forge a *transnational social citizenship* that provides protection to foreign residents and national citizens alike. Given that states historically avoided responsibility for the social protection of foreigners[2] and have used social benefits as a means to forge national citizenries,[3] the development of transnational social rights is a striking departure.

This judicial activism appears reminiscent of the Americanization of European politics associated with EU integration,[4] but the European social-rights case law is also rooted in commitments to solidarity that are uniquely European.[5] Yet because provisions for social citizenship originate in commitments to national solidarity and depend on domestic programs, efforts to extend them transnationally are contested and vulnerable to retrenchment. Welfare reforms in Europe suggest that states increasingly connect benefits to labor-market participation or vocational training, creating a system that parallels "workfare" in the United States.[6] Although a decline to U.S. standards seems unlikely, European social citizenship remains susceptible to conversion to a civil form of citizenship that reflects a move in the direction of the U.S. social model. The chapter proceeds as follows: in the next section, I develop a conceptual framework to distinguish between transnational civil and social citizenship and their corresponding rights. The subsequent section analyzes the content of EU and convention legal instruments to provide empirical support for the argument, and the final section compares European and U.S. developments.

CONCEPTUALIZING THE RIGHTS OF CIVIL AND SOCIAL CITIZENSHIP

When using the word "citizenship," I borrow from the German *staatsange-hörigkeit*, which means "belonging to a state," but I extend the boundaries to transnational communities such as the European Union or Council of Europe. The matter of who belongs to the community can be assessed in terms of who is allowed to participate in community life. Civil citizenship permits participation in civil society, including the market and other voluntary community associations. By contrast, political citizenship enables participation in the exercise of public authority, from which involuntary obligations may arise. Finally, social citizenship facilitates participation in social life, where human dignity requires access to the means of subsistence. Here I analyze the prospects for transnational civil and social citizenship in this broad sense and do not address political citizenship, which remains closely connected to nationality despite the advent of EU citizenship and its political rights.

The economic rights of contract and property are among the traditional civil rights that T. H. Marshall associated with the development of national citizenship.[7] Rights to participate in markets were once predicated largely on national membership, and the ability to engage in many economic activities remains closely associated with citizenship status. Along with the right of access to justice, economic rights are core components of transnational civil citizenship in Europe today. EU treaties and secondary legislation specify economic rights within a regional market. Meanwhile, the convention's cata-logue of human rights includes property rights as well as civil rights of an economic nature. With these rights, EU and convention law contribute to a transnational civil citizenship that expands the scope of individual freedom and opportunity.

The focus here is on social rights, however, by which I mean entitlements to resources that promote social welfare. Such resources provide for the means of subsistence. In the postwar era, these resources typically entail entitlements to education and cash payments in the event of misfortune. EU and Council of Europe legal instruments expand these entitlements by making them available to individuals who live or work in a foreign host country. The social rights that individuals gain through European institutions, therefore, depend on whether they migrate outside their home countries and where their migration takes them. As a result, European social rights manifest as a diverse set of benefits rather than any minimum common standard. Transnational citizenship is fragmented more generally, as well, because membership criteria vary across European institutions. All EU citizens benefit from the rights under the convention because all EU member states are signatories. Yet all that is required for entitlement to convention rights is personal presence in a signatory state. Transnational citizenship rights under the convention, therefore, extend beyond the universe of EU citizens. And although EU citizenship requires the nationality of an EU member state, the interpretation of European rights by the ECJ and ECtHR has generated rights for "third-country national" residents.

Two entitlements contribute to civil citizenship: social insurance and social investment, while a third entitlement, social assistance, comprises the foundation of social citizenship. Social insurance protects against particular risks, with eligibility dependent upon a status other than need. For example, being elderly, ill, disabled, involuntarily unemployed, pregnant, or the primary caregiver of dependents confers entitlement to benefits in the case of social insurance. Social investment involves resources that foster individual productivity, such as access to education and financial assistance associated with the costs of education. Social assistance, meanwhile, provides a minimum standard of living based on need. European welfare states typically determine eligibility for social insurance and investment in terms of either a history of contributions into the particular funds paying the benefits or the status of habitual resident, in which case residence implies tax contributions to general funds that finance benefits. By contrast, eligibility for social assistance typically relies on means testing and is usually contingent on national citizenship or long periods of residence. Social rights appear in legal instruments of both the European Union and Council of Europe. The treaties and regulations of the European Union and its predecessors generate the most explicit and extensive social rights for EU citizens and their family members. These EU rights overwhelmingly address entitlement to social insurance programs ("social security") and social investment programs ("social advantages"). Meanwhile, EU law explicitly excludes social assistance programs. By contrast, Article 2 of Protocol 1 is the only convention provision that explicitly confers a social right (to education). Another Council of Europe text, the Convention on Social and Medical Assistance (CSMA), specifies conditions of access to social assistance but does not provide for ECtHR jurisdiction. Despite these limits, the ECtHR has interpreted a number of convention provisions to confer social insurance and assistance entitlements.

Entitlements to social insurance and investment are strict tests of who belongs because they tell us whose welfare the community prioritizes. Entitlements to social assistance are the acid test of belonging because they indicate whose *survival* is guaranteed. The next sections illustrate that although EU and convention law has expanded all types of social entitlements, a bias toward social insurance and investment as well as contemporary welfare reforms suggest that the future of transnational citizenship in Europe is likely to be dominated by civil features.

PRODUCTION AND REPRODUCTION: EARNING SOCIAL PROTECTION IN EUROPE

Distinctions among different types of social rights in European legal texts reflect a limited form of solidarity. European judges have fortified transnational civil citizenship by actively enforcing rights in European treaties, legislation, and conventions; they have even expanded social rights beyond the intentions of their drafters to create the foundations for a nascent transnational social citizenship. In this section, however, I argue that European legislators have consistently championed "contractual" social rights that are closely linked to economic activity or traditional family relationships. These rights most often take the form of social insurance and investment for individuals who participate in the market and their dependent families. By contrast, social assistance that is based more exclusively on need either is omitted from European texts, explicitly excluded, or included in formally nonjusticiable texts. Individuals who contest their exclusion from poverty relief have found a more generous reception from European judges, who have restricted governments' ability to limit some forms of social assistance to nationals.[8] Furthermore, ECJ decisions extend rights to resident third-country nationals of countries with EU association and cooperation agreements,[9] and ECtHR decisions grant social rights universally, including to resident foreigners regardless of their national origin. Yet if social rights are separated according to their reliance on contract and need, European citizenship appears to be primarily civil in nature. Most social rights are corollaries of economic rights, and basic rights to a minimum standard of economic security are accessible to a very small set of individuals. To substantiate these claims, I examine EU and Council of Europe legal texts and the interpretation of these texts in ECJ and ECtHR case law.

Social Rights in European Treaties, Legislation, and Conventions

EU member states drafted regulations to place migrant economic activity at the center of entitlement to social rights. As a result, the primary strategy to achieve social rights through EU institutions involves labor as workers, entrepreneurs, or service providers. EU citizens "earn" entitlement to the full scope of benefits available under national social-insurance and investment programs. Council Regulation 1408/71 coordinates social-security systems, granting access to benefits regardless of the nationality or territorial restrictions member states impose.[10] Council Regulation 1612/68 also generates social rights by prohibiting discriminatory treatment of EU migrant workers and requiring that these migrants receive the same "social and tax advantages" granted to nationals.[11] These advantages include social insurance schemes such as pensions, social investment programs such as access to education, and tax incentives for particular behaviors such as raising children. Meanwhile, governments tried to avoid responsibility for poor migrants by denying access to social and medical assistance[12] and exempting a set of "special non-contributory benefits of mixed type" from the rules governing social security benefits.[13]

A secondary avenue to achieve EU social rights invokes family relationships: Spouses and dependent children or "ascending" relatives of EU citizens who have exercised their rights to movement are entitled to reside, work, and enjoy all social and tax advantages in host states.[14] Family members achieve EU rights regardless of their nationality as long as the EU citizen to whom they are related has crossed a national border within the European Union to work, establish a business, provide services, study, or reside. These benefits often entail important social rights because the states that attract the largest number of migrants typically have generous pronatalist benefits.[15]

By contrast, Council of Europe institutions provide either less explicit social rights or weaker mechanisms of enforcement. With the exception of the right to education, the convention's provisions generate no obvious social rights. The most likely implicit social right is Article 4 on the prohibition of forced labor, which could imply a right to maintenance in the absence of compulsion to work. Yet the exclusion of "any work or service which forms part of normal civic obligations" in the definition of compulsory labor does not encourage this interpretation.[16] Judicial creativity is responsible for the application of the following provisions to social benefit schemes: Article 14 prohibits discrimination on multiple grounds but makes no mention of social security. Article 1 of Protocol 1 to the convention provides for entitlement to the peaceful enjoyment of possessions but does not define possessions. Article 8 declares that everyone has the right to respect for private and family life but does not specify what such respect entails. Article 6 guarantees a fair and timely trial for the determination of civil rights but does not define what falls under the scope of civil rights. Meanwhile, like EU social security legislation, the European Council's Convention on Social and Medical Assistance (CSMA) precisely specifies rules of access to social and medical assistance. It protects nationals of signatory states from expulsion after they become dependent on assistance in a "host" state (Article 6) if they have been resident for at least five years, if they entered before age fifty-five or for at least ten years if they entered after age fifty-five, if they are not in a fit state of health to travel, or if they have close ties to the territory in which they reside (Article 7).[17] Signatory states limited their responsibility for poor Europeans, however, by allowing their deportation in other circumstances and failing to provide for judicial enforcement.

Because the CSMA protects long-term residents from expulsion, a subsidiary strategy to gain social rights relies on the intersection of EU and Council of Europe institutions. EU legislation creates positive rights to residence for certain categories of individuals, and Articles 6 and 7 of the CSMA entitle long-term resident aliens to social assistance. Together, these provisions enable individuals to circumvent restrictions that exclude foreigners from social assistance benefits that states never intended to coordinate. Stringent qualifying criteria for both sets of provisions, however, interact to limit the population that will successfully attain benefits.

The original EU directives guaranteed a right of residence only to employed or self-employed EU nationals and their families.[18] Normally valid for five years, residence permits may not be withdrawn due to temporary disability or unemployment.[19] The second wave of EU directives provided economically active EU migrants and their families with a permanent right to reside if employment caused death or permanent incapacity to work or if continuous periods of work and residence totaled two (nonoccupational disability or death) to three years (ongoing residence or retirement). Meanwhile, marriage to a national of the host state exempts migrants from time requirements.[20] The post-Maastricht wave of EU directives grants residence rights to EU citizens and their families as long as they are financially independent: All must be "covered by sickness insurance in respect of all risks in the host Member State and have sufficient resources to avoid becoming a burden on the social assistance system of the host Member State during their period of residence." States can readily control for insufficient means because they may require revalidation of "five year" residence permits after two years for economically inactive migrants, and students may be granted residence permits of only one year.[21] An impoverished EU citizen could be required to leave a host state after one or two years, therefore, whereas an impoverished worker or entrepreneur could stay for the full five years of a typical residence permit for the economically active.

Five years of residence is significant, because Article 7 of the CSMA prevents states from repatriating foreigners who become dependent on social assistance if they have lived in the host state for at least five years. This protection is important because states deny the renewal of residence permits for those dependent on social assistance.[22] EU legislation confers no explicit access to social assistance for poor migrants, and none of its minimum requirements to reside permanently qualifies individuals for social assistance under the CSMA. It is only in the intersection of EU and CSMA rights that individuals can acquire rights to move, reside, and subsist in a host state.

Social Rights in the Case Law of the ECJ and ECtHR

The priority given to contractual social rights in EU law and Council of Europe conventions facilitates enforcement of access to social insurance and investment rather than assistance. Consequently, the overwhelming majority of European litigation that addresses social rights involves claims to social insurance and investment by "productive" individuals (see Table 8.1, next page). Meanwhile, successful social assistance claims typically remain connected to conceptions of social insurance or investment rather than to a minimum standard of living. Reproduction and child rearing are increasingly recognized alongside paid labor as contributions deserving of protection, but primarily within the confines of traditional family structures. Disputes reflect a strident effort to minimize responsibility for poverty with transnational roots. This section will address the social assistance case law of the ECJ and ECtHR, privileges associated with traditional family relationships, and likely European legal viability of welfare retrenchment that makes benefits contingent on economic activity.

The ECJ has limited its extensions of social assistance to individuals who have at least some work history or family connection to the host state. In three early disputes, the ECJ denounced the five-year residence requirement for entitlement to social assistance as nationality discrimination when it applied to EU migrant workers, but not to nationals of the relevant state. The EU migrants in question had either exhausted unemployment benefits[23] or worked an insufficient number of hours to support themselves,[24] but all had exercised their right to free movement as workers. By contrast, the ECJ decided that the adult children of migrant workers remaining in the host state had no entitlement to equal treatment to social advantages, and hence to social assistance, if the advantage would not benefit the parent directly.[25] The children of migrant workers who remain in host states but fail to naturalize, therefore, face a heightened risk of indigence in the wake of prolonged dependence.

In more recent cases invoking EU citizenship, the ECJ has relaxed the requirement that individuals "not be a burden on the social assistance system" of a host state. The ECJ denounced Italian requirements to prove that students have sufficient resources as a violation of EU law, which demands only that

Table 8.1. European Social Rights Litigation by Legal Basis and Court

Legal Basis	ECJ	ECtHR
EU social security regulations and residence directives	486	No jurisdiction
Social-assistance disputes invoking EU treaty articles and legislation	51	No jurisdiction
Convention on Social and Medical Assistance	2	0
Convention for the Protection of Human Rights and Fundamental Freedoms	No jurisdiction	
Article 2 of Protocol 1 (Education)		20
Article 4 (Forced labor)		5
Article 14 and Article 1 of Protocol 1 (Discrimination and property)		47
Articles 14 and 8 (Discrimination and family life)		65
Article 6, paragraph 1 (Civil rights)		4,404
Social-insurance disputes invoking Articles 14 and 1 of Protocol 1		20
Social-assistance disputes invoking Articles 14 and 1 of Protocol 1		8
Social-insurance disputes invoking Articles 14 and 8		5
Social-insurance disputes invoking Article 6, paragraph 1		123
Social-assistance disputes invoking Article 6, paragraph 1		28

Data denote judgments of the European Court of Justice and European Court of Human Rights on the following legal bases: (1) Council Regulations 1612/68, 1408/71, 1247/92; Council Directives 364/90/EEC, 365/90/EEC, 93/96/EEC; European Parliament and Council Directive 2004/58/EC; Articles 42 EC (51 of the EC treaty), 17 EC (8 of the EC treaty), 18 EC (8a of the EC treaty); (2) Convention on Social and Medical Assistance; (3) the Convention articles specified above. Sources: Lexis searches on ECJ case law on 11 August 2006; HUDOC searches on 14 August 2006 using the HUDOC DVD and online search engines for cases until 31 December 2005. Additional search terms (social assistance, minimum subsistence, minimum w/3 subsistence) were used to identify social-assistance disputes before the ECJ. Additional search terms (social security or insurance, welfare and benefit* or assistance, and child benefit*) were used to identify social-insurance and assistance disputes before the ECtHR.

students declare sufficient resources.[26] The ECJ went on to entitle a migrant EU university student in his final year of study to social assistance in Belgium on the grounds that he had already supported himself in previous years of study and was unlikely to collect social assistance for long.[27] The ECJ also granted entitlement to subsidized loans and maintenance grants to a migrant EU student in the United Kingdom on the grounds that he had fulfilled the same three-year residence requirement as nationals.[28] Furthermore, the ECJ required Belgium to grant job seekers' allowances to graduates who completed their studies in other member states if the graduate was either a child of resident migrant workers or nationals.[29] In these cases, family relationships or completion of a program of study played a key role in gaining access to a benefit for individuals who had not yet entered the labor market. By contrast, the ECJ allowed the United Kingdom to deny its job seekers allowance to an unemployed individual who arrived without resident parents or a recent diploma.[30] Finally, the ECJ held that states could not withhold social assistance from EU citizens participating in reintegration programs for the indigent as long as the applicant held a residence permit or engaged in any "real and genuine" paid activity.[31] These cases indicate that the ECJ is fairly generous in granting social assistance when productive activity is likely to be imminent. Meanwhile, the ECJ has used the lack of dependence on social assistance as grounds to defend residence rights for the European Union and third-country national parents of resident children when states have wanted to expel individuals or families, suggesting that dependence on social assistance can be used to justify expulsion if future economic activity is unlikely.[32]

Revision of residence rights in the most recent directive reflects a less-than-enthusiastic response of states to this case law. Although the new directive acknowledges that recourse to social assistance cannot automatically result in expulsion, it also absolves states of any responsibility to pay assistance during the first three months of residence or the potentially longer period in which a new migrant seeks employment, and it removes obligations to grant maintenance aid for studies prior to the acquisition of permanent residence rights. In determining whether a claim poses an unreasonable burden on the social assistance system, the preamble indicates that states should consider claims in light of personal circumstances, the duration of residence, and the likelihood that need is temporary.[33] The legislative specification of reasonable burdens eliminates the possibility of social assistance for newcomers, therefore, and suggests that states are responsible only for the short-term needs of foreigners.

The ECJ also used the concept of EU citizenship to expand access to social insurance for parents moving across borders within the EU, but only if they are taking parental leaves from paid employment or are members of traditional families. In *Elsen and Kauer*, the ECJ required states to treat employment leaves devoted to child rearing in other member states in a nondiscriminatory manner when calculating contributions to old-age insurance.[34] When pursued as an interruption of a career, therefore, transnational child rearing receives the same remuneration as national child rearing. By contrast, the ECJ required a Spanish mother who was dependent on social assistance in Germany to be either a worker under EU law or the spouse of a worker in order to qualify for a child-raising allowance.[35] This dispute suggests that Germans prioritize the primary parent child rearing of their own nationals: this is a *child-raising* benefit not available to a parent who is employed full time rather than a child benefit available to a parent regardless of employment status. Moreover, German parents qualify for the allowance on the grounds of nationality, regardless of dependence on social assistance, but EU national parents qualify only if one or both enjoy the status of "worker" under EU law. As a result, only EU citizens exercising economic rights, or those married to EU citizens exercising economic rights, can enjoy the full range of social rights within Germany.

Dissolving family relationships also poses unique risks for transnationally mobile individuals. In *Kuchlenz-Winter*, the European Union's Court of First Instance (CFI) denied an extension of the European Union's Common Sickness Insurance Scheme to a German national on the grounds that she could not claim rights to her ex-husband's insurance even though her (national) divorce settlement entitled her to half of his pension. Kuchlenz-Winter sought the transnationally valid EU health insurance because she was resident in Luxembourg but wanted to return to Germany, where she would be denied health insurance given her lack of history of work and residence there. Because she required medical care, it would be impossible for her to return to Germany if she lacked health insurance.[36] Children of divorce fare better, however, as the ECJ ruled that public advances on child support payments constitute family benefits and therefore must be provided by a host state to the children of resident EU citizens on the same condition as national citizens; that is, when the responsible parent failed to meet his or her obligations.[37] The distinction in treatment of the divorced elderly spouse and dependent children is consistent with an approach emphasizing investment in the future rather than a broader concern for rights to minimum standards of protection.

Entitlements to EU social rights, therefore, usually reflect an effort to limit rights to those who have exercised economic rights and their "traditional" families. Access to the more generous social security regimes is predicated on the status of a worker (or dependent spouse or child), and access to the more meager and often stigmatizing social assistance is predicated on a long period of individual self-sufficiency or familial dependence. Gaining access to both will pose challenges to the transnationally mobile that nationals do not face. This environment reflects little transnational solidarity.

Meanwhile, the ECtHR has expanded social rights entitlements for individuals whose circumstances fall outside the confines of EU law.[38] ECtHR case law has contributed most dramatically by eradicating EU legal distinctions between EU citizens, associated third-country nationals, and all other foreigners, as well as between social insurance and assistance. Using Article 14's general prohibition against discrimination based on national origin, the ECtHR grants rights to resident foreigners that EU law denies on the ground that they are neither EU (or associated third-country) nationals nor the family members of migrant EU workers. Discrimination claims under Article 14 must be linked with another convention right, however, and foreign residents have invoked Article 1 of Protocol 1 or Article 8 in conjunction with Article 14 to challenge denials of benefits. Yet states remain free to reduce burdens by eliminating or reforming benefit schemes, and ECtHR case law on Article 4 suggests that reforms that link benefits to work will remain viable.

In a pioneering case, the ECtHR held that Austria could not deny an emergency-assistance benefit to an unemployed Turkish national on the grounds that he did not have Austrian nationality. The Austrians claimed that entitlement was based on need and did not automatically result from the Turkish applicant's payment of contributions into an unemployment fund, and that states could legitimately discriminate against foreign claimants because the "State has special responsibility for its own nationals and must take care of them and provide for their essential needs."[39] Observing that entitlement to this benefit was linked to the exhaustion of unemployment benefits, for which entitlement was based on contributions to a fund, the ECtHR decided that the benefit constituted a possession under Article 1 of Protocol 1.[40] Given the emphasis on the history of work and contribution to unemployment funds, this finding expanded third-country nationals' rights to social insurance programs. Although Turkish nationals could rely on association agreements to gain entitlements to similar benefits in the European Union,[41] this dispute began before Austria was an EU member, and it circumvents EU restrictions by applying universally to all foreigners in all Council of Europe states.

In two recent cases, the ECtHR interpreted Article 8 in conjunction with Article 14 to grant German child benefits to Polish nationals. Denied child benefits because they held "limited residence titles" prior to Poland's EU membership, the immigrants claimed discrimination in the exercise of their rights to respect for family life.[42] A German social court responded that the "legislature had only intended to grant child benefits to aliens who were likely to stay in Germany on a permanent basis."[43] In its defense before the ECtHR, the German government argued that child benefits did not fall under Article 8 of the convention because the "State's general obligation to promote family life did not give rise to concrete rights to specific payments."[44] Countering that states demonstrate respect for family life by granting child benefits, the ECtHR concluded that child benefits fall under the scope of Article 8 and rejected the government's discrimination between aliens who possessed stable residence permits and those who did not. By taking this position, the ECtHR echoed the Federal Constitutional Court (FCC), which ruled that treating parents differently according to the permanence of their residence permit lacked sufficient justification. The two claims continued on to the ECtHR, however, because domestic proceedings had terminated prior to the constitutional ruling for one applicant,[45] and new legislation had not yet been passed to resolve the violation for the applicants whose case had reached the FCC.[46] Once again, the ECtHR expanded transnational social rights universally to resident foreigners across most of Europe.

The ECtHR moved beyond social insurance and granted a social assistance benefit to a foreign resident on the basis of Article 1 of Protocol 1 and Article 14. An Ivory Coast national, Koua Poirrez, contested France's refusal to award him an allowance for disabled adults on the grounds that he was neither a French national nor a national of a country with a reciprocity agreement. Disabled since childhood, Koua Poirrez was adopted by a French national at the age of twenty-one, too old to naturalize. His claim for entitlement to the benefit had failed at the ECJ because his adoptive French father had never exercised his rights to free movement, which would have guaranteed any third-country family members equal access to "social advantages" such as the disability benefit.[47] In response to Poirrez's claims before the ECtHR, the French government argued that the right of property did not include non-contributory benefits that took the form of assistance. The ECtHR responded that, although it previously had decided that contributions to a fund entitled an individual to benefits, it did not mean that a noncontributory social benefit such as the disability allowance did not also give rise to pecuniary rights.[48] Once again, the ECtHR was able to exploit domestic law to justify its decision against France: The government had abolished the nationality condition in 1998 and begun to pay it out that year (but was refusing to pay it for the period before this reform), and the Court of Cassation had ruled that a refusal to grant a similar type of assistance on the grounds of nationality violated Article 14 in conjunction with Article 1 of Protocol 1.[49]

Although France was forced only to apply a policy retroactively that it already had accepted, the principle that resident foreigners can rely on Article 1 of Protocol 1 to claim a pecuniary right to social assistance is an advance over the existing level of protection. The ECtHR refused to recognize the distinctions between social insurance and social assistance that national governments had taken great pains to make in EU and Council of Europe legal instruments. And, unlike the ECJ's case law, the ECtHR decision granted access to a benefit to an individual who probably never did or will participate actively in the labor market.

In subsequent case law, the ECtHR bolstered the position that both contributory and noncontributory social benefits can give rise to pecuniary rights under Article 1 of Protocol 1. The ECtHR clarified the meaning of a possession in 2005, resolving inconsistencies and ambiguities with regard to noncontributory welfare benefits. Previously, the now-defunct European Commission of Human Rights and the ECtHR had concluded that a social benefit fell under the scope of Article 1 of Protocol 1 only when an individual contributed to the funds that financed the benefit.[50] In earlier disputes, the Council of Europe had observed that Article 1 of Protocol 1 did not confer any rights to receive social benefits, but that the making of compulsory contributions might create a right where there was a link between the level of contributions and benefits awarded.[51] The U.K. government accepted this line of decisions, arguing that proprietary claims to state benefits should be limited to those contributory benefits for which "the individual had, in effect, paid for the benefits."[52] Meanwhile, the ECtHR also had concluded that noncontributory social benefits could constitute a possession for the purposes of Article 1 of Protocol 1.[53] In disagreement with this case law, the U.K. government submitted that "the Convention and Protocol No. 1 were concerned with civil and political, rather than social and economic, rights."[54]

The ECtHR's reexamination of this issue brought noncontributory benefits solidly under the protection of the convention and its property rights provision. In the interest of coherence, the ECtHR interpreted the concept of possessions in Article 1 or Protocol 1 to be consistent with the evolution of its interpretation of the concept of pecuniary rights under Article 6, paragraph 1. Case law on the applicability of this provision also originally limited claims for "the determination of civil rights" to contributory benefit schemes because of their economic nature and similarity to private insurance.[55] Yet the ECtHR later decided that Article 6, paragraph 1 did apply to disputes about entitlements to noncontributory welfare benefits, abandoning comparisons with private insurance and any requirement of a "contract" between the individual and the state. Instead, the individual had an assertable right to social benefits.[56] By this time, the ECtHR concluded that equal treatment required the application of Article 6, paragraph 1 in the fields of social insurance and welfare assistance.[57] The ECtHR cited the U.K.'s Lord Hoffmann to support its position that the variety of funding methods, interlocking nature of welfare benefits, and contributions individual taxpayers make to benefits paid from general taxation render distinctions between contributory and noncontributory social benefits artificial.[58] Going on to assert a bold social right, the ECtHR concluded that, "in the modern, democratic State, many individuals are, for all or part of their lives, completely dependent for survival on social security and welfare benefits. Many domestic legal systems recognize that such individuals require a degree of certainty and security, and provide for benefits to be paid—subject to the fulfillment of the conditions of eligibility—as of right."[59]

This entitlement to social assistance via the convention, however, is limited by the subsidiary nature of all European social rights. The ECtHR recognizes that Article 1 of Protocol 1 creates no right to acquire property and therefore places no restriction on states' freedom to provide social benefits or determine the type or amount of benefits. The convention offers no right to receive social benefits, but once a state does offer benefits, it must do so in a manner that is nondiscriminatory.[60] Meanwhile, it remains unlikely that claims to maintenance in the absence of some compulsion to work will be successful given the current case law concerning Article 4 on forced labor. The ECtHR has found the following labor obligations to be compatible with the notion of "work or service, which forms part of normal civic obligations:" States may require individuals convicted of theft or vagrancy to earn a sufficient income from poorly paid prison labor before they are released,[61] lawyers to perform unpaid legal aid services,[62] and citizens to perform public service.[63] Given this approach to "normal civic obligations," policies that link social protections to some type of work probably will remain unchallenged.

THE TRIUMPH OF CIVIL CITIZENSHIP AND THE LIMITS OF EUROPEAN SOLIDARITY

EU law and the Council of Europe's convention promote a transnational civil citizenship in which social rights are primarily corollaries of economic rights. The main indicator of this is that most entitlements to European social protection entail social insurance and investment systems designed to reward productivity rather than social assistance programs intended to alleviate poverty. The European courts have pushed the limits of these texts to expand transnational entitlements to social assistance, but it remains possible for states to reassert their emphasis on productivity as the solution to poverty. As a result, although European courts prohibit the unequal treatment of nationals and foreigners, states and employers may construct increasingly varied forms of social protection based on differences in economic activity. This trend threatens the connection between citizenship and social protection that distinguished most of Western Europe from the United States during the postwar era.

    The United States promoted federal-scale social citizenship decades ago by allowing the indigent to move freely,[64] but the right to collect benefits upon entry coincided with a comparatively less generous system of welfare provision that no longer includes stable rights for anyone. Unlike Europe, the contemporary United States displays no commitment to social citizenship. Since the Personal Responsibility and Work Opportunity Reconciliation Act of 1996 replaced "Aid to Families with Dependent Children" with "Temporary Assistance to Needy Families" (TANF), the United States has abandoned any conception that a minimum standard of living is a right of citizenship. Content to allow individuals who exhaust the five-year lifetime limit on assistance to rely on family, local charity, or life on the streets, the United States has reverted to nineteenth-century standards of social protection that revive the prospect of being left to die in the gutter.[65] The contingency of U.S. social rights on economic activity is so strong that Gwendolyn Mink considers the coerced labor of TANF to fall under the Supreme Court's definition of involuntary servitude.[66] By contrast, commitments to social citizenship persist in Europe. Welfare programs in Europe do not impose strict deadlines to achieve economic self-sufficiency or prioritize a reduction in the welfare rolls as the primary indicator of success. Instead, Europeans focus on vocational training and investment in other social services that enable individuals to balance work and family responsibilities.[67]

Comparatively low U.S. public spending for all social programs is often contrasted with the more generous European welfare states, but U.S. exceptionalism in social policy is exaggerated. Jacob Hacker has demonstrated that what is unusual about U.S. social spending is not its level, but its source. Much of the U.S. welfare regime operates through private spending by employers rather than by public spending by the state. When public and private social spending are combined, the United States no longer appears to be an outlier among advanced industrial democracies. Yet private provision usually confers benefits only on the economically active and their families through employment contracts. Far from being universal in nature, the quality of social insurance varies: Higher-income individuals usually receive more comprehensive coverage,[68] and entitlement to benefits is increasingly contingent on obligations to work or pursue training in both the United States and states of western Europe. National reforms in most wealthy European states are linking social rights to "activity." Joel Handler argues that the "active labor market policies" and strategies for "social inclusion" being adopted throughout Europe are similar to U.S. "workfare" in the sense that they push work and training initiatives for social assistance recipients. Although the conditionality of these programs does not impose U.S.-style deadlines, they tie rights to obligations in a contractual manner. Income security becomes based on laboring status rather than on citizenship itself.[69] The linkage of most EU social rights to productive aims renders transnational social citizenship shallower than its traditional national equivalents. In the case of social assistance, governments have helped their own nationals simply because they needed it. Also, governments provide social insurance benefits to qualified nationals who are also dependent on social assistance but resist this extension of benefits to resident foreign nationals who collect social assistance. Even foreign residents who pay the five- to ten-year cover charge for social assistance, therefore, are not fully integrated into the host's system of social protection.

Even though public social insurance remains quite comprehensive and redistributive in Europe, further contemporary trends in social insurance threaten universal provision based on national citizenship. At the same time that states have begun to tie benefits more closely to labor market participation, a privatization of social provision has emerged through the proliferation of occupational, company-linked pensions and supplemental private life and health insurances.[70] Social policy analysts associate this trend with a privatization of risk and the erosion of support for more universal protection.[71] Rendering social rights dependent on economic rights, particularly in the competitive environment of transnational arenas, threatens universal social protection.[72] Given rising unemployment levels in much of western Europe and the decline of traditional families, more individuals could find themselves falling outside conventional social safety nets based on employment and family relationships.[73]

As a result, Europe may be inching toward the condition of the United States, where the economically active who are least in need of social protection are actually best insured. In a world of increased mobility, some scholars argue that contractual forms of social rights based on contribution may be the only legitimate means to extend social protections to the immigrants and resident aliens who constitute a substantial segment of the population.[74] To the extent that European courts prohibit differential treatment between nationals and foreigners, all may become subject to the contractual demands of transnational civil citizenship.

NOTES

1. Carlos Ball, "The Making of a Transnational Capitalist Society," *Harvard International Law Journal* 37 (1996): 307–388.

2. Rogers Brubaker, *Citizenship and Nationhood in France and Germany* (Cambridge: Harvard University Press, 1992).

3. Stephan Leibfried, "The Social Dimension of the European Union," *Journal of European Social Policy* 4 (1994): 239–262; Laura Jensen, *Patriots, Settlers, and the Origins of American Social Policy* (New York: Cambridge University Press, 2003).

4. R. Daniel Kelemen, "Suing for Europe," *Comparative Political Studies* 39 (2006): 101–127; R. Daniel Kelemen and Eric Sibbitt, "The Globalization of American Law," *International Organization* 58 (2004): 103–136.

5. Robert Kagan, "Globalization and Legal Change" (paper presented at the annual meeting of the American Political Science Association, Philadelphia, August 31–September 3, 2006).

6. Joel Handler, *Social Citizenship and Workfare in the United States and Western Europe* (Cambridge: Cambridge University Press, 2004).

7. T. H. Marshall and T. Bottomore, *Citizenship and Social Class* (London: Pluto Classic, 1996).

8. Lisa Conant, "Individuals, Courts, and the Development of European Social Rights," *Comparative Political Studies* 39 (2006): 76–100.

9. Lisa Conant, *Justice Contained* (Ithaca: Cornell University Press, 2002); Lisa Conant, "Contested Boundaries," in *Boundaries and Belonging*, ed. Joel Migdal (New York: Cambridge University Press, 2004): 284–317.

10. Council Regulation 1408/71, "Application of Social Security Schemes," *Official Journal of the European Communities (OJ)* II (1971), 416.

11. Council Regulation 1612/68, "Freedom of Movement for Workers," *OJ* II (1968), 475, Article 7, para. 2.

12. Council Regulation 1408/71, Article 10, para. 4.

13. Council Regulation 1247/92, "Amending Regulation 1408/71," *OJ* L 136 (June 1992), 1–6.

14. Council Regulation 1612/68.

15. Conant, 2002, Tables 7.4 and 7.5.

16. *Convention for the Protection of Human Rights and Fundamental Freedoms*, as amended by Protocol No. 11 (November 4, 1950). Rome.

17. *Convention on Social and Medical Assistance* (December 11, 1953), Paris.

18. Council Directive 221/64, "Co-ordination of Special Measures Concerning the Movement and Residence of Foreign Nationals," *OJ* P 56 (1964), 850–857.

19. Council Directive 360/68, "Abolition of Restrictions on Movement and Residence," *OJ* L 257 (1968), 13–16.

20. Commission Regulation 1251/70, "Right of Workers to Remain," *Official Journal of the European Communities (OJ)* L 142 (1970), 24–26; Council Directive 34/75, "Right of Nationals of a Member State to Remain," *OJ* L 14 (1975), 10–13.

21. Council Directive 364/90, "Right of Residence," *OJ* L 180 (1990), 26–27; Council Directive 365/90, "Right of Residence for Persons who Ceased their Occupational Activity," *OJ* L 180 (1990), 28–29; Council Directive 96/93, "Right of Residence for Students," *OJ* L 317 (1993), 59–60.

22. Virginie Guiraudon, "The Marshallian Triptych Re-ordered," Working paper EUF no. 99/1 (San Domenico di Fiesole: European University Institute, 1999); Olaf Köppe, "The Leviathan of Competitiveness," *Journal of Ethnic and Migration Studies* 29 (2003): 431–448.

23. European Court of Justice (ECJ), *Vera Hoeckx*, Case C–249/83 (1985): European Court Reports (ECR) 973; ECJ, *Scrivner*, Case C–122/84 (1985): ECR 1027.

24. ECJ, *Kempf*, Case C–0139/85 (1986): ECR 1741.

25. ECJ, *Lebon*, Case C–216/85 (1987): ECR 2811.

26. ECJ, *Commission v. Italy*, Case C–424/98 (2000): ECR I–4001.

27. ECJ, *Grzelczyk*, Case C–184/99 (2001): ECR I–6193.

28. ECJ, *Bidar*, Case C–209/03 (2005): ECR1–2119.

29. ECJ, *Commission v. Belgium*, Case C–278/94 (1996): ECR I–4307; ECJ, *D'Hoop*, Case C–224/98 (2002): ECR I–6191.

30. ECJ, *Collins*, Case C–138/02 (2004): ECR1–2703.

31. ECJ, *Trojani*, Case C–456–02 (2004): ECR1–07573

32. ECJ, *Baumbast & R*, Case C–413/99 (2002): ECR I–7901; ECJ, *Zhu & Chen*, Case C–200/02 (2004): ECR1–9925.

33. European Parliament and Council Directive 2004/58/EC, "Right of Citizens of the Union and Their Family Members to Move and Reside Freely," *OJ* L 229 (2004), 35–48.

34. ECJ, *Ursula Elsen*, Case C–135/99 (2000): ECR I–10409; ECJ, *Lieselotte Kauer*, Case C–28/00 (2002) ECR: I–1343.

35. ECJ, *Sala*, Case C–85/96 (1998): ECR I–2691.

36. Court of First Instance (CFI), *Hedwig Kuchlenz-Winter*, Case T–66/95 (1997): ECR II–637.

37. ECJ, *Offermanns & Offermanns*, Case C–85/99 (2001): ECR I–2261.

38. Conant, 2006.

39. European Court of Human Rights (ECtHR), *Gaygusuz v. Austria*, Application no. 17371/90 (1996).

40. ECtHR 1996, paras. 39–41.

41. Conant, 2002 and 2004.

42. ECtHR, *Niedzwiecki v. Germany*, Application no. 58453/00 (2005); ECtHR, *Okpisz v. Germany*, Application no. 59140/00 (2005).

43. ECtHR 2005, *Niedzwiecki*, para. 15.

44. ECtHR 2005, *Niedzwiecki*, para. 27.

45. ECtHR 2005, *Niedzwiecki*.

46. ECtHR 2005, *Okpisz,* paras. 15–16, 25.

47. ECJ, *Koua Poirrez*. Case 206/91 (1992): ECR I-6685.

48. ECtHR, *Koua Poirrez v. France*, Application no. 40892/98 (2003), para. 37.

49. ECtHR 2003, *Koua Poirrez*, paras. 40 and 48.

50. European Commission, *Szrabjet and Clarke v. the United Kingdom*, Application nos. 27004/95 and 27011/95 (1997); European Commission, *Carlin v. the United Kingdom*, Application no. 27537/95 (1997); European Commission, *Coke and others v. the United Kingdom*, Application no. 38696/97 (1999); ECtHR, *Admissibility Decision: Stawicki v. Poland*, Application no. 47711/99 (2000); ECtHR, *Admissibility Decision: Jankovic v. Croatia*, Application no. 43440/98 (2000); ECtHR, *Admissibility Decision: Kohls v. Germany*, Application no. 72719/01 (2003); ECtHR, *Kjartan Asmundsson v. Iceland*, Application no. 60669/00 (2004).

51. European Commission, *Müller v. Austria*, Application no. 5849/72 (1975); European Commission, *G v. Austria*, Application no. 10094/82 (1984); European Commission, *De Kleine Staarman v. the Netherlands*, Application no. 10503/83 (1985).

52. ECtHR, *Grand Chamber Admissibility Decision: Stec and Others v. the United Kingdom*, Application nos. 65731/01 and 65900/01 (2005), para. 34.

53. ECtHR, *Buchen v. Czech Republic,* Application no. 36541/97 (2002); ECtHR, *Wessels-Bergevoet v. Netherlands*, Application no. 34462/97 (2002); ECtHR 2003, *Koua Poirrez*; ECtHR, *Van den Bouwhuijsen and Schuring v. the Netherlands*, Application no. 34462/97 (2003).

54. ECtHR 2005, *Stec* Admissibility, para. 34.

55. ECtHR, *Feldbrugge v. the Netherlands,* Application no. 8562/79 (1986); ECHR, *Deumeland v. Germany*, Application no. 9384/81 (1986).

56. ECtHR, *Salesi v. Italy*, Application no. 13023/87 (1993).

57. ECtHR, *Schuler-Zgraggen v. Switzerland*, Application no. 14518/89 (1993).

58. ECtHR 2005, *Stec* Admissibility, paras. 50 and 21.

59. ECtHR 2005, *Stec* Admissibility, para. 51.

60. ECtHR 2005, *Stec* Admissibility, paras. 54 and 55. Although this dispute concerned sex discrimination claims and the final judgment was not favorable to the applicants (ECtHR, *Stec and Others v. the United Kingdom*, Application nos. 65731/01 and 65900/01 [2006]), the admissibility decision boldly develops interpretive principles related to property rights and their relationship to social assistance and discrimination based on Article 14.

61. ECtHR, *De Wilde, et al. v. Belgium*, Application nos. 2832/66, 2835/66, 2899/66 (1971); ECtHR, *Van Droogenbroeck v. Belgium*, Application no. 7906/77 (1982).

62. ECtHR, *Van der Mussele v. Belgium*, Application no. 8919/80 (1983).

63. ECtHR, *Karlheinz Schmidt v. Germany*, Application no.13580/88 (1994).

64. U.S. Supreme Court, *Shapiro v. Thompson* 394 US 618 (1969).

65. W. G. Sumner, *What Social Classes Owe to Each Other* (New York: Harper & Brothers, 1883).

66. Gwendolyn Mink, *Welfare's End* (Ithaca: Cornell University Press, 1998) (Rev. paperback edition, 2002).

67. Jonah Levy, "Progressive Approaches to Labor Market Activation" (paper presented at the annual meeting of the American Political Science Association, August 31–September 4, 2005, Washington D.C.).

68. Jacob Hacker, *The Divided Welfare State* (New York: Cambridge University Press, 2002).

69. Handler 2004.

70. Martin Rhodes, "A New Social Contract?" Working paper RSC 96/43 (San Domenico di Fiesole: European University Institute, 1996), 20–21.

71. Jacob Hacker, "Privatizing Risk Without Privatizing the Welfare State," *American Political Science Review* 98 (2004): 243–260; B. Jordan, "A New Social Contract?" Working Paper RSC 96/47 (San Domenico di Fiesole: European University Institute, 1996).

72. C. Closa, "A New Social Contract?" Working paper RSC 96/48 (San Domenico di Fiesole: European University Institute, 1996); Rhodes 1996; M. La Torre, "Citizenship and Social Rights," Working paper EUF 98/2 (San Domenico di Fiesole: European University Institute, 1998).

73. Rhodes 1996; Y. Kazepov, "Citizenship and Poverty," Working paper EUF 98/1 (San Domenico di Fiesole: European University Institute, 1998).

74. Ewald Engelen, "How to Combine Openness and Protection?" *Politics & Society* 31 (2003): 503–536.

CHAPTER NINE

International Imposition and Transmission of Democracy and the Rule of Law

Lessons from Central America

RACHEL BOWEN

Guatemala and Nicaragua both have struggled to achieve the rule of law within an internationalized context. Because of their acceptance of rule-of-law aid from international donor groups, they cannot readily escape from international directives from their benefactors. These international directives are informed by international norms of the rule of law. In order to understand the adoption of the rule of law in practice by a country, we must first understand the rule of law as a set of norms, how they are adopted, and how they spread. These norms guide international actors with diverse goals but have a common core of understanding involving equality and rights protection. The rule of law is transmitted internationally through the coordinated efforts of domestic and international actors who put pressure on a country to comply with its norms. Without such pressures, countries are unlikely to adopt the rule of law. However, they are also unlikely to commit seriously to the rule of law when faced solely with international pressure without also facing domestic pressure. Guatemala is an example of a country with domestic activists who have worked closely both with the judiciary and with international actors. Nicaragua's domestic activists have been much less networked than have Guatemala's and much less committed to the rule of law.

I argue that the rule of law is only possible after a state has made a profound moral commitment to the norm of the rule of law, to which it is propelled by the actions of domestic and international activists. This chapter gives consideration to the international movement in support of the rule of law. In so doing, I consider both global trends in the adoption of the norm of the rule of law as well as domestic progress within both Guatemala and Nicaragua. The first section of this chapter addresses the spread of one norm of the rule of law: the trend toward the judicialization of politics around the world. The second section examines the international transmission of norms in general, using the literature on human rights norms as its guide. The final two sections catalogue the adoption of the norm of the rule of law in Guatemala and Nicaragua, following a spiral model adopted from the human rights context.

THE GLOBAL SPREAD OF THE JUDICIALIZATION OF POLITICS

There has been an expansion of judicial power in many countries, which is related to the global spread of the rule of law. Many judiciaries have begun in recent years to turn their attention toward an expanding sphere of influence, including the confrontation of political issues. We see this in high-profile conflicts of judges with executives and in the exercise of more regulatory power by judges. We also see it in countries as diverse as Italy and Namibia, suggesting that a truly global phenomenon is afoot. There is a small body of literature that focuses on this trend. This section outlines the literature on the judicialization of politics and then places it in the context of a norm of the rule of law. The trend of the judicialization of politics is truly widespread.[1] The weakness of this literature is shown in its failure to provide an explanation for how this trend has moved from country to country and why it seems to be gathering steam.

Tate and Vallinder[2] take up the issue of the judicialization of politics or the "global expansion of judicial power." Vallinder[3] defines the judicialization of politics as either the expansion of the province of courts into areas of politics that were previously not their province or the spread of judicial decision-making methods to nonjudicial political processes. In short, "judicialization essentially involves turning something into a form of judicial process."[4] This expansion of judicial power reflects a global movement toward the rule of law. Judicialization is an important mechanism by which one part of the state (the courts) begins to enforce the rule of law as against everyone in society, as well as other parts of the state. The expansion of judicial power frequently will be necessary in order to ensure the enforcement of those rights protected in international norms and deemed essential to the strengthening of the rule of law.

Domingo[5] expands on the idea of judicialization in a way that includes several of the ideas subsumed within the concept of the rule of law. She begins with the judicialization of politics as "the process by which there is an increase in the impact of judicial decisions upon political and social processes."[6] She then suggests that conflicts are increasingly resolved at the level of the courts. These first two ideas are in close keeping with the definition provided by Tate and Vallinder. Third, she presents the notion that regime legitimacy increasingly depends on the rule of law and the public perception of the state's capacity to deliver that rule. Finally, she explains the growing trend by a variety of societal actors to use law and the courts to pursue their political goals. This definition may confuse inasmuch as some parts of it are, in reality, driven by other parts of it—for example, that societal groups that bring more conflicts to the courts largely will determine the extent to which conflicts are resolved in the courts.

We can see judicialization in our two cases, but they raise some cautions about judicialization. Both are weak democracies with loosely organized parties and with very high levels of corruption. Consequently, they often are concerned with the relationships among the executive, legislature, and judiciary. There is potential for the judiciary to hamstring the elected branches of government before they have even found their footing. There also are concerns that the judiciary could easily get caught up in the net of corruption that permeates many of the political parties and government actors, an outcome that would be to the detriment of the judiciary as well as the whole society. Finally, there is some concern that these are civil-law countries whose traditional logic does not leave much room for activist judges.[7] High levels of judicialization may not be easily compatible with traditionally understood judicial roles. Judges may find themselves criticized or sanctioned for seeking to extend their powers into political areas.

We can see judicialization in both Guatemala and Nicaragua, although levels of judicialization are much higher in Guatemala. Both have been subject to similarly high levels of international intervention into their justice systems through reform programs that supported the rule of law. These international pressures seem to have played a significant role in building the rule of law in both countries, although I place more emphasis on the role played by domestic civil society groups that pursue legal strategies. These legally oriented groups can do a great deal to push the courts toward judicialization, which then pushes the government closer to compliance with the norm of the rule of law. It is the difference in the activities of civil society groups that underlies the difference in the levels of judicialization in these two countries. In Guatemala, levels of judicialization grew considerably during the 1990s and 2000s as courts sometimes used constitutional jurisprudence in both seeking to check the legislative and executive bodies and making potentially important rulings against the military. Nicaragua enjoys the same institutional tools as Guatemala but does not use them to judicialize politics or to build the rule of law. Instead, politically dominated courts have sometimes blocked corruption prosecutions.

Judicialization has become widespread throughout the region of Latin America, although it is plagued by problems stemming from its connection to the legitimation of the regime. Where the regime is plagued by problems of corruption, vice, and lack of legitimacy, unpopular court actions will invite the charge that the court is controlled by the executive. Domingo[8] highlights the importance of the widespread judicial reform programs in the region, which have encouraged increasingly active judiciaries and tried to require that the executive submit to constraints from the courts. Mexico is an example of a country where judicialization has increased following judicial reforms. The relationship between international actors and the growth in judicialization also is highlighted. Finally, Domingo emphasizes the significance of understanding that citizenship, including citizen rights, is at the core of the process of judicialization. As courts increasingly become the guardians of citizenship, they begin to use their powers, with the support of much of the population.

The literature reviewed provides an excellent overview of the spread of judicial power, but it does not offer an explanation of how judicialization spreads and comes to be accepted. The key to the spread of judicialization lies in the growing acceptance of a norm of the rule of law. At its heart, the judicialization of politics is frequently about enforcing the rule of law against perceived attacks from the executive or legislature. The spread of judicialization thus can be understood as depending on the spread of the norms of the rule of law. We must then look at how international norms of the rule of law are transmitted between countries.

Although the literature on democratic transitions often left the rule of law outside its focus, work on democratic consolidation nearly always includes building the rule of law among its important issues. When a consolidated democracy is defined, the rule of law finds itself in a central position.[9] The rule of law has received increased attention as a part of the focus on democratic consolidation, but it continues to be poorly understood and insufficiently explicated. The rule of law probably can be most intuitively understood as the enforcement of the "rules of the game" of democracy.[10] Scholars writing in the "law and society" tradition have focused on the relative gap between the law as written and the law as lived.[11] Diamond defines the rule of law as follows: "all citizens have political and legal equality, and the state and its agents are themselves subject to the law."[12] Somewhere among these three approaches lies the general understanding reflected in most references to the rule of law: The laws as written (including the Constitution) are generally enforced; all are equal before the law; and the courts are independent and acceptably active in protecting the rights of individuals.

Many of the international funding agencies, such as the World Bank, the Inter-American Development Bank, and many bilateral aid organizations have devoted considerable time and money in the past twenty years to "Rule of Law Reforms."[13] These reforms have involved rewriting laws in order to promote economic development and protect individual rights, promoting technical innovations designed to improve the functioning of legal institutions, and in many cases, overseeing broad reorganization of judicial institutions.[14] Policy analysts involved in rule-of-law reform projects have tended to focus on the more practical issues of access to justice for the bulk of the population (especially the underprivileged), efficiency of legal institutions, and judicial independence from influence or pressure in defining the rule of law.[15]

The norms of the rule of law itself, however, often are defined broadly to encompass all of the actions done in its name. Thomas Carothers[16] organizes the rule of law into four clusters: democracy promotion, human rights and social justice, economic development, and international law enforcement. Each contain a series of goals that are pursued by rule-of-law reformers. The World Bank, through its Governance and Anti-Corruption Program, focuses on judicial reform and institutional strengthening of the judiciary.[17] The Inter-American Development Bank similarly has made a commitment to anticorruption measures and building the rule of law.[18] Corruption, an adjunct to concerns about the rule of law, is given high priority by the international donor groups because of its devastating effect on economic development. The United States Agency for International Development (USAID), by contrast, operates under a definition of the rule of law that focuses on equality and rights protection.[19]

INTERNATIONAL TRANSMISSION OF NORMS AND INSTITUTIONS

The international spread of norms has been studied primarily in the context of international human rights norms. The rule of law has become one of these international norms and is being spread primarily through programs that seek to promote democracy. In order to examine the spread of the rule of law as a norm and a practice, one must first understand the spread of international norms. It is useful to consider the spiral model of norm transmission and adoption introduced by Thomas Risse and Katherine Sikkink.[20] This model demonstrates a credible, if convoluted, path for the movement of a norm throughout a particular country. The interaction of domestic and international actors is central to this movement.

The spiral model proposed by Risse and Sikkink has five main parts. In the first stage, weak domestic opposition responds to repression by appealing to transnational networks. Those networks then invoke international human rights and apply pressure to the target state. This first step incorporates the "boomerang" model of Keck and Sikkink.[21] In the second step, the state reacts to the pressure by denying either that the violation is occurring or that the international community has any authority over it. The state also may engage in increased repression, which generally will inspire further contacts between domestic opposition and the transnational networks. The third step occurs when the state adopts tactical concessions—an action some states will not take. The domestic opposition is consequently emboldened.

According to Risse and Sikkink, the third step often is the point of no return for a violating state. After some concessions have been made and the domestic opposition begins to grow in power, it becomes more difficult for the state to maintain repression. In fact, these circumstances will lead to regime changes in some cases. The fourth step is reached when the state accepts the international norm at the level of prescription. Prescriptive status is indicated by such actions as adopting international human rights treaties and passing new laws. The final step is then rule-consistent behavior, which is seen once the state and society have become habituated to the institutionalized norms. Signs of rule-consistent behavior would include efforts to deal with a past egregious human rights record or to create oversight mechanisms to help guarantee rights.

There are thus two major struggles in the adoption of human rights norms: accepting the norm as an idea and accepting the dictates of the norm in a regime's behavior. In terms of the rule of law as a set of norms, the rule-consistent behavior state is especially interesting. As discussed below, there are many sources that seek to inculcate the norms of the rule of law. The difficulty lies, however, in persuading a regime to accept and internalize them. As Risse and Sikkink explain, "Human rights norms can only be regarded as internalized in domestic practices when actors comply with them *irrespective* of individual beliefs about their validity."[22] The same will be true of the norms of the rule of law. They will be internalized only when individuals follow their directives regardless of personal preferences or relationships.

International aid groups often are major players in these interactions, frequently pushing for the adherence to the norms of the rule of law. It is, of course, rare that a rule-of-law aid program would be exclusively formulated to foster an appreciation for these norms. More frequently, the goals of such programs are formulated with specific institutional reforms and benchmarks in mind. These goals may be as small—for example, to improve the efficiency of an existing institution. On the other hand, they may be as expansive as a plan to reorder the legal institutions altogether with regard to, for instance, the introduction of adversarial jury trials. Big concept norms like democracy, equality, or justice do loom in the background of reform programs, often shaping priorities. Big concept norms also help to determine which programs will be pursued by a particular donor agency.

THE SPIRAL MODEL IN NICARAGUA

Applying the spiral model to Nicaraguan rule-of-law development produces interesting results. Nicaragua had, by the late 1990s, fully adopted the prescriptive phase but continued to have problems achieving rule-consistent behavior. The key to ensuring rule-consistent behavior is, as ever, pressure by international and domestic groups, of which there were a significant number. Many groups have been active in agitating for the rule of law in Nicaragua, most notably international donor groups. These organizations include the World Bank, the Inter-American Development Bank, USAID, the European Union, Spain, Sweden, Norway, and Germany, among others, at one time reaching the point of eleven donor groups working with the justice sector in Nicaragua alone.[23] That pressure was not always effective, however, and governmental actors were not consistently receptive to such moves. In Nicaragua, major obstacles to enshrining the rule of law were that corruption allowed the wealthy and the elite to hold themselves above the law, and there was not a sufficiently developed system of guaranteeing rights and freedoms for Nicaraguans. The problem of corruption was further complicated by the fact that reform programs required the cooperation of at least one Supreme Court justice, which allowed the justices to use these programs for clientalist purposes.[24]

Repression and denial were constant in Nicaragua for many years, leading up to and beyond the 1979 revolution. The Sandinista Revolution marked the point when domestic and exile domestic opposition groups began to seek international support for opposing the government. The exile groups were especially successful, winning the almost unqualified support of the United States. The fact that the exile groups then went on to support an armed wing, the Contras, was a departure from the ideal type of spiral model described by Risse and Sikkink. Nonetheless, these opposition groups did place pressure on the national government through the support of powerful international actors. These actions were of course met with denial by Sandinista spokesmen, who argued in particular that their government was democratic, whereas the Contra War was illegal and a violation of human rights.

Repression, the beginning of the spiral model, has been a controversial issue in Nicaragua. It is clear that there was substantial repression under the Samoza dictatorship, which was so unresponsive to domestic and international pressure that it ultimately lost power in a revolution. The Sandinistas had a much more mixed record, however, with political opponents sometimes certainly suffering, especially as the Contra War escalated. The opposition was quite well connected and able to influence—or at least take advantage of—U.S. foreign policy in the region. Although there was little domestic pressure placed on the Sandinista government, there was tremendous international pressure from the United States, primarily through its sponsoring of the Contra army. This international pressure on the Nicaraguan government was shared only minimally by transnational activist networks, many of which in fact supported the Sandinista government. The United States tried to push its pro-capitalist and pro-democracy agenda through the provision and removal of aid.[25]

The Sandinista government initially engaged in a pattern of denial of its human rights violations and violations of the norms of the rule of law. For the most part, the Sandinistas argued that they had made strides in other areas of social democracy, which should count in favor of their record. Indeed, most basic rights were respected, and legal processes were used to carry out socialist policies such as land reform. Also, the 1985 election was considered free and fair by most European observers.[26] International pressure only grew stronger in response to these denials, however, until the Sandinistas agreed to commit to constitutional democracy (although they argued they were already democratic) in the late 1980s.[27] The 1987 constitution committed the Sandinista government to a very broad catalogue of rights, including a regimen of due process rights that should guarantee citizens a free trial. The commitment to democracy led to increased scrutiny by international actors, especially with regard to the conduct of the 1990 election, the most closely observed election to that time.[28] That election, of course, led to the end of the Sandinista government and an arguable regime change, which should have fomented a greater likelihood of rule-consistent behavior.[29]

Under pressure from the international actors involved in the Esquipulas II process, Nicaragua made strategic concessions with the decision to adopt a new constitution in 1987.[30] This constitution notably included an extensive catalogue of protected rights. More significant for our examination of the rule of law, the process of drafting the constitution included a great deal of attention to the precise wording and desired outcome in legal areas. The president of the Supreme Court helped to lead this effort, convening discussions with judges, lawyers, and ordinary citizens to consider the pros and cons of the wording in the draft constitution. This process thus allowed for some degree of pressure from domestic activists with regard to the wording of the constitution. They also held open meetings with international legal scholars, at which the constitutional drafts were debated with an eye toward, among other things, human rights and the rule of law. This penetrating attention to the rule of law at the moment of the constitution's drafting helped to ensure that the final document included nominal commitment to human rights and the rule of law.[31] What may have been intended to be a mere show of the regime's commitments in politically sensitive areas actually moved Nicaragua toward a prescriptive commitment to human rights and the rule of law.

This prescriptive commitment was quite strong. First, the constitution evidenced a deep commitment to the rule of law and human rights in all forms. It went further, however, by incorporating into the body of constitutional norms the entire contents of certain international human rights treaties.[32] These international treaties thus became the valid subjects of the constitutional jurisprudence of the Supreme Court, although it generally has shirked that responsibility. The constitution was accompanied by further aspects of the entrenchment of a prescriptive commitment, such as the introduction of a human rights ombudsman's office. The constitution also embodied the idea that Nicaragua needs a strong rule of law and that no one should be above the law. There has been a great gap, however, between the expansive language of the constitution in these areas and the actual practices of the Nicaraguan government.

As is so often the case, the ability of the Nicaraguan government to routinely display behavior consistent with the rule of law is weak. The achievement of rule-consistent behavior in Nicaragua in the past decade has been stymied by the problem of corruption more than by anything else. Although there continue to be concerns in the area of human rights, they generally are not associated with pervasive governmental repression, but rather reflect societal problems. The norm that no one should be above the law is regularly violated by the government and by politicians, among others. Corruption is a pernicious problem in Nicaraguan government.[33] Although it is sometimes prosecuted, impunity is still prevalent, especially when the perpetrator is particularly wealthy or powerful. Most troubling is the use of congressional immunity to shield politicians even from official investigation. Congressional immunity has been pierced in the well-known Alemán[34] case, but such prosecutions of powerful politicians are far too rare. Consequently, Nicaragua has a long way to go before reaching the end of the spiral model.

Civil society advocacy groups in Nicaragua do not have close ties to either the international donor groups or to the judiciary. These organizations are typically uninvolved in judicial politics, preferring instead to use political strategies such as mobilization and direct ties to the political parties. Such strategies may be successful in accomplishing more politically oriented goals, but they do little to build an overall governmental and societal commitment to the rule of law. Without working more closely with the international donor agencies, these organizations are unlikely to contribute to constructing the rule of law. Without such ties, they cannot complete the "boomerang." Because of their close ties to political parties and the widespread corruption therein, these civil society groups are unlikely to insist on holding everyone to account, especially the powerful. The domestic opposition groups currently at work in Nicaragua are unlikely to push the government on the issue of the rule of law and to move it closer to rule-consistent behavior.

The spiral model describes the early stages of rule of law adoption in Nicaragua but does not explain the lack of movement from prescriptive commitment to rule-consistent behavior. The problems with this transition are twofold. First, civil society activist groups are not strongly oriented toward the rule of law. As a consequence, they do not actively pressure the government, much less try to engage in "boomerang" connections with international organizations. Consequently, the pressure placed on the Nicaraguan government by the international community is not backed up by civil society. Second, corruption sets up a significant obstacle to achieving behavior consistent with the rule of law. The prevalence of corruption makes the government generally unresponsive to pressures from domestic or international activists. Corruption among high-ranking government officials and societal elites is antithetical to the norm of the rule of law in that it requires that citizens be treated unequally before the law depending on their connections and patronage. This is opposed to the part of the rule of law requiring that all people be treated equally before the law. Third, the international activity may have been sufficient to move Nicaragua through the symbolic prescriptive commitment phase, but it has not been enough to move it into the rule-consistent behavior phase. A stronger civil society activist community would be required for that. The spiral model does not account for these phenomena and is insufficient in that respect.

THE SPIRAL MODEL IN GUATEMALA

Ropp and Sikkink[35] trace the spiral model in Guatemala, although only up to 1998. Consequently, I will merely summarize their findings here, adding from my own research as appropriate. In particular, I will highlight issues that relate more closely to the norm of the rule of law rather than to international human rights norms, which are the primary focus of Ropp and Sikkink. I will then focus my analysis on recent events that may shed light on the current recognition of the rule of law in Guatemala.

Repression that took place primarily in the 1970s and 1980s and less so in the 1990s was extensive and involved the operation of a massive counterinsurgency campaign that targeted, among others, people connected with Maya groups and labor unions. This repression was sufficiently extensive that it severely hampered the response that might have been expected from alert civil society opponents, and the "boomerang" could not work during this period. Although some transnational actors became involved in advocating for human rights in Guatemala, they were largely unsuccessful. The governments of this period—those of Generals Lucas Garcia and Ríos Montt—engaged heavily in denial. They characterized the opposition as Marxist revolutionaries and argued that all repressive governmental actions were necessary for the successful completion of the civil war.[36]

The United States was less active in supporting democracy in Guatemala than it was in Nicaragua in the 1970s and 1980s, mostly for ideological reasons: As in Nicaragua, U.S. aid for Guatemala was cut off by the Carter administration because of the Guatemalan government's human rights record, although this had little effect on the war effort in Guatemala and ties to the authoritarian regime were later restored by the Reagan administration. The

United States did not strongly advocate for democracy or human rights in the 1980s in Guatemala. Eventually, it did lend its support to a new regime with the election of President Marco Vinicio Cerezo Arevelo of the relatively moderate Christian Democrat party,[37] although it still maintained strong support for the Guatemalan military.[38] Following this election, Guatemala was held up by the U.S. government as a model for the other countries in the region, even though it continued to be engaged in a bloody civil conflict. The U.S. government's support for real democracy in Guatemala was at best weak, however, as it continued to support the regime without seriously questioning the prominent role played by the military in civilian affairs and the human rights violations that continued to mount despite the resumption of formal democracy.[39]

The third and pivotal stage of strategic concessions was achieved in Guatemala only with the return of relatively more democratic governments. The decision to return to civilian rule in part was itself the product of a strategic concession by some elements of the military that believed the institution of the military was being harmed by having to simultaneously fight the civil war and engage in governance.[40] By releasing control of the reins of government, however, the military maintained substantial enclaves of power.[41] Regardless, the return of civilian government led to substantial concessions and even the adoption of prescriptive status for human rights, especially in the constitution itself. With regard to impunity, though, there were very few concessions, with the military attempting to maintain its "hidden hand" powers.

The rhetoric of rights became much stronger both within and without Guatemala as efforts were made to push the country toward a more democratic system. Pressure came in the early 1980s, most notably through the direct intervention of foreign governments, including the United States.[42] Transnational advocacy networks also were very active regarding Guatemala and grew stronger through the 1980s and 1990s. Organizations such as Amnesty International and Human Rights Watch were frequent critics of the Guatemalan government's human rights and legal practices for many years after the formal adoption of democracy. Even more pronounced criticism came from the solidarity organizations based in Europe and the United States. These networks frequently applied pressure both to the Guatemalan government and to foreign governments in order to hold Guatemala to higher standards, as they still do.[43]

The rhetoric and idea of rights was especially pronounced among civil society advocacy organizations, although these could not safely express themselves before the advent of formal democracy. Indeed, the assassinations of human rights leaders in the 1990s highlighted the dangers that faced domestic human rights activist networks. These organizations, however, continued to raise the dual banners of human rights and of the rule of law. They advocated nationally and internationally, relying on the provisions of international human rights documents. For example, Rigoberta Menchú Tum and other Maya activists frequently invoked ILO treaty 169, which provides certain rights to indigenous communities.[44] In the 1990s, several organizations were founded that had a specifically legal orientation for their mission. The consequence was a heightened focus on the idea of rights and the rule of law, as these organizations were now attempting to ensure the enforcement of both.

Ropp and Sikkink place the achievement of the fourth stage, prescriptive status, with the new constitution. In the area of human rights, this may be accurate, given the extensive nominal protection of human rights in the 1986 constitution. However, entrenched rights are only one-half of the rule of law. The other half is that no one should be above the law, which in practice in Guatemala refers to the issue of impunity. The problem of impunity is deeply seated in Guatemalan society. There is no clear commitment that all will be prosecuted, even those who are part of the powerful elite or the military. I argue that a nominal promise regarding the rule of law was only made as a part of the 1996 peace accords.

The shift from the fourth stage to the final stage, rule-consistent behavior, is largely yet to be achieved. To the extent that there has been progress, it is a product of the pressure brought to bear by both domestic and transnational actors. A somewhat different set of actors became involved in exerting pressure in the area of the rule of law following the 1996 peace accords. The presence of a UN mission played a significant role in exerting pressure for the rule of law, as did the presence of rule-of-law aid projects. Through these projects, organizations like USAID, the World Bank, and the Inter-American Development Bank came to play a substantial role for promoting the rule of law. Finally, focus on the issue of impunity helped to mobilize a variety of organizations to place a greater emphasis on the rule of law, especially on the norm of the rule of law that says that no one shall be above the law.

One of the most significant international actors in Guatemala was MINUGUA, the United Nations Verification Mission in Guatemala. MINU-GUA was charged with "verifying" the peace process in Guatemala in the mid-1990s.[45] Because the peace accords were so expansive, MINUGUA could reasonably monitor many aspects of Guatemalan society, but most notably human rights and the rule of law. It not only provided verified accounts of the human rights violations that were occurring in Guatemala during its tenure, but it also made calls for an end to these violations and an end to impunity. MINUGUA was able to be unusually influential because it had a substantial domestic presence, making it at once almost a domestic actor and an international presence.

Another significant set of international actors in Guatemala has been the rule-of-law aid donor groups. Many groups have been represented in Guatemala, which has been a major target for these organizations. The most prominent donor groups represent the banks, specifically the World Bank and the Inter-American Development Bank. The Organization of American

States has engaged in democracy promotion programs in Guatemala as well, although it is not a donor group per se. Unilateral donor groups are also well represented. USAID has a very large mission, along with several European countries including Spain, Germany, and Sweden. Collectively, these organizations contribute a great deal of pressure on the Guatemalan government to embrace the rule of law.[46]

Coordination among these groups has been a significant concern. One agency official identified lack of coordination as a major obstacle in agencies pursuing their programmatic goals. Although this is certainly true when it comes to realizing specific programs, it is less true when considering the norms of the rule of law. Agencies do differ somewhat in how they prioritize different aspects of the rule-of-law project, but they typically share a core set of goals. These core goals correspond to the norms of the rule of law. The oft-cited attention to access to justice and greater efficiency are integral to the core value that no one should be above the law. Many agencies have aspects of their programs that focus directly on human rights. Through their aid program activities, these donor groups have placed, since the mid-1990s, sustained pressure on the Guatemalan government to accept and behave in accordance with the norms of the rule of law.

Many civil society advocacy groups have placed pressure on the Guatemalan government to embrace the rule of law. One important sector includes the Mayan organizations, including the Widow's Group (CONAVIGUA), the Rigoberta Menchu Foundation, and others. Human rights organizations such as the Myrna Mack Foundation play an important role as well. There are also educational and investigative agencies at San Carlos University, at private universities, and in the private sector. The most obviously related organizations are the legal activist groups of the Human Rights Legal Action Center (CALDH) and the Archbishop's Office on Human Rights (ODHA).

The legal activist organizations are the ones most obviously related to promoting the norms of the rule of law, but other organizations can also play a substantial role. The importance of nonlegal organizations stems from the significance of the focus on impunity by many such organizations, for the issue of impunity was a very important one for civil society actors during the process of negotiating and then implementing the peace accords. The two Guatemalan truth commissions were important efforts to combat impunity. Yet during the same period, human rights activists were being assassinated by military agents. Numerous human rights organizations rose up to call for the prosecution of those responsible and, in a few cases, to participate directly in those trials. As a consequence of both of these phenomena, there was a great deal of attention placed in society on the issue of impunity and on the value that no one should be above the law.

The spiral model better explains the adoption of rule-consistent behavior in Guatemala than it does in Nicaragua, yet there are serious difficulties with the last phase. The civil society activist community in Guatemala is relatively strong and is also well connected to the international organizations in the area of the rule of law. It has put significant pressure on the government of Guatemala and has seen some progress toward commitment to the rule of law, particularly in the tenure of the current president, Oscar Berger. This pattern follows the "boomerang" aspect of the spiral model of norm adoption. Of course, Guatemala continues to have serious problems with the rule-consistent behavior phase of the spiral model, for example, in the case of the unsolved murders of young women in Guatemala City that have been ongoing for the past several years, with inadequate police and governmental response.[47] To be sure, neither corruption nor impunity has ended, but it would be naïve to expect that either can easily be vanquished.

CONCLUSION

The rule of law must be embraced by nations as a set of norms before it can be implemented as part of an overall pattern of behavior in accord with these norms. As a set of norms, the rule of law includes both a body of rights that must be protected and the important value that no one should be above the law. Much of the difficulty in enshrining the rule of law in Guatemala and Nicaragua lies with the notion that no one should be above the law. Indeed, issues such as reserved powers for the military and other entrenched elites and continuing corruption pose persistent problems for achieving this part of the rule of law.

This chapter has used the spiral model proposed by Risse and Sikkink to help explain the patterns regarding transmission of the norms of the rule of law. Their model suggests that the uptake of norms is the product of international pressure supported by domestic actors. The spiral model looks at distinct processes of tactical concession, prescriptive status, and compliant behavior. Throughout the efforts to have a state adopt rule-of-law norms, the crucial factor is the pressure brought to bear on the recalcitrant states by both by domestic actors and by international actors who often have intervened in response to appeals from domestic actors. This model is a helpful way to understand this process of norm transmission regarding the rule of law precisely because it highlights the relationship between the state and those domestic and international actors.

NOTES

1. The judicialization of politics has been discussed in countries as diverse as Israel (Yoav Dotan, "Judicial Accountability in Israel: The High Court of Justice and the Phenomenon of Judicial Hyperactivism," *Israel Affairs* 8, no. 4 [2002]: 41–68), Switzerland (Christine Rothmayer, "Towards the Judicialization of Swiss Politics?" *West European*

Politics 24, no. 2 [2001]: 77–94.), and Namibia (Nico Steytler, "The Judicialization of Namibian Politics," in *The Global Expansion of Judicial Power*, ed. C. Neal Tate and Torbjörn Vallinder [New York: New York University Press, 1995]).

2. C. Neal Tate and Torbjörn Vallinder, eds., *The Global Expansion of Judicial Power* (New York: New York University Press, 1995).

3. Torbjörn Vallinder, "When the Courts Go Marching In," in *The Global Expansion of Judicial Power*, ed. C. Neal Tate and Torbjörn Vallinder (New York, New York University Press, 1995).

4. Ibid., 13.

5. Pilar Domingo, "Judicialization of Politics or Politicization of the Judiciary? Recent Trends in Latin America," *Democratization* 11, no. 1 (2004): 104–126.

6. Ibid., 110.

7. Many have argued that the civil law tradition is changing and converging with the common law tradition, even to the point of allowing judges to become more political. Jorge L. Esquiroi, "The Fictions of Latin American Law (Part I)," *Utah Law Review* (1997): 425–470; Mary Ann Glendon, "The Sources of Law in a Changing Legal Order," *Creighton Law Review* 17 (1984): 663–684.

8. See note 5.

9. Juan Linz and Alfred Stepan, for example, include in *Problems of Democratic Transition and Consolidation: Southern Europe, South America, and Post-Communist Europe* (Baltimore: Johns Hopkins University Press, 1996) the rule of law as one of five arenas in which democracy needs to be strong in order to become consolidated. Larry Diamond suggests in *Developing Democracy: Toward Consolidation* (Baltimore: Johns Hopkins University Press, 1999, 11) that "Freedom and pluralism, in turn, can be secured only through a 'rule of law,' in which legal rules are applied fairly, consistently, and predictably across equivalent cases, irrespective of the class, status, or power, of the subject of the rules."

10. Adam Przeworski, "Some Problems in the Study of Transitions to Democracy" in *Transitions from Authoritarian Rule: Comparative Perspectives*, ed. Guillermo O'Donnell, Phillippe C. Schmitter, and Laurence Whitehead (Baltimore: Johns Hopkins University Press, 1986).

11. This view is also reflected in Paulo Sergio Pinheiro's introduction to *The (Un)Rule of Law and the Underprivileged in Latin America* (Notre Dame: University of Notre Dame Press, 1999), in which he suggests that a fundamental weakness of citizenship in the weak democracies of Latin America allows traditional elites to manipulate state institutions, and produces (or at least tolerates) lawless violence, discrimination, and lack of access to justice.

12. Larry Diamond, *Developing Democracy: Toward Consolidation* (Baltimore: Johns Hopkins University Press, 1999), 11.

13. Pilar Domingo and Rachel Sieder, eds., *Rule of Law in Latin America: The International Promotion of Judicial Reform* (London: Institution for Latin American Studies, 2001).

14. In Guatemala, for instance, numerous laws have been rewritten, the courts have been equipped with computerized case-tracking systems, and adversarial jury trials have been instituted in the past fifteen years.

15. See, e.g., William C. Prillaman, *The Judiciary and Democratic Decay in Latin America: Declining Confidence in the Rule of Law* (Westport, Conn.: Praeger, 2000); Mark

Ungar, *Elusive Reform: Democracy and the Rule of Law in Latin America* (Boulder: Lynne Rienner Publishers, 2002).

16. Thomas Carothers, "The Many Agendas of Rule-of-Law Reform in Latin America" in *Rule of Law in Latin America: The International Promotion of Judicial Reform*, ed. Pilar Domingo and Rachel Sieder (London: Institute of Latin American Studies, 2001).

17. Online at http://www.worldbank.org/wbi/governance/about.html (visited July 12, 2006).

18. Online at http://www.iadb.org/integrity/oii_ar05/introduction.cfm?language =english, updated 2006.

19. United States Agency for International Development, "Strengthening the Rule of Law & Respect for Human Rights," online at http://www.usaid.gov/our_work/ democracy_and_governance/technical_areas/rule_of_law/, updated 2005.

20. Thomas Risse and Kathryn Sikkink, "The Socialization of International Human Rights Norms in Domestic Practices: Introduction" in *The Power of Human Rights: International Norms and Domestic Change*, ed. Thomas Risse, Stephen C. Ropp, and Kathryn Sikkink (Cambridge: Cambridge University Press, 1999).

21. Margaret Keck and Kathryn Sikkinik argue in *Activists Beyond Borders: Transnational Advocacy Networks in International Politics* (Ithaca: Cornell University Press, 1998) that domestic activists may magnify their influence by appealing to "transnational advocacy networks," who then influence third-party governments such as the United States to put pressure on the offending government.

22. See note 20 above at 16.

23. Luis Salas, "From Law and Development to the Rule of Law: New and Old Issues in Justice Reform in Latin America" in *Rule of Law in Latin America: The International Promotion of the Judicial Reform*, ed. Pilar Domingo and Rachel Sieder (London: Institute of Latin American Studies, 2001).

24. Ximena Carreto, personal interview, August 11, 2004, Managua, Nicaragua.

25. See, e.g., "U.S. to Give Nicaragua Some Humanitarian Aid," *New York Times*, May 13, 1978; "Never Popular, Foreign Aid is Even More on the Ropes," *New York Times*, April 6, 1980; "U.S. Planning Loans and Other Aid for Nicaragua," *New York Times*, August 17, 1979; "U.S. Halts Nicaragua Aid Over Help for Guerrillas," *New York Times*, January 13, 1981.

26. John A. Booth, Christine J. Wade, and Thomas W. Walker, *Understanding Central America: Global Forces, Rebellion, and Change*, fourth edition (Boulder: Westview Press, 2006); Thomas W. Walker, "Introduction" in *Reagan Versus the Sandinistas: The Undeclared War on Nicaragua*, ed. Thomas W. Walker (Boulder: Westview Press, 1987).

27. The regional conflict that included the Contra War in Nicaragua and the civil wars in El Salvador and Guatemala attracted the interest of a large number of countries, primarily through the Organization of American States. Argentina, Brazil, Peru, and Uruguay provided special support in the period, along with lesser contributions by Mexico and Spain. The focus of the Contradora group, as they were called, was primarily on a peaceful solution to the conflict with a rather agnostic stance on the questions of democracy and social justice. Democracy found its way firmly into the regional peace process with the Arias plan embodied in the Esquipulas II accord. The premise of that accord was that all of the signatory countries in the region would commit to democracy internally and to peace externally. Although most countries

believed they had already done enough to meet the bar for democracy, the adoption of that rhetoric soon opened the door for a more expansive notion of liberal democracy. Jack Child, *The Central American Peace Process 1983-1991: Sheathing Swords, Building Confidence* (Boulder: Lynne Rienner Publishers, 1992).

28. Leslie Anderson, "Elections and Public Opinion in the Making of Nicaraguan Democracy" in *Elections and Democracy in Central America, Revisited*, ed. Mitchell A. Seligson and John A. Booth (Chapel Hill: University of North Carolina Press, 1995).

29. Thomas W. Walker, *Nicaragua: Living in the Shadow of the Eagle* (Boulder: Westview Press, 2003); Katherine Hoyt, *The Many Faces of Sandinista Democracy* (Athens, Ohio: Ohio University Center for International Studies, 1997); Stephen Schwartz, *A Strange Silence: The Emergence of Democracy in Nicaragua* (San Francisco: Institute for Contemporary Studies Press, 1992).

30. See note 27 above.

31. Alejandro Serrano Caldera, "The Rule of Law in Nicaraguan Revolution," *Loyola of Los Angeles International and Comparative Law Journal* 12, no. 2 (1990): 341–468.

32. Constitution of Nicaragua, Article 46.

33. Katherine Isbester, "Nicaragua 1996-2001: Sex, Corruption, and Other Natural Disasters," *International Journal* 56, no. 4 (2001): 632–648.

34. Former Nicaragua President Arnoldo Alemán was convicted of money laundering, embezzlement, and corruption in December 2003 and sentenced to twenty years. He is the highest-ranking public official to ever be charged with corruption in Nicaragua, a country in which corruption cases often go without prosecution. His conviction was opposed actively by his party (the Liberal Constitutional Party), which eventually succeeded, working with the Sandinistas, in shortening his sentence by fifteen years. However, his conviction was entirely overturned by the Nicaraguan Supreme Court on January 16, 2009.

35. Stephen C. Ropp and Kathryn Sikkink, "International Norms and Domestic Politics in Chile and Guatemala" in *The Power of Human Rights: International Norms and Domestic Change*, Thomas Risse, Stephen C. Ropp, and Kathryn Sikkink, eds. (Cambridge: Cambridge University Press, 1999).

36. John A. Booth, Christine J. Wade, and Thomas W. Walker, *Understanding Central America: Global Forces, Rebellion, and Change*, 4th ed. (Boulder: Westview Press, 2006).

37. "U.S. is Said to Favor Request for Increase in Aid for Guatemala," *New York Times*, May 13, 1987.

38. Susanne Jonas, "Dangerous Liaisons: The U.S. in Guatemala," *Foreign Policy* 103 (1996): 144–160.

39. Juan Carlos Zarate, *Forging Democracy: A Comparative Study of the Effects of U.S. Foreign Policy on Central America* (Lanham, Md: University Press of America, 1994).

40. Jennifer Schirmer, *The Guatemalan Military Project: A Violence Called Democracy* (Philadelphia: University of Pennsylvania Press, 1998).

41. Jennifer Schirmer, "The Guatemalan Politico-Military Project: Legacies for a Violent Peace?" *Latin American Perspectives* 26, no. 2 (1999): 92–107.

42. Kathryn Sikkink, *Mixed Signals: U.S. Human Rights Policy and Latin America* (Ithaca: Cornell University Press, 2004).

43. NISGUA (Network in Solidarity with the People of Guatemala) 2006, online at http://www.nisgua.org/, updated June 21, 2006.

44. Rigoberta Menchú Foundation 2006, online at http://www.frmt.org/ (visited July 19, 2006).

45. United Nations "MINUGUA," online at http://www.un.org/Depts/dpko/ dpko/co_mission/minugua.htm, updated 2003.

46. Oscar Chaverria, personal interview, March 29, 1994, Guatemala City, Guatemala.

47. Amnesty International, "Guatemala: No Protection, No Justice: Killings of Women (an Update)," online at http://web.amnesty.org/library/pdf/ AMR340192006ENGLISH/$File/AMR3401906.pdf (visited August 1, 2006).

CHAPTER TEN

The Role of International Actors in Promoting Rule of Law in Uganda

JOSEPH M. ISANGA

INTRODUCTION

There is a perception that Uganda, like several African nations held to be beacons of hope in the late 1980s and 1990s, had made a break from bad governance and was headed toward democratization; however rule by men (i.e., the military) rather than by law persists. Yet the rule of law is critical to sustained political and economic development. The lack of respect for the rule of law has adversely affected the emergence of democracy in Uganda. The need for strong, principled, and concerted political leverage by international actors is clear. International insistence on constitutionalism and the rule of law are the keys to Uganda's democratic transformation.

In an increasingly integrated world, characterized by notions of limited sovereignty,[1] development assistance is linked to good governance and rule of law. Unfortunately, there are simply too many stakes in global politics, some of them undergirded by self-interest,[2] that make this process painfully slow. Nevertheless, it would still be in the interest of international actors to exercise political leverage, which seems to be the only effective antidote to intractable violent conflicts in many African states, including Uganda, whose governments have promulgated progressive constitutions, but have ignored their provisions.[3] The slogan is "Trust the bullet, but despise the ballot." In particular, the Museveni administration in Uganda has encouraged judicial review, but only as a façade to placate the international community. Such international action, however, would present an alternative that might forestall insurrection and military conflict. Conflict prevention ultimately costs less than international peacekeeping, humanitarian assistance, and other forms of intervention in the interest of international peace and security, not to mention the high costs of human suffering.[4]

African conflicts have been caused in part by regimes that do not respect democracy. Uganda is an illustrative case. International actors have played along under an undeclared policy of constructive engagement, but this has essentially served only to delay democratic evolution. As a result, Ugandan leaders have become increasingly autocratic. In such circumstances, reliance on the military and personal rule based on patronage—as opposed to democracy and the rule of law—have become critically important in governance. Yet forceful measures often only beget forceful reactions. The best hope for democracy is for courts to enforce the will of the people as expressed in the laws enacted by their elected representatives. This would depend on both the effective, uncorrupted actions of the legislature[5] and an emboldened and independent judiciary. There is still much work to be done in Uganda. At present, the executive turns courts into legitimization instruments for its otherwise undemocratic actions. Real change ultimately will depend upon an enhanced role of international actors and an emboldened and independent judiciary.

UGANDA: AN EMERGING DEMOCRACY?

Upon its promulgation in 1995 the current Uganda constitution (herein "Constitution")—the fourth constitution in Uganda's forty-four years of independence from the British—represented a culmination of a progressive departure from years characterized by draconian laws, absence of judicial review, lack of independent judiciary, gross human rights violations, partisan militaries, and life presidencies.[6] It was against that backdrop that by 1994, President Bill Clinton called current Uganda president Yoweri Museveni one of the "new breed,"[7] or new generation, of African leaders—the others being Paul Kagame of Rwanda, Issayas Aferwoki of Eritrea, Meles Zenawi of Ethiopia, Bakuli Muluzi of Malawi, Gerry Rawlings of Ghana, and the late Laurent Kabila of the Democratic Republic of Congo—who raised hopes that they would deliver peace, prosperity, good governance, respect for human rights, and the rule of law. Although still struggling, these countries represented emerging democracies in Africa. They represented beacons of hope on a continent that had endured a long plague of bad governance characterized by life presidents, despots, and brutal dictators like Emperor Bokasa of the Central African Republic, Emperor Haile Selassie of Ethiopia, Mobutu of Zaire, Jerry John Rawlings of Ghana, Charles Taylor of Liberia, and Idi Amin of Uganda, to mention only a few. The international community thought it had seen the end of a seemingly intractable governance problem in Africa. Between

1986 and 1996, Museveni's efforts at political stability and economic growth were rapid, phenomenal, dramatic, and unprecedented.[8] Under his tenure, the country weathered one of the greatest threats to humanity with one of the most effective national responses to HIV/AIDS in Africa.

Occurring equally fast was a radical reversal—as opposed to mere setbacks—and the "new breed" idea is now discredited and all but dead. Increasingly, the Museveni administration became synonymous with personal rule. Yet this did not deter international actors from placating Museveni's administration. For instance, President George W. Bush visited Uganda in 2003, two years after the highly disputed elections that provided a critical test for the rule of law under the new Constitution.[9]

International actors could have used their leverage to require adherence to good governance and the rule of law. Instead, that option was pursued inconsistently and never forcefully enough. A group of international donors meets regularly with the Ugandan government and negotiates budget items, including defense spending. The economic contribution of international actors in this respect is significant and, at least in the long term, almost indispensable. Human Rights Watch reported that these donors provide half of the budget of the Ugandan government, their funds going directly to the treasury after the budget has been agreed on. Although the U.S. government is not part of this donor group, it has provided military assistance and training to Uganda's military, but with no special human rights or good-governance conditions attached.[10] Human Rights Watch further observed that in January 2006, the U.K. government's development ministry announced the withdrawal of US$26 million of direct funding to the government due to concerns about a lack of democratic and economic reform. The United Kingdom, the Netherlands, Norway, Sweden, and Ireland also had reduced aid in 2005. According to the EU Election Observation Mission to Uganda, the February 2006 elections fell short of full compliance with international principles for genuine democratic elections, in particular because a level playing field was not in place.[11]

These developments in Uganda are not mere setbacks or hitches in an inevitably imperfect process. There is a determined reliance on the military rather than on normal democratic processes for retention of political power. The military extends presidential term limits and does not worry about holding elections because it knows the outcome beforehand. Confident in its firm control of electoral commissions, the military intimidates both the electorate and the judiciary if election results are challenged. The consequences are inevitable: cronyism, corruption, decadence, repression of dissent and other freedoms, and economic stagnation or recession. These are the hallmarks of personal rule—the very antithesis of constitutionalism and the rule of law. The regime respects the rule of law only as long as its hold on power is not threatened.

In an increasingly globalized world, the possibility of prosecution of ex-presidents under international and transnational law only serves to compound the difficulties of political evolution in emerging nations such as Uganda.[12] Nevertheless, with concerted and consistent political leverage by international actors, the momentum of democratic evolution could be sustained. In recent years, international actors have expressed the desire to tie their development assistance and partnership only with countries in the African region character-ized by good governance, rule of law, and democracy.[13] Despite their estimable intentions, they have not acted consistently or firmly enough. As a result, African leaders have been able to "have their cake and eat it." They have been able to get away with their actions under misplaced claims to sovereignty.

Good governance includes the rule of law, respect for human rights, free and fair elections, open political processes, and decision making that is transpar-ent and accountable. In the sections that follow, two key and strategic areas of globalizing justice—constitutionalism and the independence of the judiciary—are examined. In emerging nations such as Uganda, these two areas constitute indispensable elements of democratic transition on which international actors should focus to establish the rule of law and firm foundations for development and thus avoid a return to a chaotic past. The international community cannot continue to placate African leaders who may at first wear democratic clothing but whose true dictatorial characteristics emerge a few years later.

In 2005, just ten years after the promulgation of the seemingly pro-gressive Constitution, the current Uganda administration removed limits on presidential terms, in effect providing the necessary conditions for life presi-dencies, by bribing and intimidating members of Parliament. In the 2001 Uganda presidential elections, won by the incumbent (President Museveni), the military intimidated the electorate. Just before the 2006 presidential elec-tions, the government pressed what were condemned as trumped-up charges of treason and rape against Dr. Kizza Besigye, the strongest political opponent to Museveni.[14] When the court granted bail to Dr. Besigye, the government sent members of a militia to besiege the High Court in an effort to prevent the bail from taking effect.[15] The Uganda Constitutional Court condemned this attack in *The Uganda Law Society v. The Attorney General* (2006)[16] as hav-ing "violated the Judiciary's independence in Articles 128 (1), (2), and (3) of the Constitution."[17] This was not the first time Ugandans saw the judiciary silenced by the government. In 1971, during the dictatorship of Amin,[18] the military captured and killed the chief justice of Uganda.[19] Besigye simulta-neously had to answer charges of terrorism before the General Court Mar-tial—the military tribunal. Yet even these high-handed tactics of the Museveni administration did not appear to be consequential enough to get the atten-tion of international actors.[20] There is a troubling perception that developing countries should not be pressed to adhere to the same standards as obtained elsewhere simply because they are developing countries. Yet foreign assistance to these countries is of no use unless the donors insist on the development of democratic institutions and respect for the rule of law.

JUDICIAL REVIEW IN UGANDA:
LEGITIMIZING PERSONAL RULE?

Constitutionalism, understood here as the maintenance of constitutional supremacy, requires judicial review of the constitutionality of laws enacted by Parliament and the acts of governments. Judicial review is crucial to the maintenance of a democratic dispensation based on the notions of checks and balances of the central powers, the rule of law, and individual rights. The framers of the Constitution appreciated these notions.[21] Judicial review became the power of the judiciary to bring state organs under the superior rule of law[22] and thus control the excesses of government that are often used to subvert democracy.

The supremacy of constitutional rules is genuine only if it is guaranteed by an institution that is independent of the political authorities whose acts are being reviewed.[23] This is perhaps the best rationale for judicial review. In an autocracy, in which judicial independence is nonexistent and judicial review is not exercised, constitutional supremacy is a myth. The Constitution provides for judicial review, under which governmental acts and laws can be challenged before the Constitutional Court and, on appeal, the Supreme Court.[24] Judicial review is entrenched in the Constitution, because it provides that the people of Uganda are sovereign and that the constitution is supreme.[25] In *Paul K. Ssemogerere et al. v. The Attorney General* (2002),[26] the Uganda Supreme Court invoked that provision while observing that Parliament cannot clothe itself with "[s]upremacy which in Uganda lies in the majesty and sanctity of the Constitution," and that "[I]n Uganda, it is in the people and the Constitution that sovereignty resides." Ugandan courts handed down numerous decisions that evidenced this progressive understanding of the source of the Constitution's legitimacy and authority. In just ten years from the time the Constitution went into effect, there have been close to forty constitutional cases.[27] Although some applied cross-border legal norms on the supremacy of constitutions in constitutional democracies, most relied on the views and the intentions of the framers of the Constitution.[28] However, after twenty years in power, the increasingly personal rule of Museveni has begun to adversely affect the progress made earlier in establishing the rule of law through judicial review. In fact, there have been instances in which judicial review was used to advance a contrary purpose—the legitimization of personal rule.

In a series of cases brought by the political opposition, the government endured stinging losses in the Constitutional Court. To that extent, it seemed like there was an increasing respect for the rule of law. Yet later decisions that involved challenges to the political establishment faced hostile reactions from Parliament and the executive. In *Major General David Tinyefuza v. Attorney General* (1996), the Constitutional Court delivered its first landmark decision under the Constitution, setting a progressive trend.[29] In *Dr. Paul K.*

Ssemogerere et al. vs. Attorney General of Uganda (2002),[30] the Constitutional Court seemed to advance the rule of law when it struck down certain provisions of the Political Parties and Organisations Act and declared that the ruling "Movement"[31] amounted to a one-party system. The court reasoned that "[P]luralism is a core concept in democracy and that political parties are not always negative and can offer constructive criticism to the government." The court held that the restrictions in the impugned statute were unjustifiable in a free and democratic society.

In *Paul K. Ssemogerere and Zachary Olum v. Attorney General* (1999),[32] the Constitutional Court struck down another Act of Parliament—the Referendum and Other Provisions Act (1999)—on the ground that it was passed without the requisite quorum. The government respected the decision and sought to enact a new referendum law consistent with parliamentary procedure. The new law, debated for only two hours, was in form and substance a replica of the old one. Two petitions swiftly challenged the new referendum law on grounds of retrospectivity and contravention of parliamentary procedures. In the meantime, the national referendum was held and, if the results are to be believed, the people of Uganda favored Museveni's preferred "Movement"[33] system to a multiparty system. Thereafter presidential elections were held under that "Movement" system, and Museveni was said to have won the elections. When this new referendum law came before the Constitutional Court, the outcome was the same as in *Paul K. Ssemogerere & Anor. v. Attorney General* (1999).[34]

When Justice Twinomujuni held that "no political system was ever put in place," the constitutionality of Museveni's election was placed under question. An enraged Museveni promptly and publicly condemned what he called the court's usurpation of people's power, which he called "totally unacceptable." He maintained:

> [I]f the people do not have the power, then who are the judges? You're even less qualified. . . . It is clear, legislative power belongs to Parliament, executive power belongs to the President, and judicial power belongs to the courts. But when you get a court trying to legislate—now trying to make law or to write a constitution—then if you don't correct that you get into problems.

The president's argument suggested that there were areas where the Constitutional Court could exercise its judicial power, but that there were also some prohibited areas. The Museveni administration's outrage about judicial review escalated in *Paul K. Ssemogerere et al. v. The Attorney General* (2002)[35] and *Charles Onyango Obbo and Andrew Mujuni Mwenda v. The Attorney General* (2004).[36] In the latter case, the Uganda Supreme Court held that "meaningful participation of the governed in their governance, which is the hallmark of democracy, is only assured through optimal exercise of the freedom of expression. This is as true in the new democracies as it is in the old ones." Yet the government's reaction made it clear that it would tolerate judicial oversight and the rule of law only to the extent that it did not jeopardize its overall objective of retaining political power. The government warned that if the judiciary ignored that critical interest it would resort to military power—the very antithesis of democracy and the rule of law. While stating that he could ignore the striking down of the "false news" provisions in the *Onyango* case—which in his view amounted to the court sanctioning "telling lies"[37]—Museveni warned that the government and its military would not tolerate court rulings that represented potential threats to the current political establishment. In a statement that would have a chilling effect on the capacity of courts to uphold the rule of law and democracy, Museveni warned:

> [T]he ones who are playing these games, should play them in other areas like they normally do and we ignore. Like for instance a judge who declared recently that telling lies is legal. . . . We fought Kony, defeated him, we fought these other groups ADF [Allied Democratic Forces], FOBA [Force Obote Back Again] to defend the NRM [National Resistance Movement] system, to defend Uganda and to defend the sovereignty of the people. That sovereignty can't be taken away by court maneuvers by Ssemogerere and his group. It will not happen. . . . I am repeating that the government, including the national executive will not allow any institution including the court to usurp the power of the constitution in any way.[38]

Such statements fundamentally undercut the rule of law and independence of the judiciary. The current chief justice of Uganda, Benjamin Odoki, responded to these threats:

> [A]s regards the Judiciary, its independence means that it is not in a position to consult or compromise with any of the other two organs of the State in making judicial decisions. The Judiciary has taken this constitutional role seriously in adjudicating constitutional and other issues. This has sometimes provoked undue and harsh responses from the executive. For as long as the Judiciary is alive to its institutional role, constitutional mandate and jurisdictional limitations, it should be left free to administer justice impartially and equally between citizens and the government. . . . The three organs of the State must learn to respect the functions and powers of each other. . . . Each organ must avoid intimidation. . . . Unless such tendency is avoided, it may create a dictatorship of one organ against the rest, and the entire country.[39]

The bases for personal rule in Uganda are the use of the military in politics and the relegation of law to a secondary place in the resolution of political difference.[40] The military is loyal to a single person—its founder—and is not sufficiently institutionalized and professionalized. The provisions of the Constitution alone cannot stop the use of the military in domestic politics.

The courts' impotence in the face of the executive's reliance on the military or intimidation to protect the political establishment is best illustrated in three recent instances. In the first, the courts have been powerless in political cases that challenged the conduct of presidential elections. In 2001, when Museveni faced the stiffest challenge to his grip on power, he quickly deployed the military to intimidate the electorate. In a split three-to-two decision, the Supreme Court largely accepted the evidence in *Kizza Besigye v. Y.K. Museveni and the Electoral Commission* (2001)[41] but ambiguously ruled in the favor of Museveni, stating, "The fact that these malpractices were proved to have occurred is not enough . . . the petitioner had to go further and prove their extent, degree, and the substantial effect they had on the election."[42]

In the second instance, as if the repressive conduct of elections was not enough to undermine the democratic process, the Museveni administration amended the Constitution to provide for what effectively amounts to "life presidency"[43] and a significantly diminished competence of judicial review of executive and legislative action. The Constitution originally provided for only two presidential terms, but as a result of the amendment, Museveni—who came to power in 1986 through a protracted military struggle and has remained in power without any interruptions—became eligible for reelection in 2006 and for infinite times thereafter. In addition, Museveni's government amended the Constitution to limit the extent to which courts would be able to review the constitutionality of laws passed by Parliament. In essence, the amendments excluded the jurisdiction of judicial review if a law was "repealed," "spent," "expired," or "had its full effect at the date of delivery of judgment."[44] Moreover, even if the state did not repeal a particular piece of legislation before the court delivered its review of it, the amendment provided that such judgment would not affect any acts of the state completed under the impugned legislation. This meant that the court would be rendered impotent with regard to the review of laws or acts of government patently enacted or perpetrated in contravention of the Constitution. The fundamental objective was to place the political establishment's actions beyond the reach of law. These developments effectively undermined the constitutional provisions relating to judicial review in Uganda.[45]

These developments left a sense of constitutional desperation—the sense that although the Constitution was a largely progressive document in its letter and spirit, in practice it was only a façade to assuage international criticism and an instrument for the legitimization of the administration's attempt to hold on to power. Yet these developments did not move international actors to step up and renounce the government's actions. This reluctance to act did not augur well for Uganda's constitutional development and the rule of law. The United States did not help, with the State Department issuing ineffectual, fence-sitting rhetorical statements such as, "Democratisation could suffer a setback if members of the National Resistance Movement are successful in removing presidential term limits from the Constitution," and declaring that neither Parliament nor the judiciary in Uganda is "[s]trong enough to serve as a counterbalance to the powerful executive. Constitutional changes proposed by President Museveni's cabinet, which are scheduled for a vote this year, would make the executive still more powerful."[46]

The third instance concerns the Museveni administration's arrest of Col. Dr. Kizza Besigye. The charges involving treason and rape were brought before the High Court and those involving treason, terrorism, and illegal possession of firearms were brought before the military court-martial. Furthermore, the government sought to exclude its most formidable presidential contender from the race by challenging the validity of his candidacy on the grounds that he was in prison (on the government's charges). The Constitutional Court dismissed the latter claims in *Kabagambe, Farajabdullah and the Attorney General v. The Electoral Commission and Dr. Kizza Besigye*,[47] maintaining that there was no requirement in the law that the presidential candidate must be physically present before he is nominated. These circumstances cast serious doubt on the government's commitment to democracy and the rights to political participation and due process.[48] However, in an act of brute political power, the government deployed the military to besiege the High Court premises and prevented the court order granting bail to Besigye from taking effect. The government disregarded the views of Justice James Ogoola, who in granting bail observed that in light of the imminent presidential elections, it was imperative to secure the liberty of the accused until his conviction.[49] Despite the devastating effect of these momentous events on the rule of law and democracy in Uganda, the United States, the British Commonwealth, and the European Union stood idly by, failing to exert any significant political pressure.[50]

ROLE OF INTERNATIONAL ACTORS

The international community could and should have done better in assisting democratization in Uganda. Uganda, like other emerging nations, needs help in its transition toward democracy and the rule of law. More effective political pressure on the Ugandan government and greater insistence on the respect for the rule of law and independence of the judiciary were needed from the international community.[51] Because the more developed democracies generally command greater authority based on their significantly established respect for the rule of law, they could and should have used that authority to send clear, unambiguous messages demanding that emerging democracies, such as

Uganda, respect such international standards. For example, such leverage has been put to good use by the EU, which insists that nations seeking to join the EU respect human rights and the rule of law.

The return to democratic governance and the rule of law in countries like Nigeria[52] and South Africa was due in part to lessons these countries learned from constitutional democracies around the world. It was also due to the role of the international community. The South African case aptly illustrates how effective external pressure by international actors—legitimized by their own traditions of respect for the rule of law—can be in complementing and advancing internal efforts toward greater democracy.[53] After a remarkable transition, South Africa became the exemplar of democracy, constitutionalism, and the rule of law in Africa. Its new Constitutional Court soon established a reputation as being one of the finest in the world.

The Constitutional Court also played a key role in South Africa's move away from its long, dismal, and antidemocratic apartheid past, characterized by repression and states of emergency, to become a multiracial democracy that respects rights, human dignity, and the rule of law. In its first politically important and publicly controversial decision, the South African Constitutional Court struck down the death penalty.[54] The court emphasized that the transitional constitution established a new order in South Africa in which human rights and democracy are entrenched and in which the constitution is supreme. The justices emphasized that the court "must not shrink from its task" of review.[55] Even with the recognition that public opinion seemed to favor the retention of the death penalty, the Constitutional Court answered with the clear statement that it would not "allow itself to be diverted from its duty to act as an independent arbiter of the Constitution,"[56] and that public opinion in itself is "no substitute for the duty vested in the courts to interpret the Constitution and to uphold its provisions without fear or favor."[57] Justice Arthur Chaskalson reasoned that if public opinion were to be decisive, "there would be no need for constitutional adjudication."[58] This should provide an answer to the populist arguments used in attacking judicial decisions by the Ugandan courts of judicial review.

Another decision by the South African Constitutional Court whose reception in South Africa stands in stark contrast to the Ugandan experience was *Executive Council of the Western Cape Legislature v. President of the Republic of South Africa* (1995).[59] In this case, the court declared that s.16 (A) of the Local Government Transition Act 209 of 1993 (LGTA) amounted to an unconstitutional delegation of legislative power to the executive. The conflict erupted when President Nelson Mandela, acting in accordance with amending powers granted to the executive in s.16 (A) of the LGTA, took action to counter the attempt by the provincial government in the Western Cape, dominated by the National Party, to demarcate the Cape Town metropolitan areas, removing all the resource-poor African areas from the wealthy, white-dominated areas. In striking down Mandela's action, the Constitutional Court was hailed by the National Party, opponents of the government, as defenders of the constitution for standing up to the African National Congress (ANC)-dominated executive and legislature and for fulfilling the promise of judicial review. In a surprising move, President Mandela praised the court's decision, stating that "this judgment is not the first, nor will it be the last, in which the Constitutional Court assists both the government and society to ensure constitutionality and effective governance."[59] The court had successfully walked the tight line between law and politics, and the government respected its ruling. This notable case demonstrates how a Constitutional Court can use its power of judicial review, uphold the supremacy of the constitution over the actions of the party in power, and draw acceptance from all parties.

CONCLUSION

Credit must be accorded to Ugandan courts for some courageous decisions they have pronounced amid extremely arduous conditions. Uganda is a fledgling democracy and cannot be expected to instantly achieve standards obtained elsewhere in more developed democracies. However, all emerging nations must strive toward the same democratic ideals in virtue of the universality of human dignity—the grounding principle for human rights.[60] The question is whether or not the state is doing enough given the sociopolitical realities in Uganda. The challenge for Uganda and other emerging democracies consists of demilitarizing its politics,[61] respecting the rule of law, and complying with court orders pursuant to judicial review.

In an increasingly globalized world in which a particular country may not be capable of ignoring international opinion for a long time, the international community should exercise political pressure through the various measures available in an effort to demilitarize political conditions and promote respect for the rule of law. Such pressure would be legitimate because Uganda is a signatory to several international legal instruments, particularly with regard to international human rights, and is sensitive to its international image.[62] As part of the effort to bring political pressure to bear, international actors should be less willing to cooperate with despotic governments. Strict international criteria of political accountability, financial transparency, and development-friendly social and economic policies should be enforced and used in the evaluation of international relations and the future course such relations should take.

NOTES

1. See Article 2 of the United Nations Charter (June 26, 1945, 59 Stat. 1031, T.S. 993, 3 Bevans 1153, entered into force October 24, 1945). Limited state sovereignty

was also endorsed by the unanimous adoption of resolution on the international "responsibility to protect" by the world's heads of state and government at the UN World Summit in September 2005. See 2005 World Summit Outcome September 2005, paras. 138–139, A/60/L and UN Security Council Resolution 1674 (April 28 2006), S/RES/1964 (2006) para. 4.

2. Tony Blair called it "enlightened self-interest." See World Economic Forum, "Special Address by Tony Blair, Prime Minister of the United Kingdom," January 27, 2005, online at http://www.weforum.org (visited December 12, 2005).

3. The Uganda Constitution (1995) and the Uganda judiciary borrow from constitutions of many democratic countries—consistent with the increasing cross-border flow of legal norms or transnational law. The Uganda Constitutional Commission reported: "[T]he final source has been the comparative study of constitutional arrangements of other countries and studies and developments in constitutional matters and all matters related to democracy, human rights and the rule of law. The aim was to discover relevant lessons for Uganda." See Uganda Constitutional Commission, *Report of the Uganda Constitutional Commission*, 7 (1993). In *Charles Onyango Obbo and Andrew Mujuni Mwenda v. The Attorney General*, Uganda Supreme Court, Constitutional Appeal No. 2 of 2002 (Judgment of February 11, 2004) (unreported), the Uganda Supreme Court held that foreign judicial decisions are of persuasive value and, when invoked by counsel, must be considered and would be rejected only for *good reason*. However, beyond that borrowing, there has been no consistent adherence to constitutionalism and the rule of law. See *Paul K. Ssemogerere et al. v. The Attorney General*, Uganda Supreme Court, Constitutional Appeal No. 1 of 2002 (unreported) (Justice Kanyeihamba citing Professor Nwabueze that there are "many countries in the World to-day with written constitutions but without constitutionalism" and that in "a number of developing countries, constitutions are perceived by those in power, not as protectors of human rights and the liberties of the individual but as instruments for legitimizing the exercise of power"). Justice Kanyeihamba then concludes that the "founders and makers of the Uganda 1995 Constitution were determined to avoid the situation described by the learned professor."

4. The United States Agency for International Development makes a similar observation. It states: "U.S. interests in Uganda are twofold. Uganda is a critical player in the region in leading efforts to address regional conflicts peacefully; development and political stability in Uganda is key to East Africa's integration into the global marketplace." USAID, "Democracy and Governance in Uganda," online at http://www.usaid.gov/our_work/democracy_and_governance/regions/afr/uganda.html (visited May 30, 2007).

5. Justice George Kanyeihamba (Uganda Supreme Court) observes that the Uganda Parliament is "impotent" and "weakened to the extent that whatever the Executive will, it must be done or must occur without resistance from the Parliament." *New Vision*, online at "Parliament Is Impotent—Judge," http://www.newvision.co.ug/ (visited December 11, 2005).

6. The Uganda constitution (1995) had the objective, inter alia, to "demarcate division of responsibility among the State Organs of the Executive, the Legislature and the Judiciary, and create viable checks and balances between them." Uganda Constitutional Commission Statute, Statute No. 5 (1988), § 4.

7. BBC, "Profile: Uganda's Yoweri Museveni," online at http://news.bbc.co.uk/1/hi/world/africa/4124584.stm (visited February 25, 2006).

8. During the last decade, Uganda averaged annual growth rates of roughly 7 percent. See the White House, "Why Is The President Proposing This New Initiative?" March 14, 2002, online at http://www.whitehouse.gov/infocus/developingnations/newinitiative.html (visited December 12, 2005).

9. The 2001 presidential and parliamentary elections provided a critical test for the rule of law under the new constitution, which provides for free and fair elections. Article 1(4), Uganda constitution (1995). The U.S. State Department reported: "[D]uring the presidential and parliamentary campaigns, there were many reports of arbitrary detention. . . . Many supporters of the opposition were arrested and detained." See U.S Department of State, "Country Reports on Human Rights Practices" (Uganda) (2001), March 4, 2002, online at

http://www.state.gov/g/drl/rls/hrrpt/2001/af/8409.htm (visited December 12, 2005). Nevertheless, the Uganda Supreme Court did not find that the presidential election was fundamentally and substantially flawed—essentially endorsing the status quo. In *Kizza Besigye v. Y.K. Museveni and the Electoral Commission* (hereinafter *Besigye I case*) Uganda Supreme Court Election Petition No. 1 of 2001 (unreported), the Uganda Supreme Court noted that it had been proven that there had been state-inspired military violence in those elections. Yet the Supreme Court acquitted the president of wrongdoing, holding that it had been proven that election malpractices committed by state agents had not been committed with his knowledge or approval. The Uganda Supreme Court came to the same conclusion in *Rtd. Col. Dr. Kizza Besigye v. Electoral Commission and Yoweri Kaguta Museveni* (hereinafter *Besigye II case*), Uganda Supreme Court, Election Petition No. 1 of 2006 (unreported), which challenged the 2006 Uganda presidential elections held under the new multiparty political dispensation. Although the court agreed with the petitioner that there had been noncompliance with the law in the disenfranchisement of voters, counting and tallying of results, bribery and intimidation or violence, multiple voting, and vote stuffing in some areas of the country, it found that the conduct of the election did not affect the results in a substantial manner.

10. Human Rights Watch, "World Report 2005," January 13, 2005, online at http://hrw.org/english/docs/2005/01/13/uganda9862.htm (visited October 30, 2007).

11. Human Rights Watch, "World Report 2007," January 11, 2007, online at http://hrw.org/englishwr2k7/docs/2007/01/11/uganda14719.htm (visited October 30, 2007). See also *Besigye case II*.

12. The Ugandan military wreaked havoc in the Democratic Republic of Congo while President Museveni—who currently enjoys sovereign immunity—was in command. In *Armed Activities on the Territory of the Congo (Democratic Republic of the Congo) v. Uganda,* Provisional Measures, Order of 1 July 2000, I.C.J. Reports 2000, p. 111, the International Court of Justice observed: "[I]t is not disputed that Ugandan forces are present on the territory of the Congo . . . that the fighting has caused a large number of civilian casualties in addition to substantial material damage . . . and . . . that grave and repeated violations of human rights and international humanitarian law, including massacres and other atrocities, have been committed on the territory of the Democratic Republic of the Congo."

13. African poverty is partly due to bad governance. The George W. Bush administration noted that: "Good governance, rooting out corruption, upholding human rights, and adherence to the rule of law are essential conditions for successful development." See the White House, "Helping Developing Nations," March 14, 2002, online at http://www.whitehouse.gov/infocus/developingnations/ (visited December 12, 2005). Tony Blair admitted, "Global poverty in Africa will be fought not just by aid but by good governance, the absence of corruption and an end to the ravages of unnecessary conflict." See 10 DOWNING STREET, "PM Says World Should Tackle Trade Injustice," November 14, 2005, online at http://www.number-10.gov.uk/output/Page8524.asp (visited December 12, 2005). On October 12, 2005, the European Commission launched a new, ambitious initiative called the "European Union Strategy for Africa." The strategy mentions "good and effective governance" as a key requirement for sustainable development. See EUROPA, "European Commission Adopts "European Union Strategy for Africa," December 10, 2005, online at http://europa.eu.int/rapid/pressReleasesAction.do?reference=IP/05/1260&format=HTML&aged=0&language=EN&guiLanguage=en (visited December 12, 2005).

14. Rejecting the rape charges, the Uganda High Court in *Col. (Rtd.) Dr. Kizza Besigye v. Uganda*, Uganda High Court, Criminal Session No. 149/2005 (unreported) castigated the prosecution for bringing "monstrous" evidence to "ruin the honour of a man who offered himself as a candidate for the highest office in this country." While treason charges against Kizza Besigye and others were pending before the High Court of Uganda, the government brought charges of treason and terrorism against the same persons before the General Court Martial. This course of action was challenged in *Uganda Law Society v. The Attorney General, Constitutional* (hereinafter *Law Society case*) Uganda Constitutional Court, Constitutional Petition No. 18 of 2006 1/31/2006 (unreported). Citing transnational legal norms, in particular, the *Manual for Court Martial United States*, 1995 ed., 11–10, the Court held that, as a matter of state policy, a person who is pending trial or has been tried by a state court should not be tried simultaneously by the court martial for the same act/omission. Despite this decision, the General Court Martial continued with the trial of the civilians. See also International Commission of Jurists, "Uganda—General Court Martial Must Respect Ruling by Constitutional Court," February 2, 2006, online at http://www.icj.org/news_multi.php3?id_groupe=2&id_mot=407&lang=en (visited October 30, 2007).

15. According to principal judge of the High Court of Uganda, Justice James Ogoola, this incident was "a very grave and heinous violation of the twin principles of the Rule of Law and Judicial Independence." See Justice James Ogoola, "The Current State of Affairs in the High Court and the Role of Division Heads and Registrars," (paper, Judges Conference, Sheraton Hotel, Kampala, Uganda, February 2006) 15, online at http://www.judicature.go.ug/uploaded_files/1141051083PJ-presentation.pdf.

16. *Law Society case*, Uganda Constitutional Court, Constitutional Petition No. 18 of 2006 (unreported).

17. Subsequent events did not demonstrate government willingness to change course. On March 1, 2007, the Uganda police again sealed off the High Court in order to rearrest persons allegedly belonging to a rebel movement who had been granted bail. The outraged Ugandan judiciary went on strike, accusing the government of invading the judiciary and disobeying court orders. See Anne Mugisa, "Tracing Roots of the Debate about Independence of the Judiciary," *New Vision*, March

8, 2007, online at http://www.newvision.co.ug/D/8/459/553039/judges%20strike (visited October 30, 2007).

18. Amin's brutal subjugation and near obliteration of the judiciary was the culmination of what Uganda's first postindependence president, Milton Obote, set in motion when he militarized the political process and abrogated the first Uganda constitution (1962). In response to the subsequent constitutional challenge in *Uganda v. Commissioner of Prisoners, ex parte Matovu*, East African Law Report (Uganda) (1966), 514, the court merely rubber-stamped Obote's actions, holding that there had been successful revolution establishing a new Grundnorm and as such, the new constitution could not be impeached based on the previous (1962) constitution.

19. Subsequently, Amin ruled by decree. In particular, he enacted the Proceedings Against the Government (Protection) Decree [Uganda Decree No. 8 of 1972], which provided that courts could not grant relief in any actions brought against the military government for injuries sustained as a consequence of measures taken to maintain public order and security. The Amin regime was characterized by complete emasculation of judicial power and any remaining notions of judicial review and constitutionalism. There were no cases on constitutional law brought before the courts of Uganda from 1972 to 1979, the year Amin was overthrown by military struggle. However, even after 1979, courts remained subjugated by a strong executive backed by the military. See Joe Oloka Onyango, *Judicial Power and Constitutionalism in Uganda* (Kampala: Centre for Basic Research, 1993), 31.

20. However, following the arrest of Kizza Besigye, a prominent political opponent, the Netherlands withdrew $8 million in aid. But the British Commonwealth simply continued with its plan to hold its 2007 summit in Uganda, the implications of these developments for democracy notwithstanding.

21. Ralf Rogwski and Thomas Gawron, "Constitutional Litigation as Dispute Processing: Comparing the U.S. Supreme Court and the German Federal Constitutional Court," in *The Constitutional Courts in Comparison: The U.S. Supreme Court and the German Federal Constitutional Court* (Rogowski and Gawron, eds., 2002), 1.

22. Allan R. Brewer-Carías, *Judicial Review in Comparative Law* (Cambridge: Cambridge University Press, 1989), 90.

23. Louis Favoreu, "Constitutional Review in Europe: The Influence of the United States Constitution Abroad" in *Comparative Constitutional Law*, 2nd ed., Vicki C. Jackson and Mark Tushnet (New York: Foundation Press, 2006), 469–485.

24. Uganda Constitution (1995), arts. 137 and 132(3).

25. Uganda Constitution (1995), art. 1(1) provides that "[A]ll power belongs to the people who shall exercise their sovereignty in accordance with this Constitution." Article 2 provides that "[T]his Constitution is the supreme law of Uganda. . . . If any other law or any custom is inconsistent with any of the provisions of this Constitution, the Constitution shall prevail, and that other law or custom shall, to the extent of the inconsistency, be void."

26. Uganda Supreme Court, Constitutional Appeal No. 1 of 2002 (unreported).

27. See Nsibambi Apollo, "A Comment on the Functional Relationship between the Three Arms of the State in Uganda," *East African Journal of Peace & Human Rights* 7, no. 2 (2001): 160.

28. See note 3.

29. *Major General David Tinyefuza v. Attorney General*, Uganda Constitutional Court, Constitutional Petition 1 of 1996 (unreported) concerned the constitutionality of the letter of the minister of state for defence rejecting the petitioner's resignation from the army and requiring him to follow military laws. Rejecting the proposition to dismiss the petition on technical grounds (defective affidavits), the court heard the petition on merits.

30. Uganda Constitutional Court, Constitutional Petition No. 5 of 2002 (unreported).

31. Upon coming to power in 1986, President Museveni established a de facto one-party political dispensation—the "Movement." Although President Museveni described it as broad-based, all-embracing, and not as divisive as multiparty politics, in practice it only provided an instrument for his personal rule and monopolization of political space.

32. Uganda Constitutional Court, Constitutional Petition No. 3 of 1999 (unreported).

33. The political system required candidates to contend for elective political office on the basis of the so-called all-inclusive, broad-based "Movement" that did not provide for political party sponsorship of such candidates.

34. Uganda Constitutional Court, Constitutional Petition No. 6 of 1999 (unreported).

35. Uganda Supreme Court Constitutional Appeal No. 1 of 2002 (unreported). The case questioned the constitutionality of the Constitutional Amendment Act No. 13 (2000), which provided, inter alia, that information in the custody of Parliament may not be adduced in evidence without its special leave. The Supreme Court held that the procedures for making this law had not been followed and that provisions on the right to a fair hearing had been impliedly amended, as it was not possible to have a fair hearing if access to information necessary for litigation was denied.

36. Uganda Supreme Court, Constitutional Appeal No. 2 of 2002 (Judgment of February 11, 2004) (unreported). The decision in which freedom of speech (expression) was in issue, the appellants challenged the constitutionality of s.50 of the Uganda Penal Code, which prohibited the publication of "false news."

37. The government tended to respect orders of the court if they concern personal rights as opposed to political rights.

38. *New Vision*, "Museveni Mad with Judges Over Nullifying 2000 Referendum Act," online at June 30, 2004, http://www.newvision.co.ug/ (visited January 21, 2005). Whereas Kony, ADF, and FOBA were armed rebel groups that could lawfully and legitimately be confronted by the military, "Ssemogerere" group was a civilian political opposition. Nevertheless, President Museveni signaled that the military would be deployed even against the latter group as well if the courts ruled in its favor and critically prejudiced or threatened the establishment's grip on political power.

39. Benjamin J. Odoki, *The Search for a National Consensus: The Making of the Uganda (1995) Constitution* (Kampala: Fountain Publishers, 2005), 353–354.

40. In cases when the government has not used the military, it has employed or acquiesced in activities of paramilitary groups, police and/or other groups committed to the use of physical force to silence legitimate political opposition and demonstrations. See, e.g., Patrick Jaramogi, "CMI Boss Praises Kiboko Squad," *New Vision*, June

1, 2007, online at http://www.newvision.co.ug/D/8/13/568308?highlight&q=kiboko (visited October 30, 2007).

41. Uganda Supreme Court, Election Petition No. 1 of 2001 (unreported).

42. On "substantial effect," see Monica Twesiime, "The State of Constitutional Developments in Uganda—2001," online at http://www.kituochakatiba.co.ug/Monica2001.htm, noting that the electoral law is silent about the test for determining a "substantial manner"—whether it should be quantitative (number of votes) or qualitative (violation of law). The majority of the court agreed with the president that it should be quantitative. Be that as it may, the result of the petition seems to have turned on judicial fear of plunging the country into another cycle of chaos, political instability, and bloodshed. The chief justice, Benjamin Odoki, thus opines: "This is not an ordinary case but an important case involving the election of the President of the Republic of Uganda. It raises serious constitutional and legal issues.... The effect of the decision on the governance and development of the country, and on the well-being of the people of Uganda, cannot be overemphasized." Arguments in favor of political stability may be sustained in the short term, but in the longer term they must yield to the argument that it is legal—as opposed to political—decisions that constitute the bedrock of the rule of law, engender respect for the law and guarantee ultimate political stability and development.

43. Extension of presidential mandate in Africa has been attempted (e.g., Nigeria, Malawi, and Zambia) or secured (e.g., Namibia and Burkina Faso) in many African countries by amendments to constitutions that limited presidential term limits.

44. Uganda Constitutional (Amendment) Bill, (2005), clause 58. This bill was later withdrawn by the state as it was an omnibus bill that did not meet the procedural requirements for amending provisions of the constitution. The proposed amendments respecting judicial review do not appear in the subsequent Constitutional (Amendment) Act (2005).

45. Article 137 (3) of the Uganda Constitution (1995) provides for judicial review of Acts of Parliament.

46. U.S. Department of State, "Supporting Human Rights and Democracy: The U.S Record 2004-2005," March 28, 2005, online at http://www.state.gov/g/drl/rls/shrd/2004/43108.htm (visited April 1, 2005).

47. Constitutional Petition No. 1, 2006 [Uganda Constitutional Court] (unreported).

48. *Law Society case*. With regard to terrorism charges, the Constitutional Court held that the right to a fair trial was violated, as the General Court Martial did not have the necessary subject matter jurisdiction.

49. *Monitor*, "Besigye: To Grant To Deny Bail," December 5, 2005, online at http://www.monitor.co.ug/ (visited November 21, 2006).

50. Ambassador Frazer, the U.S Assistant Secretary of State for African Affairs, attempted an explanation in these terms: "I don't know how it [response] cannot be as forceful when we specifically say that we have tremendous concerns about the arrest of Dr. Besigye.... The thing about it is he [President Museveni] did it constitutionally.... The fact that they're trying him both in a civilian court and in a military court—all of this is quite problematic." See U.S Department of State, "State's Frazer Heralds Spread of Democracy in Africa," December 7, 2005, online at http://usinfo.

state.gov/af/Archive/2005/Dec/08-749713.html (visited October 30, 2007). Speaking at the commonwealth in Malta in the wake of the arrest of Besigye, Prime Minister Tony Blair went no further than stating, "The UK has made clear its concerns about what is happening in Uganda. It is one of the basic principles of the Commonwealth that there should be proper respect for the proper functioning of democracy." See *The New Vision* (November 27, 2005). The European Union stated only: "The EU views with deep concern the arrest of the FDC leader, Dr. Kizza Besigye, and 22 others on charges including treason....The move to a pluralist democratic system in advance of the next elections in February or March 2006 is seen by the EU as a crucial step in the political development of Uganda."

51. The underlying premise of the reluctance of international actors to exert more effective political pressure is that the developments in Uganda fell within the country's constitutional framework—an understanding to which the United States makes express reference. However, the concern of international actors should be whether or not an emerging nation has a "constitution without constitutionalism," which encompasses the rule of law and independence of the judiciary. The irony is that in Africa there is "interest in constitutional reforms even by leaders that have established a long-standing reputation of disregard for the rule of law and their existing constitutions." Julius O. Ihonvbere, "Constitutions Without Constitutionalism? Towards a New Doctrine of Democratization in Africa," in *The Transition to Democratic Governance in Africa: The Continuing Struggle* (Westport: Praeger Publishers, 2003), 148. The "making of a constitution is one thing and implementing is quite another," for "in order to implement a constitution, the government must create, among other things, an enabling atmosphere for the 'protection of basic human rights and the rule of law.' " Benjamin J. Odoki, "The Challenges of Constitution-Making and Implementation in Uganda," in *Constitutionalism in Africa: Creating Opportunities, Facing Challenges* (Kampala: Fountain Publishers, 2001), 263, 281.

52. Kayode Oladele observes, "[S]uffice it to say that Nigeria's return to democracy was made possible by the intense efforts of the pro-democracy and human rights groups as well as the opposition to the military government in Nigeria by the International Community." Kayode Oladele, "Nigeria in the Threshold of Constitutional Crisis," November 21, 2006, online at http://www.nigeriavillagesquare.com/index.php/content/view/4327/46/ (visited October 30, 2007). In Nigeria, the judiciary is increasingly capable of performing its role without interference from the executive. The latest instance of that was the Supreme Court's ruling that the Independent National Electoral Commission (INEC) had no constitutional powers to disqualify any candidate found eligible for election by his political party, thereby allowing Vice President Atiku to feature as a candidate in the April 21, 2007, presidential election. However, beyond allowing Nigerian judges to express their opinions, executive compliance with court orders has been disappointing.

53. It is worth recognizing the efforts of South Africa in the wake of the arrest of the main political opponent to Museveni. South African president Thabo Mbeki promptly paid a visit to Uganda, presumably to exert political pressure on the Museveni administration. The reaction of the media to this visit included a statement to the effect that Mbeki should teach his host how to hand over power peacefully. The reaction of Mbeki was that naturally the two leaders had addressed the matter of the arrest of Dr. Besigye.

54. *S. v. Makwanyane and Another*, South African Constitutional Court, 1995 (6) BCLR 665 (CC).

55. Ibid.

56. Ibid.

57. 1995 (6) BCLR 665 (CC) [88].

58. 1995 (6) BCLR 665 (CC) [88].

59. Heinz Klug, *Constituting Democracy: Law, Globalism and South Africa's Political Reconstruction* (Cambridge: Cambridge University Press, 2000), 150.

60. Article 1, Universal Declaration of Human Rights, 1 G.A. Res. 217, U.N. GAOR (III 1948), adopted by the UN General Assembly on December 10, 1948.

61. The Uganda Catholic Episcopal Conference has called on the state to demilitarize politics as one of the conditions for democracy to flourish in Uganda. See Uganda Episcopal Conference, "Toward a Democratic and Peaceful Uganda Based on the Common Good: The Transition from the Movement System of Governance to Multiparty Politics," (Pastoral Letter, Kampala, November 11, 2005).

62. President Museveni acknowledged that the holding of the Commonwealth Heads of Government Meeting (CHOGM) in Kampala in November 2007 would, among other benefits, lead to the "promotion of Uganda's image internationally." He also indicated that he appreciated the consequences of the failure to adhere to the rule of law, stating: "[C]ontrary to the insinuation that after Chogm the government will be extremely repressive, I want to re-assure the Nation that the government will continue to uphold and enforce the rule of law." "State of the Union Address," *Daily Monitor,* June 9, 2007, online at http://www.monitor.co.ug/news/news06096.php (visited June 9, 2007). With respect to his own ruling style, he maintained, "[A]fter November, as chairman of the Commonwealth for the next two years, I will have to be very careful not to damage the status of the chairman." See Emmanuel Gyezaho, "I Won't Be Repressive After Chogm," *Daily Monitor*, June 8, 2007, online at http://www.monitor.co.ug/news/news06081.php (visited June 8, 2007).

PART IV

Transnational Law and the Boundaries of Sovereignty

CHAPTER ELEVEN

Blurring Sovereignty

The Human Rights Act of 1998 and British Law

MARY L. VOLCANSEK

Many nations voluntarily abdicated a measure of sovereignty in the late twentieth century as regionalism and globalization took hold, and the Council of Europe that promulgated the European Convention on Human Rights (ECHR) in 1950 represents one example of that trend. The United Kingdom ratified the convention in 1951, but it was not incorporated into U.K. law and therefore not directly applicable in a U.K. court until October 2000. This chapter examines how British sovereignty was blurred by the European Convention on Human Rights prior to its incorporation into U.K. law in 2000 by the Human Rights Act of 1998 and what changes have been wrought in the intervening years. Observers in the United Kingdom predicted an executive authority trampling individual rights without incorporation of the convention or, conversely, an activist judiciary usurping the authority of Parliament once incorporation was accomplished. A tentative appraisal of the validity of those competing visions also will be offered.

Similarly extreme predictions were made in the United Kingdom as it entered the EU (then the European Economic Community, or EEC) in 1973, and a vast literature has been generated to explain how and why the various national courts in the EU accommodated the EU treaties, secondary legislation, and decisions by the European Court of Justice into domestic law.[1] Each nation and its national judiciary responded differently, and the U.K. judges charted their own unusual course to bring domestic law into line with that required by EU membership.[2] A similarly unconventional route could naturally be expected as portions of the ECHR were incorporated into British law. Was passage of the Human Rights Act of 1998 "a landmark in the constitutional history of the nation," as Christopher Jenkins asserts,[3] or was it what Mark Tushnet labels a mere weak form of judicial review in which "legislative majorities can displace judicial interpretations"?[4]

This section will assess those evaluations by, first, briefly treating the concept of parliamentary sovereignty and then addressing the ECHR and its incorporation by the Human Rights Act. Next, the record of U.K. courts on protecting rights before and after the Human Rights Act took effect on October 2, 2000, will be examined to ascertain if there are, indeed, significant differences in the treatment that petitioners receive in them.

National human rights regimes generally have been achieved through pressure from NGOs such as Amnesty International, along with citizen activities[5] international community pressure,[6] or through transnational movements.[7] The U.K. experience involved none of those. Rather, the process of expanding rights and ultimately incorporating aspects of the ECHR was led by legal elites. That unusual course stands as particularly puzzling because the "British legal culture and the judiciary are remarkably conservative,"[8] and both are wed to the principle of parliamentary sovereignty. Charles Epp has proposed that, contrary to other explanations, rights revolutions rely on judicial attention, judicial support, and judicial implementation, but there must be legal mobilization to place cases before the judges.[9] The Epp model clearly explains the U.K. experience.

PARLIAMENTARY SOVEREIGNTY

The basic foundation of the nation-state as conceived in the sixteenth century was the notion of absolute sovereignty.[10] When referring to sovereignty today, most people have in mind the 1648 Westphalian notion that grants nations the authority to exercise a monopoly of power within their borders and prevents any nation from intervening in the domestic affairs of another.[11] In the United Kingdom, sovereignty has been equated with Parliament and usually relies on the definition offered by A. V. Dicey in 1885: Parliament holds the "right to make or unmake any law whatever," and "no person or body is recognized by the law of England as having a right to override or set aside" the laws that it passes.[12] Notably, however, no Act of Parliament acknowledges its supremacy; rather, parliamentary sovereignty has as its source a "judicial recognition of the historical fact that England has two sovereigns, who share power, and that there is no higher authority than these two sovereign authorities coming together formally to agree to a measure."[13]

Parliamentary sovereignty was limited, prior to the passage of the Human

Rights Act of 1998, by two other developments in the last quarter of the twentieth century. The first was the European Communities Act of 1972, by which the United Kingdom entered into the EEC (now EU) and thereby subjected itself to laws emanating from Brussels and to judicial decisions from Luxembourg. Then, in 1998, devolution delegated some lawmaking authority to parliaments in Scotland, Northern Ireland, and Wales.[14] Parliament can, however, revoke membership in the EU or devolution by passage of an ordinary statute.

In most countries, the principal institution protecting individual rights is the judiciary.[15] However, the British concept of liberty has been a very Lockean one of negative rights. One has total liberty to do anything, according to William Blackstone, unless a law specifically prohibits the action. Liberty, therefore, is "no other than natural liberty so far restrained by human laws (and no farther) as is necessary and expedient for the general advantage of the publick."[16] Most constitutional democracies list a series of positive rights that are beyond legislative curtailment and rely on courts for enforcement. Britain's system of negative rights relied, however, on political rather than legal accountability and assumed a "self-correcting democracy" in which rights are protected through the political processes of ministerial responsibility and parliamentary elections.[17]

Individuals in Britain may complain of alleged abuses of their liberties through a device called judicial review, not to be confused with constitutional review or American-style judicial review. Rather, the claim for judicial review is a mechanism to complain about the legality of a particular administrative decision and is designed to keep the executive accountable. All executive actions must have a basis in law to be valid. This form of judicial review is less than half a century old, but by 1984 the courts had developed the law sufficiently for it to be summarized into three categories of unacceptable executive decisions: illegality, irrationality, and procedural impropriety.[18] Claimants must request permission from the court to make a substantive application, and there is a good deal of judicial discretion both in granting permission and in applying the criteria to the challenged executive action. Only a few of the cases brought typically concerned the central government, and even those involved only a few departments; most involved local government agencies. The process is both costly and chancy, and many special tribunals have been instituted to handle judicial review claims.[19] More than half of the claims brought involve immigration, homelessness, and crime.[20] Judicial review is an administrative law device that can be highly effective in redressing a grievance, but it lacks easy access. Even so, it has been the principal means for protection of human rights in the United Kingdom during the last half century and can check abuses of power.

HUMAN RIGHTS ACT OF 1998

The ECHR was signed in 1950, ratified by the United Kingdom in 1951, and entered into force in 1953. Despite being the first nation to ratify the treaty, the United Kingdom exercised its option to deny the compulsory jurisdiction of the European Court of Human Rights (ECtHR) in Strasbourg that enforces the treaty and did not allow the right of individual petition to the court until 1966. The policy was reviewable every five years and, notably, has been renewed by all succeeding governments.[21] Litigants were required, however, to exhaust all remedies in domestic courts before approaching the ECtHR, but were unable to rely on the convention's prohibitions in U.K. courts. The convention has not, though, been incorporated in any uniform fashion by all of the signatories to the convention.[22]

Since 1970, bills to incorporate the ECHR have been introduced in Parliament twenty-five times, and in twelve of those instances, the bills originated in the House of Lords. Finally, in 1997, Lord Irvine's bill passed both houses and became law.[23] The Human Rights Act of 1998 specifically incorporated Articles 2 to 12 and 14 of the convention, Articles 1 to 3 of the First Protocol, and Articles 1 and 2 of the Sixth Protocol, as read with Articles 16 to 18 of the convention. The following rights were thereby made effective in U.K. courts: right to life; protection from torture and inhuman or degrading treatment; protection from slavery and forced or compulsory labor; right to liberty and security of person; right to a fair trial; protection from retrospective criminal offenses; protection of private and family life; freedom of thought, conscience, and religion; freedom of expression; freedom of association and assembly; right to marry and found a family; freedom from discrimination; right to property; right to education; right to free and fair elections; and the absence of capital punishment in peacetime.

Courts in the United Kingdom are obliged by the Human Rights Act to consider existing and future case law from the ECtHR and from the European Commission on Human Rights, and to the extent possible, existing legislation in domestic law is to be interpreted in a fashion compatible with rights in the convention. However, domestic legislation cannot be invalidated. Should a law contravene a convention right, courts may declare its incompatibility, but the law remains valid. A Minister of the Crown may, however, should he have "compelling reasons," order that the incompatible law be amended to remedy the incompatibility.[24]

RIGHTS PROTECTION PRIOR TO 2000

Negative rights of the kind that the British enjoyed prior to October 2, 2000, were the norm as constitutionalism developed. They are rights of a protective character and are the "hard core of human rights protection" because they prohibit public authorities from certain actions. The generation of rights that began to be recognized in the late eighteenth century was of a very different nature.[25] Indeed, some of the earliest limitations on the prerogatives of government were created in the United Kingdom. The Magna Carta (1215) and the Bill of Rights (1688) confirmed limitations on the power of the crown vis-à-vis, in the latter case, Parliament and formed the basis for negative rights secured through the political process or the common law. Two problems have been identified with this approach. First, such rights can always be taken away by statutory law; second, these rights are always residual, constituting only what is left after limitations have been imposed through law.[26]

David Feldman emphatically states that there has always been "an assumption that [the United Kingdom] is a free country . . . [and that there is] a minimum of state intervention."[27] Interventions in individuals' freedoms occurred only after serious debates in the House of Commons, and the courts protected other liberties through the common law. Blackstone wrote eloquently in the eighteenth century about the "absolute rights of every Englishman . . . founded on nature and reason, so they are coequal with our form of government; though subject at times to fluctuate and change: their establishment (excellent as it is) being still human."[28] There was no sense that human rights in the United Kingdom were at risk, and U.K. residents generally were complacent about rights. That began to change in the 1970s. Some attributed the shift in attitudes, at least among legal and judicial elites, to excesses by the Thatcher government,[29] to the United Kingdom's losing record before the ECtHR in Strasbourg,[30] and to the broader "Europeanization" of the United Kingdom through its membership in the EU.[31] A confluence of all of these factors likely served as the catalyst for seeking a more legal than political vehicle for ensuring rights.

The common law traditionally had been thought to stand as a bulwark against incursions on rights should political mechanisms fail. The common law could be invoked through the judicial review mechanism, and the irrationality element of that review has been driven by the *Wednesbury* test articulated by the court of appeal in 1948. The test defined what might constitute an "unreasonable" use of discretion in *Wednesbury*: "If a decision on a competent matter is so unreasonable that no reasonable authority could ever have come to it, then the courts can interfere." However, "to prove a case of that kind would require something overwhelming."[32] The high bar of proof that must be demonstrated for a discretionary action of a government agency to qualify as sufficiently unreasonable to be overturned judicially would, nearly fifty years later, be deemed insufficient by the ECtHR to pass muster under Article 13 of the convention that requires effective remedies in member nations' systems to adjudicate convention rights and freedoms.[33]

A growing number of U.K. petitioners took their cases to the European Court in Strasbourg, and the United Kingdom was often found to have run afoul of the convention. Between 1959 and 1989, the United Kingdom had the highest number of cases brought against it of any country (thirty-seven) and was found to be in violation most often (twenty-three).[34] Clive Walker and Russell Weaver examined the figures from 1959 through 1997 and found that the United Kingdom was second only to Italy in the number of adverse judgments by the ECtHR. They then, however, took into account the relative populations of the countries under consideration. Looking at the number of violations per year per 100,000 population, they found that the United Kingdom was lower than Belgium, France, and Italy. Even so, that meant about five findings of violations per year.[35] A disproportionate number of the cases against the United Kingdom that reached the ECtHR were, moreover, a consequence of procedures used in an attempt to counter terrorism in Northern Ireland.[36]

Following are some cases illustrative of how English and Welsh judges treated alleged rights infringements in the three decades before the Human Rights Act. The range of subjects extended beyond treatment of alleged terrorism. Freedom of expression was also at issue in some cases. The *Handyside* case in 1976 illustrates how the European Court's doctrine of "margin of appreciation" that recognizes variations among national practices and national cultures allowed the United Kingdom to ban a book as obscene, even though it had also been published in Belgium, Denmark, Finland, France, Germany, Greece, Iceland, Italy, the Netherlands, Norway, Sweden, and Switzerland and was circulating freely in Austria and Luxembourg. The European Court found that the English authorities had acceptably condemned the book to protect the morals of youth and, recognizing the national authorities' margin of appreciation, had not, therefore, run afoul of the convention's protection of freedom of expression.[37]

The *Spycatcher* case that began in 1986 in the United Kingdom and was ultimately concluded in 1991 in Strasbourg illustrates how the United Kingdom fared worse before the ECtHR. Peter Wright had worked for the U.K. security services (MI5) from 1955 until retiring in 1976 and subsequently wrote a book, *Spycatcher*, about his work, which included accounts of wiretappings and burglaries, planned assassinations, high-level double agents, and plots to destabilize the government. Wright had allegedly committed a breach of confidence by revealing what he knew from his service in MI5, but the United Kingdom did not pursue that charge, choosing rather to block publication. Interlocutory injunctions were obtained against two newspapers, and later, a breach of confidence suit was obtained against another. Ultimately, within the U.K. courts, the House of Lords upheld the temporary injunctions until, in trial, both of the newspapers were exonerated of breach of confidence charges. However, the third newspaper was found to have breached confidence and was fined.[38]

The dispute then moved, as anticipated, to the ECtHR in Strasbourg, where the argument revolved around Article 10, freedom of expression. The full complement of twenty-four judges heard the case, and fourteen of them upheld the initial injunctions because of the margin of appreciation allowed to national courts. However, they unanimously agreed that the injunctions lost any purpose after *Spycatcher* was published in the United States.[39]

The *Brind* case defined the limits of applying the European Convention in the context of a judicial review proceeding. By the time *Brind* was heard by the House of Lords in 1991, it was well established in the common law that if a statute was ambiguous or subject to different interpretations, the courts would always assume that Parliament intended to comply with its international treaty obligations and would interpret the law to conform to the convention. Brind and other journalists objected to a decision of the home secretary to prohibit, under the Broadcasting Act of 1981, broadcasting the voice of anyone representing a banned organization. Brind applied for judicial review, claiming that the ban was unreasonable (the *Wednesbury* test) and also that it disproportionately violated the European Convention's right to freedom of expression in Article 10. The House of Lords rejected the claim. What is important, though, is how the lords treated application of the convention. The general rule is to interpret domestic legislation in light of the convention, but "where Parliament has conferred on the executive an administrative discretion without indicating the precise limits within which it must be exercised, to presume that it must be exercised with Convention limits would be to go far beyond the resolution of an ambiguity."[40] In short, the House of Lords clearly rejected a form of judicial incorporation of the convention. Brind subsequently took his complaint to the European Court, but the commission rejected his application on the grounds that the home secretary's action was not disproportionate.[41]

The United Kingdom's policy of dismissing anyone from the military forces for being a homosexual was challenged in 1997. Jeanette Smith, a lesbian, and Graeme Grady, an allegedly gay man, both were discharged from the Royal Air Force when their sexual preferences were revealed. Both also were subjected to intrusive interrogations, as were their presumed partners, prior to their involuntary separations from the military. The U.K. High Court had first considered their respective claims and, applying the *Wednesbury* test of reasonableness, determined that even when a fundamental human right is in question, "the threshold of unreasonableness is not lowered." The court of appeal further agreed that the policy was not, citing *Wednesbury*, unreasonable. Subsequently, the ECtHR found that Article 8 of the convention requiring respect for one's private life was infringed, despite a margin of appreciation for national security issues, by the discharge of the two service people and also by the demeaning investigations to which they were subjected. More importantly for U.K. law, the European Court determined that Article 13, requiring that there be effective remedies for rights grievances in national courts, was violated by the irrationality test: "[T]he threshold at which the High Court and the court of appeal could find the Ministry of Defence policy irrational was placed so high that it effectively excluded any consideration in domestic courts of the . . . applicants' rights."[42] The ECtHR's rebuke was even more stinging because the case was decided after the passage of the Human Rights Act of 1998 but before it came into force in October 2000. Three months before the Human Rights Act took effect in the United Kingdom, the European Court awarded damages in the amount of 78,200 pounds sterling to each of the petitioners and 32,000 pounds sterling in costs.[43]

It is particularly relevant, given that the U.K. constitution relies on political as well as legal means for protecting right, that in the years prior to 1998 some significant pieces of legislation were passed aimed at achieving greater equality and human rights. The Murder Act of 1965 abolished the death penalty and replaced it with a sentence of mandatory life imprisonment. The Equal Pay Act of 1970 sought to bring men and women to an equal economic footing for the work they did. The Sex Discrimination Acts of 1975 went further by attempting to eliminate sex discrimination. The Race Relations Act of 1976 similarly was directed at ending racial discrimination. The Criminal Justice Act of 1991 was passed in response to a decision by the Strasbourg court in *Thynne, Wilson and Gunnell v. U.K.*[44]

Although these are only a few illustrative examples of both parliamentary and judicial handling of rights in the United Kingdom prior to the coming into force of the Human Rights Act in October 2000, these cases highlight four consistent themes. First, the political constitution did work to achieve greater protection of rights as seen through parliamentary measures enacted. Also, the judges, particularly in the House of Lords, strove to maintain the rules of the common law, as in *Brind*. At other times, when there was a legitimate choice in interpreting domestic law, the lords typically nodded to the convention, even if they did not follow it, through their interpretation of domestic legislation. The glaring exception is the case of *Smith and Grady*. Finally, no arm of the U.K. administration attempted after 1966 to prevent individuals from taking their claims under the convention to Strasbourg; presumably the United Kingdom went along with the decisions of the Strasbourg court when the U.K. administration was found to be in noncompliance.

INCORPORATION OF THE CONVENTION

Anticipating increased demand for judicial review of official actions once the Human Rights Act came into force in October 2000, a number of administrative reforms were put in place to achieve more pre-permission settlements (i.e., settlements before the courts decide whether to permit a hearing on the merits of a claim). The Public Law Project examined all civil judicial review applications during a three-month period in 2002 and tracked those granted permission during a six-month period.[45] Of 652 claims filed, 316 (46 percent) actually raised Human Rights Act issues, and the overwhelming majority of those were related to immigration and asylum cases.[46] Of 652 claims raising Human Rights Act issues that were tracked during six months in 2002, 13 percent were settled in favor of the claimant, 43 percent were denied permission, and only 20 percent were granted permission to move to court.[47]

As of January 2009, twenty-six declarations of incompatibility had been made by British courts. Seventeen declarations were final. Of those, ten had been remedied by new legislation, and in three cases, the legislation had already been altered to achieve compliance before the declaration. One law was altered administratively, and three remained in stage of consultation to determine the appropriate response. Eight declarations were overturned on appeal and three remain subject to further appeal.[48]

After the Human Rights Act came into force in the United Kingdom, there was an almost inevitable clash between the *Wednesbury* rule and ECHR jurisprudence in the *Daly* case early in 2001. Daly was in prison and objected to a policy promulgated by the home secretary in 1995 involving searches of prisoners and their cells. One element of that policy provided that during a cell search, "staff must examine legal correspondence thoroughly in the absence of the prisoner" but "only so far as necessary to ensure that it is bona fide" legal correspondence and "does not conceal anything else." When the House of Lords decided the case, Lord Bingham noted that even though prisoners were removed from their cells to avoid intimidation and even though by definition the fact of being in prison involves curtailment of some rights enjoyed by other citizens, three rights remained unaltered: "the right of access to court; the right of access to legal advice; and the right to communicate confidentially with a legal adviser under seal of legal professional privilege." The ECtHR previously had held that correspondence with a prisoner's lawyer is privileged under Article 8 of the convention and allowed that a letter might be opened, but never read, and even then only when there existed a reasonable cause to believe it contained something illicit. Lord Bingham concluded that the blanket policy of reading prisoners' legal correspondence was a violation of the common-law rights of prisoners and also under the convention and the rulings of the ECtHR. In other words, both the common law and the convention produced the same result. Another law lord added that when the two forms of judicial analysis achieve different conclusions, those of the convention must prevail. Another went further and predicted that *Wednesbury* will be recognized at some point as "an unfortunately retrogressive decision in English administrative law."[49]

Another convergence of the convention and the common law was found in the *Shayler* case. David Shayler worked for the Security Service from 1991 until 1996 and had, at both the beginning of his employment and on leaving it, signed declarations requiring that he not disclose, without official authorization, any information relative to security, defense, or international relations that he might come across in his work. The following year, Shayler gave some twenty-nine documents to the *Daily Mail* that resulted in several articles, including one carrying his byline. Shayler voluntarily returned to the United Kingdom from France in 2000 and claimed that his disclosures were protected by his freedom of expression under the common law, the Human Rights Act, and the convention. His appeal to the House of Lords involved a decision by a lower court judge in preparatory hearings and, therefore, preceded any trial or formal determination of facts or culpability. Shayler claimed that he disclosed the documents in the public and national interest, but if the prosecution's allegations were true, Shayler had acted in contravention of the Official Secrets Act of 1989 and the Security Service Act of 1989.[50]

The lords acknowledged a "fundamental right of free expression" under the common law but noted that it had not rested on statutory authority until passage of the Human Rights Act. Lord Bingham relied on Article 10 of the convention to note that freedom of expression was not an absolute right, concluding that "it is on the question of necessity, pressing social need and proportionality that the real issue between the parties arises." He recognized the distinction offered earlier in *Daly* and took pains to apply the principle of proportionality, as adopted by the ECtHR, to determine whether the Official Secrets Act and the Security Services Acts violated Article 10. Because both acts included provisions for seeking authorization for disclosure, there was no incompatibility.[51]

Until the end of 2004, the House of Lords had not found any action incompatible with the European Convention, but on December 16, 2004, that was to change when the Court was confronted with an appeal from nine foreign nationals who had been certified by the home secretary under the Anti-Terrorism, Crime and Security Act of 2001. Two had exercised their rights to leave the United Kingdom, one had been placed in a hospital as mentally ill, and one had been released on bail, but under strict conditions. The other five remained in custody for approximately three years before their appeal was heard by the House of Lords, yet none had been charged with a criminal offense and none was facing the prospect of a trial. Prior to the detention of the nine people, the home secretary had made a Derogation Order from the convention because of the terrorism threat following the September 11, 2001, attacks in the United States. The Anti-Terrorism Act had specifically authorized the challenged detentions: "A suspected international terrorist may be detained under a provision . . . despite the fact that his removal or departure from the United Kingdom is prevented (whether temporarily or indefinitely)." Lord Bingham questioned the choice of an immigration measure to address a security problem because it allowed only detention of non-U.K. nationals unwilling to leave the country and left U.K. suspected terrorists at large. He concluded that the relevant section of the 2001 Anti-Terrorism Act was incompatible with Articles 5 and 14 of the European Convention because it was disproportionate and discriminated on the ground of nationality or immigration status. Lord Nicholls added that "indefinite imprisonment without charge or trial is an anathema in any country which observes the rule of law."[52]

The true value of the Human Rights Act of 1998 was then put to the test, as the highest court could do no more than declare a statute incompatible with the incorporated sections of the convention. Slightly more than one month after the declaration of incompatibility, the government announced a plan to reconstruct its antiterrorism policy. The proposal gave the home secretary the authority, when dealing with suspected terrorists, to impose curfews, tag with electronic bracelets, limit access to telephones and the Internet, restrict contact with named individuals, or restrict to house arrest.[53] Twelve suspects were expected to be released from custody under the changed policy.[54] The government's proposed amendments to the Anti-Terrorism, Crime and Security Act of 2001 were passed by Parliament as the Prevention of Terrorism Act 2005.

The fates of the original nine detainees in the 2004 case gave rise to a follow-up case before the House of Lords. The issue arose of whether the Special Immigrations Appeals Commission (SIAC), when certifying and detaining foreign terror suspects, could use evidence that may have been procured through torture in another nation, without the complicity of the British authorities. All of the lords expressed their total disdain for torture in any form and noted the extensive case law, treaty law, common law, and other national laws or cases that condemn it. The division of opinion arose as to the burden of proof required to demonstrate that information before the SIAC had been obtained by torture and, therefore, must be excluded from evidence. The majority of the lords preferred a rule that leaned slightly in favor of accepting the evidence and accepted a test that SIAC "must direct its inquiry to what has happened in the past," with a focus on whether it has been "*established*, by means of such diligent inquiries into the sources that it is practicable to carry out and on a balance of probabilities, that the information [emphasis added]" was obtained by torture; if the answer is yes, then the evidence must be excluded.[55]

The House of Lords applied the Human Rights Act again in a major case in June 2007, when it held that the act applied in "those exceptional situations" when a U.K. public authority violates the rights enumerated in the act outside the territorial jurisdiction of the U.K. Families of five Iraqi civilians who had been killed in Basra by U.K. soldiers and the family of a sixth Iraqi who died in a U.K. detention facility, allegedly beaten to death by U.K. soldiers, brought suit for damages under the Human Rights Act. The majority of the House of Lords held that the sixth victim was, for purposes of the Human Rights Act, under U.K. jurisdiction at the time of his death and remanded the case to the trial court for factual determinations.[56]

Because approximately one-third of the cases decided by the House of Lords since implementation of the Human Rights Act raised a human rights claim, coverage of all of them exceeds the scope of this chapter. However, the Department of Constitutional Affairs determined that only about 10 percent of the outcomes were affected in any substantial way by the Human Rights Act.[57] In addition to the cases discussed here, cases were brought involving criminal law, sentencing, prisons, immigration and asylum, family law, inquiries and inquests, mental health, travelers and gypsies, administrative decision making, education, and discrimination.[58] In most areas, U.K. practices were found to be consistent with the requirements of the European Convention.

CONCLUSION

Beginning in the 1980s, human rights became a common theme in U.K. jurisprudence, but no evidence suggests that a British "rights revolution" was driven by pressure from international NGOs, as one theory argues.[59] Indeed, U.K. citizens largely have tended historically to be complacent about their rights, and in the 1997 general elections, human rights were not considered a salient issue to voters (only regional government was rated lower); in the 2001 general elections, human rights were only viewed as more salient than regional government and local government.[60] Nor have human rights been driven in the United Kingdom by transnational legal movements[61] or by international pressures. Rather, the legal elites—the judges and the lawyers in the United Kingdom—attempted to fashion a means for protecting rights through the judicial review mechanism while also striving to incorporate the European Convention into domestic law.

As Charles Epp found, in advance of the Human Rights Act of 1998, more than 30 percent of the House of Lords appeals by 1990 involved rights claims.[62] What drove the so-called "rights revolution" in the United Kingdom was legal mobilization to get cases onto court dockets and a judiciary that was attentive to and supportive of those claims.[63] Where possible, the highest appellate judges, those in the House of Lords, embedded rights into the fabric of the common law. Thus access to courts, access to legal advice, and the privilege of confidential communication with one's lawyers could be protected through the common law.[64] Failing that approach, the courts have looked to the United Kingdom's international treaty obligations on the assumption that "Parliament has not maintained on the statute book a power capable of being exercised in a manner inconsistent with the treaty obligations of this country."[65] This was the same approach U.K. judges had employed to reconcile a U.K. statute with EU law decades earlier.[66]

Judges continued to grapple with the restrictive definition of what constituted "irrational" administrative decisions as dictated by the *Wednesbury* decision. Some law lords chafed under the precedent and struggled to reconcile both EU law and the Human Rights Act with *Wednesbury*. The lords had, until 1966, refused to depart from one of their own precedents. In that year, however, they issued a Practice Statement, declaring that they would not be inextricably bound by their own precedents. Even so, the House of Lords appears to be most reluctant to overrule prior decisions.[67] The *Wednesbury* irrationality test may, nonetheless, be discarded in the future to more readily allow U.K. courts to accommodate the Human Rights Act and ECHR jurisprudence.

Was the coming into force of the Human Rights Act "a landmark in the constitutional history of the nation?" Have "activitist" judges embraced the act to legislate from the bench? A review of cases at the House of Lords level since the Human Rights Act came into force in 2000 suggests that neither prediction has been borne out. The law lords continue to show great deference both to parliamentary enactments and to the executive. This was clearest in the decision in late 2005 to exclude from administrative decisions evidence obtained through torture in another country. The lords chose to adopt the requirement that it must be established, not merely plausible, that the information was obtained through torture.[68] The lords acted more boldly, however, in the *Al-Skeini* case by extending the reach of the Human Rights Act to U.K. public authorities extraterritorially. Importantly, Parliament and the executive have also been deferential to judicial decisions. In the single instance in which the House of Lords found a statute incompatible with the European Convention, the government and Parliament acted swiftly to amend the law and remove the offending section. Even so, Parliament can, should it choose, repeal or amend the Human Rights Act simply by passing an ordinary statute.

Human rights can be protected by a variety of mechanisms. A catalog of rights does not ensure that the enumerated rights will be respected by the executive, by the legislature, or in the courts. A culture of rights and a culture of democracy must provide the infrastructure for rights to flourish. The United Kingdom embodied both before and after the passage of the Human Rights Act of 1998. More importantly, U.K. sovereignty on rights claims was already beginning to blur as judges, particularly on the highest court, were cognizant of treaty obligations including and beyond the ECHR and strained, despite the *Wednesbury* precedent and within the confines of the common law's requirements, to bend domestic legislation to meet international treaty obligations. Human rights and the extent of their protection continue, however, to "reflect the fundamental ambiguities in the prevalent political culture."[69]

NOTES

1. See, for example, Karen J. Alter, *Establishing the Supremacy of European Law* (Oxford: Oxford University Press, 2001); and Anne-Marie Slaughter, Alec Stone Sweet, and Joseph H. H. Weiler, eds., *The European Courts and National Courts* (Oxford: Hart Publishing, 1997).

2. Danny Nicol, *EC Membership and the Judicialization of British Politics* (Oxford: Oxford University Press, 2001).

3. Christopher D. Jenkins, "The Institutional and Substantive Effects of the Human Rights Act in the United Kingdom," *Dalhousie Law Journal* 24 (Fall 2001): 219.

4. Mark Tushnet, "Alternative Forms of Judicial Review," *Michigan Law Review* 101 (August 2003): 2786.

5. Tim Dunne and Nicholas J. Wheeler, "Introduction: Human Rights and the Fifty Years' Crisis," in *Human Rights in Global Politics*, ed. Tim Dunne and Nicholas J. Wheeler (Cambridge: Cambridge University Press, 1999), 2.

6. Thomas Risse and Kathryn Sikkink, "The Socialization of International Human Rights Norms into Domestic Practices: Introduction," in *The Power of Human Rights: International Norms and Domestic Change*, ed. Thomas Risse, Stephen C. Ropp, and Kathryn Sikkink (Cambridge: Cambridge University Press, 1999), 20.

7. Alison Brysk, *From Tribal Village to Global Village: Indian Rights and International Relations in Latin America* (Stanford: Stanford University Press, 2000), 285.

8. Charles R. Epp, *The Rights Revolution* (Chicago: University of Chicago Press, 1998), 131.

9. Ibid., 7–18.

10. Gabriel A. Almond, "Political Science: The History of the Discipline," in *A New Handbook of Political Science*, ed. Robert E. Goodin and Hans-Dieter Klingemann (Oxford: Oxford University Press, 1996), 58.

11. Stephen D. Krasner, "Abiding Sovereignty," *International Political Science Review* 22 (2001): 234.

12. Albert Venn Dicey, *Introduction to the Study of the Law of the Constitution* (London: E.C.S. Wade, 1956 [1885]), 40.

13. Adam Tomkins, *Public Law* (Oxford: Oxford University Press, 2003), 48–49.

14. David Jenkins, "Both Ends against the Middle: European Integration, Devolution, and the Sites of Sovereignty in the United Kingdom," *Temple International and Comparative Law Journal* 16 (Spring 2002): 16.

15. Ariel L. Bendor and Aeez Segal, "Constitutionalism and Trust in Britain: An Ancient Constitutional Culture, A New Judicial Review Model," *American University International Law Review* 17 (2002): 705.

16. William Blackstone, *Commentaries on the Laws of England* (reprinted Buffalo: William S. Hein & Co., Inc, 1992), i, 121.

17. Lord Irvine of Lairg, "Sovereignty in Comparative Perspective: Constitutionalism in Britain and America," *New York University Law Review* 76 (2001): 19.

18. Tomkins, *Public Law*, 170–172.

19. Carol Harlow and Richard Rawlings, *Law and Administration* (London: Butterworths, 1997), 530 531.

20. Ibid., 538.

21. Mary Baber, "The *Human Rights* Bill [HL] Bill 119 of 1997-98" (House of Commons Library: Research Paper 98/24, 1998), 8.

22. J. E. S. Fawcett, *The Application of the European Convention on Human Rights* (London: Oxford University Press, 1969), 20.

23. Baber, "The *Human Rights Bill*," 65–66.

24. Human Rights Act 1998, online at www.opsi.gov.uk/acts/acts1998/ukpga_19980042_en_1 (visited August 9, 2009).

25. Tim Koopmans, *Courts and Political Institutions: A Comparative View* (Cambridge: Cambridge University Press, 2003), 214.

26. Timothy H. Jones, "Fundamental Rights in Australia and Britain: Domestic and International Aspects," in *Understanding Human Rights*, ed. Conor Gearty and Adam Tomkins (London: Mansell Publishing, 1996), 92.

27. David Feldman, *Civil Liberties and Human Rights in England and Wales* (Oxford: Clarendon Press, 1993), 60–61.

28. Blackstone, *Commentaries on the Laws of England*, i, 121.

29. K. D. Ewing and C. A. Gearty, *Freedom under Thatcher: Civil Liberties in Modern Britain* (Oxford: Clarendon Press, 1990); and Michael Zander, *A Bill of Rights?* (London: Sweet & Maxwell, 1985), 45.

30. Feldman, *Civil Liberties and Human Rights in England and Wales*, 98.

31. Ibid., 99.

32. *Associated Provincial Picture Houses Ltd v. Wednesbury Corp.* [1948] 1 KB 223.

33. *Smith and Grady v. United Kingdom*, 29 EHHR 493 [2000].

34. Donald W. Jackson, *The United Kingdom Confronts the European Convention on Human Rights* (Gainesville: University Press of Florida, 1997), 17

35. Clive Walker and Russell L. Weaver, "The United Kingdom Bill of Rights 1998: The Modernisation of Rights in the Old World," *University of Michigan Journal of Law Reform* 33 (Summer 2000): 513.

36. For a complete treatment of many of these cases through 1996, see Jackson, *The United Kingdom Confronts the European Convention on Human Rights*, chap. 3.

37. *Handyside v. United Kingdom*, 24 Eur. Ct. H.R. (ser. A) 23, (1976).

38. *Attorney-General v. Guardian Newspapers and Others*, 1 WLR 1248 [1991].

39. *The Observer and Guardian v. U.K.; Sunday Times v. U.K.*, 14 EHHR 153 [1991].

40. *R. v. Secretary of State for the Home Department, ex parte Brind* [1991] 1 AC 696.

41. Application No. 18714/91, decision of 9 May 1994.

42. Case of *Smith and Grady v. United Kingdom* [1999] 29 EHHR 493.

43. Case of *Smith and Grady v. United Kingdom*, 2000.

44. *Thynne, Wilson and Gunnell v. U.K.* 13 EHHR 66 [1990].

45. Varda Bondy, *The Impact of the Human Rights Act on Judicial Review: An Empirical Research Study* (London: The Public Law Project, 2003), 2.

46. Ibid., 4.

47. Ibid., 17.

48. *Responding to Human Rights Judgments: Government Response to the Joint Committee on Human Rights' Thirty-first Report of Session 2007-08* (London: Ministry of Justice, 2009), 41.

49. *R. v. Secretary of State, ex parte Daly* [2001] UKHL 26 (23 May 2001).

50. *R. v. Shayler* [2002] UKHL 11 (21 March 2002).

51. Ibid.

52. *A and others v. Secretary of the Home Department; X and another v. Secretary of the Home Department* [2004] UKHL 56.

53. Lizette Alvarez, "Britain Offers Plan to Restrain, Not Jail, Foreign Terror Suspects," *New York Times* (January 27, 2005), online at http://query.nytimes.com/gst/fullpage.html?res=940CE1D7163BF934A15752C0A9639C8B63 (visited August 9, 2009).

54. "Terror Suspects Face House Arrest," online at http://news.bbc.co.uk/2/hi/uk_news/politics/4207295.stm (visited August 11, 2009).

55. *A and others v. Home Secretary; A and others and others v. Home Secretary* [2005] UKHL 71 (8 December 2005).

56. *Al-Skeini and others v. Secretary of State for Defence* [2007] UKHL 26.

57. Department for Constitutional Affairs, *Review of the Implementation of the Human Rights Act* (London: DCA, 2006), 10.

58. Ibid., 12–16.

59. Dunne and Wheeler, "Introduction," 2.

60. Robertas Pogorelis, Bart Maddens, Wilfried Swenden, and Elodie Fabre, "Issue Salience in Regional and National Party Manifestos," *West European Politics* 28 (November 2005): 1003.

61. Brysk, *From Tribal Village to Global Village*, 285.

62. Epp, *The Rights Revolution*, 133.

63. Ibid., 7–18.

64. *R. v. Secretary of State for the Home Department, ex parte Daly* [2001] UKHL 26.

65. *R. v. Secretary of the Home Department, ex parte V.* and *R. v. Secretary of the Home Department, ex parte T.* [1997] UKHL.

66. Mary L. Volcansek, *Judicial Politics in Europe* (New York: Peter Lang, 1986), 220.

67. Epp, *The Rights Revolution*, 125.

68. *A. and other v. Secretary of the Home Department; A. and others v. Secretary of Home Department* [2005] UKHL 71.

69. Hugo E. Fruhling, "Human Rights in Constitutional Order and in Political Practice in Latin America," in *Constitutionalism and Democracy*, ed. Douglas Greenberg, Stanley N. Katz, Melanie Beth Oliviero, and Steven C. Wheatly (New York: Oxford University Press, 1993), 97.

CHAPTER TWELVE

Fundamental Rights, the European Court of Justice, and European Integration

MICHAEL C. TOLLEY

INTRODUCTION

Under the law of the United Kingdom, the retirement age for men and women is sixty-five and sixty years, respectively. In February 2002, Sarah Margaret Richards applied to the secretary of state for Work and Pensions for a retirement pension to be paid from February 28, 2002, the date when she turned sixty. In March 2002, the application was refused on the ground that her birth certificate registered her as male and the retirement age for men in the United Kingdom is sixty-five. Ms. Richards brought an appeal to the Social Security appeal tribunal, arguing that in 2001 she underwent gender reassignment surgery and, therefore, was eligible for a retirement pension at age sixty. When the appeal tribunal dismissed her case, Ms. Richards appealed to the Social Security commissioner. She claimed that the refusal to pay her a retirement pension at the age of sixty violated Article 8 of the European Convention on Human Rights (ECHR) and Directive 79/7, which implemented the community law principle of equal treatment for men and women in matters of state pensions. In 2004, the Social Security commissioner referred the following question to the European Court of Justice (ECJ) for a preliminary ruling under Article 234 EC: "Does Directive 79/7 prohibit the refusal of a retirement pension to a male-to-female transsexual until she reaches the age of sixty-five and who would have been entitled to such a pension at the age of sixty had she been held to be a woman as a matter of national law?"[1]

In 2006, the ECJ ruled that "the right not to be discriminated against on grounds of sex is one of the fundamental human rights the observance of which the Court has a duty to ensure." The court went on to explain that "Article 4(1) of Directive 79/7 must be interpreted as precluding legislation which denies a person who, in accordance with the conditions laid down by national law, has undergone male-to-female gender reassignment entitlement to a retirement pension on the ground that she has not reached the age of sixty-five, when she would have been entitled to such a pension at the age of sixty had she been held to be a woman as a matter of national law."

The ECJ's ruling in *Sarah Margaret Richards v. Secretary of State for Work and Pensions* (2006)[2] raises many questions about the protection of rights in Europe. The most obvious question concerns the legitimacy of the ECJ's rights jurisdiction. On what authority may the ECJ recognize fundamental rights and use them to strike down national laws or policies to the contrary? The 1957 Treaty Establishing the European Economic Community (Treaty of Rome) lacked an express bill of rights, and in 1959, the ECJ ruled that the protection of fundamental rights was not part of its jurisdiction.[3] During the next fifty years, the ECJ has recognized a fairly substantial list of fundamental rights, including the right of transsexuals to obtain pensions free from discrimination.[4] Two commentators have called it "the progressive construction of a charter of rights for the Community."[5] Because fundamental rights as such were not matters originally within the ECJ's competence, questions about the legitimacy of this court-engineered development naturally arise.

Another question is related to the capacity of the ECJ to develop a coherent and effective system of rights protection for all of Europe. The European Union (EU) today is a diverse, supranational polity of 27 member states and more than 490 million people. With each enlargement, the European Union has changed in many ways. Despite the European Union's motto, *in varietate concordia* (unity in diversity), there are still questions regarding whether the ECJ can possibly succeed in finding a common standard of fundamental rights when the historical, cultural, and linguistic differences between member states are so great. Rights are often closely related to cultural values. The rights recognized and enforced by the ECJ may not always reflect the values of citizens in all parts of Europe. The potential for a clash of values has increased dramatically since 2004, when ten Eastern Bloc countries and former Soviet republics were brought into the European Union. The challenges of an expanded European Union are not simply economic. There is also the challenge of declaring and ultimately enforcing rights vertically in a diverse and expansive supranational political system.

This chapter examines the transnational flow of human rights norms among the ECJ, the European Court of Human Rights (ECtHR), and the constitutional courts of member states. Europe's unique supranational arrangements produce parallel and sometimes overlapping systems of rights protection.

Questions about the legitimacy and capacity of the ECJ's rights jurisdiction are examined within this context. In conclusion, I argue that the ECJ's development of a fundamental rights jurisprudence helped to consolidate common principles of liberty, respect for human rights and fundamental freedoms, and rule of law; and advanced the movement toward a more integrated Europe.

EMERGENCE OF A RIGHTS JURISPRUDENCE

The development of fundamental rights in the law of the European Community (EC)/European Union has progressed through four distinct stages. The first, spanning from the founding in 1957[6] to 1969, was a time when the ECJ ruled consistently that fundamental rights were not part of its jurisdiction. The second stage began in 1969, with the first recognition in ECJ case law that fundamental human rights could not be easily separated from the economic freedoms at the core of the Treaty of Rome. In a series of cases during the 1970s and 1980s, the ECJ ruled that fundamental rights were an integral part of community law and could be used in the review of community measures, such as commission decisions, regulations, and directives. The third stage came in 1989, when the ECJ ruled for the first time that these newly recognized rights extended to the acts of member states to the extent that their acts came within the field of community law. Featured in the third stage were the expansion of the rights recognized and applied as general principles of EC, and later EU law, and the tension this development caused between courts at the national and supranational levels. The fourth stage began in 1999, the year the European Union committed to drafting a Charter of Fundamental Rights (CFR). The CFR brings together all the existing rights of EU citizens, many of which had been recognized in ECJ judgments during the past few decades. Featured in this latest stage in the development of fundamental rights in the law of the EU are questions about the new institutional arrangements and the legal status of the CFR after the reforms of the Lisbon Treaty went into effect (December 1, 2009). Now that the Lisbon Treaty has been ratified by all member states and the CFR—which is part of the new treaty—has become legally binding, EU citizens can use it to challenge actions taken or not taken by EU institutions and member states.

The CFR was agreed to by the Intergovernmental Conference in 2000 (Nice Treaty), but its legal status was uncertain. In 2004 it was appended to the proposed Treaty for Establishing a Constitution for Europe. Because the "no" votes by France and the Netherlands in 2005 halted the constitution's movement toward ratification, the CFR's status had remained uncertain. In June 2007, though, EU leaders meeting in Brussels agreed to the so-called "Reform Treaty," which included an explicit reference to making the CFR legally binding.[7] Details of the new treaty were worked out in the Intergovernmental Conference in Lisbon and at the time of writing all member states have approved the treaty. EU citizens now have their first bill of rights.

The Treaty of Rome lacked what might be called a traditional bill of rights. Nevertheless, it contained several fundamental rights, such as the right to equal pay for men and women (Article 141) and the right to freedom from discrimination based on nationality (Article 12). In 1957, at the time of the founding of the community, rights in Europe were protected at the national level by the member states' constitutions, bills of rights, and court systems, and at the international level by membership in the Council of Europe and acceptance of the mechanism set up by the ECHR. These arrangements were believed to be sufficient. Later, it became clear that the ECJ's responsibility in making sure that community law was interpreted and implemented in conformity with the founding treaties of the European Community could not be carried out by ignoring fundamental rights.

The ECJ at first denied, but later came to recognize, fundamental rights as "general principles of Community law." In *Freidrich Stork v. High Authority of the European Coal and Steel Community* (1959),[8] the ECJ decided that it could not rule on the compatibility of community measures with fundamental rights. Stork, a German citizen, argued for annulment of a decision of the High Authority, an institution established by the EEC treaty, on the grounds that the decision violated the fundamental right to economic freedom protected by Articles 2 and 12 of the German Basic Law. In rejecting that argument, the ECJ explained: "Under Article 8 of the Treaty the High Authority is only required to apply Community law. It is not competent to apply the national law of the Member States." Ten years later, in *Stauder v. City of Ulm, Sozialamt* (1969),[9] the ECJ made its first, albeit vague, reference to fundamental rights in community law. The question was whether the commission's measure to stimulate the sale of surplus butter by authorizing member states to make butter available to the needy at reduced prices violated the right to privacy. Strauder alleged that his right to privacy, protected by the German Basic Law, was breached by the requirement that he had to disclose his name on the coupons needed to purchase the butter at reduced rates from retailers. In ruling that the challenged measure in this case could and should have been interpreted so as not to require an action that might compromise fundamental rights, the ECJ indicated its willingness to review community measures for compatibility with fundamental rights:

> It follows that the provision in question must be interpreted as not requiring—although it does not prohibit—the identification of ben-eficiaries by name. . . . Interpreted in this way the provision at issue contains nothing capable of prejudicing the fundamental human rights enshrined in the general principles of Community law and protected by the Court.

The following year, the ECJ, in *Internationale Handelsgesellschaft Mbh v. Einfuhr-und Vorratsstelle Fur Getreide und Futtermittel* (1970), referred less obliquely to its role in judging the validity of community measures on rights grounds:

> Recourse to the legal rules or concepts of national law in order to judge the validity of measures adopted by the institutions of the Community would have an adverse effect on the uniformity and efficacy of Community law. The validity of such measures can only be judged in the light of Community law. In fact, the law stemming from the Treaty, an independent source of law, cannot because of its very nature be overridden by the rules of national law, however framed, without being deprived of its character as Community law and without the legal basis of the Community itself being called in question. Therefore, the validity of a Community measure or its effect within a Member State cannot be affected by allegations that it runs counter to either fundamental rights as formulated by the constitution of that State or the principles of a national constitutional structure.
>
> However, an examination should be made as to whether or not any analogous guarantee inherent in Community law has been disregarded. In fact, respect for fundamental rights forms an integral part of the general principles of law protected by the Court of Justice. The protection of such rights, whilst inspired by the constitutional traditions common to the Member States, must be ensured within the framework of the structure and objectives of the Community.[10]

Several years later, the community measure requiring national coal producers to sell only to large wholesalers was challenged on fundamental rights grounds by a small wholesaler named Nold. The measure was adopted in a time of economic recession with the aim of achieving greater efficiency in the production and distribution of coal. Though the measure was upheld against Nold's claims that its fundamental rights to property and freedom to engage in economic activity were being denied, the ECJ explained more fully the sources of the rights now understood to be part of the general principles of community law:

> In safeguarding these rights, the Court is bound to draw inspiration from constitutional traditions common to the Member States, and it cannot therefore uphold measures which are incompatible with fundamental rights recognized and protected by the Constitutions of those States.

Similarly, international treaties for the protection of human rights on which the Member States have collaborated, or of which they are signatories, can supply guidelines which should be followed within the framework of Community law.[11]

The sources for the fundamental rights comprising the "general principles of Community law" were the constitutional traditions of member states and the ECHR. The first reference to the ECHR in the database of the ECJ's case law appeared in *Nold* (1974). After the ECHR was recognized as a source for fundamental rights in community law, references to the European human rights treaty and the ECtHR's case law became more frequent. The number of ECJ cases with explicit references to the ECHR increased over time. The ECHR has been cited by the ECJ nearly twice as many times in its second decade (1996-2005) as in its first twenty-two years (1974-1995). Thus the ECJ has come to rely increasingly on the ECHR when giving expression to fundamental rights in community law.

The previous discussion described when and how the ECJ began to develop its fundamental rights jurisprudence. The question why is the subject of some academic debate, dividing those scholars who favor the "strategic power" explanation and those who favor its rival, the "neo-functionalist" explanation. Coppel and O'Neill[12] argue that the ECJ extended its jurisdiction to include rights to expand the reach of the community over more activities of the member states. Weiler,[13] Stone Sweet,[14] and the author of this chapter take the position that the ECJ's new rights jurisdiction was the natural extension of the doctrine of supremacy, the fundamental organizing principle of community and later EU law.

That is why the view expressed in *Stork* (1959) (the ECJ was not competent to consider the traditions of fundamental rights of member states when applying community law) had to change. After the court's decision in *Costa v. Ente Nazionale per l'Energia Electtrica (ENEL)* (1964),[15] national courts began to see the danger posed by EC supremacy without fundamental rights. To allay these concerns, the ECJ had to develop this new competence.

In *Costa v. ENEL* (1964), the ECJ established the doctrine of supremacy of community law over conflicting laws of member states:

The precedence of Community law is confirmed by Article 189 [now 249], whereby a regulation "shall be binding" and "directly applicable in all Member States." This provision, which is subject to no reservation, would be quite meaningless if a State could unilaterally nullify its effects by means of a legislative measure which could prevail over Community law.

Constitutional courts in Italy and Germany were the first to question the supremacy of community law over deeply entrenched rights in their national constitutions.[16] To reconcile this problem, the constitutional courts in these member states persuaded the ECJ to develop a rights jurisprudence. If the doctrine of supremacy was going to endure, community law had to safeguard the fundamental rights traditions of the member states. In the words of one commentator, "Without supremacy, the ECJ had decided, the common market was doomed. And without a judicially enforceable charter of rights, national courts had decided, the supremacy doctrine was doomed."[17]

In *Solange I* (1974), the German Constitutional Court ruled that "[a]s long as the integration process has not progressed so far that Community law also receives a catalogue of fundamental rights . . . of settled validity, which is adequate in comparison with the catalogue of fundamental rights contained in the [German] Constitution," it would decide for itself whether community law would be supreme. The ECJ's newfound respect for fundamental rights in the 1970s (e.g., *Nold v. Commission* (1974)[18] and *Hauer v. Land Rheidland-Pfalz* (1979)[19]) is, therefore, best understood as a response to this challenge. Its concerns allayed, the German Constitutional Court in *Solange II* (1986)[20] accepted the supremacy of community law "so long as the EC, and in particular the ECJ, generally ensures an effective protection of fundamental rights." By responding to the concerns of member states, the ECJ transformed the community from its beginnings as essentially an economic unit, committed to advancing the four trade-related freedoms (free movement of goods, free movement of workers, free movement of capital, and freedom to provide services) into a more integrated political unit committed to principles of liberty, democracy, and respect for fundamental rights.

In the 1970s and 1980s, the ECJ was careful to restrict its emerging fundamental rights principles to review of community measures. Although it was restrained in this respect, the ECJ had moved aggressively to enforce the fundamental right to equality and equal treatment. The ECJ's rulings on equal pay and gender equality[21] stand out as notable legal developments during this early stage when the ECJ was just beginning to recognize fundamental rights as general principles of community law.

This court-engineered development was approved in 1977 in a Joint Declaration by the European Parliament, the council, and the commission. What is interesting from a comparative constitutional law perspective is that there was not much controversy about the introduction of ECJ review of community measures for compliance with fundamental rights principles. In the United States, for example, judicial review of the acts of the coordinate branches of the national government (horizontal review) still manages to excite considerable controversy.[22] As will be explained in the next section of this chapter, the introduction of vertical review in community law—that is, ECJ review of member state measures implementing community law for compliance with principles of fundamental rights—has caused much more controversy in Europe than has the introduction of vertical review in American law.[23] With its ruling in *Martin v. Hunter's Lessee* (1816),[24] the U.S. Supreme Court asserted its authority to review state law matters that presented federal constitutional questions, and the power has been widely accepted. The difference cannot be explained solely on the basis of the U.S. Constitution's supremacy clause.[25] The doctrine of supremacy is, of course, also recognized in European law. The fact that the issue of vertical review still manages to rankle in Europe suggests that center-periphery relations there are different. In comparison with that in the United States, the European legal system is much less hierarchical or, in the words of one commentator, a kind of "inverse hierarchy":

> The Member States remain sovereign, in the international law sense of the term, and they ultimately are free to leave the Union for any reason. The Union, for its part, does not have the competence to decide freely on its own competences (Kompetenz-Kompetenz) and thus is denied sovereignty. . . . Thus, the political authority of the Union is best described as a union of States, where sovereignty and thus the ultimate responsibility for the Union's course of action rests with the constituent Member States.[26]

DEVELOPING A MORE EXPANSIVE RIGHTS JURISPRUDENCE

The ECJ introduced fundamental rights to community law gradually, first by applying fundamental rights norms horizontally to community law measures that would have direct effect in member states and then by extending fundamental rights norms vertically to review member state action within the sphere of community law. The critical year for this development was 1989. In *Hubert Wachauf v. Bundesamt für Ernahrung und Forstwirtschaft* (1989),[27] the ECJ declared for the first time that actions of member states would be reviewed for conformity with fundamental rights.

Wachauf was a tenant dairy farmer in Germany who brought suit against the Federal Office for Food and Forestry (Federal Office) in the Verwaltungsgericht Frankfurt am Main (the Administrative Court). When his landlord decided not to renew his lease, Wachauf decided he would exercise his rights to compensation, which an EC regulation provided to dairy farmers who ceased the production of milk. The Federal Office responsible for implementing this regulation denied Wachauf's claim because he had not obtained the written consent of the landowner. The law in Germany, passed pursuant to this EC regulation, specified that if the individual requesting compensation under this scheme is a tenant farmer, the application must provide evidence of the landlord's written consent. Because the landlord had withdrawn his consent, the Federal Office denied Wachauf's claim. The Verwaltungsgericht stayed the proceedings and referred two questions to the ECJ for a preliminary ruling. In its ruling, the ECJ expanded its protection of fundamental rights in community law to include review of member state action within the scope of EC law:

> The Court has consistently held, in particular in its judgment . . . in . . . *Hauer v. Land Rheinland Pfalz* (1979), that fundamental rights form an integral part of the general principles of the law, the observance of which is ensured by the Court. . . .
>
> Having regard to those criteria, it must be observed that Community rules which, upon the expiry of the lease, had the effect of depriving the lessee, without compensation, of the fruits of his labour and of his investments in the tenanted holding would be incompatible with the requirements of the protection of fundamental rights in the Community legal order. Since those requirements are also binding on the Member States when they implement Community rules, the Member States must, as far as possible, apply those rules in accordance with those requirements.

Instead of overruling the German rule requiring the landlord's consent in these cases, the ECJ instructed the Verwaltungsgericht to read the act so as not to offend Wachauf's fundamental rights to the "fruits of his labour and of his investments in the tenanted holding." The Verwaltungsgericht complied and awarded Wachauf compensation and costs.

The ECJ expanded the scope of its decision in *Wachauf* to include review of member state measures that are related only indirectly to community law. Elliniki Radiophonia Tileorassi (ERT), the radio and television broadcasting company that had received from the Greek government the exclusive right to broadcast television programs, sued Dimotike Etairia Plirofosississ (DEP) and the mayor of Thessaloniki for setting up a rival television station. Realizing that the case raised many questions of community law, the national court stayed the proceedings and sought a preliminary ruling from the ECJ. In *Elliniki Radiophonia Tileorassi v. Dimotike Etairia Plirofosississ* (1991), the ECJ ruled that "[c]ommunity law does not prevent the granting of a television monopoly for considerations of a non-economic nature relating to the public interest."[28] The ruling directed the national court to focus on "the manner in which the monopoly was organized" and on the actions taken to justify the exclusive right. The ECJ reasoned that where a member state seeks to derogate from the freedom to provide services, in this case denying a rival television station's right to broadcast, its justifications for doing so must be compatible with community-based principles of fundamental rights in the same way actions directly related to community law must be:

> [W]here a Member State relies on the combined provisions of Articles 56 and 66 in order to justify rules which are likely to obstruct the exercise of the freedom to provide services, such justification, provided for by Community law, must be interpreted in the light of the general principles of law and in particular of fundamental rights.

By 2000, the ECJ had extended its review on fundamental rights grounds of the following measures: community measures, including commission decisions, regulations, and directives; national measures taken in pursuance of EU law or in implementing a directive; and the national measures, as in the ERT case, that are only indirectly related to community law. In extending its reach, the ECJ was careful not to displace the fundamental rights jurisprudence of member states or the ECtHR. The community's fundamental rights system coexists alongside the national and international systems when member states are not acting within the sphere of community law. But when member states are acting within the sphere of community law, the three systems overlap and sometimes there is tension between the national and supranational levels. The ECJ has tried to manage this conflict by adopting a cooperative or dialogic approach. In the words of two commentators, the interplay between the ECJ and the national courts regarding this issue of fundamental rights had the positive effect of deepening legal integration:

> Despite being conflictual in origin, the dialogue on fundamental rights has served to deepen legal integration, to widen the scope of EC constitutional politics, and to strengthen the supranational aspects of the Community.[29]

The expansion of the ECJ's rights jurisprudence to include review of member state action soon raised some questions of judicial capacity. The first, and perhaps most urgent, issue involved the challenge of handling conflicts with the national courts. After *Wachauf* and *ERT*, it was not clear which level—national constitutional court or ECJ—had the final decision in disputes about whose fundamental rights law should apply. The second issue stemmed from the difficulty in determining the proper standard to be used to give expression to a protected right. The parallel and, since *Wachauf* and *ERT*, sometimes overlapping systems of rights protection result in more than one standard for the protection of the same fundamental right. It is entirely possible in Europe's multilevel system to have the same right apply differently because the standard established by the constitutional courts of member states in applying community law may be different from the standard established by the ECJ or the ECtHR. The lack of a coherent standard for what is supposed to be a fundamental right is closely related to the third issue—the general uncertainty about the definition and scope of what essentially are unwritten rights incorporated into EU law at the discretion of the ECJ on a case-by-case basis.

A. Who Has the Final Decision in Cases Raising Conflicts about Fundamental Rights?

Decisions of the constitutional courts of Germany and Italy suggest that there are still some questions about who will be the final arbiter of rights. In *Brunner and Others v. The European Union Treaty* (1993),[30] the Bundesverfassungsgericht (Federal Constitutional Court) may have accepted the primacy of community law when it upheld the constitutionality of the German law ratifying the Treaty on European Union, but it reserved for itself the competence to ensure that the fundamental rights in the Basic Law would not be diminished. The Bundesverfassungsgericht made it clear that EU measures, as applied in Germany, would be scrutinized for compliance with national law standards:

> Acts of the particular public power of a supranational organization which is separate from the State power of the member states may also affect those persons protected by the basic rights in Germany. Such acts therefore affect the guarantees provided under the Basic Law, and the duties of the Federal Constitutional Court, which include the protection of basic rights in Germany, and not only in respect of German governmental institutions. However, the Federal Constitutional Court exercises its jurisdiction regarding the applicability of derivative Community law in Germany in a "cooperative relationship" with the ECJ.[31]

The Italian Constitutional Court came to the same conclusion about the question of who has the final decision on matters of fundamental rights. In *Frontini* (1974)[32] and later in *Granital* (1984),[33] the Corte Costiuzionale conditioned its acceptance of community law with the following proviso: The protection of fundamental rights guaranteed by the Italian constitution is ultimately its responsibility.[34] According to one commentator, decisions by national courts showing the same "defiance" also can be found in Denmark, Belgium, and Spain.[35]

B. Which Standard Applies?

The parallel systems of rights protection sometimes result in more than one standard for the protection of fundamental rights—the standard established by the constitutional courts of member states in applying community law, the standard established by the ECtHR, and the standard established by the ECJ. With its divided competences, Europe's multilevel system of protecting rights creates the potential for a constitutional crisis. What if there is a conflict between the ECJ and the ECtHR about the interpretation and effect to be given a convention right? There have been instances when an interpretation by the ECJ on the meaning of a right inspired by the ECHR is subsequently contradicted by an interpretation of that same right by the ECtHR.[36] The national constitutional court may be acting contrary to the ECHR if it follows the ECJ's interpretation and may be acting contrary to community law if it follows the interpretation of the ECtHR.

The problem with standards can be seen in all the litigation emerging from the Irish right-to-life case called *Society for the Protection of Unborn Children (SPUC) v. Grogan* (1991).[37] The SPUC sought to enjoin Grogan and other student organization officers from distributing information about abortion clinics in countries where abortion is legal, such as the United Kingdom. Grogan and the other defendants argued that the community law principle of free movement of services protected their right to publish and disseminate literature about the availability of abortion services in the United Kingdom. After the community law issue was raised, the Irish High Court asked the ECJ for a preliminary ruling. In the meantime, the SPUC appealed to the Irish Supreme Court, arguing that the lower court's refusal to grant immediate relief was a violation of the provision in the Irish constitution, which protects the right to life (Article 40).

Without waiting for the ECJ's ruling, the Irish Supreme Court issued the injunction sought by the SPUC based on the court's previous decision that prohibited physicians and family planning counselors from discussing abortion options with women. In its preliminary ruling, the ECJ decided that abortion was a "service" within the meaning of the community law principle freedom to provide services and that the conflict between the right to life in Irish law would have to be considered in light of the fundamental rights within the "general principles of Community law" that were implicated in this case. In balancing freedom to provide services with right to life in Irish law, the ECJ came down on the side of the latter:

> Although the national court's questions refer to Community law in general, the Court takes the view that its attention should be focused on the provisions of Article 59 of the EEC Treaty, which deal with the freedom to provide services, and the argument concerning human

rights. . . . As regards, first, the provisions of Article 59 of the Treaty, which prohibit any restriction on the freedom to supply services, it is apparent from the facts of the case that the link between the activity of the students associations of which Mr. Grogan and the other defendants are officers and medical terminations of pregnancies carried out in the clinics in another Member State is too tenuous for the prohibition on the distribution of information to be capable of being regarded as a restriction within the meaning of Article 59 of the Treaty.[38]

Although the ECJ had managed to avoid a decision on whether the prohibition in Irish law on the dissemination of information about abortion services violated freedom of expression, the issue soon came before the ECtHR. In *Open Door Counseling and Dublin Well Women v. Ireland* (1992), the ECtHR ruled that the Irish ban violated Article 10 of the ECHR: "In sum, the restraint imposed on the applicants was disproportionate to the aims pursued."[39]

The *Grogan* case resulted in three different interpretations of the right to free expression. At the national level, the Irish Supreme Court ruled that the right to free expression had to give way to competing constitutional value—the right to life. At the international level, the ECtHR applied its test of proportionality and found that the ban on speech could not be saved by any "pressing social needs." And at the supranational level, the ECJ ruled that the free speech issue raised by defendants in this case was outside the scope of community law: "[T]he information constitutes a manifestation of freedom of expression and of the freedom to impart and receive information which is independent of the economic activity carried on by clinics in another Member State."

C. How Does the ECJ Find and Determine the Scope of Unwritten Rights?

Since its decision in *Stauder* (1969), which recognized that fundamental human rights were enshrined in the general principles of community law, the ECJ has developed a fairly impressive catalogue of rights. Although there were some guidelines, such as the ECHR, which the ECJ said had "special status,"[40] and the constitutions of the member states, which the ECJ declared would be an important source of fundamental rights to be protected, the ECJ has had considerable discretion both in declaring these unwritten rights and in determining the scope of their application. Thus another problem with this development has been the general uncertainty about the nature and scope of the rights recognized on a case-by-case basis.

The need for clearly understood limits on EU power becomes more pressing as the scope of EU power increases. Currently, the ECJ's power to interpret the scope of EU law determines whether the EU's fundamental rights will apply. For example, the ECJ's decision in the Irish right-to-life case turned on its belief that the defendant's speech was in context beyond the reach of EU law. If the fundamental rights recognized as general principles of community law are to be real checks on the exercise of power, then the field of application of community law cannot be decided on a case-by-case basis.

TOWARD A "BILL OF RIGHTS" FOR EUROPE

The approach of the new millennium brought a realization that the European Union lacked a coherent system for the protection of fundamental rights. The desire for greater certainty and clarity led to the call to draft a "charter of rights" for the European Union.

In December 2000, the European Council met in Nice and signed the draft CFR. The aim of the CFR was to make clear that these rights were legally binding not only on the institutions, agencies, and bodies of the European Union, but also on the member states. In October 2004, the heads of state of the then twenty-five member states and the three candidate countries signed the Treaty Establishing a Constitution for Europe, which incorporated the CFR in Part II. Until June 2005, the proposed constitution had been going through the formal ratification process. Prior to France's "no" vote on May 29, 2005, fourteen countries had voted to ratify. But after the "no" votes in France and in the Netherlands (June 1, 2005), the European Council called for a "period of reflection" and suspended the votes that had been scheduled in the remaining countries. The "no" votes in 2005 and the period of reflection through 2006 appear to have only delayed the process of making the CFR legally binding. In June 2007, heads of the twenty-seven member states agreed to the so-called Reform Treaty, which included a declaration making the CFR legally binding. The Intergovernmental Conference meeting in Lisbon later that year approved it, and the Lisbon Treaty, as it came to be known, which included the CFR and the changes needed to allay the concerns of those who had opposed ratification of the constitutional treaty, began the process of ratification. Now that all member states have ratified the Lisbon Treaty, fundamental rights in the European Union have attained a new, quasi-constitutional status.

References to the CFR have appeared in ECJ records since 2001. The first reference came in an advocate-general's opinion.[41] The second came in an Order of the President of the Court in *Commission v. Technische Glaswerke Ilmenau GmbH* (2002).[42] Over the past five years, there have been seventy-three references to the CFR in ECJ judgments.

Before the CFR was legally binding, it had already influenced the work of the European Commission. On April 27, 2005, the commission issued its policy on the effect of the CFR on matters related to community law. "The main aim," the commission explained in its document titled *Compliance with the Charter of Fundamental Rights in Commission Legislative Proposals*, "... is to allow Commission services to check all Commission legislative proposals systematically and rigorously to ensure they respect all the fundamental rights concerned in the course of normal decision-making procedures."[43] Before the Brussels Summit in June 2007, the CFR enjoyed considerable support among the most important institutions of the European Union. Nevertheless, it was the subject of some controversy, especially among the British who demanded a veto over the CFR's effect on domestic law. The United Kingdom's objections were voiced and concessions made,[44] but in the end the Reform Treaty and subsequently the Lisbon Treaty included the declaration that the CFR would be legally binding under the new arrangements.

Bringing the new treaty arrangements and the CFR into effect might very well promote the twin aims of greater certainty and clarity in Europe's law of fundamental rights. The jurisdictional confusion that has sometimes resulted in conflicting interpretations of fundamental rights is likely to be lessened. A clearer understanding of the rights that would then be explicitly provided for in the text would help to constrain the ECJ's discretion in determining whether the right may be enforced against EU measures. Also, uncertainty over whether the ECJ's or ECtHR's standard ought to apply is likely to be dramatically reduced.[45] But, as long as multilevel constitutionalism remains the distinctive feature of the European Union's supranational polity, and there are objections from member states, such as the United Kingdom, over the reach of the CFR, there will still be conflicts that will require resolutions. Thus, the next stage in the development of fundamental rights in the law of the European Union would comprise the ECJ's attempts to resolve the issues arising from the newly entrenched CFR.

CONCLUSION

Fundamental rights have played a key role in the movement toward increased integration and what has been called the "constitutionalization of Europe."[46] Though the word *constitution* was not supposed to be mentioned after the "no" votes in France and the Netherlands,[47] there can be no denying that the first step in the gradual construction of a more integrated Europe was the establishment by the ECJ of the principle of supremacy of community law (*Costa v. ENEL*). The next critical step was when the ECJ developed a fundamental rights jurisprudence in defense of the challenges by member states to the doctrine of supremacy. After establishing horizontal review of community law and action based on fundamental rights principles (*Nold*), the ECJ established vertical review of member state law and action designed to carry out community law (*Wachauf*). The drafting of the CFR follows logically from the entrenchment of the idea that the ECJ would review both community action and member state action on behalf of community law for conformity with principles of fundamental rights.

Now that the new arrangements envisioned by the Lisbon Treaty (and with it the CFR) have gone into effect, the ECJ's role in protecting the rights of EU citizens will certainly increase. This will complete the ECJ's transformation into Europe's preeminent constitutional court and will ensure that it will remain a key player in the European project in the future.

NOTES

1. *Sarah Margaret Richards v. Secretary of State for Work and Pensions*, Case C-423/04, 2006 ECJ CELEX LEXIS 190 (April 27, 2006).

2. Ibid.

3. *Freidrich Stork v. High Authority of the European Coal and Steel Community*, Case 1/58 [1959] ECR 17.

4. The following rights and freedoms have been recognized in the case law of the ECJ and the CFI: equal treatment (right to be free from discrimination on the basis of gender, ethnicity, religious belief, and sexual orientation); right to a fair hearing; right to be defended and to call witnesses; right to an effective judicial remedy; the right to human dignity; right to respect for private life, family life, right to confidentiality in one's correspondence and one's health records; right to property; right to vote and to stand for election; freedom of religion; freedom of expression; freedom of association (including both right to protest and to join a trade union); freedom from retroactive criminal sanctions; freedom to engage in economic activity; and freedom of movement. See generally, Koen Lenaerts and Piet Van Nuffel, *Constitutional Law of the European Union*, 2d ed. (London: Thomson/Sweet & Maxwell, 2005), 735–738.

5. Alec Stone Sweet with Thomas Brunell, "Creating a Supranational Constitution," in Alec Stone Sweet, *The Judicial Construction of Europe* (New York: Oxford University Press, 2004), 87.

6. The Treaty Establishing the European Economic Community (EEC) was signed in Rome on March 25, 1957.

7. "The Conference declares that: 1. The Charter of Fundamental Rights, which has legally binding force, confirms the fundamental rights guaranteed by the European Convention on Human Rights and Fundamental Freedoms and as long as they result from the constitutional traditions common to Member States. . . ." European Council, "Presidency Conclusions," (11177/07), Brussels, 23 June 2007, 25.

8. Case 1/58 [1959] ECR 17.

9. Case 29/69 [1969] ECR 419.

10. Case 11/70 [1970] ECR 1125.

11. *J. Nold, Kohlen-und Baustoffgro v. Commission of the European Communities*, Case 4/73 [1974] ECR 491, at 507.

12. Jason Coppel and Aidan O'Neill, "The European Court of Justice: Taking Rights Seriously?" *Legal Studies* 12 (1992): 227–239.

13. J. H. H. Weiler, "The Transformation of Europe," *Yale Law Journal* 100 (1991): 2403–2483.

14. Alec Stone Sweet, *The Judicial Construction of Europe* (New York: Oxford University Press, 2004).

15. Case 6/64 [1964] ECR 585.

16. *Internationale Handelsgesellschaft mbH v. Einfuhr- und Vorratsstelle fur Getreide und Futtermittel (Solange* I) 37 BVerfGE 271 (1974); *Frontini v. Ministero delle Finanze,* Case 183 [1974] Il Foro It. 314.

17. Alec Stone Sweet, *Governing with Judges: Constitutional Politics in Europe* (New York: Oxford University Press, 2000), 172.

18. Case 4/73 [1974] ECR 491.

19. Case 44/79 [1979] ECR 3727.

20. *In re Application Wunsche Handelsgesellschaft (Solange II),* 73 BVerfGE 339 (1986).

21. See, for example, *Defrenne v. Sabena,* Case 43/75 [1976] 1 ECR 455 (equal pay for women and men/comparable worth standard); *Commission v. United Kingdom,* Case 61/81 [1982] ECR 2601 (need for an authority within member states to decide whether work has same value as other work); and *Bilka-Kaufhaus GmbH v. Von Hartz,* Case 170/84 [1986] ECR 1607 (shifts burden of proof to employers in cases of indirect discrimination against women in employment). See also Ingeborg Heide, "Supranational Action Against Sex Discrimination: Equal Pay and Equal Treatment in the European Union," *International Labour Review* 138 (1999): 381–410.

22. See, for example, Larry D. Kramer, *The People Themselves: Popular Constitutionalism and Judicial Review* (New York: Oxford University Press, 2004). Kramer casts doubt on the idea that courts have a monopoly on constitutional interpretation, arguing that over the years, judicial review supplanted the founding generation's idea that the people would play a vital role.

23. See generally, George A. Bermann, "Judicial Review and the European Union: Marbury v. Madison and European Union 'Constitutional' Review," *George Washington International Law Review* 36 (2004): 557–566.

24. 14 U.S. 304 (1816).

25. "This Constitution, and the Laws of the United States which be made in Pursuance thereof; and all Treaties made, or which shall be made, under the Authority of the United States, shall be the supreme Law of the Land; and the Judges in every State shall be bound thereby, . . ." U.S. Constitution (1789), Article VI, section 2.

26. Volker Röben, "Constitutionalism of the European Union after the Draft Constitutional Treaty: How Much Hierarchy?" *Columbia Journal of European Law* 10 (2004): 339–377 at 343–344.

27. Case 5/88 [1989] ECR 2609.

28. Case C-260/89 [1991].

29. Alec Stone Sweet with Thomas Brunell, "Constructing a Supranational Constitution," in Alec Stone Sweet, *The Judicial Construction of Europe* (New York: Oxford University Press, 2004), 90.

30. (The Maastricht Treaty Case) 89 BverfGE 155 (1993).

31. Juliane Kokott, "Report on Germany," in Anne-Marie Slaughter, Alec Stone Sweet, and J. H. H. Weiler, eds., *The European Court and National Courts—Doctrine and Jurisprudence* (Oxford: Hart Publishing, 1998), 108.

32. Case 183 [1974] Il Foro It. 314.

33. *Granital v. Amministrazione delle Fianze dello Stato*, Case 170/84 [1984] Il Foro It. 2062.

34. See, generally, Marta Cartabia, "The Italian Constitutional Court and the Relationship between the Italian Legal System and the European Community," *Michigan Journal of International Law* 12 (1990): 173 and Francesco P. Ruggeri Laderchi, "Report on Italy," in Anne-Marie Slaughter, Alec Stone Sweet, and J. H. H. Weiler, eds., *The European Court and National Courts—Doctrine and Jurisprudence* (Oxford: Hart Publishing, 1998).

35. J. H. H. Weiler, "Epilogue: The Judicial Apres Nice," in *The European Court of Justice*, eds. Grainne de Burca and J. H. H. Weiler (New York: Oxford University Press, 2001), 220–221.

36. Compare *Hoechst AG v. Commission*, Case 46/87 and 227/88 [1989] ECR 2859 (right to privacy does not extend to a business) with *Chappell v. United Kingdom*, Eur. Court HR, Series A, Vol. 152 (1990), 12 EHRR 1 (right to privacy might apply to a business).

37. Case C-159/90 [1991] ECR I-4740.

38. *Society for the Protection of Unborn Children (SPUC) v. Grogan*, Case C-159/90, 1991 ECR I-4740, para. 23.

39. Eur. Court HR, Series A, No. 246 (1992), at para. 463.

40. Opinion 2/94 on the Accession by the Community to the ECHR.

41. Opinion of Advocate General Alber, *TNT Traco SpA v. Poste Italiane SpA and Others*, Case C-340/99 (2001).

42. Case C-232/02 (2002).

43. Commission of the European Communities, COM (2005) 172 Final (Brussels, April 27, 2005).

44. The United Kingdom secured from the Brussels Summit (June 2007) the following concession: "To the extent that a provision of the Charter refers to national laws and practices, it shall only apply in the United Kingdom to the extent that the rights or principles that it contains are recognised in the law or practices of the United Kingdom."

45. Article 52.3 of the CFR reduces some of the ambiguity over which standard applies: "In so far as this Charter contains rights which correspond to rights guaranteed by the Convention for the Protection of Human Rights and Fundamental Freedoms, the meaning and scope of those rights shall be the same as those laid down by the said Convention. This provision shall not prevent Union law providing more extensive protection."

46. Alec Stone Sweet and Thomas Brunell define the term in the following way: "The constitutionalization of the EC refers to the process by which the Rome Treaty evolved from a set of legal arrangements binding upon sovereign states into a vertically integrated legal regime conferring judicially enforceable rights and obligations on legal persons and entities, public and private, within the EC territory. The phrase thus captures the transformation of an intergovernmental organization governed by international law into a multi-tiered system of governance founded on higher-law constitutionalism." *The Judicial Construction of Europe* (New York: Oxford University Press, 2004), 65.

47. Marcin Grajewski, "EU told not to mention the constitution," (Reuters, June 20, 2007).

CHAPTER THIRTEEN

Spreading the Word

Australia's National Human Rights and Equal Opportunity Commission as Transnational Legal Entrepreneur

RHONDA EVANS CASE[1]

Human rights norms were internationalized during the second half of the twentieth century through a multitude of declarations, treaties, and conventions. Nearly all nation-states have accepted obligations pursuant to these instruments, but supranational enforcement of their terms has proven problematic. United Nations (UN) treaty bodies may only issue what amounts to advisory opinions, and beyond Europe, regional human rights regimes remain inadequate and largely impotent. Two sets of recent developments, however, have created new national avenues for holding governments accountable to transnational human rights standards.

First, national courts, many of them newly empowered through domestic bills of rights, have shown an increased willingness to incorporate into their decision making not only principles of international conventions and customary law but also relevant decisions issued by their peers in other countries. Cumulatively, these judicial practices have given rise to a burgeoning body of transnational jurisprudence. Second, national human rights institutions (NHRIs), quasi-governmental agencies intended to promote and protect human rights, have proliferated internationally. The number of national human rights commissions, probably the most popular form of NHRI, at least quadrupled between 1990 and 2000, bringing the total number to near eighty.[2] Although these institutions lack coercive power vis-à-vis governments, they nevertheless can promote conformity with transnational human rights standards in myriad ways, including through the national courts. Given the growing attentiveness of many judges to transnational sources of law, NHRI lawyers may expect to find a receptive audience on the bench.

This chapter focuses on the intersection of these two developments. It examines the extent to which Australia's Human Rights and Equal Opportunity Commission (HREOC) has acted as a transnational legal entrepreneur, using its authority to intervene in litigation as a means of promoting the incorporation of human rights treaty obligations and transnational human rights jurisprudence into the decision making of domestic courts. It also evaluates HREOC's impact on the courts in this regard.

Concentrating on the sixteen immigration and refugee cases in which HREOC intervened, the analysis demonstrates that the commission's lawyers consistently relied in their legal arguments on Australia's international human rights obligations and the corpus of transnational jurisprudence that has developed in recent years. In so doing, they apprised national judges of cross-national trends and promoted a symbiotic relationship between the national and transnational legal orders. HREOC's impact in immigration and refugee cases, however, was limited. Although it scored one major victory in an immigration case before the Australian High Court in 1995, subsequent victories in three separate cases involving refugees were eviscerated on appellate review. Most of the cases in which the commission intervened involved issues concerning the government's controversial policy of detaining, indefinitely if necessary, all unlawful noncitizens who arrive on Australia's shores seeking refugee status. The analysis indicates that in the face of a recalcitrant government that controls the judicial appointments process, transnational legal entrepreneurship before the courts may prove an ineffective strategy for holding the government accountable to its international human rights obligations.

THE LITERATURE

Judicial use of international law and transnational precedent, particularly with respect to human rights, has attracted considerable scholarly attention.[3] Because of the communications and technological revolutions that have made cross-national legal information readily available, as well as a growing number of international judicial conclaves that promote cross-national socialization, today many judges regard themselves as "cosmopolitan transnational actors."[4] Judges, however, do not ordinarily incorporate international and foreign jurisprudence into their decisions *sua sponte*. Lawyers also serve as conduits of transnational legal ideas, especially in common law systems, where they play a key role in framing issues and crafting legal arguments. Therefore, it makes sense to examine the ways in which they serve as "transnational legal entrepreneurs" before domestic courts.[5]

Research has shown that NHRIs can serve as "institutional homes" for activist lawyers well versed in transnational human rights law.[6] These bodies can provide the requisite support for sustained litigation campaigns.[7] For example, Karen J. Alter and Jeannette Vargas found that Britain's Equal Opportunities Commission (EOC), the quasi-state body charged with enforcing the Sex Discrimination Act 1975, used European law and courts to develop national gender equity policy in favorable ways despite a hostile Thatcher government.[8] In its structure and operation, the EOC resembles the typical national human rights commission. However, organizations need not undertake the costly and time-consuming task of sponsoring litigation to have an impact; rather, they may elect to file an amicus curiae ("friend of the court") brief or, where permissible, intervene in existing litigation, as has been the case with HREOC. Within the literature on organizational litigation, scholars continue to debate the effectiveness of these strategies in effecting political change.[9] Moreover, as Robert A. Dahl demonstrated with regard to the U.S. Supreme Court, because of the judicial appointments process, "the policy views dominant on the Court are never for long out of line with the policy views dominant among the lawmaking majorities."[10]

Nevertheless, many scholars expect NHRIs to act as transnational human rights entrepreneurs, mediating the space between the international and national politico-legal orders. Sonia Cardenas, for example, asserts that they can "contribute to the overall development of human rights jurisprudence,"[11] and Anne Gallagher suggests that these institutions can "de-mystify universal principles and translate them into practical measures at the level where it most matters."[12] However, the literature on NHRIs, which Cardenas characterizes as "largely ad hoc and descriptive," thus far has failed to establish exactly how, as well as the conditions under which, NHRIs can exercise these effects.[13] The subsequent analysis seeks to redress this lacuna by focusing on HREOC's record of interventions in existing litigation.

AUSTRALIA'S HUMAN RIGHTS REGIME

Hilary Charlesworth characterizes Australia as exhibiting a "split personality" with regard to human rights.[14] In stark contrast to other Western democracies, the country has resisted efforts to adopt a national bill of rights in either statutory or constitutional form.[15] Yet its domestic misgivings have not been matched in the international realm. With only one exception, Australian governments have signed all of the major UN human rights conventions.[16] These conventions do not, however, give rise to domestic rights or causes of action until they have been "transformed" into domestic rules through a deliberate lawmaking act. Not all treaty obligations have been transformed into legislation. Whereas federal antidiscrimination laws were enacted in the

1970s and 1980s pursuant to ratification of the UN's International Convention on the Elimination of All Forms of Racial Discrimination (ICERD) and the Convention on the Elimination of All Forms of Discrimination Against Women (CEDAW), comparable efforts to implement the International Covenant on Civil and Political Rights (ICCPR), which would have amounted to some sort of bill of rights, failed. As an alternative, the ICCPR was appended to the Human Rights and Equal Opportunity Commission Act 1986 (HREOCA), the act that brought the HREOC into being. The terms of this act provide that additional international instruments can be attached by ministerial declaration, and in 1992, the Convention on the Rights of the Child (CRoC) was added.[17]

Australia also has subjected itself to international monitoring of its human rights record. In 1991, it acceded to the First Optional Protocol to the ICCPR, thereby accepting the jurisdiction of the UN Human Rights Committee (UNHRC). This allows individuals in Australia to submit what amount to complaints, but technically are called "communications," to the committee for alleged breaches of the ICCPR by the state. In response to these communications, the UNHRC issues nonbinding "views" rather than "decisions."[18] As indicated, the formal terms used in the protocol to describe the UNHRC's work in this area are distinctly nonjudicial in nature. Today, however, UN publications employ judicial terms, such as "complaints," "decisions," and "jurisprudence," when discussing the UNHRC's functions under the protocol.[19] In addition to its work under the protocol, the committee also publishes its interpretation of the ICCPR's provisions through a series of general comments, and it issues concluding observations on the periodic reports filed by signatory states. Its views, comments, and observations all serve as resources that may be used by NHRI lawyers in the courts.

These developments gave rise to a number of questions concerning the relationship between Australia's legal system and the increasingly dense web of international law and transnational jurisprudence. Two of these emerged as particularly salient in the area of immigration and refugee law. First, under what conditions, if any, should Australia's international human rights obligations aid in the interpretation and development of domestic statutory, constitutional, and common law? Second, what is the practical effect of the international instruments that have been appended to the HREOCA? The subsequent analysis will reveal how HREOC lawyers sought to influence the courts' answers to both questions.

AUSTRALIA'S HUMAN RIGHTS AND EQUAL OPPORTUNITY COMMISSION

HREOC was designed to be a passive institution. In contrast with similar bodies established in other Anglo-American democracies,[20] it has never been empowered to initiate or direct any type of litigation before the courts. Perhaps unwittingly, HREOC's political architects gave it one potentially powerful tool—the authority to seek leave to intervene in existing litigation that involves issues of discrimination or human rights.[21] At the commission's creation in 1986, this tool was unappreciated by HREOC's friends and foes alike. In contrast with amici curiae, interveners are parties to the proceedings, they may file pleadings or lead evidence, and they may lodge an appeal. Although in some lower court cases HREOC lawyers have exercised the additional prerogatives that interveners enjoy, in most cases they have behaved much like amici, submitting written submissions and participating, with the court's permission, in oral arguments. Given HREOC's tight budget and small legal staff, intervention, compared to sponsorship of cases, constitutes a cost-effective means of working through the courts.

HREOC's role as an intervener is especially important in Australia because the country's courts have historically been suspicious, if not hostile, to nonparty interventions.[22] A comparison of Australia's High Court with North American supreme courts is instructive. Between 1947 and 2005, nearly a sixty-year period, Australia's High Court gave leave to 1,212 nonparty interveners.[23] The United States Supreme Court, by contrast, accepted almost five thousand amicus curiae briefs between 1986 and 1995,[24] and the Supreme Court of Canada granted 469 nongovernmental bodies leave to intervene in Charter of Rights cases alone between 1985 and 1999.[25]

In the late 1970s, the rate of nonparty interventions before Australia's High Court began to increase dramatically as the result of a 1976 change in the law that granted state and commonwealth attorneys general (AGs) an automatic right to intervene in cases that raise constitutional issues.[26] Since then, AGs account for 91 percent of all High Court interventions. After the AGs, however, HREOC is the most frequent intervener before the High Court. No other single organization comes close.[27] Between 1991—the year of HREOC's first intervention before the High Court—and 2005, the High Court gave leave to seventy-six non-AG interveners. HREOC accounts for seventeen of these over this fourteen-year period. Thus it occupies a position comparable to that of the Women's Legal and Education Action Fund (LEAF) in Canada, which, during a similar period (1984–1999), was the most frequent non-AG intervener before the Supreme Court of Canada, with nineteen such interventions.[28] LEAF has served as the subject of several books and articles,[29] but HREOC's record as an intervener has not yet served as the focus of scholarly analysis.

RESEARCH DESIGN AND DATA COLLECTION

HREOC must receive leave from the court before it can intervene in a case. To date, only one court has denied its application for leave.[30] The commission first exercised its intervention function in 1988, and between that year and 2007, it intervened in fifty-one different cases.[31] In six of these, it intervened at multiple levels of the appellate process, thereby bringing the total number of interventions to fifty-eight.[32] Although HREOC has participated in litigation that involves a wide array of issues, including discrimination, family law, and indigenous land rights, 36 percent (21) of its interventions involved issues of immigration and refugee law. Family law accounts for the second highest proportion of the commission's interventions, at 22 percent (13). Immigration and refugee cases, which serve as the focus of the following analysis, thus account for the single largest share of HREOC's intervention work. These types of cases also have assumed special political salience during the last fifteen years because of Australia's controversial policy of subjecting "unlawful non-citizens" to mandatory administrative detention and the dramatic rise in the volume of refugee cases in the federal courts.[33]

I read each of HREOC's submissions and the corresponding court opinions. Data for this project were available on HREOC's Web site, where, with two minor exceptions, it has posted copies of its written submissions and links to the courts' decisions.[34] First, one of the requisite submissions was missing from the site.[35] However, HREOC had also intervened before the lower federal court in this case, and these submissions were available. I shall assume that the commission advanced substantively similar arguments to the appellate court. Second, a decision by the Refugee Review Tribunal in *AM*, a case in which HREOC intervened, is unavailable. As a result, this case was simply eliminated from the qualitative analysis, bringing the total number of cases to fourteen and the total number of interventions to twenty.

In order to assess the extent to which HREOC lawyers behaved as transnational norm entrepreneurs, we evaluated each submission's arguments according to the following four criteria: first, the extent to which they promote methods of legal interpretation that presume a symbiotic relationship between transnational and domestic law; second, the extent to which they cite Australia's international treaty obligations; third, the extent to which they cite other international sources, including but not limited to UN treaty monitoring views, comments, and reports; and fourth, the extent to which they cite decisions issued by foreign national courts. Of course, in addition to relying on the foregoing materials, HREOC's lawyers consistently used domestic precedents and sources in its arguments. This analysis, however, focuses solely on the transnational dimension of their submissions.

The approach used to assess HREOC's impact was borrowed from the largely American literature on interest groups acting as amicus curiae.[36] Many of these studies were able to employ statistical methods because of the sheer volume of amicus curiae participation before U.S. courts.[37] Such methods, however, were less useful here given the relatively small number of cases under examination. Drawing on qualitative work in this area, HREOC's impact was assessed in two ways: case outcome and judicial reasoning. Each case was coded in terms of the party that prevailed—either the individual or the representative of the federal government. In all of the cases examined, HREOC's arguments supported the interests of the individual.

Judicial reasoning was evaluated in three main ways. First, following Karen O'Connor and Lee Epstein, we recorded the number of cases in which a judge "specifically mentioned" HREOC's submission.[38] As O'Connor and Epstein admit, the resultant data constitute "blunt indicators of the usefulness of interest group *amicus curiae* briefs to the Court."[39] This study, therefore, focuses on a smaller set of cases and analyzes the judicial decisions in greater detail. As a second measure of impact, we recorded the number of cases in which a member of the majority discussed any one of HREOC's arguments, whether or not he or she explicitly attributed these arguments to HREOC.[40] And, third, we recorded the number of cases in which a dissenting judge adopted any one of HREOC's arguments, whether or not he or she explicitly attributed these arguments to HREOC. Gregg Ivers and Karen O'Connor, who employed a similar approach, suggest that this type of analysis provides "a good preliminary surrogate measure of effectiveness."[41] They readily admit, though, that it is difficult for those beyond the inner sanctum to know the extent to which lawyers' arguments affect judicial decision making.[42]

Because the facts of each case will not be discussed in great detail, a brief overview of the issues that each presents is warranted. Five cases involved the fate of detainees facing indefinite detention because deportation arrangements could not be secured despite government efforts to do so.[43] One case challenged the policy of keeping children in mandatory detention.[44] In another, the issue was whether a man who had escaped from a detention facility could use evidence of its deplorable conditions as part of his defense to charges of escape.[45] Two involved the rights of detainees, including the right to legal counsel,[46] and two others involved challenges to statutory privative clauses intended to insulate administrative decisions from judicial review.[47] The remaining cases involved the executive's power to prevent the entry of noncitizens into Australia,[48] the deportation of a father of Australian citizens,[49] and the refugee status of individuals seeking asylum because of China's one-child policy.[50]

HREOC AS TRANSNATIONAL LEGAL ENTREPRENEUR

HREOC consistently acted as a transnational legal entrepreneur across the fourteen immigration and refugee cases. Of the main UN treaties, HREOC invoked the ICCPR most frequently, in 93 percent of the 14 cases. This was followed by the CRoC (36 percent); the Convention Against Torture (CAT) and the Universal Declaration of Human Rights (UDHR) (both 29 percent); the International Covenant on Economic, Social and Cultural

Rights (ICESCR) (21 percent); and the Convention on the Elimination of All Forms of Discrimination Against Women (CEDAW) in a single case. For the remaining instruments, with the exception of CEDAW, for which it invoked only a single provision, HREOC lawyers cited a variety of provisions. Over time, HREOC's submissions became more elaborate. Its first submission in an immigration or a refugee case, *Minister of State for Immigration and Ethnic Affairs v. Teoh* (1995), is one of its briefest and invokes only a single provision of a single convention, the CRoC. By contrast, HREOC's submission in *Re Woolley* (2003) invokes five provisions of the ICCPR and six provisions of the CRoC.

In addition to citing UN conventions, HREOC lawyers frequently referenced views, comments, and reports issued by the UN bodies charged with monitoring state compliance. Perhaps unsurprisingly considering the number of ICCPR references, they most frequently cited the UNHRC's interpretations of the ICCPR. In twelve of the fourteen cases, they cited views issued by the committee pursuant to the First Optional Protocol. Counsel also invoked the UNHRC's general comments in eight cases and its responses to country reports in four cases. In addition, they cited reports issued by both the UN Committee on the Rights of the Child (five cases) and the UN Committee on Economic, Social and Cultural Rights (two cases). HREOC lawyers, however, did not treat these materials as though they were legally binding. Rather, they asserted that because the UNHRC serves as "the pre-eminent interpreter of the ICCPR," one could "expect Australian Courts to have regard to the UNHRC's views where questions of interpretation of the ICCPR arose."[51] Furthermore, they noted that the committee's views had been characterized as "considerable persuasive authority" and "highly influential, if not authoritative" by New Zealand chief justice Thomas Eichelbaum and Australian jurist Elizabeth Evatt, respectively.[52]

HREOC lawyers also made frequent use of transnational jurisprudence. They cited precedents from courts in other countries, including Britain (in eleven of the fourteen cases), Canada (in eight cases), the United States (in seven cases), and New Zealand (in four cases). Decisions of the European Court of Human Rights (ECtHR) were also cited in six cases. For example, HREOC lawyers argued that in construing Article 2(3) of the ICCPR Australian courts should follow the jurisprudence developed by the ECtHR concerning Article 13 of the European Convention on Human Rights (ECHR), which is similarly worded.[53] In one set of cases, HREOC and counsel for the federal government sparred over the applicability of a principle derived from the ECtHR's jurisprudence for purposes of interpreting the Australian constitution.[54] On this particular occasion, HREOC argued against use of the principle, noting the distinctive nature of the European system and citing British case law to support its alternative construction.[55]

Of its twenty-one interventions, courts ruled in favor of the individual and hence in favor of HREOC, on only four occasions.[56] Yet by our other indicators, HREOC's influence belies this dismal record. Judges expressly acknowledged HREOC's submissions in nine of the twenty interventions.[57] In three of the four occasions on which HREOC prevailed, its arguments concerning Australia's international obligations were an important component in the reasoning of at least one member of the majority.[58] Moreover, in five of HREOC's unsuccessful interventions, at least one judge in the majority engaged HREOC's arguments, sometimes in considerable detail.[59] Finally, in six of its unsuccessful interventions, at least one dissenting judge accepted HREOC's transnational arguments.[60] Thus HREOC's arguments were consistently recognized and engaged.

Moreover, the record suggests that in some cases, counsel for the party challenging the government relied on HREOC's submissions. For example, in *VCCL and Vadarlis v. MIMIA* (2001), federal court judge Anthony North noted that Eric Vadarlis "expressly adopted the submissions filed by HREOC as his own."[61] Judge Wilcox, in *NAAV*, observed that although counsel for the refugee claimants addressed the constitutional issues in their written submissions, they nevertheless "left the main burden of the argument" to counsel for the HREOC.[62] Finally, in *Luu*, the court observed that in raising one particular argument, the individual party "appears to have been prompted to do so by submissions of the Commission."[63] Thus HREOC lawyers exercised influence in a number of different ways.

HREOC's first intervention in an immigration case involved it in one of Australia's most famous international law cases, *Minister of State for Immigration and Ethnic Affairs v. Teoh* (1995), and constitutes its most notable success in this policy area. *Teoh* involved the planned deportation of a noncitizen who had been convicted of drug offenses but was also the father of multiple children with Australian citizenship. Deportation, his counsel argued, would bring a terrible hardship on his family and would abridge Article 3(1) of the CRoC, which provides that "in all actions concerning children, whether undertaken by public or private social welfare institutions, courts of law, administrative authorities or legislative bodies, the best interests of the child shall be a primary consideration." The High Court was asked to determine whether this provision was relevant to the government official's exercise of the statutory discretion involved in the deportation; and if so, whether Australia's ratification of the convention gave rise to a legitimate expectation that the decision maker would either exercise this discretion in conformity with the terms of the convention or, alternatively, provide notice, reasons, and an opportunity to be heard on the issue. The full Federal Court answered these questions in the affirmative.

HREOC intervened before the High Court, urging it either to sustain the lower court's decision concerning procedural fairness,[64] or more boldly, to find that upon the CRoC's entry into force for Australia, "the decision-maker became *indefeasibly bound*" to comply with its terms, in this case treating "the best interests of the child as 'a primary consideration.' "[65] In advocating for the latter position, HREOC lawyers sought to distinguish a contrary British case, noting that it had been criticized by the New Zealand Court of Appeal.[66] They further noted that even before the United Kingdom incorporated the ECHR into its domestic law through the Human Rights Act (1998), British judges had accepted that they should have close regard to the ECHR in expanding and protecting common law and statutory remedies dealing with human rights.[67] HREOC's lawyers suggested that Australian judges, whose role may be analogous to that of British judges before the Human Rights Act went into effect, should regard the CRoC in a similar manner. The federal government's lawyers, by contrast, vigorously contended that a convention ratified by Australia but not incorporated into its domestic law could have neither of the effects claimed by HREOC.

The High Court sustained the lower court's ruling. Although none of the justices specifically acknowledged HREOC, Chief Justice Anthony Mason and Justice William Deane endorsed HREOC's arguments, including its reading of the British and New Zealand cases. Justice Mary Gaudron concurred as to the effect of the CRoC on Australian law, although it was not key to her reasoning. Even in dissent, Justice Michael McHugh devoted substantial effort to refuting HREOC's arguments.[68] Although *Teoh* raised a political furor, precipitating a joint statement by the minister for foreign affairs and AG in which they denounced the decision,[69] on further reflection, legal scholars have characterized it as an "unexceptional, even conservative, decision" that represents "a modest step towards the assimilation of international standards and norms in the development of the domestic common law."[70]

HREOC's second victory came in a case arising from the "*Tampa* Affair." In 2001, the MV *Tampa*, a Norwegian cargo ship, rescued more than four hundred persons who intended to seek refugee status in Australia, off the coast of Christmas Island, an Australian territory. A diplomatic row ensued, as the Australian government, heading into an election, did not want to admit these persons, all of whom remained on board the *Tampa* in deteriorating conditions. The Victorian Civil Liberties League and attorney Eric Vadarlis filed suit in the federal court, claiming, among other things, that by not allowing the rescued asylum seekers to disembark in Australia, the federal government was unlawfully detaining them. At trial, federal court judge Anthony North found that the asylum seekers were entitled to be released by the government and brought to the Australian mainland, although he neither recognized nor engaged HREOC's transnational arguments. On appeal before the full federal court, however, Judges Bryan Beaumont and Robert French overturned the lower court's decision, also without engaging HREOC's arguments. By contrast, the third member of that panel, Chief Justice Michael Black, would have sustained the lower court, drawing in part on arguments advanced by HREOC. This proved to be the final decision, as the High Court denied an application for special leave to appeal. By this time, the asylum seekers on board the *Tampa* had been relocated to either Nauru or New Zealand pursuant to arrangements negotiated by the federal government, known as the "Pacific Solution," and thus were no longer being detained.

HREOC's two remaining victories occurred before the full federal court in two cases that involved the issue of indefinite detention, *VFAD* and *Al Masri*. Both involved appeals by the commonwealth government from decisions issued by federal court justice Ron Merkel, who had ruled that a detainee who could not be deported must be released rather than held indefinitely in custody. Some of Merkel's peers on the federal bench not only criticized these two decisions but also reached the opposite conclusion in litigation before their courts.[71] The same three-judge panel of the full federal court, composed of Chief Justice Michael Black and Justices Ross Sundberg and Samuel Weinberg, heard the appeals in both *VFAD* and *Al Masri* within four months of each other. HREOC intervened in both cases at this stage of the litigation, defending Merkel's decisions, and in both cases, the full federal court sustained the decisions.

In so doing, the appellate judges explicitly acknowledged HREOC's arguments and incorporated transnational jurisprudence into their analysis. In *VFAD*, the three-judge panel, speaking through a single opinion, stated that it was "fortified" in its conclusion by the principle that statutory provisions "should, so far as the language permits, be interpreted and applied in a man-ner consistent with established rules of international law and which accords with this country's treaty obligations."[72] In *Al Masri*, the judges reiterated this point and devoted substantial time to considering British and American case law, jurisprudence developed by the ECtHR, and views expressed by the UNHRC, most of which had been cited by HREOC in its submissions. The High Court denied the federal government's application for special leave to appeal the *Al Masri* decision, but the following year, it finally heard arguments in two cases that involved this same issue of indefinite detention.

In *Al-Kateb* and *Al Khafaji,* which essentially were jointly considered, HREOC again argued that in light of international and transnational jurispru-dence, the statute at issue should be interpreted as failing to provide authority for indefinite detention. If, however, the statute was determined to provide for indefinite detention, HREOC argued that the statute should be declared unconstitutional, again, in light of international and transnational jurisprudence. A narrow majority (four to three) of the High Court, comprising Justices Michael McHugh, Kenneth Hayne, Ian Callinan, and Dyson Heydon, upheld the government's policy of indefinite detention and overruled the full federal court's decisions in *Al Masri* and *VFAD*. In interpreting the statute, the major-ity decided that recourse to international law and transnational jurisprudence was unwarranted because the law's language was clear and unambiguous. Two of the justices went further and attacked the transnational arguments that had been offered by HREOC. Although Justice McHugh accepted that the use of international law in statutory interpretation had been endorsed in a number of Australian cases, he nevertheless asserted that "the rationale for the rule that [statutes] should be construed to conform with international law bears no relationship to the reality of the modern legislative process."[73] Justice Hayne also rejected that "reference to international instruments" or "resort to decisions of other [foreign] courts" could transform the meaning of the statute.[74] In addition, McHugh and Callinan also denied the relevance of international law and transnational jurisprudence to constitutional interpretation. The former described the idea as "heretical," and the latter endorsed the views of U.S. Supreme Court justices Antonin Scalia and Clarence Thomas.[75]

The minority in *Al-Kateb*, composed of Chief Justice Murray Gleeson and Justices William Gummow and Michael Kirby, did not express this same hostility to these uses of transnational human rights jurisprudence. Although none of the justices expressly acknowledged HREOC, Gleeson and Kirby engaged some of HREOC's arguments. Considerations of domestic law predominated in Gummow's opinion, but Kirby, in concurring with Gummow, demonstrated the ways in which his colleague's views were buttressed by international law.[76]

The High Court considered two additional, related cases, *Behrooz* and *Re Woolley*. In *Behrooz*, the same competing arguments concerning the relationship of transnational jurisprudence to domestic statutory and constitutional law were rehearsed by Kirby and McHugh. In a nearly unanimous decision, with Kirby as the lone dissenter, the High Court found that the conditions of mandatory detention, no matter how harsh, could not serve as a valid defense to a charge of escaping from immigration detention. In reaching his decision, Kirby drew upon the ICCPR, which was a cornerstone of HREOC's submission.[77] Finally, in *Re Woolley*, the court decided unanimously that the federal government's power to detain also included children who were unlawful noncitizens, ignoring the special physical and emotional vulnerability of children and the protections enshrined in international law. In this case, Kirby concluded that the language of the statute and Parliament's intent were clear. Therefore, the court was bound to uphold the law irrespective of countervailing international human rights instruments. As a result of these High Court decisions, the government's policy of mandatory detention essentially was sanctioned by the court.

A litigation strategy's success ultimately depends on the nature and composition of the court and whether the judges can be persuaded to accept the groups' or interveners' legal arguments. The federal bench in Melbourne has been known for its liberal tendencies, particularly in the area of refugee law.[78] Three of HREOC's victories occurred before federal court judges based in Melbourne: Justice North in *Vadarlis* and Chief Justice Black and Justices

Sundberg and Weinberg in both *Al Masri* and *VFAD*. Moreover, upon retiring in 2006, former federal court judge, Ron Merkel, whose decisions were
sustained in *Al Masri* and *VFAD*, became a vocal critic of the government's
refugee policies and developed a legal practice focusing on public interest and
indigenous matters.[79] In a 2006 interview with ABC Radio National, Merkel
made the following observation:

> The law has been going through a period of almost stagnation over
> recent years, where the internationalization of Australian law, the broad
> view taken by the High Court of the Constitution in the late '80s,
> early '90s, an endeavor to keep Australian law in conformity with
> developments in other Commonwealth countries like Canada and
> New Zealand, the United Kingdom, the United States, all of that,
> has come to an end.[80]

Later in that same interview, he expressed hope at "the new possibility
of trying to get human rights back onto the legal agenda. They've not fared
all that well over the last ten years or so."[81]

HREOC's fortunes before the High Court also appear to have been
conditioned by judicial attitudes. It intervened before the court on seven different occasions. The first, *Teoh*, occurred at the end of Anthony Mason's tenure
as chief justice (1987–1995), during which time the High Court experienced
a significant role transformation, moving from what Jason L. Pierce describes
as an "orthodox" role into a "new politicized judicial role." This transformation was marked by the court's involvement in some of the country's most
controversial issues and its adoption of "new, controversial modes of legal
reasoning."[82] *Teoh* exemplifies both trends. HREOC's next six interventions
before the High Court between 2001 and 2004 all proved unsuccessful.

By this time, the composition of the bench had changed significantly as
the result of a change in government—from Labor to a conservative Liberal-
National Coalition—following the 1996 election and the constitutional requirement that federal judges retire at the age of seventy. The coalition government
deliberately filled the High Court vacancies with avowedly legalistic jurists.
By 2003, it had appointed a majority of the court's bench, including Hayne
(1997), Callinan (1998), Gleeson as chief justice, (1998), and Heydon (2003).
Since then, the court generally has employed a more traditional interpretative methodology, which the majority decisions in *Al-Kateb* and *Al Khafaji*
aptly demonstrate. Kirby, who has become a frequent dissenter, often stands
as the lone exception. He was appointed to the High Court a month before
the pivotal 1996 election, and although he was not a member of the Mason
Court, he nevertheless seems to embody its progressive spirit. Most important
for present purposes, Kirby is the court's strongest advocate of the symbiotic
relationship between the transnational and national legal orders.

It is, of course, impossible to know for sure how the retired Mason Court judges would have decided the series of mandatory detention cases if they had remained on the bench. I have reason to believe that their opinions would have been more receptive of international law and transnational jurisprudence. Moreover, one cannot conclude that a Labor government, had it continued in power, would have appointed jurists inclined to challenge its immigration and refugee policies. Consider the following: Gummow, the Labor government's last High Court appointment, was regarded as a "legalistic judge," representing a compromise between the Labor Party and the Opposition.[83] The policy of mandatory detention was actually initiated by a Labor government in 1992, and the party remains divided about the issue today. Also, it was a Labor government that reacted in a hostile manner to the High Court's decision in *Teoh*. Thus faced with a burgeoning refugee caseload in the federal courts and segments of the federal bench sympathetic to refugee claims, it is not unreasonable to conclude that a Labor government also might have become more conservative in its judicial appointments.

CONCLUSION

The purpose of this research has been to analyze HREOC's amicus curiae participation in immigration and refugee cases before Australian federal courts. It established that HREOC lawyers have, indeed, acted as transnational legal entrepreneurs. Although it is difficult to know for sure just what HREOC's impact was on the courts, the findings strongly suggest that judges consistently engage HREOC's arguments. Furthermore, individual parties sometimes rely on HREOC for its expertise in international law and transnational jurisprudence. Future research should compare HREOC's submissions with those of the other litigants to determine more accurately which arguments may have been introduced to the litigation purely by virtue of HREOC's participation. And for comparative purposes, it should also evaluate HREOC's impact in other issue areas, particularly those concerning less politically charged policies. Finally, despite being unsuccessful in court, HREOC's arguments may have had indirect effects; for example, by reshaping views within the legal community or influencing the development of the law through other means.

NOTES

1. The author thanks East Carolina University, Claremont McKenna College (CMC), and the Keck Center for International and Strategic Studies at CMC for their generous support, and her CMC research assistants, Candice Camargo, Phoebe Kinzie-Larson, and Kevin Okie, for their assistance with this project.

2. Sonia Cardenas, "Adaptive States: The Proliferation of National Human Rights Institutions." Carr Center for Human Rights Policy, Kennedy School of Government, Harvard University. Working Paper Series T-01-04 (2001), 56, p. 9.

3. See Anne-Marie Slaughter, *A New World Order* (Princeton: Princeton University Press, 2004), chap. 2.

4. Paul Schiff Berman, "The Supreme Court, Constitutional Courts and the Role of International Law in Constitutional Jurisprudence: Judges as Cosmopolitan Transnational Actors," *Tulsa Journal of Comparative & International Law* 12 (2004) 109, 110.

5. See Martha Finnemore and Kathryn Sikkink, "International Norm Dynamics and Political Change," *International Organization, International Organization at Fifty: Exploration and Contestation in the Study of World Politics* 52, no. 4 (1998): 887–917; Catherine Powell, "The Role of Transnational Norm Entrepreneurs in the U.S. 'War on Terror,'" *Theoretical Inquiries in Law* 5, no. 47 (2004): (online edition).

6. Chris Bonastia, "Why Did Affirmative Action in Housing Fail during the Nixon Era? Exploring the 'Institutional Homes' of Social Policies," *Social Problems* 47, no. 4 (2000): 523–542.

7. Charles R. Epp, *The Rights Revolution* (Chicago: University of Chicago Press, 1998).

8. Karen J. Alter and Jeannette Vargas, "Explaining Variation in the Use of European Litigation Stratgies," *Comparative Political Studies*, 33, no. 4 (2000): 452–482, 456–457. On the EOC's litigation strategy, see also Epp, 1998, chaps. 7, 8.

9. Gerald N. Rosenberg, *The Hollow Hope* (Chicago: University of Chicago Press, 1991); Michael McCann, *Rights at Work* (Chicago: University of Chicago Press, 1994).

10. Robert A. Dahl, "Decision Making in a Democracy: The Supreme Court as a National Policy Maker," *Journal of Public Law* 6, no. 279 (1957): 285.

11. Sonia Cardenas, "Emerging Global Actors: The United Nations and National Human Rights Institutions," *Global Governance* 9, no. 23 (2003): 26.

12. Anne Gallagher, "Making Human Rights Treaty Obligations a Reality," in *The Future of UN Human Rights Treaty Monitoring*, ed. Philip Alston and James Crawford (Cambridge: Cambridge University Press, 2000), 201–227, 203.

13. Cardenas, 2001, 7.

14. See Hilary Charlesworth, "Australia's Split Personality: Implementation of Human Rights Treaty Obligations in Australia," in *Treaty-making and Australia: Globalization Versus Sovereignty*, ed. Philip Alston and Madelaine Chiam (Annandale, NSW: Federation Press, 1995), 136–137.

15. The Australian Capital Territory (ACT), the small, self-governing territory in which the federal capital of Canberra is located, and the State of Victoria are the only jurisdictions that currently have bills of rights. Both do not empower courts to strike down legislation that contravenes the rights recognized therein.

16. Australia has not ratified the International Convention on the Protection of the Rights of All Migrant Workers and Members of Their Families.

17. In addition to the ICCPR, the International Labour Organization Convention No. 111, the Declaration on the Rights of the Child, the Declaration on the Rights of Mentally Retarded Persons, and the Declaration on the Rights of Disabled Persons were also originally scheduled to the act. The Declaration on the Elimination of All Forms of Intolerance and of Discrimination Based on Religion or Belief was added in 1993.

18. See First Optional Protocol, Articles 1 and 5(4).

19. For example, see "Fact Sheet No. 7/ Rev. 1, Complaints Procedures" produced by the Office of the United Nations High Commissioner for Human Rights, online at http://www.ohchr.org/english/about/publications/docs/fs7.htm, and "Jurisprudence of the Treaty Monitoring Bodies," Office of the High Commissioner for Human Rights, online at http://www.unhchr.ch/html/menu2/8/jurispr.htm.

20. For example, see Rhonda Evans Case, "Enforcing New Zealand's Anti-discrimination Laws: The State as Public Interest Litigator in New Zealand" in *Public Interest Litigation: New Zealand Experience in International Perspective*, ed. Rick Bigwood (Wellington: LexisNexis NZ Limited, 2006), 133–160.

21. See Racial Discrimination Act 1975 (Cth), s 20(1)(e); Sex Discrimination Act 1984 (Cth), s 48(1)(gb); Disability Discrimination Act 1992 (Cth), s 67(1)(l); Human Rights and Equal Opportunity Act 1986 (Cth), s 11(1)(o) and s 31(j).

22. See Jason L. Pierce, *Inside the Mason Court Revolution: The High Court of Australia Transformed* (Durham, N.C.: Carolina Academic Press, 2006), 95–99; George Williams, "The Amicus Curiae and Intervener in the High Court of Australia: A Comparative Analysis," *Federal Law Review* 28 (2000): 365–402.

23. All data on High Court interventions through 2001 are taken from Pierce, 2003, 94–102. The author gathered the data for the period 2002 to 2005.

24. Joseph D. Kearney and Thomas W. Merrill, "The Influence of Amicus Curiae Briefs on the Supreme Court," *University of Pennsylvnia Law Review* 148 (January 2000): 743, 752.

25. Ian Brodie, *Friends of the Court: The Privileging of Interest Group Litigants in Canada* (Albany: State University of New York Press, 2002), 43.

26. Judiciary Act 1903 (Cth), s 78B.

27. Although no data exist on interveners before the federal courts, it is probably safe to assume that there, too, HREOC occupies a similar position.

28. Brodie, 2002, 44.

29. See, e.g., Shrene Razack, *Canadian Feminism and the Law: The Women's Legal Education and Action Fund and the Pursuit of Equality* (Toronto: Second Story Press, 1991); and Christopher P. Manfredi, *Feminist Activism: Legal Mobilization and the Women's Legal Education and Action Fund* (Vancouver: University of British Columbia Press, 2004).

30. *The Queen v. GJ* [2005] NTCCA 20.

31. This figure excludes *Howe v. QANTAS* [no citation given] and *ACCC v. Radio Rentals* [2005] FCA 1133, both of which appear to have been discontinued. Since 2000, the individual commissioners of HREOC have been empowered to seek leave to act as amici curiae in cases involving complaints of unlawful discrimination. *Human Rights Legislation Amendment Act No. 1 1999* (Cth). These cases are not included in this analysis.

32. Although HREOC included its arguments for a trio of related cases—*Al-Kateb v. Godwin* [2004] HCA 37, *MIMIA v. Al Khafaji* [2004] HCA 38, and *Behrooz v. Secretary of the Department of Immigration, Multicultural and Indigenous Affairs* [2004] HCA 36—in a single submission, I have counted each separately for purposes of arriving at this figure.

33. See Juliet Curtin, " 'Never Say Never': *Al-Kateb v. Godwin*," *Sydney Law Review* 27 (2005): 355–370; Mary Crock, "Judging Refugees: The Clash of Power and Institutions in the Development of Australian Refugee Law," *Sydney Law Review* 26 (2004): 51–73.

34. Online at http://www.hreoc.gov.au/legal/intervention_info.html.

35. HREOC's submission before the Full Federal Court in *Long Guan Chun, et al. v. Minister for Immigration, Local Government & Ethnic Affairs* (1996) 64 FCR 245.

36. Karen O'Connor and Lee Epstein, "The Rise of Conservative Interest Group Litigation," *Journal of Politics* 45 (1983): 479–489.

37. Donald R. Songer and Reginald S. Sheehan, "Interest Group Success in the Courts: Amicus Participation in the Supreme Court," *Political Research Quarterly* 46 (1993): 339–354; Kearney and Merrill, 2000; Paul M. Collins Jr., "Friends of the Court: Examining the Influence of Amicus Curiae Participation in U.S. Supreme Court Litigation," *Law & Society Review* 38 (2004): 807.

38. O'Connor and Epstein, 1983, 42.

39. O'Connor and Epstein, 1983, 43.

40. In contrast to the American system, Australian appellate courts typically issue seriatim opinions. This means that rather than a single judge writing an opinion on behalf of the entire court, each judge writes an individual opinion, even when a majority exists.

41. Gregg Ivers and Karen O'Connor, "Friends as Foes: The Amicus Curiae Participation and Effectiveness of the American Civil Liberties Union and Americans for Effective Law Enforcement in Criminal Cases, 1969-1982," *Law & Policy* 9 (1987): 161–178, 166.

42. Ivers and O'Connor, 1987, 166. For the argument that legal advocacy exercises negligible effect upon judicial behavior, see Jeffrey A. Segal and Harold J. Spaeth, *The Supreme Court and the Attitudinal Model* (Cambridge: Cambridge University Press, 1993); cf. Andrea McAtee and Kevin T. McGuire, "Lawyers, Justices, and Issue Salience: When and How do Legal Arguments Affect the U.S. Supreme Court?" *Law & Society Review* 41 (2007): 259–278.

43. *Luu v. MIMIA* [2002] FCAFC 369; *MIMIA v. VFAD* [2002] FCAFC 390; *MIMIA v. Al Masri* [2003] FCAFC 70; *Al-Kateb v. Godwin* [2004] HCA 37; *MIMIA v. Al Khafaji* [2004] HCA 38.

44. *Re Woolley; Ex parte Applicants M276/2003 by their next friend GS* [2004] HCA 49.

45. *Behrooz v. Secretary of the Department of Immigration, Multicultural and Indigenous Affairs* [2004] HCA 36.

46. *Fang v. Minister for Immigration and Ethnic Affairs* (1996) 64 FCR 245; and *Odhiambo v. MIMIA* [2002] FCAFC 194.

47. *NAAV v. MIMIA* [2002] FCAFC 228; and *S134/2002 v. MIMIA* [2003] 195 ALR 1.

48. HREOC intervened at three levels: *Victorian Council for Civil Liberties Inc. (VCCL) & Vadarlis v. MIMIA* [2001] FCA 1297; *MIMIA v. Vadarlis & VCCL* [2001] FCA 1329; and *Vadarlis v. MIMIA* M93/2001 (27 November 2001) (Special leave application to the High Court of Australia).

49. *Minister of State for Immigration and Ethnic Affairs v. Teoh* [1995] 183 CLR 273.

50. *Chun v. Minister for Immigration and Ethnic Affairs* [1996] 136 ALR 303.

51. HREOC Submission, *Al-Kateb*, para. 27, fn. 39.

52. HREOC Submission, *Al-Kateb*, para. 27, quoting *Nicholls v Registrar Court of Appeal* [1998] 2 NZLR 385 at 404; and Elizabeth Evatt, "The Impact of International

Human Rights on Domestic Law," in *Litigating Rights: Perspectives from Domestic and International Law*, eds. Grant Huscroft and Paul Rishworth (Oxford: Hart Publishing, 2002), 281–303, 295.

53. HREOC Submission, *VFAD*, para. 32; and *NAAV*, paras. 72–76.

54. HREOC Submission, *Al-Kateb*, para. 38.

55. HREOC Submission, *Al-Kateb*, para. 38.

56. *Teoh; VCCL and Vadarlis v. MIMIA* [2001] FCA 1297 (Federal Court); *VFAD*; and *Al Masri*.

57. See *Odhiambo* (C. J. Black, J. Wilcox, J. Moore), paras. 67-77; *Al Masri* (C. J. Black, J. Sundberg, J. Weinberg), paras. 45–48, 133, 138, 142, 165; *VFAD* (C. J. Black, J. Sundberg, J. Weinberg), paras. 77–82, 88; *Luu* (J. Gray, J. North, J. Mansfield), paras. 31, 68, 69, 70, 73, 88, 89, 93, 95; *Behrooz* (J. Kirby), para. 72, 131; *C, L, J, and Z v. Minister for Immigration and Ethnic Affairs* (unreported, O'Loughlin, 30 March 1995), para. 3; *Fang* (Federal Court), para. 1; *Fang* (Full Federal Court) J. Jenkinson, para. 1; J. Carr. para. 1; *Re Woolley*, (C. J. Gleeson), para. 10, (J. McHugh), para. 105, and (J. Gummow), paras. 120, 162.

58. See *Teoh* (C. J. Mason and J. Deane); *Al Masri* (C. J. Black, J. Sundberg, J. Weinberg); and *VFAD* (C. J. Black, J. Sundberg, J. Weinberg).

59. See *Odhiambo* (C. J. Black, J. Wilcox, J. Moore), paras. 67-77; *Luu* (J. Gray, J. North, J. Mansfield), paras. 31, 68, 69, 70, 73, 88, 89, 93, 95; *Re Woolley* (C. J. McHugh), paras. 107–115, (J. Kirby), para. 201; *Al-Kateb* (McHugh), paras. 62–72, (J. Callinan), paras. 282–285; *Teoh* (McHugh), paras. 3, 6-7, 34–44.

60. See *Fang* (J. Carr); *NAAV* (J. Wilcox); *Al-Kateb* (J. Kirby and J. Gaudron); *Behrooz* (J. Kirby), para. 72, 131; *Re Woolley*, (C. J. Gleeson), para. 10, (J. McHugh), paras. 105, 107–115, and (J. Gummow), paras. 120, 162; *Vadarlis* (Full Federal Court) (C. J. North).

61. See *MIMIA & Ors v. Vadarlis and VGCCL* [2001] FCA 1329 (Full Federal Court).

62. *NAAV*, para. 303.

63. *Luu* [2002] FCAFC 369, para. 77 (J. Gray, J. North, and J. Mansfield).

64. HREOC Submission, *Teoh*, para. 10.

65. HREOC Submission, *Teoh*, para. 12.

66. *R. v. Home Secretary, ex parte Brind* [1991] 1 AC 696; *Tavita v. Minister of Immigration* (1993) 1 HRNZ 30 (Cooke, Richardson, and Hardie Boys).

67. See HREOC Submission, *VFAD*, fns. 34–37; HREOC Submission, *NAAV*, paras. 87–90; HREOC Submission, *Teoh*, paras. 8, 13.

68. *Teoh* (McHugh), paras. 34–45.

69. Joint Statement by the minister for foreign affairs, Senator Gareth Evans, and the attorney general, Michael Lavarch, *International Treaties and the High Court Decision in Teoh*, May 10, 1995.

70. Gavan Griffith and Carolyn Evans, "*Teoh* and Visions of International Law," *Australian Year Book of International Law* 21 (2001): 75, 77.

71. See *WAIS v. MIMIA* [2002] FCA 1625 per French J., *NAES v. MIMIA* [2003] FCA 2 per Beaumont J., *Daniel v. MIMIA* [2003] FCA 20 per Whitlam J. and *SHFB v. MIMIA* [2003] FCA 29 per Selway J.

72. *VFAD*, para. 114.

73. *Al-Kateb*, para. 65.

74. *Al-Kateb*, Hayne, paras. 238, 240.

75. *Al-Kateb*, McHugh, para. 65, Callinan, para. 284; 533 US 678 at 703–705 (2001).

76. *Al-Kateb*, para. 150.

77. *Behrooz*, Kirby, paras. 125–133.

78. Pierce, 2006, 68.

79. John Toohey Oration 2007: "Flawed Justice": Hon. Ron Merkel QC presents the John Toohey Oration 2007, University of Western Australia, Perth (University Club Auditorium, 10 May 2007), online at http://www.mcnaught.com.au/barristers.cfm?action=145.

80. ABC Radio National, The Law Report, "Leaving high office for a higher purpose," 23 May 2006, interview of federal court judge Ron Merkel by Damien Carrick, online at http://abc.net.au/rn/lawreport/stories/2006/1644195.htm (visited June 14, 2007).

81. ABC Radio National, The Law Report.

82. Pierce, 2006, 4 [emphasis omitted].

83. Pierce, 2006, 277.

CHAPTER FOURTEEN

Judicial Globalization

How the International Law of Human Rights Changed the Argentine Supreme Court

WALTER F. CARNOTA

This chapter seeks to explain how the international law of human rights changed the way Argentine judges (particularly, the Argentine Supreme Court justices) approach law in general, and how they introduced new human rights norms and canons of constitutional interpretation into Argentine law. International law and norms supplemented domestic law and, as a result, the constitutional material involved in this operation increased manifold. Janet Koven Levit described the impact of international human rights on the Argentine constitution in the following way:

> The Argentine Constitution is no longer [after 1994] a succinct document containing 110 constitutional provisions but rather a compendium of the constitutional text and the nine human rights treaties which, by virtue of their constitutional status, are effectively incorporated into the constitutional text. Therefore, every right, every privilege, every guarantee, that the anointed human rights treaties grant are part of Argentina's Constitution.[1]

In the case of Argentina, the influx and reception of international law shifted the locus from the traditional boundaries of the nation-state to the paradigms of the international bodies entrusted with human rights compliance.[2]

The traditional notion of state sovereignty has been deeply affected in the process. Human rights are not only to be found and discovered in the constitution or in domestic law in general. International law has begun to play an active role as a source for newer fundamental rights in Argentina and elsewhere.

The famous French political philosopher Jean Bodin characterized state sovereignty back in the sixteenth century as "absolute" and "indivisible."[3] This concept, which emerged during the French Wars of Religion, became a *legal* notion after the advent of constitutionalism. Thus constitutions were deemed "supreme law" and embodied the top legal order of the nation-state. One prominent example was the U.S. Constitution, which recognized the supremacy of "[t]his Constitution, and the Laws of the United States which shall be made in Pursuance thereof" in Article VI. However, after World War II, the clear distinction between national and international law became blurrier as states began to integrate politically, legally, and economically. Globalization in the late twentieth century became an open challenge to the traditional nation-state and constitutional law.

ARGENTINE HISTORICAL BACKGROUND

The Argentine Supreme Court had been historically reluctant to use international law standards. One famous case, *Merck Quimica Argentina*,[4] decided in 1948, involved Argentina's declaration of war on Germany just as World War II was ending. Due to mounting pressure led by American then-ambassador Spruille Braden and the incoming UN structure, Argentina belatedly produced a war statement and confiscated German assets. Chemical manufacturer Merck sued, in turn, for compensation.

Juan Perón had removed the Supreme Court the year before (1947) after a highly politicized impeachment process. The new court was adamant to oppose Perón's regime (Perón had been vice president during the brief 1945 conflict with Germany). To validate these policies, the Perón Court developed an infamous double standard: The Argentine constitution was considered supreme in peaceful and normal times. However, during times of war, the court said, international guidelines (i.e., war powers) prevailed, and constitutional guarantees had to take the backseat.

After the military takeover of 1976 to 1983, during which the so-called "dirty war" against guerrillas took place, Argentine lawyers realized that domestic protection of human rights was insufficient to ensure that future violations would never happen again. During the late 1970s and early 1980s, efforts spearheaded by the administration of U.S. president Jimmy Carter and the Organization of American States, among others, had highlighted the international protection of human rights. When democracy was restored in December 1983, the new Argentine government of President Raúl Alfonsín took significant steps to foster human rights and prevent new abuses from occurring in the future. In 1984, the Argentine Congress approved the American Convention of Human Rights (or San José Treaty), which was promptly ratified, and two years later, both the International Covenant on Civil and Political Rights and the International Covenant on Economic, Social and Cultural Rights, under the aegis of the UN, were approved and ratified. A new habeas corpus law was enacted, and human rights became the cornerstone of the Alfonsín administration. Military tribunals were placed under final civilian supervision. As a consequence, the former military junta was put on trial, an unprecedented development in Latin American politics, and many lower court judges had to cope for the first time with the unpleasantries of trying and sentencing men in uniform.

Increasing armed forces pressures led the Alfonsín administration to persuade the congress to pass some kind of limitation on overall military responsibility. The so-called full-stop law (law number 23.492) set a sixty-day deadline for new prosecutions to be launched. Because this legislation did not prevent the prosecution of significant number of defendants, the congress approved in 1987 the due obedience law (law number 23.521), which granted immunity from prosecution to all military personnel, except for top commanders.[5]

THE DIFFICULT ROAD TOWARD
A CULTURE OF HUMAN RIGHTS

Argentine legal culture has two pillars: American constitutionalism and French civil law. But the French influence ran deeper and also pervaded the realm of administrative law. Public law at the top mirrored the U.S. institutional framework (i.e., the presidential system and federalism), whereas at the bottom it paid tribute to France's *regime administratif*. Spanish colonial heritage also may account for the degree of centralization:[6] the president thus was more powerful than his American counterpart, and Argentine federalism considerably weaker. Sovereignty was in this respect a key notion, because the "sovereign" (albeit now republican in nature) was the center of the legal system (for instance, the president as "supreme head of the Nation,"Section 99 (1), Argentine constitution).

This culture was ill prepared for this dramatic sea change, in which human rights considerations were paramount in the political and constitutional discourse. Over the years, many constitutional scholars had in fact justified the actions of different military governments simply by placing its norms and statutes above the constitution. It started in 1930, when the first military government took office. The Argentine Supreme Court was informed of this coup and gave it an immediate seal of approval by issuing a decision based on the de facto doctrine of Canadian constitutionalist Albert Constantineau. In

1943, just after another military takeover, the court rendered a similar decision. As mentioned earlier, the Perón Court had no trouble at all in placing the constitution after the "war powers" so as to avoid economic consequences. In 1955, 1966, and 1976, the de facto governments removed the existing Supreme Court altogether.

The concept of human rights remained elusive. For nearly half a century, courts generally were deferential to both the president and congress when dealing with different kinds of government emergency powers. Judges were generally deferential in the social and economic arenas, but this was especially the case regarding questions of the validity of a de facto regime. These matters were absolutely off-limits.

Although political tradition did not help much, the Alfonsín government was eager to implement, through education, those changes advanced in constitutional, criminal, and procedural law. In 1986, for instance, formal teaching of human rights began at the Law School of the University of Buenos Aires, the nation's most important legal center. It was very hard then to extricate rights from classical constitutional discourse, which emphasized government functions and executive and legislative powers. In the first semester of 1986, a tutoring preparatory course was fashioned by a philosopher named Eduardo A. Rabossi, then Human Rights secretary. He emphasized philosophical and international considerations more than he did strictly "legal" matters, introducing works by Norberto Bobbio and Karél Vasak. A new team of professors was assembled the following year, new syllabi were crafted, and new legal materials were prepared on this subject.

Military and police education also were enhanced. For the first time, new "human rights" courses were introduced to those being trained in these professions. Even though a presidential commission, books, movies, and the like were devoted to this subject, Argentine judges were reluctant to directly apply international human rights regulations (the phenomena of "national resistance" and "constitutional patriotism"). Many judges did not know these rules well. Some were skeptical that a nation with a dismal human rights record[7] would ever begin to grasp and assert the full notion of international human rights safeguards. Others argued that when discussing these issues, national sovereignty was at stake and that, consequently, internal law should take precedence.

PRECONSTITUTIONAL REFORM MOMENTS

In a number of cases in which the issue involved the hierarchy of international norms, the Argentine Supreme Court generally decided them by following U.S. case law.[8] By 1992, however, these standards were found to be inadequate.

One such case involved a well-known constitutional law professor, Miguel Ekmckdjian, who filed suit against a popular television host, asking for a "right to reply" regarding religious issues.[9] This so-called "right to reply" had been enshrined in Article 14 of the American Convention on Human Rights, but no internal Argentine law admitted it. Ekmekdjian argued that international recognition was self-executing and needed no further regulation for proper implementation.

The Argentine Supreme Court faced a dilemma in this case. It could have repeated its doctrine established in a previous case also brought by Ekmekdjian, in which the court disregarded direct application of the "right to reply" provision in the American Convention of Human Rights.[10] It also could have rejected altogether this line of reasoning and adopted a new model in accordance with the increasingly global nature of law. It chose this second course of action. In a famous passage, the court held that the convention was "self-executing" in nature, because Argentina had previously ratified the Vienna Convention on Treaties. This international instrument precluded countries from alleging the need for domestic legislation in order to avoid compliance with treaties, by act or omission.[11] The court also stressed that needs of international cooperation, harmonization, and integration called for this solution.

Janet Koven Levit argued that "*Ekmekdjian* placed international treaties on a supra-statutory level and, by holding that they were presumptively self-executing documents, transformed them into a potent source of law which the court itself harnessed to decide the case."[12] Although this decision was qualified the following year (*Fibraca*),[13] it represented a clear attempt by the Menem Court to act in synchronicity with international jurisprudence.

The Menem Court started to take international law more seriously in several key decisions beginning with *Ekmekdjian* and *Fibraca*. It continued to do so after the 1994 revision in the following cases: *Café La Virginia*,[14] *Giroldi*,[15] *Bramajo*,[16] *Acosta*,[17] and *Fellicetti*. In 1994, this vast constitutional reform took place. The main feature of the whole process was to allow the sitting president to stand for reelection. However, other issues were on the constitutional agenda set up by the two main political parties, the Justicialista movement (formerly Peronista) and the Radical party. One notable issue was the proper rank of international human rights obligations.

Different options were considered, ranging from conferring supreme status to international human rights law in general to joint higher standing for both the constitution and international human rights rules. Finally, the latter stance prevailed in the new wording of Section 75 (22). As a result, treaties including the UN Declaration of Human Rights (1948); International Covenant on Civil and Political Rights (1966); International Covenant on Economic, Social, and Cultural Rights (1966); and the American Convention on Human Rights were elevated to constitutional preeminence. New treaties also could achieve this rank, provided that no inconsistencies existed with the constitution itself. Some scholars derived from this premise the argument that international norms were still inferior to the constitution, as before 1994. But more mainstream jurists contend that a "constitutional block" existed (borrowing from the French idea of *bloc de constitutionalité*) consisting of the constitution and the international treaties mentioned in Section 75 (22).[18]

A new method of interpretation began to emerge. In addition to literal, historical, systemic, and dynamic models,[19] a new internationalist approach was appearing. U.S. case law, omnipresent in nineteenth-century jurisprudence, faded away and was replaced with international standards. The introduction of this new approach was not without controversy. Although some believed that by employing the new internationalist approach the court was eroding its authority and jeopardizing its legitimacy, others argued that international law provided a needed fresh perspective on controversial issues.

A COURT IN CRISIS

In 1990, President Carlos Menem enlarged the Supreme Court. He added four more seats and filled them with political cronies with scant legal credentials. Although this court had rubber-stamped all of the former president's policies, efforts to impeach the justices failed in 2002. When President Nestor Kirchner took office in May 2003, he vowed to remove the Menem Court, which was derided as an "automatic majority" tribunal. Two justices resigned to avoid impeachment, and this time, two others were successfully removed.

As it began to take shape, the new court issued a series of decisions regarding labor rights in 2004. It struck down key provisions of the occupational hazards legislation passed during the Menem years (*Castillo*, *Aquino*, *Milone*), placing workers at the center of a protective system (*Vizzoti*).

Another area of some controversy involved health law matters. In several cases from the previous court (*Asociación Benghalensis*, *Campodonico de Beviacqua*), plaintiffs had sued both the federal and provincial governments, winning specific health benefits under existing legislation. This trend continued under the Kirchner Court. "Right to health" cases represent a trickle-up influence (as opposed to the traditional trickle-down approach) as first- and second-instance judges eagerly decided in favor of the claimants.

The year 2005 proved to be an important one for the Supreme Court. In *Verbitsky*, the court decided to allow collective habeas relief to monitor prison conditions in the province of Buenos Aires and subject them to international guidelines. Yet by far the most significant case decided by the new court was the *Simón* case, which involved reviewing the amnesty legislation passed during the administration of President Raúl Alfonsín back in 1986 and 1987. Congress had decided then that courts could try only the highest-ranking military officers in matters related to human rights violations during the "dirty war" on guerrillas pursued by the de facto government of 1976 to 1983. All other military personnel were exempt of criminal responsibility.

In 1998, the congress finally repealed these laws and in 2003 declared that they were null and void. Although this legislation had been in effect for more than a decade, many military officers had not faced trial at all.

In 2003, a new international convention banning statute of limitations on crimes against humanity[20] was approved and given constitutional rank in the terms of Article 75 (22). A new political and legal drama ensued regarding whether military personnel should be tried, as their alleged crimes had not elapsed. Some scholars and analysts argued that this was a fair option, because the crimes involved were sufficiently heinous to warrant criminal prosecution whenever possible.[21] Others maintained that those crimes were covered by valid amnesty laws and that this interpretation involved an ex post facto action forbidden by statute of limitations and the constitution's due process clause (Section 18). It is interesting to see, in strict constitutional terms, that this debate shows the emphasis placed by different interpreters on the same legal material. Whereas human rights activists prefer to read Section 75 (22) without any further conditions, conservative legal scholars point out that Section 27 of the constitution is still binding[22] and that international treaties should not run counter to the constitutional text itself.[23]

This discussion is reflected in the two positions taken by the justices in the *Simón* case, decided in a seven-to one vote with one abstention. Although the majority saw no legal hurdles in applying this and other treaties, the minority opinion, written by veteran justice Carlos S. Fayt, challenged that this solution left legal definition of crimes, due process, res judicata, vested rights, and other traditional constitutional principles in the lurch.

Chief Justice Enrique Petracchi, who previously had upheld the amnesty legislation as constitutional, changed his view in deference to the evolving criteria of the Inter-American Court of Human Rights. Other justices followed converging lines of argument, based on diverse viewpoints and literature. Justice Zaffaroni stressed that the norms now included in the convention on crimes against humanity were *jus cogens* when the amnesty was declared. Justice Lorenzetti relied on the dynamics of the different legal sources. He emphasized in this context the character of international human rights law. Some observers have even argued that Lorenzetti had in fact equated international human rights with natural law.

The new Supreme Court also found the *Chocobar* precedent on pensions lacking in legal weight and socially inconvenient. In May 2005, this decision was overturned by *Sanchez*. *Sanchez* returned to the body of pre-*Chocobar* pension law. The court allowed for cost-of-living increases, because it considered that these adjustments were mandated by the constitution and were not covered by anti-inflation legislation enacted under Menem in 1991. It also stated that international human rights treaties, particularly the American Convention, did not cap pension benefits because this treaty could never preclude better protection conferred by internal constitutional or legal provisions (Justices Zaffaroni and Argibay, concurring). The Supreme Court majority stressed that the "progressive development" clause encompassed new or better benefits and had no bearing on existing ones. Another judge linked present pensions with property rights, quoting classical Argentine jurisprudence and the Inter-American Court of Human Rights decision adopted in *Cinco Pensionistas v. Peru* (2003).[24]

Another important social security decision had been issued in a case called *Itzcovich* (2005). This case dealt with Supreme Court jurisdiction in pension matters. The court was intent on becoming a constitutional court, leaving aside "minor" matters such as reviewing the decisions of the lower courts.[25] Constitutional court aspirations were reaffirmed in *Verbitsky*, the collective habeas case, and in 2006 in the first significant environmental law decision, *Beatriz Mendoza*.

Property rights fared worse under the new court, as *Bustos* (2004), *Massa* (2006), and *Rinaldi* (2007) upheld emergency legislation passed during the previous administration placing restrictions on bank deposits and fixing a new currency exchange rate. Perhaps property was not clearly seen as a "human right," a problem with which international law also has had to deal.[26]

Although some opinions reflect increasing use of international standards, others do not. In the *Madorran* case (2007), for example, the opening opinion stressed public employees' special status and relied on international criteria, but the concurring opinion limited itself to a strict constitutional analysis.

NEW MECHANISMS FOR JUDICIAL RECRUITMENT

When Nestor Kirchner became president in May 2003, he attempted to fashion a new court. He issued an executive order (*Decreto 222/03*) that governed all future appointments. As the justices from the Menem era resigned or were removed by impeachment, Kirchner named prestigious law professors and former court of appeals judges to the court. His first appointment was Eugenio Raul Zaffaroni. Zaffaroni had been a former judge of the criminal court of appeals in Buenos Aires, had a highly regarded academic career as a criminal law professor (he holds nine honorary doctorates from universities in Europe and Latin America), is a prolific author, and also had helped to draft both the 1994 federal constitutional revision and the 1996 City of Buenos Aires Constitution. Many citizens opposed this nomination. Yet because human rights organizations supported him, the president overruled these objections and sent Zaffaroni's name to the senate anyway.

In his last book, *El Enemigo en el Derecho Penal*, Zaffaroni criticizes the U.S. Supreme Court for reestablishing the death penalty, which was "re-legitimized by the Republican judges elevated to the Court by this party's Presidents, starting with President Nixon's appointees."[27] He contends,

"International Criminal Law is set to diminish an uncontrolled power area, which in times resembles Hobbes's *bellum*."[28] In *Arancibia Clavel* (2003), he stressed that the international law of human rights could create new crimes not previously punished.

Another Kirchner appointee, current chief justice Ricardo Lorenzetti, was a well-known contracts law professor and lawyer from the province of Santa Fe. He has written extensively on environmental, consumer protection, and tort law. He argues, "Law is being totally transformed by the incorporation of human rights, which are guaranteed by the Constitution and the international treaties, and that embody a 'protection paradigm.' " In his dissent in *Mujeres por la Vida* (2006), he states that the Argentine constitution is not guided by the American document.

Justice Elena Highton also has a long-standing reputation as a civil law professor and judge. The newest justice, Carmen Argibay, sat as an ad hoc judge on the International Criminal Tribunal for the former Yugoslavia. Highton and Argibay were the second and third women to be named to the court, the first being Margarita Arguas, who was appointed in the early 1970s.

As external forces gathered momentum and significance during the confirmation hearings[29] of the new nominees,[30] the justices became increasingly aware of the importance of civil society, especially NGOs. Amicus briefs were introduced in 2004 (*Acordada 28/*04), following U.S. and Inter-American Court practices. Transparency was bolstered across the board. New Web resources, easier access to decisions, banning of ex parte meetings with justices, and an entire communications strategy were implemented. By 2007, a new format was designed for *cert* petitions that was based on the American model (*Acordada 4/*07). These guidelines attempted to put the court's chaotic docket in order. In 2006, Congress had ordered that no new court vacancies would be filled in the future, gradually reducing the court from nine to five members.

THE ROLE OF INTERNATIONAL LAW IN THE MENEM AND KIRCHNER COURTS

International law is certainly performing a different function in the Kirchner Court, compared with the Menem Court of the 1990s. The Menem Court used international law as a basic tool for economic globalization. It was an integral part of the former president's strategy to make Argentina a first-world country where global capitalism could exist unimpeded. Social rights were rolled back and economic liberties flourished. By contrast, the Kirchner Court is struggling with evils from the past (crimes against humanity, human rights violations, pension reforms), while at the same time trying to achieve social and political legitimacy. For instance, in earlier times, amnesty laws would have been easily branded as political questions, and courts would have deferred to executive or legislative action. Today that label is suspect because courts in Argentina and elsewhere have become increasingly politicized, a phenomenon known as the judicialization of politics. By turning to international law in its attempt to promote a human rights regime, the Kirchner Court has attained the new legitimacy it desperately sought in order to avoid its predecessor's fate.[31]

Globalization is a complex process with many aspects. There is an economic aspect of globalization: markets, corporations, and transactions are increasingly intertwined. And there is certainly a political aspect of globalization comprising new areas of cooperation in combating the illegal drug trade, working toward increased environmental protection, and in advancing democratization and institution building. But there is also a legal aspect of globalization. Courts increasingly rely on other's arguments and rationales. Constitutional interpretation canons travel widely and are increasingly relevant, particularly in the area of human rights. Several contributors to this book would agree with Professor Vicki Jackson, who writes that "constitutional courts around the world engage more regularly in transnational discourse about human rights than about other issues in constitutional law."[32]

Over time, the new court cited the American legal tradition less and relied more on international human rights norms and case law. It became increasingly apparent that the Kirchner Court was more progressive, more receptive to claims of human and social rights, and more internationalist in its orientation. But the frequent use of foreign and international sources begs a question: Is it just a tactical move, or does it involve a deeper change? Based on their observations of the U.S. Supreme Court, Lee Epstein and Jack Knight predict that it is just a tactical move to advance a justice's policy preferences:

> We could discuss other cases in which concerns over institutional legitimacy served as the primary motivation for judicial decisions. We could also discuss other goals that scholars have posited. And we could point to justices who not only seemed unconcerned with moving policy in the direction of their preferences but who also took steps to ensure that their policies were not etched into law. But the general point would be the same: although justices occasionally pursue other goals and the occasional justice never pursues policy, *most justices in most cases seek to establish law as close as their own policy preferences.*[33]

As I have shown, the international law of human rights serves both purposes: It advances the policy preferences of the justices on the new court, and it provides a deeper, more secure foundation for law in Argentine society. Nevertheless, the biggest challenge is to make these provisions so they will work effectively in difficult social and economic contexts.

NOTES

1. Janet Koven Levit, "The Constitutionalization of Human Rights in Argentina: Problem or Promise?" *Columbia Journal of Transnational Law* 37 (1998–1999): 312.

2. For this trend in general, see Mary L. Volcansek and John F. Stack Jr., "Judicialization and Sovereignty," in *Courts Crossing Borders: Blurring the Lines of Sovereignty*, eds. Mary L. Volcansek and John F. Stack Jr. (Durham, NC: Carolina Academic Press, 2005), 11.

3. Jean-Jacques Chevallier, "Histoire de la pensée politique," vol. 1, Paris, Payot, 267.

4. Argentine Supreme Court 211 "Fallos" 162 (1948).

5. The Argentine Supreme Court held that this law was constitutional. See *Camps*, Argentine Supreme Court 310 "Fallos" 1162 (1987).

6. There is, however, a strong Spanish tradition of judicial review of administrative acts. See Jesús González Pérez and Juan Carlos Cassagne, *La justicia administrativa en Iberoamérica* (Buenos Aires: Lexis-Nexis, 2005).

7. A study reveals that "unfavorable history proved to be even more closely connected to the collapse of democracy. Only a small minority of the collapsed democracies had strong democratic historical backgrounds (10 percent), compared to a majority of the stable democracies (71.9 percent)." See Abraham Diskin, Hanna Diskin, and Reuven Y. Hazan, "Why Democracies Collapse: The Reasons For Democratic Failure and Success," *International Political Science Review* 26 (2005): 300.

8. See, for background, the seminal work of Jonathan Miller, "The Constitutional Authority of a Foreign Talisman: A Study of U.S. Practice as Authority in 19th Century Argentina and the Argentine Elite's Leap of Faith," *The American Law Review* 46 (1987): 1483. For an unorthodox view, see Carlos F. Rosenkratz, "Against Borrowings and Other Nonauthoritative Uses of Foreign Law," *International Journal of Constitutional Law* 1 (2003): 269.

9. Argentine Supreme Court 315 "Fallos" 1492 (1992).

10. Argentine Supreme Court 311 "Fallos" 2497 (1988).

11. See Jo M. Pasqualucci, *The Practice and Procedure of the Inter-American Court of Human Rights* (Cambridge: Cambridge University Press, 2003), 330. "Provisions in human rights treaties which are sufficiently definite should be considered to be inherently self-executing and, therefore, automatically incorporated into the law of domestic States that ratify the human rights convention."

12. See Janet Koven Levit, "The Constitutionalization of Human Rights in Argentina: Problem or Promise?" *Columbia Journal of Transnational Law* 37 (1998–1999): 308.

13. Argentine Supreme Court 316 "Fallos" 1669 (1993).

14. Argentine Supreme Court 317 "Fallos" 1283 (1994).

15. Argentine Supreme Court 318 "Fallos" 514 (1995).

16. Argentine Supreme Court 319 "Fallos" 1840 (1996).

17. Argentine Supreme Court 321 "Fallos" 3555 (1998).

18. The "constitutional block" is a densely populated legal area.

19. In 1980, German author Peter Häberle wrote about a "fifth method of interpretation," meaning the comparative method.

20. Its evolution, in Margaret McAuliffe deGuzman, "The Road from Rome: The Developing Law of Crimes against Humanity," *Human Rights Quarterly* 22 (2000): 335.

21. America's director at Human Rights Watch, José Miguel Vivanco, said, "The crimes of the 'dirty war' are far too serious to be amnestied and forgotten." See HRW's report, "Argentina: Amnesty Laws Struck Down (Supreme Court's Long-Awaited Ruling allows prosecution of 'Dirty War' Crimes," online at www.hrw.org/english/docs/2005/06/14/argent1119.htm (June 14, 2005, visited January 13, 2006).

22. It was drafted with the original 1853 constitution and it states that treaties must conform to "constitutional public law principles."

23. Statement given by the country's most important legal authority, Academia Nacional de Derecho y Ciencias Sociales de Buenos Aires, August 25, 2005, "Dictamen sobre los Tratados Internacionales y la supremacía de la Constitución Nacional," in *El Derecho* 214 (2005): 1035.

24. Ana Salado Osuna, *Los casos peruanos ante la Corte Interamericana de Derechos Humanos* (Lima: Norma Legales, 2004) 97.

25. Walter F. Carnota, "La nueva fisonomía del control de constitucionalidad argentino," *Revista Iberoamericana de Derecho Procesal Constitucional* 6 (2006): 155.

26. Both covenants, on civil and political rights and on economic and social rights, are elusive on the subject. "The right of property, already recognized by the Universal Declaration of Human Rights, appears in neither covenant; while there was general agreement that it was to be respected, there was a stalemate among delegates as to the limitations that might be imposed on it." Terence Daintith, "The Constitutional Protection of Economic Rights," *International Journal of Constitutional Law* 1 (2003): 58–59.

27. Eugenio Raul Zaffaroni, *El Enemigo en el Derecho Penal* (Buenos Aires: Ediar, 2006).

28. Ibid., 180.

29. About the U.S. Supreme Court, Davis writes: "The combination of news coverage, group appeals (which stimulates more news coverage), and polling facilitates public opinion as a factor in judicial selection." Richard Davis, *Electing Justice: Fixing the Supreme Court Nomination Process* (New York: Oxford University Press, 2005), 103. During the first round of appointments, nominees (notably Zaffaroni) became household names, an unprecedented fact in Argentine politics. It is generally understood that the new mechanism "strengthened the citizens' culture." *La Corte y los Derechos* (Buenos Aires: Asociación por los Derechos Civiles, 2005), 29.

30. The first experience can be traced in *Aportes para una mejora en la calidad institucional. El nuevo procedimiento para la designación de jueces de la Corte Suprema de Justicia de la Nación* (Buenos Aires: Comisión de Acuerdos Honorable Senado de la Nación and Instituto Federal de Estudios Parlamentarios, 2004).

31. By the time the new court took office, it was measuring 4.25 of 10 possible points in public trust. See Antonio María Hernández, Daniel Zovatto, and Manuel Mora y Araujo, *Encuesta de Cultura Constitucional Argentina: Una Sociedad Anomica* (Mexico City: UNAM, 2005), 76.

32. Vicki C. Jackson, "Comparative Constitutional Federalism and Transnational Judicial Discourse," *International Journal of Constitutional Law* 2 (2004): 100.

33. Lee Epstein and Jack Knight, *The Choices Justices Make* (Washington, D.C.: Congressional Quarterly Press, 1998), 49. Emphasis added.

Conclusion

DONALD W. JACKSON, MICHAEL C. TOLLEY, AND MARY L. VOLCANSEK

What have these fourteen chapters written by sixteen different hands added to our knowledge about the globalization of law? Though globalization as "the process of increasing interconnectivity and interdependence among nation-states" is treated as a relatively new and novel phenomenon,[1] the process in legal circles, as David O'Brien reminds us in the first chapter, can be traced at least to 1815, when Chief Justice John Marshall nodded toward foreign legal norms as aids in judicial decision making. Perhaps, though, recent developments including transnational judicial institutions and treaties such as the General Agreement on Tariff and Trade (GATT), the World Trade Organization (WTO), International Court of Justice (ICJ), International Criminal Court (ICC), International Center for Settlement of Investment Disputes (ICSID), World Bank, International Monetary Fund (IMF), United Nations Commission on International Trade Law (UNCITRAL), and invocations of universal jurisdiction in matters such as crimes against humanity are accelerating the process. Globalization takes various forms, but this volume emphasizes its effects on law, politics, trade, commerce, and society.

In many ways, the case of *Medellin v. Texas*,[2] decided by the U.S. Supreme Court in 2008, serves as an apt metaphor for the dilemmas of a system of global justice. In this case, José Ernesto Medellin, a foreign national from Mexico, was charged, tried, convicted, and sentenced to death for the rape and murder of two teenage girls before he was told of his right to consular access. Article 36 of the Vienna Convention on Consular Relations, adopted in 1963 and ratified by the U.S. Senate in 1969, provides that foreign nationals who are detained by a signatory of the treaty must be told of their right to contact their nation's embassy. The State of Texas failed to notify Medellin and fifty other Mexican nationals of this right, and Mexico filed suit over the situation in the International Court of Justice (ICJ), winning in 2004.

The court ruled that the United States government had a duty to review and reconsider the foreign nationals' convictions and sentences. President George W. Bush directed the Texas courts to comply with the ruling, but the reluctance of the Texas courts to do so resulted in a lawsuit that reached the U.S. Supreme Court.

In a six-to-three decision, the U.S. Supreme Court held that Texas courts did not have a duty to give a new hearing to Medellin and the others, despite the decision of the ICJ, the Vienna Convention, and the entreaty from President Bush. Chief Justice John Roberts reasoned that the Vienna Convention was not "self-executing" and thus required congressional action to make the treaty enforceable in U.S. courts. Justices Stephen Breyer, Ruth Bader Ginsburg, and David Souter dissented, with Justice Breyer lamenting the likely implications of the majority's decision in "a world where commerce, trade and travel have become ever more international."[3]

The roles played by politics, law, and international affairs, along with the efficacy of international human rights and humanitarian law, in the face of domestic resistance all met in José Ernesto Medellin's case. Many questions implicated in the tapestry of the *Medellin* case were confronted in this book: how effective are international treaties and obligations in domestic politics and policy making; what are the implications of claims of universal jurisdiction; are prophecies of the demise of the notion of Westphalian sovereignty and the nation-state premature; and are hegemonic powers insulated from the reach of international norms? Few complain that globalization has wrought the spread of ideas about the desirability of good governance, due process or—more broadly—the rule of law, judicial independence, liberal democracy, and the increasing prominence of human rights and political freedom in countries around the world. But what if globalization and its concomitant weakening of the nation-state also hampered the ability of the nation-state to respond to domestic problems caused by globalization? Clearly, as Hans Peter Schmitz wrote in chapter 7, there is a domestic bias in how we look at human rights and democratic change in light of real-world events. The *Medellin* case also illustrates how domestic politics, in this case the continuation of the death penalty in the United States, can run counter to world opinion. Execution has, according to Schmitz, been outlawed by the Second Optional Protocol to the International Covenant on Civil and Political Rights, and 129 nations have signed it, with only sixty-eight (including the U.S.) retaining the death penalty.

ECONOMIC AND RIGHTS GLOBALIZATION

The contributors to this book focused largely on the diffusion of human rights norms through transnational, international, and supranational regimes. A parallel aspect of legal globalization has occurred in the economic sphere, but the human rights and commercial globalization phenomena are quite distinct in the motivations behind them and the impetus for states to enter willingly into transnational legal arrangements. Alec Stone Sweet and Wayne Sandholtz explain that the commercial integration of Europe and by extension other transnational trade regimes was based on cross-border transactions. Nonstate actors engage in commercial and communications transactions that are hampered by the absence of rules, standards, and a means to settle disputes. National rules create transaction costs, and those costs "come to be seen as obstacles to the generation of wealth and the achievement of other collective gains."[4] Even though national governments have their own interests, the impediments to commerce and national wealth eventually overcome government resistance to the formation of transnational mechanisms to foster trade and commerce, even if only incrementally.[5] Although competing versions have also been offered of how and why economic integration has occurred, all revolve around access to markets. Thus free trade legal arrangements developed, such as GATT, WTO, IMF and more than one hundred regional trade associations, to allow access to markets and to reduce transaction costs.[6] A rising concern for the rights of investors then demanded a transnational means to protect investors' interest in the regulation of financial markets. Likewise, to protect intellectual property, a legal mechanism known as TRIPS (Trade-Related Aspects of Intellectual Property Rights) was created. Interestingly, TRIPS imposed the intellectual property concepts from Europe and the United States on the rest of the world as, for example, in pharmaceuticals and the prices of medications.[7]

Human rights treaties with enforcement mechanisms evolved differently. At the conclusion of World War II, a natural law doctrine of human rights was launched that directly impinged "upon the relationships between each state and its citizens."[8] That incursion on national sovereignty was quite direct—more so than trade and commerce—and harder to sell to governments. The UN Universal Declaration of Human Rights of 1948 stands as a statement of aspirational principles, but enforcing its lofty ideals proved difficult then and, as Schmitz, Isanga, and Evans Case have shown here, now. Nonstate actors, such as Amnesty International and Human Rights Watch, form advocacy networks and, working with domestic rights organizations, have proved essential to the internalization of human rights norms.[9] Enforcement then relies on legal mobilization, whereby "widespread and sustained litigation in support of civil rights and civil liberties" occurs.[10]

Both commercial and human rights obligations at the transnational level have significant domestic political implications. Human rights enforcement at the transnational and international level affects the social fabric of society as well as the political arena. The global spread of human rights norms has created one prong of the new cosmopolitanism.[11] Globalization of information has made us more aware of places where rights are not respected and has aided not only advocacy groups, but also has facilitated the migration of legal ideas and norms from lawyer to lawyer and from judge to judge. In turn, new pressures for international regimes in areas of private law, family law, and adoption are emerging. Even though cosmopolitans may "suppose that all cultures have enough overlap in their vocabulary to begin a conversation . . . they don't suppose . . . that we could all come to agreement if only we had the same vocabulary."[12]

DOMESTIC EFFECTS OF LEGAL GLOBALIZATION

Banner, Miller, and Provine chose the term "conversation" in chapter 2 to describe the use of foreign judicial decisions in legal arguments in the United States. Indeed, based on findings revealed in this volume about the effects of international legal norms on domestic law, policy, and society, a conversation may be the precise term; we may have come to some agreements, but how those agreements are followed and enforced may mean that only a conversation has begun. Yet, as Joseph Isanga reminds us in chapter 10, all nations must strive to promote the "universality of human dignity—the grounding principle for human rights."

One of the questions asked at the outset of this book was that of the effects of globalization on domestic law, policy, and society. Legal globalization's influence on domestic policy can be seen perhaps most starkly in countries lacking a constitutional enumeration of rights, such as Australia. As Rhonda Evans Case points out in chapter 13, the Australians entered into a web of international human rights treaties, but no treaty has the force of law unless it is adopted or given force through statutes. Adoption has not necessarily followed. However, Australia's Human Rights and Equal Opportunity Commission (HREOC), acting as a transnational legal entrepreneur, served as a nonparty intervenor in Australian courts to promote human rights in fifty-eight instances between 1988 and 2007. Evans Case's analysis found that the judges consistently engaged the arguments presented by HREOC, even though they were not always persuaded.

The United Kingdom, as Mary Volcansek explains in chapter 11, reacted differently to its treaty obligations under the European Convention on Human Rights (ECHR), and, contrary to experiences elsewhere, was led in its effort to bring Convention guarantees into domestic law by the legal elites. Although a signatory to the ECHR in 1951, the United Kingdom did not allow the "conversation" to take place in domestic courts. In 1998, however, the Human Rights Act was passed that incorporated most provisions of the ECHR into U.K. law. A comparison of decisions by the House of Lords, the U.K.'s highest court, both before and after implementation of the Human Rights Act in 2000 found that rights had been protected before the Human Rights Act came into force as well as afterwards. The judges simply had more tools with which to work following the enactment. Through 2007, the House of Lords had ruled that only one statute was incompatible with the Human Rights Act, and the government and Parliament acted swiftly to bring the law into compliance with the decision of the House of Lords.

Uganda represents the unhappy side of the globalization of law. There, treaties other than the UN Charter have not served as a force for domestic policy change; what change there has been can be attributed to donor nations that used aid money as a carrot and withdrawal of it as the stick. Even so, presidents relying on personal rule and backed by the military trample on individual judges and the judiciary when attempts are made to apply the legal norms embodied in the 1995 Ugandan constitution. Courts, as Joseph Isanga tells us in chapter 10, were reduced to legitimizing personal rule despite a few courageous attempts to protect rights and limit executive power. International donor actions and international pressure did yield positive results, though, in Nigeria and South Africa.

The Argentine case presents a different study in legal globalization. Argentina has been a signatory to most human rights treaties and many economic ones, and some have been granted constitutional status. Different presidents and the courts they fashioned have, as Walter Carnota reported in chapter 14, used those international legal norms to different ends. President Menem's court saw international law as a vehicle for economic change to move Argentina toward global capitalism. Kirchner's court that followed relied on international law to confront violations of human rights.

Perhaps the more interesting twist on legal globalization can be found in the United States, where congressional furor and pointed judicial opinions greeted the citation of foreign law in Supreme Court decisions. The commotion may, however, have been, as Mark Tushnet concluded, more about judicial power than about citing foreign law.[13] The controversy appears, as David O'Brien notes in chapter 1, "more smoke than fire," because the citations to foreign law are typically found in *dicta* and only appeared in eight majority opinions during the era of the Rehnquist court. Similarly, Francine Banner, Ken Miller, and Doris Marie Provine (chapter 2) found that after examining 722 amicus curiae briefs filed with the Supreme Court in 2003, citations of foreign law or judicial decisions appeared in only thirteen cases.

The effects of legal globalization on domestic law and policy then are various, but there are some common threads. Who controls the judiciary is primary. In Australia the judges are overtly political appointees, while in Uganda, judges can be severely harassed for deciding contrary to the executive. Argentina has a tradition of packing, removing, or impeaching judges with each change of president, such that the executive can ensure judges share the same political leanings. In all three cases, noting that the rights violations found in the three countries are often leagues apart, fewer international legal norms have penetrated domestic law. Argentina presents the exception, because international legal norms are regularly invoked, but the executive's priorities determined which sets of norms were primary. In the United Kingdom, on the other hand, where judicial independence has long been prized and judges are not appointed based on their partisan politics,[14] human rights were protected through resort to the common law before the Human Rights Act provided the judges with a more versatile tool. Also, the vehicles that bring international legal norms into the judicial system (or not) are variable. In Australia, transnational legal entrepreneurs have been active, in the United Kingdom the legal elite led the way, and in Uganda, South Africa, and Nigeria donor nations and international pressures were at the forefront. The United States remains an outlier, where the judges and those who argue before them have relied minimally on international legal norms or even examples of how a judicial problem might be solved from external perspectives.

ACCEPTING GLOBALIZED RIGHTS

The second question posed in the introduction to this book addressed variations in acceptance of legal globalization in different countries and at different times. International legal norms must have some source, and the decisions of transnational and international courts often provide that source because they interpret the various treaties and covenants that constitute human rights law and international criminal law. One intention behind the multiple treaties and the judicial institutions that apply them is that the international legal norms will be internalized by national actors, particularly national courts. In chapter 3, Christopher Whytock reminds us in his discussion of the use of foreign law in U.S. courts of the difficulties of even measuring the degree of internalization that occurs. Would the courts decide differently without introduction of external norms? Indeed, Hans Peter Schmitz tells us in chapter 7 that the quantitative research by political scientists in the area of human rights paints a dismal picture. The "increasing global human rights 'talk' is not necessarily followed by improvements of human rights conditions (even decades after joining a human rights treaty)." The qualitative literature provides a more hopeful view of the transformative effect of transnational human rights networks and their domestic counterparts in socializing and pressuring repressive regimes into compliance. Of course, as Schmitz notes, most qualitative research has been conducted in Eastern Europe and Latin American, not in Africa and Asia. Moreover, as Donald Jackson cautions in chapter 5, the international tribunals created to prosecute perpetrators of crimes against humanity can be charged with exacting victor's justice, and their legitimacy depends on perceptions of their fairness, impartiality, and effectiveness, a theme that he extends in chapter 4. The problems of international criminal law are compounded when countries like the United States, in prosecuting its war on terrorism, declared themselves immune to international legal norms and often insure immunity through bilateral agreements.[15]

An additional problem with enforcement of international criminal law is the difficulty in apprehending indictees. Lilian Barria and Steven Roper in chapter 6 assessed the potential effectiveness of the ICC on that score by extrapolating from the experiences of the ad hoc tribunals charged with trying those charged with genocide, crimes against humanity, and other war crimes in Rwanda and the former Yugoslavia. In almost all cases, the state authorities, not the court, must locate, arrest, and surrender defendants. The effectiveness of the ICC in prosecuting potential violators will be tested as it acts on cases from the Democratic Republic of the Congo, Sudan, Uganda, and the Central African Republic. Donald Jackson in chapter 4 also questions the sources of legitimacy for the ad hoc tribunals, which require that the prosecutions are perceived to be consistent with "widely shared beliefs and values and [with] broad consent." Another major question that Jackson raises is who to try, high officials or low-level perpetrators, when widespread rights abuses occur. The former presents difficulties of proof, and the latter requires a substantial staff and budget.

Michael Tolley in chapter 12 and Lisa Conant in Chapter 8 focus on Europe and the two transnational courts whose jurisdictions and those of national courts overlap. Conant explains that the European Court of Justice and the European Court of Human Rights jointly extended social benefits to foreign residents as well as nationals and created transnational civil citizenship. Tolley, on the other hand, looks at how the European Court of Justice gradually developed a jurisprudence on fundamental rights, ultimately deciding in 1989 that member states' actions were reviewable for conformity with the European Union's fundamental rights.

When we move from the transnational and international levels to look at individual country's differential acceptance of legal globalization, a framework is useful. Christopher Whytock's typology in chapter 3 for classifying nondomestic law in cross-border norm migration offers a mechanism to consider the seven nation-states covered in this volume. The five categories that Whytock proposed are binding law (what *must* we decide); nonbinding legal norm (what *should* we decide); interpretative aid (what does it mean); functional comparison (what are the consequences), and factual information (what are the relevant facts). For example, in its treatment of the ECHR prior to 2000, the House of Lords treated the treaty as a nonbinding legal norm, but after implementation of the Human Rights Act accepted the Convention as a binding legal norm. Guatemala and Nicaragua achieved different results in their attempts to bring the rule of law to their countries in the aftermath of conflict, as Rachel Bowen explains in chapter 9. The Inter-American Court of Human Rights serves as the only regional institution demarcating rights for the two Central American nations. However, pressures came to bear on both countries to achieve a consistent national rule of law, based often on a more distant concept of human rights. Therefore, external law for both Guatemala and Nicaragua remains nonbinding and offers only functional comparisons, factual information, and interpretive aids. Similarly, Uganda's and Argentina's reception of external norms must be measured against a general understanding of human rights rather than by a specific court's jurisprudence, even though Uganda has a modern constitution that provides for a number of rights protections. Australia, on the other hand, is a signatory to almost all human rights treaties, but few have been incorporated into domestic law. The examples that Evans Case cites in her study of HREOC's activities in Australia suggest that in the areas of asylum and refugees, the Australian courts also treat external law as nonbinding.

SOVEREIGNTY AND THE NATION-STATE

The third question that was posed in the introduction to this book deals with the effects, if any, that the reception of international human rights norms has had on nation-states and the concept of national sovereignty. Indeed, most agree that the spread of human rights norms, increased emphasis on rights and the rule of law in the process of democratization, and mechanism to hold dictators, despots, and war criminal accountable are all positive aspects of legal globalization of human rights norms. Yet on the other hand, among the negative effects are found the diminution of national sovereignty, creation of new global governance institutions lacking a democratic element, and the widening divide between rich and poor nations and developed and developing nations.

The seventeenth-century Westphalian concept of sovereignty may not fit well into the globalized world of the twenty-first century. The years following World War II witnessed not only a new concern for human rights, but also a willingness of some countries to forego a measure of sovereignty to achieve a greater goal. Six nations in western Europe made that decision in 1951 with the signing of the European Coal and Steel Treaty, an act that began the odyssey to the current European Union, with twenty-seven member states and others vying to be admitted. The quest for economic growth and national prosperity drove the European experiment, but many of the same member nations also willingly signed the ECHR and were willing to bind themselves to treat the citizens and residents of their nations humanely. Economic motive drives the GATT and the WTO, along with myriad regional trade associations, whereas loftier ideals have served as the catalysts for the spread of human rights.

How globalization has affected the nation–state has been studied from a number of angles in different disciplines. Not only can goods and services migrate easily across national boundaries, but ideas can flow as well. The marketplace replaces, in both instances, some functions of the traditional nation-state[16] or at least contributes to the "attenuation of the state."[17] The diminished position of the state also has undercut the idea of immunity for state actors who violate international law or abuse their own citizens.[18] New forms of governance have arisen at the regional, supranational, and international levels to regulate and police new global interactions. Disputes about the rules that once were resolved by diplomats now are more likely decided by judges applying treaty provisions.[19] As Anne-Marie Slaughter notes, however, most of the webs of treaties governing human rights, trade, and international criminal law also are designed to encourage nations to follow their own rules, to try their own criminals, and to police themselves.[20] Rather than replacing the state, she sees a growing vertical integration in which judges, legislators, bureaucrats, and regulators maintain a dialogue that runs from the supranational to the national, and this network enforces and implements the rules.[21]

CROSS-BORDER MIGRATION OF LEGAL NORMS

Law was once studied as falling into one of two distinct spheres, either national or international. As a consequence, "scholars of international law have historically tended to ignore the multifaceted ways in which legal norms are disseminated, received, resisted, and imbibed 'on the ground' in daily life, thereby missing much of the complexity of how law operates."[22] Whereas the diffusion and reception of human rights are often described, the processes by which that occurs are rarely explained. The acculturation model derived from sociology stands in marked contrast to the realism of international relations theory that still focuses on the nation-state as the principal actor in a Hobbesian international world. Acculturation theory emphasizes the micro-processes that influence states actors. States tend to act, the theory holds, in accordance with expectations and roles that they have internalized. Actors conform, because of the "social psychological costs of nonconformity . . . and social-psychological benefits of conforming to group norms and expectations."[23] Policy actors at the national level conform to roles and purposes that originate at the global level, in part because global actors serve as their reference group and define desirable and appropriate polices. In other words, state action is socially based, rather than a response to pressure and coercion.[24] Put differently, global scripts affect domestic law and policy.[25] If that account can be validated, then the means to make international human rights norms more effective requires reconsideration.[26]

Globalization, whether of law or economics, is not without its critics. The global human rights norms proclaimed in the UN's Universal Declaration and indirectly enforced by the ICC and the ad hoc tribunals are the measures by which nations are judged and violators are held accountable. Are those rights truly universal, or are they a form of Western imperialism being imposed on non-Western countries? Indeed, are the trade rules that drive global capitalism also merely another form of Western imperialism? Are advanced economies benefiting more from globalization than less developed ones, and as a result, are the poorer countries becoming even poorer? Indeed, is the globalization of information and drive for cosmopolitanism a Trojan horse for Western culture to invade the non-Western world?[27] Are the ad hoc tribunals and the ICC potential vehicles for reconciliation or instruments of vengeance? These are normative and also empirical questions for which the essays in this book offer no definitive answers. That does not render them less urgent as the various waves of globalization rise. As the works collected here reveal, the comparative study of law and courts from a social science perspective may hold the best chance of bringing useful insights and empirical findings to bear on many of these new questions about law and justice in an increasingly globalized world.

NOTES

1. Thomas L. Friedman, *The World is Flat: A Brief History of the Twenty-First Century* (New York: Farrar, Straus, and Giroux, 2005).

2. 552 U.S. _____, 128 S.Ct. 1346 (2008) slip opinion.

3. Ibid.

4. Alec Stone Sweet and Wayne Sandholtz, "Integration, Supranational Governance and the Institutionalization of the European Polity," in *European Integration and Supranational Governance,* ed. Alec Stone Sweet and Wayne Sandholtz (Oxford: Oxford University Press, 1998), 11.

5. Ibid., 12.

6. Mary L. Volcansek, "Courts and Regional Trade Agreements," in *Courts Crossing Borders: Blurring the Lines of Sovereignty,* ed. Mary L. Volcansek and John F. Stack, Jr. (Durham: Carolina Academic Press, 2005).

7. Joseph E. Stiglitz, *Making Globalization Work* (New York: W.W. Norton and Company, 2007); Joseph E. Stiglitz, *Globalization and Its Discontents* (New York: W.W. Norton and Company, 2002).

8. Antonio Cassese, *Human Rights in a Changing World* (Cambridge: Polity Press, 1994), 16.

9. Thomas Risse and Kathryn Sikkink, "The Socialization of International Human Rights Norms into Domestic Practices: Introduction," in *The Power of Human Rights: International Norms and Domestic Changes,* ed. Thomas Risse, Stephen C. Ropp, and Kathryn Sikkink (Cambridge: Cambridge University Press, 1999), 11.

10. Charles R. Epp, *The Rights Revolution: Lawyers, Activists, and Supreme Courts in Comparative Perspective* (Chicago: University of Chicago Press, 1998), 18.

11. Kwame Anthony Appiah, *Cosmopolitanism: Ethics in a World of Strangers* (New York: W.W. Norton and Company, 2006).

12. Ibid., 57.

13. Mark Tushnet, "The Possibilities of Comparative Constitutional Law," *Yale Law Journal* 108 (1999): 1225–1308.

14. See Kate Malleson and Peter H. Russell, eds., *Appointing Judges in an Age of Judicial Power: Critical Perspectives from around the World* (Toronto: University of Toronto Press, 2006).

15. See, for example, the American Servicemembers' Protection Act (2002), Pub. L. No. 107–206 §§ 2001–2015, 116 Stat. 820, 899–909 (codified at 22 U.S.C. §§ 7421–7432).

16. Peter Evans, "The Eclipse of the State?" *World Politics* 50 (1997): 62–87.

17. Malcolm Water, *Globalization* (New York: Routledge, 2001).

18. Ramesh Thakur and Peter Malcontent, eds., *From Sovereign Impunity to International Accountability: the Search for Justice in a World of States* (New York: United Nations University Press, 2004).

19. Mary L. Volcansek, "Courts and Regional Trade Agreements," in *Courts Crossing Borders: Blurring the Lines of Sovereignty*, eds. Mary L. Volcansek and John F. Stack, Jr. (Durham: Carolina Academic Press, 2005), 35.

20. Anne-Marie Slaughter, *A New World Order* (Princeton: Princeton University Press, 2004), 26–27.

21. Ibid., 20–21.

22. Peter Schiff Berman, "From International Law to Law and Globalization," *Columbia Journal of Transnational Law* 43 (2005). 492.

23. Ryan Goodman and Derek Jinks, "How to Influence States: Socialization and International Human Rights Law," *Duke Law Journal* 54 (2004): 621.

24. Ibid.

25. Bruce G. Carruthers and Terence C. Halliday, "Negotiating Globalization: Global Scripts and Intermediation in the Construction of Asian Insolvency Regimes," *Law and Social Inquiry* 31 (2006): 521–584.

26. See Anthony McGrew and David Held, *Globalization Theory: Approaches and Controversies* (Oxford: Polity, 2007) and Anthony McGrew and David Held, *Governing Globalization* (Oxford: Polity, 2002).

27. Charles Jones, *Global Justice: Defending Cosmopolitanism* (Oxford: Oxford University Press, 1999).

List of Contributors

Francine Banner is an attorney and Ph.D. candidate in the School of Justice and Social Inquiry at Arizona State University. She has published articles on terrorism and the death penalty.

Lilian A. Barria is assistant professor of political science at Eastern Illinois University and a visiting assistant professor and assistant dean for academic affairs in the Georgetown University School of Foreign Service in Qatar. Her research interests focus on international law and human rights. She has coauthored a book with Steven D. Roper titled *Designing Criminal Tribunals: Sovereignty and International Concerns in the Protection of Human Rights* (2006), and her articles have appeared in journals including *The International Journal of Human Rights, Journal of Human Rights,* and *The Journal of Conflict Resolution.* She is the vice president elect of the Human Rights Section of the American Political Science Association.

Rachel Bowen is assistant professor at The Ohio State University in Mansfield, Ohio, where she teaches courses in American politics, comparative politics, and legal politics. She researches judicial politics, focusing on the growth of the rule of law and the judicialization of politics. Her current research focuses on Central America.

Walter F. Carnota is professor of constitutional law in the School of Economics at the University of Buenos Aires, where he also serves as director of the constitutional law graduate program in the Law School.

Lisa Conant is associate professor of political science at the University of Denver and author of the book *Justice Contained: Law and Politics in the European Union* (2002). Her current research explores transformations in citizenship that derive from judgments of national and supranational courts interpreting European Union law and the European Convention on Human Rights.

Rhonda Evans Case is assistant professor in the department of political science at East Carolina University. Her research interests lie at the intersection of law and politics and include topics related to public interest litigation and the judicialization of politics. She is currently finishing a project that examines the legal and political impact of National Human Rights Institutions in Australia and New Zealand.

Joseph M. Isanga is assistant professor of law at Ave Maria School of Law in Naples, Florida. Prior to becoming a lawyer, he worked in Catholic social justice ministry and on the Interdisciplinary Teaching of Human Rights Project of Makerere University's Human Rights and Peace Center in Uganda. He has also advocated for African issues at the Maryknoll Office for Global Concerns in Washington, D.C. His current research focuses on international human rights law, African regional human rights protection mechanisms, and the intersection of religion and human rights.

Donald W. Jackson is the Herman Brown Professor of Political Science at Texas Christian University, where he also serves as the director of the Center for Civic Literacy. His research usually involves the intersection of law and politics, and recently it has involved the impact of international or transnational law on the sovereignty of nation-states. He has had a particular interest in the European Court of Human Rights (*The United Kingdom Confronts the European Convention on Human Rights* [1997]) and on the emergent tribunals that try cases under international criminal law.

Ken Miller received his J.D. from the University of Arizona and is an instructor and a Ph.D. candidate in the School of Justice and Social Inquiry at Arizona State University. His research and teaching focus on the intersection of law, courts, and social justice. He has written and published on the politics of the death penalty, the role social science plays in Supreme Court decision making, and the limitations that courts place on capital juries. His current research focuses on how courts approach morally difficult end-of-life issues, such as physician-assisted suicide.

David M. O'Brien is the Leone Reaves and George W. Spicer Professor of Government and Foreign Affairs at the University of Virginia. He is the author of several books, including *Storm Center: The Supreme Court in American Politics*, 7th ed. (2005) and the two-volume casebook *Constitutional Law and Politics*, 6th ed. (2005).

Doris Marie Provine is professor in the School of Justice and Social Inquiry at Arizona State University. Her research focuses on courts, often in comparative perspective, and on racial disadvantage. She is the author, most recently, of *Unequal Under Law: Race and the War on Drugs* (2007).

Steven D. Roper is professor of political science at Eastern Illinois University. His research focuses on constitutional development, conflict resolution, and human rights. He is the author of *Romania: The Unfinished Revolution* (2000), coauthor, with Lilian A. Barria, of *Designing Criminal Tribunals: Sovereignty and International Concerns in the Protection of Human Rights* (2006), coeditor of *Party Finance and Post-Communist Party Development* (2008), and coeditor of *The Development of Human Rights Institutions* (forthcoming).

Hans Peter Schmitz is associate professor of political science at the Maxwell School of Citizenship at Syracuse University. He is the author of *Transnational Mobilization and Domestic Regime Change: Africa in Comparative Perspective* (2006). His articles have appeared in *Comparative Politics, International Studies Review, Human Rights Quarterly*, and other journals, as well as in edited volumes. His current research focuses on the legitimacy and accountability of transnational nongovernmental organizations.

Michael C. Tolley is associate professor of political science at Northeastern University. He is the author and coauthor of several books related to American constitutional development and judicial process. He is also interested in the comparative study of law and courts, and his article "Parliamentary Scrutiny of Rights: Assessing the Work of the Joint Committee on Human Rights" appeared recently in the *Australian Journal of Political Science*. He was convenor of the Research Committee on Comparative Judicial Studies, an affiliate of the International Political Science Association, from 2003 to 2008.

Mary L. Volcansek is professor of political science at Texas Christian University. She has published five monographs and four edited volumes on law, courts and politics, primarily in Europe or at the transnational level. The most recent was a coedited volume with John F. Stack Jr., *Courts Crossing Borders: Blurring the Lines of Sovereignty*. She is currently working on a project to synthesize the vast literature on non-U.S. courts to determine what, if any, generalizations may be gleaned about the roles of law, courts and politics in contemporary democracies.

Christopher A. Whytock is associate professor of law at the University of Utah S.J. Quinney College of Law. He received a Ph.D. in political science from Duke University and a J.D. from Georgetown University and has published in both political science and law journals. His current research examines the role of domestic courts in global governance, and his broader research interests include international law and international relations, comparative law and comparative politics, and empirical legal studies.

Index

Case names are in *italic* font. Page numbers with tables are indicated with **bold** font.